STEAL
★ THIS ★
VOTE

STEAL ★ THIS ★ VOTE

DIRTY ELECTIONS AND THE ROTTEN HISTORY OF DEMOCRACY IN AMERICA

ANDREW GUMBEL

☆ ★ ☆ ★ ☆

NATION BOOKS
NEW YORK

STEAL THIS VOTE
DIRTY ELECTIONS AND THE ROTTEN HISTORY OF DEMOCRACY IN AMERICA

Published by
Nation Books
An Imprint of Avalon Publishing Group Inc.
245 West 17th St., 11th Floor
New York, NY 10011

AVALON
publishing group incorporated

Nation Books is a co-publishing venture of the Nation Institute and
Avalon Publishing Group.

Library of Congress Cataloging-in-Publication Data is available.

ISBN 1-56025-676-1

9 8 7 6 5 4 3 2

Book design by Maria Elias
Printed in the United States of America
Distributed by Publishers Group West

To my friends in Albania, especially the extended Stefani and Rama families, who have experienced both a sham version of electoral democracy and the real thing, and know how to tell the difference

CONTENTS

★ ☆ ★ ☆ ★ ☆ ★

★ **PART TWO** ★

Voting in the Machine Age

Remember clearly that for the public to have faith in the government, they first have to have faith in the process that elected the government.

—R. Doug Lewis, executive director, The Election Center

Not alone the triumphs and the statesmen; the defeats and the grafters also represent us, and just as truly. Why not see it so and say it?

—Lincoln Steffens

PREFACE

★ ☆ ★ ☆ ★ ☆ ★

THIS BOOK HAS its origins in an article I wrote about the advent of touch-screen computer voting for *The Independent* in October 2003. Like my readers, I was stunned by the lack of commitment shown by many state and county election officials to the integrity of the voting process, particularly in the wake of the Florida debacle in 2000 and the alarms it had sounded about accuracy and democratic accountability. Why were so many parts of the country throwing out their old voting machines only to buy up hugely expensive replacements that some of the country's brightest computer scientists found to be sloppily programmed, dangerously insecure, short on backup data, and incompatible with the conduct of manual recounts? This was not just a matter of corruption or stupidity, although both were evident in the more obviously dirty jurisdictions. Even officials who seemed acceptably honest and qualified for their jobs—which was most of them—demonstrated a worryingly lackadaisical attitude toward the system's basic transparency and fairness. One had the impression that safeguarding democratic integrity was on their to-do list, but not at the top.

The second thing that surprised me, and the biggest spur to writing this book, was the reaction of many readers who seemed to think there was something unusual or novel about these systemic failures. They suggested America's electoral democracy had been in fighting-fit shape, or close to it, before the 2000 election, and saw the avalanche of problems cascading into the public consciousness thereafter as some wild deviation from the norm. On the left, this deviation was blamed on the ever-expanding power of corporations that, having corrupted so much else, were now setting their sights on the inner sanctum, the holy of holies, of America's civic institutions. There was certainly some truth to this interpretation, but it also rested, perhaps inadvertently, on one of the oldest and hoariest themes in America's national mythology: that of a country perennially confronted with the loss of its innocence. It didn't seem to me the United States had a whole lot of innocence left to lose, especially when it came to the management of elections. People have been manipulating and stealing votes more or less since the dawn of the republic. Far from being a departure from normal practice, the computer voting machine controversy struck me as just one more stage in a long and inglorious tradition. That, too, seemed worthy of further exploration.

Here's what Joseph P. Harris, a reformist political scientist and one-time poll worker in Prohibition-era Chicago, had to say when he examined the system on behalf of the Brookings Institution in 1930: "There is probably no other phase of public administration in the United States which is so badly managed as the conduct of elections. Every investigation or election contest brings to light glaring irregularities, errors, misconduct on the part of precinct officers, disregard of election laws and instructions, slipshod practices, and downright frauds . . . The truth of the matter is that the whole administration—organizations, laws, methods and procedures, and records—are, for most states, quite obsolete." He could have written the same paragraph, more or less verbatim, at any time since. Not that Harris had all the answers. He spent thirty years of his life trying to come up with a voting system that would be impervious to both frauds and fools. His grand invention, rolled out in the early 1960s, was the now infamous Votomatic punch-card machine, the one that caused all the chad trouble in Florida. The history of electoral democracy in the United States is full of such instances where the best of intentions go sadly awry. Too often, reformist zeal has run into a brick wall of unforeseen technical difficulties, bureaucratic torpor, and political ill-will.

Some of the most interesting reactions to my *Independent* piece came from readers on the right. Naturally, many of them scoffed at the suggestion, voiced by a number of nascent anti–touch screen campaigners I talked to, that the machines were open to particular abuse by the Republicans. A handful, though, not only took this suggestion at face value, but said it was a good thing, too: the Democrats had been stealing elections for years, and it was high time the Republicans found a way to play the same dirty game. This analysis was not especially accurate—neither party can claim to have clean hands in this business—but in its bracing cynicism it nevertheless reflected the mercenary attitudes of many in the political establishment whose interest lies in fighting and winning elections by any and all available means. Similar sentiments have been expressed on and off for the past century and a half. In 1868 a Republican newspaper in Cincinnati urged the party faithful to follow the example of their rivals and raise tens of thousands of dollars for the express purpose of buying votes. "The devil must be fought with fire," the paper said, "and the Democrats have enjoyed the exclusive privilege of 'ranching' long enough."

In this book I am not interested in playing referee to determine which party has been the greater cheat and which the greater victim. Books like that have been written, on both sides' behalf, and invariably they make for deeply unconvincing reading. Cheating in elections is usually a matter of power, opportunity, and the closeness of pivotal races, not party ideology per se. It's not that the parties are always equivalent in their disregard for the rules, or in the ruthlessness with which they set out to circumvent the will of the electorate. As many of the examples in this book show, one side is frequently more at fault than the other. If the Republicans have made more of the running in the past ten or fifteen years, it is because they have been in the ascendant politically, and because their unusually radical brand of right-wing politics contains many elements, from Christian fundamentalism to the embrace of Machiavellian schemes and deceptions, that are explicitly hostile to democratic openness and pluralism. That does not mean that the Democrats have been blameless, or that they have cast off the political culture that led them in the past to toss ballots in rivers, or run city wards like minidictatorships, or form alliances with organized crime. In the end, the parties belong to one and the same political culture, which has given them shape and been shaped by them in return. Studying what they have in common can often be more fruitful, in fact, than focusing on what divides them. Historically, the zero-sum logic of two-party competition has given rise to a number of abuses at the ballot box, as well as an effort to keep those abuses hidden from the general public. In crunch moments, the attitude has been not only: *They're probably cheating, so we'd better cheat, too.* It has also often been: *We won't say anything about what they've done, because that will only encourage them to rat on us in return.* It has rarely been productive for a candidate or a party to complain that an election has been stolen, leading as it does to invariable accusations of bad faith, paranoia, and the stirring of needless alarm among voters. Races do get contested, and sometimes overturned, but nobody wins popularity points for dragging the process out through the courts. The understanding, in almost all the great ballot-box standoffs of the past two centuries, has been that a fight is a fight, and the measure of a winner lies in the ability to finish ahead, whether by observing the Queensbury Rules or not.

The first time I witnessed a stolen election was in Albania in 1996, when Sali Berisha's unpopular and increasingly authoritarian government thought it could get away with squashing the opposition at the polls because it was seen by the West as a bastion of stability in an otherwise turbulent Balkan region. Berisha's Democratic Party so overdid it with stuffed ballots, forged signatures, and armed thugs scaring opposition supporters away from polling stations that the counting had to be stopped in midstream and adjusted to make the theft a little less blatant. Many of the abuses were perpetrated within full view of international election monitors, who reported repeated instances of multiple ballots being handed to individual voters, of counts revealing greater numbers of votes than voters, and of precincts announcing 100 percent turnout and shutting their doors early even though eligible voters were still standing in line outside. In one regional capital where party operatives were a little more scrupulous, an Albanian-speaking foreign observer overheard the chairman of a local precinct voting board apologizing on the telephone that he could not "deliver the required result," because an international monitoring team was watching his every move.

The opposition, made up of both heirs to Enver Hoxha's hard-line Communist Party and anti-Communist former allies of Berisha's, chose to boycott the election as soon as the scope of the fraud became clear. The next day, they organized a mass protest rally in the main square of the capital, Tirana, only to be attacked without provocation by baton-wielding riot police, hauled off to jail, and beaten again in custody. Foreign governments gave Berisha a virtually free pass on all this, quietly telling him to cool it, with the understanding that no serious challenge would be made to the legitimacy of his election. "I don't think it would help to do anything overhasty," one European ambassador told me breezily. Some of Berisha's more ardent foreign fans even took the trouble to insist that the election had been entirely free and fair, painting all evidence to the contrary as cleverly concocted Communist propaganda and hailing Berisha, once a confidant and personal physician of Hoxha's, as the true savior of Albanian democracy.

The lesson I eventually took from this experience was that no long-term good can come of such distortions and betrayals of the democratic process. Within months, Berisha had driven the economy into the ground due to the collapse of pyramid investment schemes endorsed by his government, the people had begun an armed insurrection by looting every last police and army weapons depot, and a country already fragile from decades of material deprivation and Stalinist isolationism had become the very antithesis of the Balkan stability that Western capitals so craved. For three months it wasn't clear if Albania was headed for civil war, or if any authority could be established at all. Then, after the democratic betrayal came something of a democratic miracle. New elections were held in the summer of 1997 under the eye of an ad hoc coalition of international peacekeepers. Despite daunting security odds, these passed off peacefully and fairly, resulting in an opposition victory and a slow, if checkered, return to normality.

Post-Communist Eastern Europe wasn't a bad place in general to savor the power of popular resistance to undemocratic leadership. I was lucky enough to see it in action in East Germany as the Berlin Wall came down, and again in Belgrade when hundreds of thousands of nonviolent protesters, incensed by the attempted cancellation of legitimate municipal elections won by the opposition, took to the streets for weeks on end. They heaved mightily to topple Slobodan Milosevic and eventually, after a two-year hiatus punctuated by the war in Kosovo, succeeded. By the time I arrived in the United States, in the middle of the Clinton impeachment imbroglio in 1998, I had a pretty good idea of what democracy at its best should look like, and I knew it wasn't embodied by the likes of Tom DeLay, Henry Hyde, and the rest of the relentless gang of presidential persecutors. Then, in 2000 the bizarre election-night roller coaster of high emotions, false announcements, exit-poll screwups, and concessions given and retracted filled me with a singularly queasy feeling that persisted throughout the extraordinary thirty-six-day battle that followed. America's crisis of democratic faith didn't stoop, of course, to the physical brutality or blatant unsubtlety of Albania four years earlier. But occurring as it did in the world's richest, most sophisticated country, it was also a whole lot odder.

For all these reasons, the relatively modest premise of this book is that *representative democracy is a good thing*. The more representative the better, in fact. I would argue that the health and dynamism of a society is almost invariably to be measured by the extent to which its disparate voices engage one another and battle openly for public acceptance. If parts of the electorate are apathetic, they need to be engaged, not ignored. If they are ignorant, they need to be educated, not alienated. That is—or should be—what democracy means.

In reality, of course, it does not always work out that way. For all the lip service paid to democracy, it has proved a much more troublesome concept than the mythology of America's civic institutions might lead us to believe. Most of the framers of the Constitution were suspicious of the very idea of popular elections; the idea that they were great democrats in the modern sense was essentially an invention of the Civil War era. Conservative thinkers have often pointed out that the United States is a republic, not a democracy, and all the better for it. Alexis de Tocqueville, of course, worried about the "tyranny of the majority," and many of his subsequent

American admirers took care to destroy the most tangible potential manifestation of that majority, the Populist movement, which erupted across the Great Plains and the South in the latter years of the nineteenth century. Even today, proponents of greater participation in U.S. elections, the least well attended in the Western world, can find themselves under attack as partisan hacks interested primarily in stuffing registration lists with the names of vagrants, felons, and noncitizens whose votes can later be controlled or stolen.

Granted, there have been times in American history when such accusations have been entirely warranted. Since the early nineteenth century this country has been both a living experiment in the expansion of democratic rights and also a world-class laboratory for vote suppression and election-stealing techniques. Antidemocratic forces have dressed themselves up as well-meaning reformers every bit as often as genuine reformers have been accused of perverting the system for their own ends. Nobody ever said democracy was simple, and in America its progress has been rife with complications and paradoxes unrivaled anywhere else on the planet.

Curiously, America's democratic culture has all too often gone unexamined and unquestioned, especially by Americans themselves. The 2000 meltdown forced people to pay attention for a while, but already there are signs that the country is sinking back into complacency. The fact that the 2004 presidential election did not turn into another Florida, as widely forecast, has been taken by many as a sign that the controversies over computer voting, registration, provisional ballots, felon disenfranchisement, and the rest have been overblown. But the only reassuring thing about 2004—for those in a mood to be reassured—is that President George W. Bush's margin of victory was wide enough to prevent the shortcomings of the system from becoming excessively visible. The shortcomings are still very much there, and ignoring them will not make them go away.

It's gratifying that a book about democratic participation has often felt like a collaborative effort. Many people not only gave of their time and expertise, but also did so with remarkable selflessness, reflecting their commitment to the subject and their desire for of all of us to edge toward greater knowledge and understanding. A few of them must remain anonymous, but my thanks are no less heartfelt for that. Most, however, were only too happy to stand up and be counted. Thanks, first and foremost, to my friend, neighbor, and favorite American politics specialist, Chuck Noble of Cal State Long Beach, who acted as a felicitous combination of mentor, sounding-board, thesis director, interlocutor, and critic, suggesting all the right books for me to read and fetching quite a few from the library himself. His observation early on that free and fair elections in the United States are "almost an oxymoron" acted as an informal motto for the entire project. Particular thanks also to Rebecca Mercuri, who first inducted me into the topsy-turvy world of election management and helped me make sense of it; to Kim Zetter, a fine colleague and friend with an unerring nose for nonsense; to Kim Alexander, who always had great ideas and the right phone numbers; and to indefatigable activists like Roxanne Jekot in Georgia and Jeremiah Akin in Riverside County, California, who, despite the runaway passions the topic so often inspires, always took care to get it right and reliably passed on what they had found. Others who read portions of the manuscript and provided valuable comment include Bob Gumpert, Pierre Gervais (who first put the idea of an antidemocratic tradition into my head), Tim Pershing, Rob Richie, Michael Pauls, Larry George, Gary Humphreys, and Gioconda Belli.

I would also like to thank Doug Chapin and Sean Greene of Electionline.org; Steven Hertzberg and Eva Waskell of Votewatch; David Dill at Stanford; and the Fair Election International team at Global Exchange, including Ted Lewis, Tim Kingston, Mat Rosen, Shannon Biggs, and Walter Turner, as well as their international monitors, especially Dr. Brigalia Bam and Neerja Choudhury. In Florida, thanks to Lida Rodriguez-Taseff, Courtney Strickland, Joe Egan, Steve Clelland, Lew Oliver, Ion Sancho, Kevin Wood, Kendall Coffey, Robert Wexler, Jim Sebesta, Charlotte Danciu, Susan Van Houten, Echo Steiner, and Arthur Anderson. In Georgia, Denis Wright and Mark Sawyer. In Maryland, Linda Schade and

Tom Iler. In Texas, Adina Levin and the Austin ACLU office. In California, Ron and Bernadette Burks, Mike and Linda Soubirous, Art Cassel, Brian Floyd, Greg Luke, Fred Woocher, Bob Varni, Bill Rouverol, Paul Barbagelata, and Tony Miller. In Louisiana, Peppi Bruneau. In New Mexico, Mike Laurance, Al Solis, Bill Wheeler, Chuck Davis, and Bill Barnhouse. In Chicago, Jan Rieff, by way of Andrew Apter and Robin Derby. In Brazil, Pedro Rezende and Amilcar Brunazo.

Leonard Doyle, Jan Thompson, and Simon Kelner at *The Independent* were exceptionally accommodating about giving me the time and the assignments I needed to complete this project. Carl Bromley at Nation Books was a delight to work with. The book would not have been possible without the excellent library services of the city of Santa Monica, Santa Monica College, UCLA, Cal State Long Beach, and USC. And it would have been a lot less pleasant without the facilities and the warm welcome extended to all writers by my two favorite coffee shops in Santa Monica, the 18th Street Café and the Talking Stick. A big thank-you, finally, to Kathleen, who piled her plate extraordinarily high so I could keep my own clear, and to my children, Max and Raffaella, the voters of the future, who asked smart questions and always knew how to make me laugh. Raffaella thought this book should be called *Elections Don't Work*, and she was probably right. Max thought it ought to be subtitled *Making Elections Work Is Harder Than Making $100 at a Lemonade Stand*, and he was probably right, too.

For any lapses or mistakes that may have crept into the manuscript —any repeating (of the obvious), floating (of dubious ideas), transcription errors, or faulty counting—I take full responsibility, of course.

1
HOW TO STEAL AN ELECTION

★ ☆ ★ ☆ ★ ☆ ★ ☆ ★ ☆ ★ ☆ ★ ☆ ★

If you do everything, you'll win. —Lyndon Johnson

A FEW DAYS before the November 2004 election, Jimmy Carter was asked what would happen if, instead of flying to Zambia or Venezuela or East Timor, his widely respected international election-monitoring team was invited to turn its attention to the United States. His answer was stunningly blunt. Not only would the voting system be regarded as a failure, he said, but the shortcomings were so egregious the Carter Center would never agree to monitor an election there in the first place. "We wouldn't think of it," the former president told a radio interviewer. "The American political system wouldn't measure up to any sort of international standards, for several reasons."

What, after all, was to be done with a country whose newest voting machines, unlike Venezuela's, couldn't even perform recounts? A country where candidates, in contrast to the more promising emerging democracies of the Caucasus or the Balkans, were denied equal, unpaid access to the media? There were a number of reasons, in the

1

sharply partisan atmosphere surrounding the Bush-Kerry race, to wonder whether campaign conditions didn't smack more of the Third World than the First. Every day, newspapers recounted stories of registration forms being found in garbage cans, or of voter rolls padded with the names of noncitizens, fictional characters, household pets, and the dearly departed. The *Chicago Tribune*, a paper that knows its voter fraud, having won a Pulitzer for its work on the infamous Daley machine, found 181,000 dead people on the registration lists of six key battleground states.

Some of these stories were touted by Republicans to discredit their Democratic Party opponents. Students at Democrat-leaning campuses, for example, were reported to be registering twice, once at their college address and once at their family's home, as were snowbirds with addresses in both Florida and liberal northern states like New York. Many more stories, though, were peddled by Democrats to discredit the Republicans. In Michigan, a Republican state senator came in for a roasting after announcing his party's intention to "suppress" Detroit's overwhelmingly African American, overwhelmingly Democratic vote. In Nashville, African Americans complained they were receiving phone calls and flyers giving out erroneous polling station locations, or even the wrong election date. In Ohio, where the top election official was doubling as cochair of President Bush's state reelection campaign, one bizarre ruling after another sought to disqualify voter registration forms submitted on anything other than eighty-pound stock paper, or to invalidate provisional ballots if they were cast at the incorrect polling place. The bulk of these measures were deemed detrimental to the Democrats. In Florida, where President Bush's brother Jeb was governor, the Republican secretary of state was on an unwavering mission to abolish recounts—raising suspicions about what exactly she was trying to hide—and also to throw out the registration forms of Democrat-leaning, foreign-born voters who forgot to tick every last box attesting to their U.S. citizenship.

Florida, of course, was where the cracks in America's much-vaunted democratic system had become obvious to all in the wake of the agonizing Bush-Gore standoff four years earlier. The official line coming out of Tallahassee and almost every other state capital was that everything was now immeasurably better, thanks to official commissions and investigations, a new federal election law promising billions of dollars in funding, and the introduction of state-of-the-art voting technology to replace the troublesome old punch-card machines. From the viewpoint of grassroots political activists, however, things did not feel remotely better. In many places, and especially in Florida, election bureaucrats seemed overwhelmed, if not also buffeted by alarmingly underhand political pressures. In Broward County, around Fort Lauderdale, sixty thousand completed absentee ballots inexplicably went missing. In Miami's Little Haiti, also a Democratic Party stronghold, activists complained that more than 20 percent of new voters had not received voting cards, or had been sent new ones ahead of the primaries with the wrong party affiliation, making it next to impossible to participate. In Orlando, get-out-the-vote organizers in black neighborhoods were subjected to a seemingly specious vote fraud investigation by the state police, and leaders of the local firefighters' union, which had endorsed John Kerry, were hauled in for questioning on suspicion of corruption and embezzlement of city funds.

Beyond the dirty partisan politics, growing numbers of voters were expressing disquiet at new touch-screen computer voting machines, which were experiencing errors and breakdowns almost everywhere they were deployed and did not provide an independently verifiable paper record in case of disputes or mechanical failure. Members of both major parties found this disquieting, but Kerry supporters were especially alarmed, since the major touch-screen manufacturers were all Republican Party donors. The chief executive of the most widely reviled of them, Diebold Election Systems, had even written a fund-raising letter the previous year in which he said he was "committed to helping Ohio deliver its electoral votes to the president." Bush opponents were all too inclined to believe, in fact, that the Republicans were about to steal the presidency, just as they believed it had been stolen the last time. The Republicans, for their part, laughed this off as conspiratorial nonsense, but they also weren't shy about announcing how hard or how dirtily they were prepared to fight if it came down to another Florida-style tug-of-war. Long Island's GOP congressman Pete King, caught on camera by the documentary maker Alexandra Pelosi during a White House function on election day, bragged even as the first polls were closing that Bush had already won. When Pelosi asked him how he knew, he answered, perhaps jokingly, perhaps not: "It's all over but the counting. And we'll take care of the counting."

Election day itself, at least in the battleground states, was a deeply jarring experience for America's trusting majority, which had led itself to believe that all was for the best in the best of all possible democracies. Outside many polling stations, clumps of voting rights activists, party workers, and paralegals were primed for trouble, lining up with clipboards and pens, printed regulations, election code extracts, and lists of emergency numbers. Some were there to defend the interests of one party, others to defend the integrity of the process itself. Many, especially the Democratic partisans, had crisscrossed the country to set up in strategic locations, believing only hawkeyed vigilance could prevent the wholesale theft of all they held dear. "This is the core of democracy," one volunteer from the Election Protection Coalition, an umbrella organization of many smaller groups, said outside a precinct in Cleveland, Ohio. "If we can't control this, we've really lost everything."

Everyone bristled with suspicion and mutual mistrust. The Republicans accused the Democrats of trying to sneak ineligible voters to the polls and threatened to deploy official challengers to sniff out the mischief—something much discussed ahead of time but that ultimately failed to materialize on any scale, perhaps because of a flurry of negative publicity stirred up on the eve of the election. The Democrats, meanwhile, could barely keep up with their own seemingly endless list of grievances. Across the country, voters in urban, heavily African American precincts complained their polling places had far too few voting machines to accommodate the crowds, creating lines as long as seven or eight hours toward the end of the day and deterring an unknown number of voters. In suburban Cincinnati, observers erupted in fury when they and the media were thrown out of county election headquarters for the duration of the vote count. They were told there had been a terrorist threat, but the FBI later denied all knowledge of it. Ohio in general underwent a microscopic examination from one end to the other, since it was considered the single most important state in the election, and all manner of irregularities and glitches emerged as a result. Some precincts had more votes than voters. Others showed anomalous totals for lower-order candidates or obscure third parties. In Columbus, a computer glitch in one precinct, later corrected, gave four thousand votes too many to President Bush. Miami County found an extra nineteen thousand unexplained votes after asserting that 100 percent of its precincts had reported their results.

The poisoned atmosphere scarcely improved as Bush was declared the winner, with a comfortable popular margin of well over three million and a lead of more than one hundred thousand in Ohio. After the most hotly contested election in a generation, many of the president's detractors simply refused to believe it could be so. How come the official results were so much at variance with exit polls predicting a Kerry victory? Why had some television networks called Ohio for Bush prematurely, not only while the count was still in progress, but also while some voters caught in the longest lines were actually still waiting to cast their ballots? Within a couple of days, the headline "Kerry Won" popped up on a progressive Web site, the argument being that when questionable punch-card ballots were recounted by hand and provisional ballots were factored in, the world would see that Bush had not been elected to a second four-year term after all. (When the Ohio ballots were duly recounted and the provisionals factored in, Bush was still 118,000 votes ahead.) Statistical analyses of varying degrees of professional competence also sought to bring out the numbers behind the numbers, pointing to inconsistencies and fluke occurrences in a number of states to make the case that Kerry had somehow been cheated. In Florida, well-known voting rights activist Bev Harris claimed to have found the backup data to Volusia County's computer tabulation machines sitting in garbage bags ready for disposal, the suspicion being that county officials might have falsified the official count and then set about destroying the evidence. But she never actually produced the allegedly discarded data, or even the videotapes she said she had made of her find.

Whatever the merits of these unsubstantiated claims, the suspicion and rancor they portended were clearly at variance with America's idealized image of its own political integrity. All the high-minded talk on the Kerry campaign trail of creating a "more perfect Union" was manifestly being undermined by a noisy minority of Kerry supporters who fervently believed the Union had been hijacked and perverted by a ruthless cabal of cheats and crooks. On the Republican side, the antitax guru Grover Norquist opined that the Democrats should learn to calm down and accept their ever-dwindling minority status with equanimity and grace—a not-so-subtle way of telling them to roll over and play dead now that the big boys were in charge. It all seemed so strange. Until the Florida meltdown of 2000, conventional wisdom would have had us believe the machinery of American democracy ran smoothly and peacefully, that victors played fair, and that the vanquished conceded graciously. Now, seemingly out of nowhere, it was open season for frauds, manipulators, corrupt election officials, dishonest voting machine manufacturers, bully-boy winners, and paranoid sore losers. Where did they come from so suddenly?

In truth, the 2004 election was far from an aberration. Nothing has been more normal, over the past two hundred-plus years, than for one side in an American election to push, shove, and strong-arm its way across the finishing line, praising the strength and fairness of the process as it goes, while the other side stares forlornly at the inevitability of defeat and yelps in frustration about the perpetration of an outrageous theft that threatens the very fabric of the nation. This pattern is hardly good for a democracy (though it is certainly better, if transparency and fair play are lacking, to have a tightly fought contest and relatively high turnout than a moribund one and a foregone conclusion). Equally, it should not come as a surprise, given the tempestuous history of elections in this country. John Quincy Adams stole the presidency from under the nose of Andrew Jackson in 1824, and Rutherford B. Hayes stole it again, even more brazenly, from Samuel Tilden in 1876. George W. Bush no more deserved to win Florida in 2000 than John F. Kennedy deserved to win Illinois in 1960. And that's just the presidency, a far more serenely contested office than the often ferocious dogfights at the state or local level. At different times in American history, the sanctity of the ballot box has been violated by intimidation, kidnapping, bloodshed, bribery, embezzlement, intoxication, under-the-table bargaining, stuffed voter rolls, creative vote-counting, and, above all, grotesque bureaucratic incompetence and corruption. Ballots have been bought and sold on the open market, stolen, forged, spoiled, and tossed into lakes, rivers, and oceans. In 1868 the *Cincinnati Gazette* reported there were men "who would think no more of going to the polls and voting without being paid for it, than a cow does of going to her rack when there is no fodder in it." In these days of wholesale rather than retail politics, the money is more likely to be spent on deceptive television advertising or wholesale character assassination (or, as emerged in the wake of the 2004 race, paying pliant television commentators to use their airtime as undisclosed White House publicity puffs), but pockets of vote purchasing persist nonetheless. In rural Texas, "vote whores" paid by the political parties still hand out cash or favors in exchange for support on election day. Elsewhere, the transactions have moved online, to Web sites like eBay, where the digital police periodically spot them and pounce to shut them down.

There is nothing new, either, about technological miracle solutions that turn all too quickly to bitter disappointment. Before electronic voting, punch cards were hailed as the salvation of American democracy, even though they habitually lost up to 5 percent of the votes entrusted to them. Before punch cards came lever machines, which proved less impregnable than their manufacturers claimed and couldn't be double-checked, because they, too, did not provide a paper backup. Before lever machines came the innovation of the secret ballot itself—an unimpeachable contribution to electoral democracy, one would have thought, except that it was shamelessly abused as a battering ram to disenfranchise half the electorate at a time when universal suffrage, far from being trumpeted as a great American virtue, was widely deemed to be deleterious to the health and economic well-being of the nation.

Some people might think that the days of elections fought illegally, won unfairly, and lost ungraciously belong to some distant past, but really they never went away. True, polling places and election offices tend to be calmer than they were, say, in Kansas City in 1946, when a notorious local gangster and election fixer named Morris "Snag" Klein raided the Jackson County courthouse under cover of darkness, blew open a safe, and removed crucial evidence supporting the indictments of sixty-one people, himself included, on fraud charges relating to a dirty congressional primary. The decline of big-city machine politics and the growing complexity of the technology of voting have also made it less common for election officials from one party to bribe, twist, intimidate, or cut deals with their counterparts on the other side—or, for that matter, to arrange for them to be kidnapped, Chicago-style, for the duration of voting hours, or to slip Ex-Lax in their coffee so they would be otherwise engaged during the most important phase of the count. Gone are the days when Democrats in certain Baltimore wards would arrange for the voting machines to "break down" during the peak hours of Republican attendance at polling stations, then magically right themselves when the union boys showed up in force.

But it is important not to confuse an outward appearance of calm with transparency or fairness. Take, for example, the governor's race in Alabama in 2002, when the Democratic incumbent, Don Siegelman, appeared to have won by a narrow margin, only to be undone by the sudden discovery of a computer glitch in rural Baldwin County. The county's probate judge in charge of elections had taken it upon himself to check the tabulation machinery in the dead of night, long after poll watchers and most of his staff had gone home, and concluded that Siegelman had accidentally been awarded seven thousand votes too many—enough to tip the entire race to his Republican challenger, Bob Riley. County officials were distinctly vague about the cause of the supposed error, furnishing no details other than a passing reference to a lightning strike. Of course, it may have been just a coincidence that the judge was a Republican, just as it may have been unimpeachable legal precedent that led Alabama's attorney general, also a Republican, to refuse authorization for a recount or any independent inspection of the ballots. A subsequent analysis of the voting figures by James Gundlach, a sociologist at Auburn University, showed all sorts of wild deviation from the statistical norms established by this and previous elections. Gundlach observed: "There is simply no way that electronic vote counting can produce two sets of results without someone using computer programs in ways that were not intended. In other words, the fact that two sets of results were reported is sufficient evidence in and of itself that the vote tabulation process was compromised."

Despite the technical changes of recent decades, America remains beset by a patchwork of electoral rules and practices that can vary wildly from state to state and from county to county. The lack of uniformity or of an independent central electoral commission to enforce minimum standards are further reasons cited by the Carter Center why the United States is unsuited to observation by an international election-monitoring mission. A dirty county, one prone to the abuses of a tight local power network, can conduct dirty elections more or less routinely with little or no accountability to higher authority. If an outsider candidate for school board or water board feels cheated, what, realistically, are the available remedies? Voter fraud is notoriously difficult to prove under the best of circumstances, and next to impossible when the challenger's political opponents happen to control the elections office and, with it, access to materials necessary to establish proof of malfeasance or miscounting sufficient to alter the outcome. In some jurisdictions, such as Alabama in 2002, the authorities can simply refuse to authorize a recount. In others, the adoption of electronic touch screens, as with the earlier adoption of lever machines, makes recounts impossible from the outset.

If America's electoral system is more corrupted than any of its Western counterparts, many of the reasons are to be found in the workings of the county elections office. The United States has never successfully produced a professional class of technocrats, and the field of election management has, by common consent, been treated too often as a dumping ground for dimwits, time-servers, crooks, and small-time political appointees who are too incompetent to be given anything else to do. The worst of them get fired, forced into early retirement, or prosecuted on fraud charges. The administrators in turn rely on the services of dozens, sometimes hundreds or even thousands, of shoddily paid temporary workers and volunteers, who may come forward for all the right reasons but are thrown into the job with inadequate training and little or no supervision. In the 1930s the chief clerk of a big-city elections office complained to the author of a government report: "It would be difficult to imagine a more incompetent and drunken lot of loafers anywhere than the non-descript outfit that was put on registration and election work, with a few exceptions." Things have scarcely improved since, not least because of the disdain heaped on the very concept of public office since the Reagan era and the repeated budget cuts that have been endured as a consequence. In December 2000 as the Bush-Gore battle in Florida was reaching its endgame, the *Los Angeles Times* interviewed a former county election director from rural Washington State who quit to become a waitress at Sizzler, where the money was better. Lousy pay also explains why it is so hard to find and keep competent voting machine technicians. "You make more money servicing laundry machines," New York City election commissioner Douglas Kellner complained.

Mediocrity and sparse resources make election offices ripe for abuse, especially when the political culture around them becomes degraded by the overweening ambition of prominent officeholders, their injudicious choice of political allies, or the corrupting influence of a patronage machine. This can happen just about anywhere, under Republicans or Democrats, in big cities or in remote rural areas. Take San Francisco, a city hardly lacking in its stated commitment to progressive democratic politics. In 1975 the mayoral election was stolen by thousands of members of Jim Jones's Peoples Temple—then, eerily, very much in vogue with California's political elite—who went from precinct to precinct casting repeat ballots, not unlike the marauding gangs of Boss Tweed's New York, and bused in friends, relatives, and acquaintances fraudulently registered as San Francisco residents. When the beneficiary, George Moscone, took office, he rewarded Jones first by elevating him to the city's human rights commission and then to the chairmanship of the housing authority. Jones's personal lawyer, Timothy Stoen, was appointed assistant district attorney and placed in charge of a dedicated voter fraud unit, which was inundated with complaints but chose to ignore almost all of them. Temple dropouts and survivors of the horrific mass suicide orchestrated by Jones in Guyana later admitted that their efforts had almost certainly swayed the election. But official San Francisco, then undergoing a decisive leftward shift, was not remotely interested in taking steps to undermine its own legitimacy.

Moscone's narrowly defeated opponent, Republican supervisor John Barbagelata, tried for a while to stir up public indignation, attracting enough death threats from Temple members and other fringe groups to warrant a twenty-four-hour armed guard outside his house and police escorts on constant kidnap alert for his eight children. Partly thanks to Barbagelata's efforts, fifty out-of-towners were eventually indicted for registration fraud, although none were Temple members. A federal prosecutor also launched an investigation into the district attorney's office, but made little headway after the city told him that voter lists for the mayoral election had somehow vanished along with four hundred precinct registration books. Barbagelata himself gave up the fight after someone—he never quite worked out who—mailed a quarter-stick of dynamite concealed in a box of See's candy to his home, addressed to "the people's choice." Two of Barbagelata's teenage daughters unwittingly tossed

11

the package around the living room before their father came home and called the bomb squad.

Two decades later, San Francisco was in trouble again, eating its way through six election chiefs in the eight years of Willie Brown's flamboyant tenure as mayor. Brown, a wily operator who had spent fifteen years as speaker of the California State Assembly (and before that helped found the Democratic Party machine that embraced Jim Jones), specialized in an idiosyncratic brand of patronage politics in which a well-placed job always seemed to be available to friends, acquaintances, business contacts, and ex-girlfriends. He created no fewer than 350 mayoral "special assistants," at a cost to taxpayers of more than $45 million a year, and extended his personal influence over almost every aspect of city hiring and firing. The effect on the elections office, which had a direct line to the mayor through the city administrator, was less than impressive. In 1997 when a controversial proposal to build a $535 million stadium and mall to house the 49ers football team came before the voters, prosecutors and local news reporters found evidence that hundreds of people in the Brown stronghold of Bayview–Hunters' Point, next to the proposed construction site, had been registered to vote more than once, and that an additional 744 people were recorded as being dead at the time they went to the polls. A number of polling stations that were deemed likely to record a high "yes" vote opened early on election day, while others likely to vote "no" were closed down ahead of schedule. Thousands of ballots were left out in the rain in open boxes, obliging enterprising poll workers to dry them off in microwave ovens so they could still be counted. A precinct captain in Bayview–Hunters' Point was found to have voted twice and prosecuted accordingly. The ballot measure, strongly backed by both Mayor Brown and his friends in the construction business, squeaked home by less than fifteen hundred votes. But the stadium-mall was never built—for entirely unrelated reasons of political corruption.

The elections office itself was left in turmoil. Over the next four years, 80 percent of the experienced staff quit, as did four successive chiefs. In one 1998 election the vote count was halted for the night less than a quarter done, because poll workers were tired and wanted to go to bed. In 1999 one ballot box in twenty was found to have come into the tabulation center unlocked and unsealed, an open invitation to foul play, and several thousand votes were compromised by computer failures and a printing error in the voter guide. By 2000 the situation had become so dysfunctional that the secretary of state's office ordered an investigation, which showed a shockingly high, and unexplained, variance of 8.8 percent between the number of ballots supposedly completed by the voters in the Bush-Gore election and the number later produced for inspection.

In 2001 troubling questions emerged about another controversial ballot measure, this one proposing the creation of a public power authority to counter the dominance of Pacific Gas and Electric, which had failed to keep the lights on during a recent power crisis and passed the cost of the overpriced electricity it purchased from out-of-state suppliers on to its customers. The measure was narrowly defeated, as Mayor Brown and PG&E had hoped, but not without a furor about eight ballot-box lids found floating in San Francisco Bay, the chance discovery of 240 marked but uncounted ballots dumped in voting machine storage bins, and the unsecured transportation of thousands of absentee and provisional ballots on election night from city hall to two alternate locations. Election chief Tammy Haygood said she had moved the absentee ballots in response to an anthrax scare and didn't have time to implement full ballot security procedures. And she insisted the errant ballot-box lids picked up by the Coast Guard were nothing to worry about. They had gone astray, she said, after election workers decided to give them a wash and left them on a dock near Fisherman's Wharf to dry. Given the contentiousness of the power issue and the tiny five-hundred-vote margin of victory for the "no" camp, people weren't especially inclined to believe her.

The same election saw voter approval for the creation of an independent election commission, which wasted no time in firing Haygood after it discovered she had pushed the department $5.6 million over budget in a matter of months. Some of that money was spent paying temporary poll workers who never showed up, and some of it on lavish overtime payments for Haygood's one-time deputy, who continued to receive her remarkably generous salary long after she had left her job. Haygood fought her dismissal for the better part of a year, during which time she ceased working but continued to be paid her own $125,000 annual salary. Bizarrely, it turned out that her prime motivation for clinging to the city payroll was to qualify her domestic partner for insurance coverage on a sex-change operation. Mayor Brown had recently endorsed the extension of health benefits to include elective surgery for the transsexual partners of city employees, apparently—so city insiders said—with Haygood's situation specifically in mind.

There is no one way to steal an election in the United States. With the infrastructure of democracy split into fifty states and more than four thousand counties, the permutations for mischief are almost endless. What works in one jurisdiction with one kind of electoral machinery can easily run into a procedural brick wall in the next. Still, the historical record shows that precinct bosses and party machines have tended to learn from each other, borrowing the most successful techniques and then adding new ones of their own. In the nineteenth century, loopholes involving registration lists were exploited from the very outset, as voters known as "floaters" would hop across to the next ward, the next county, or even the next state to cast extra ballots. Paying for votes was standard practice across the country, as was the lavish distribution of free liquor on election day. In New York, Boss Tweed's Tammany braves perfected the art of repeat voting, visiting the same precincts in the same wards in a variety of disguises and changes of clothes. Tweed also perfected a way to fast-track the naturalization process to generate tens of thousands of new immigrant votes, an idea he originally filched from his archrival, Fernando Wood. In Pittsburgh, a city memorably described by Lincoln Steffens as "hell with the lid off" physically and "hell with the lid on" politically, boss Chris Magee took the time to travel to New York to study the Tammany model and take the lessons home with him. In Philadelphia, the Gas Ring also copied New York and learned to pad out the voter rolls with the names of fictional characters, children, household pets, and the dead.

In the South after the Civil War, the former Confederate states followed one another's lead as they pioneered ways to exclude black voters and illiterate whites from the polls. In the North and Midwest, bosses in Chicago, Philadelphia, and Kansas City figured out that the best response to the secret ballot was to stop corrupting individual voters and start corrupting precinct election officials and neighborhood canvassing boards instead. Tight ward-by-ward control of the city was key to this operation and frequently the object of ferocious partisan battles in and of itself. When lever machines came in, political control of voting became all the more crucial. Governor Earl Long of Louisiana once boasted that with the right election commissioners he could get the machines to sing "Home Sweet Home." (He also said that when he died, he wanted to be buried in Louisiana so he could remain active in politics.)

The age of computer voting machines has brought its own innovations and peculiarities, most notably the greasing of palms in contract negotiations in certain states, which has led to the criminal prosecution of several machine company executives and election officials, often at the same time. The fact that vote tampering can now be conducted secretly and invisibly through software manipulation is also a perfect cover for the would-be crook. If we can't document with certainty the cases where this may have occurred already, it is precisely because digital ballots, without a paper backup, can be handled in any number of ways without leaving fingerprints. Everything is in place for the perfect electoral crime, which is of course the dirty politician's favorite kind. This avenue, one senses, has hardly begun to fulfill its potential.

One important thing to understand about vote theft is that it is not merely a question of personal morality. It is not something that divides the world into bad politicians, who do it habitually, and good politicians, who take scrupulous care to avoid it at all costs. It is first and foremost a matter of opportunity, and that in turn depends on the broader political context. If a race is particularly close, or if the stakes are regarded as particularly high, then the temptation to play to the very limit of the rules, if not beyond, will become compelling. If a political machine boss or party leader believes he can control a certain number of votes, then he will do everything to get out that vote, and never mind the exact nature of the "control" that needs exerting. If each side has reason to suspect that the other will resort to cheating, then thievery will invariably be justified as self-defense against the dastardly tactics of the other side. Often, mere accusations of vote fraud can be political weapons that are every bit as ruthless as vote fraud itself.

One of the central themes of this book is that there are no dirty elections without dirty politics, and indeed as long as the politics are not clean, it is almost impossible to prevent the electoral process from becoming tainted. After all, rules work only if they are enforced. America is a country that thrives on ferocious competition —the sink-or-swim ethic of capitalist adventurism, forever flirting with the fringes of the permissible—and few competitive arenas are more cutthroat than elective politics. To believe that smooth elections are merely a question of updated machinery and proper procedure, as many election officials and mainstream media outlets appear to have done since 2000, is to slip deep into denial and self-delusion. The system functions not on the principle of the common good, but on how much its participants think they can get away with. There is nothing virginally pure about American democracy, and there never has been.

Why do such dirty politics exist? In contrast to many corrupted parts of the world, where democracy has been threatened or subverted by an excess of ideology, the answer, curiously, may be that the two major parties have not been ideological enough. Both Republicans and Democrats have represented such a grab bag of constituencies and interests over the course of their history that it has often been difficult to say what exactly each of them stands for. The GOP, in addition to its reputation as the advocate of big business and conservative social values, has at various times been the party of the antislavery movement, the reformist impulses of the Progressive Era, and the environmentalism of both Teddy Roosevelt and Richard Nixon. The Democrats, for their part, spent much of their history as an utterly improbable coalition of white Southern racists, Northern industrialists, and immigrant workers. Such oddities could take root and persist only because of the devolved nature of American politics, and because executive power happened to be vested in the presidency, not a British-style parliamentary system. The disparate factions in each party have not generally had to try too hard to find common ground and work for a common program; often, coexistence has been enough. Such radical devolution of party organization has not been without its benefits, particularly in the diversity of political cultures spanning the country, but it has also given rise to a strikingly grasping attitude when it comes to competing for public office. Because the parties have only a fuzzy set of ideas to defend—the conservatives are not necessarily the fiscal conservatives, nor the liberals necessarily the big spenders— their supporters rally around them much like sports fans around a favorite team. Democrats call themselves Democrats and Republicans call themselves Republicans as a matter of personal identity more than ideology. What the party is, or claims to be, is often more important than what the party actually does. Partisanship, in other words, is the primary organizing principle at election time. And that makes winning everything—not just the goal, but an end in itself.

Defending the candidate, not the program, is what it has always been about. Indeed, the notion of a European-style slate of candidates, chosen according to the overall vote tallies of each party, seems almost laughable in the American context. The clash of personalities is not only given primacy over the clash of ideas; in these days of politics infected by the cult of celebrity, personality is often the only thing under consideration. Playing dirty becomes not only understandable; it is virtually the norm. Call it the *American Idol* model of election practice. The audience—which is to say the voters—are told that the choice is all theirs, but really the key decisions on form and content have already been made, the contest is skewed in advance by the television producers for maximum entertainment value, and the only meaningful criterion left is to determine which candidate projects the greater charisma and the more pleasing character traits. The whole system reeks of deception from top to bottom.

Few historical figures attest to the abiding ferocity of electoral competition better than Lyndon Johnson, one of the pioneers of modern American politics who radically altered both parties' ideas on campaigning and the wielding of elective office. He always played the system ruthlessly to his own advantage—which is another way of saying he could be as brazen, skillful, and meticulous an election thief as anyone when circumstances warranted. Few politicians, in fact, have adhered as closely to Charles de Gaulle's maxim to be petty in the pursuit of power but magnanimous in the exercise of it. Johnson never pretended to be a nice guy, or even a particularly honest one, appealing to the very worst in the electorate when it served his purposes to do so. At the same time, he racked up some genuinely impressive achievements in the course of his career: landmark civil rights legislation, including the Voting Rights Act; the creation of Medicare; the food stamp program; and the beginnings of a vision to address the growing social and economic inequalities of American society. Had it not been for the calamity of Vietnam, he might have gone down as one of the great presidents of his century. As it was, Johnson shredded America's international reputation and self-confidence, was responsible for hundreds of thousands of needless deaths in Southeast Asia, and torpedoed his own career while it was at its height.

Some have sought to draw a moral equivalence between his failings as a leader and the manner in which he conducted his political battles. According to his biographer Robert Caro: "His morality was the morality of the ballot box, in which nothing matters but victory and any maneuver that leads to victory is justified, a morality that was amorality." But it is also important to see Johnson as a creature of his times and of the Texas system from which he emerged.

Curiously, while his vision of a government-driven Great Society has gone radically out of fashion, his lying, stealing, cheating approach to the elemental battleground of American politics—his singular ability to craft an expedient and effective political identity for himself while crushing his opponents without pity or twinge of conscience—has become his most striking legacy.

Johnson cheated in the first race he ever ran, for senior class representative on the student council of Southwest Texas State Teachers College in San Marcos. He and his campus buddies, known as the White Star Gang, went systematically from class to class pretending to be enrolled where they had no right to be, made sure one of their own was named temporary chairman, and recorded the class vote as an aye for Johnson regardless of the actual outcome. In 1934, three years before he first ran for Congress, Johnson was working for a Democratic representative named Maury Maverick and spent election day sitting in the Plaza Hotel in San Antonio peeling five-dollar bills off a large roll and handing each one to a Mexican American voter from the West Side slums. When Johnson made his first run for the Senate in 1941, he remembered to make sure the West Side Mexicans were taken care of, but—making a mistake he would take care never to repeat—he neglected to have his own campaign workers oversee them on election day, resulting in a crucial shortfall in his vote totals. As the journalist John Gunther observed at the time, paying off the Mexicans was no guarantee that someone else would not try to buy them out afterward. "An honest Mexican," he wrote wryly, "is one who stays bought."

In 1940s Texas everyone's votes were seemingly for sale, especially in the poorer rural areas of the state, including the heavily Mexican border regions along the Rio Grande. Illiterate Mexican Americans would be escorted to the polls by pistoleros, who would pay off their poll taxes and offer them a shot of tequila in exchange for their vote. Sometimes the ballots would be marked in advance, and sometimes the voters would be given strings with knots that lined up with the names of the candidates they were supposed to vote for. Illegal voters from Mexico proper would routinely come across the border to swell the numbers for favored candidates. Opposition poll watchers and election judges rarely objected to these procedures, since they were paid handsomely to look the other way. In six border counties centered on Duval County, about halfway between Laredo and Corpus Christi, the votes were controlled by a local boss by the name of George Parr, better known to Anglos as the Duke of Duval, and to Mexicans as Tacuacha, or "sly possum." Johnson's rival in the 1941 Senate race, the folksily corrupt Pappy O'Daniel, had enjoyed Parr's support when he ran for governor in 1940, winning 95 percent of the vote in his six-county domain. But one year later he was outmaneuvered by Johnson, who put in a personal phone call to the Duke of Duval following some assiduous legwork by one of his most trusted lieutenants. O'Daniel's total in the border counties plummeted to 5 percent in the Senate race, while Johnson picked up more than 90 percent. The reversal was denounced at the time as nauseatingly corrupt, worse than the city machines of Chicago, Kansas City, and Jersey City combined. But it was not enough to get Johnson elected.

LBJ's second big mistake, after his failure to "ride the polls" in San Antonio, as the phrase had it, was to announce his crushing advantage in the Rio Grande Valley too soon. As the Texas newspapers went to bed on election night, they were under the strong impression he had won. "Johnson with 5,152 lead, appears elected," trumpeted the next day's *Houston Chronicle*. But he had already exhausted his hand, and in East Texas the O'Daniel campaign set to work making up the shortfall with the help of pliant county judges who had taken their ballot boxes home for safekeeping, along with keys to open them. Paradoxically, O'Daniel was helped by the fact that his foes were as eager to see him elected as his friends. He was a Prohibitionist, which meant that Texas would be starved of liquor for as long as he remained in power in the state. Kicking him upstairs to Washington was the ideal way to get rid of him. Even supporters of the third-placed candidate, Martin Dies, were happy to see their votes switched to Pappy, and Johnson's lead soon melted away. A frustrated LBJ got on the phone again to George Parr to see if he couldn't rustle up a few hundred extra votes, but Parr told him: "Lyndon, I've been to the federal penitentiary, and I'm not going back for you."

The defeat of 1941 had a lot to do with Johnson's determination not to be caught on the losing side again when he made his second run for the Senate seven years later. So, too, did the fact that his career was now at an uncomfortable crossroads. To qualify for the 1948 Senate campaign, Johnson had to agree not to run for reelection to his House seat, which meant he was rolling the dice on his entire political future. His problem was that he was running against a popular conservative governor, Coke Stevenson, who finished seventy thousand votes ahead of him in the first round of the Democratic primary—Democratic primaries being the only elections that counted in the one-party, segregationist South. For the runoff, Johnson knew he would have to sweat out every last vote. Money was no object, thanks to the patronage of the construction and military contractor company Brown and Root (these days a subsidiary of Halliburton, and still very much in the political game). Johnson commissioned numerous opinion polls, a political tool then in its infancy, which persuaded him the only way to win was to run to Stevenson's right. He blasted the radio airwaves with advertisements to ram home his message, another relative novelty. He also took to campaigning by helicopter, creating a frenzy of excitement in every rural town where he landed his "Johnson City Windmill." None of this was enough, however, for him to overtake Stevenson in the first round. So he had to resort to more devious strategies. He orchestrated a succession of negative stories about his opponent that were so incendiary that Stevenson felt it beneath him even to respond. Stevenson was pilloried as a Communist sympathizer and a union shill, both outrageous claims, and was pilloried all over again as Johnson seized on Stevenson's silence to accuse him of quivering before uncomfortable home truths.

Johnson held meetings with the political kingpins in San Antonio and lavished them with inducements, including fat rolls of dollar bills to cover poll worker "expenses," to woo their support away from Stevenson, who had taken the city by a two-to-one margin in the first round. He also kept the Duke of Duval firmly on his side. When all was said and done, turnout in Duval County was an utterly implausible 99.6 percent, and Johnson won there with a similarly preposterous 99 percent of the vote. First, though, the two sides spent several days engaged in a nerve-racking game of Texas Hold 'Em, in which neither candidate dared announce more than a handful of results from his strongholds for fear of what might get stacked up against him once the numbers were on the table. On election night, Stevenson was ahead by 854. The following night, Johnson made up almost all the difference, thanks to late-breaking returns from Houston and one precinct in Duval County. Four days after the election, though, Stevenson was up again by a seemingly insurmountable 362. After six days, with nothing obvious left to count, Stevenson was still leading by 113. Johnson needed a miracle, and he got one, courtesy of an enforcer by the name of Luis Salas in Jim Wells County, one county over from Duval. At the Thirteenth Precinct in Alice, the Jim Wells county seat, Salas artfully had a 7 in one of the vote totals changed into a 9 by the addition of a simple loop, giving Johnson an extra 200 votes and with them the election.

The Stevenson campaign exploded in indignation, refusing to believe for an instant the figures could be genuine. (Several decades later, with Johnson in his grave, Salas came clean and confirmed that the late returns from Box 13 were entirely fraudulent.) Stevenson himself traveled down to Alice in the company of Frank Hamer, a legendary Texas Ranger who had set up the ambush that killed Bonnie and Clyde. Together they examined the electoral register and noticed that the last two hundred names appeared in strict alphabetical order and were written in a different color of ink from the rest. The two men were not permitted to copy the list, but they memorized as many names as they could and then set about tracking down the individuals in question, many of whom said they had not been to the polls at all. Soon, Johnson faced a dangerous new problem. Having stolen the election, he now had to fight to get away with it. His greatest fear was that the race would be thrown into the courts, and from there subjected to a full-blown criminal investigation. To avoid that, he had to persuade both the Texas Democratic Party and the secretary of state's office to sign off on the results as submitted. Seven members of the state certification board were too afraid to show up to their own meeting, much less offer an opinion on the validity of the result, but Herman Brown of Brown and Root sent his private plane to pick up three of them at their homes and made sure they put their seal on Johnson's eighty-seven-vote margin of victory. The party, which held ultimate responsibility for its own primaries, was a tougher nut to crack, with many members of the state executive committee arguing in favor of a court contest to resolve the controversy one way or the other. At the decisive meeting, the committee first voted 29-28 for Johnson, then, after one member had a change of heart, reverted to a 28-28 split, enough to allow the legal contest to proceed. Johnson's aides, with their backs right up against the wall, hunted the building high and low for any committee stragglers and eventually found one, a certain Charley Gibson, hiding in the toilets. Gibson's reluctant vote sealed Johnson's victory and with it perhaps the most outrageous single act of vote fraud in American history.

The legal challenges continued for a while, with subpoenas issued to more than fifty witnesses in Jim Wells, Duval, and Zapata Counties. All but a handful of the witnesses vanished, however, leaving word that they had gone "on vacation" to Mexico. Luis Salas was ordered to produce the paperwork on Box 13, but he perjured himself in court and said both copies of the list of voters had been stolen from his car one night while he was out drinking. Normally, one of the copies would have gone into the safekeeping of the local Democratic Party secretary, but the secretary had unaccountably gone missing and was never interviewed. An increasingly frustrated Stevenson then sued to have the ballot boxes opened and the votes examined and recounted, but in the absence of concrete proof of fraud he could not make the case. When even the Supreme Court refused to hear him, he gave up for good. Johnson, meanwhile, sought to minimize the stench of criminality that followed him to the Senate by turning the whole thing into a joke. He relished being nicknamed "Landslide Lyndon," and at all subsequent elections made a public show of picking up the phone to call George Parr. The Senate could have refused to seat him, the Democratic Party could have repudiated him, or the voters could have punished him by picking a different senatorial candidate in 1954. But all rolled over in the end, preferring to retain the services of a fearsome political operator and maintain the fiction of America's democratic integrity rather than ask awkward questions that could only bring disrepute upon the country's core political institutions.

More than half a century later, it is difficult not to see some reflection of Johnson's take-no-prisoners attitude in the political style of his fellow Texan George W. Bush, and especially in the maneuverings of Bush's canny campaign strategist, Karl Rove. Despite their different party affiliations and the very different eras that spawned them, Johnson and Bush tapped into much the same well of Southern populism. Just as Johnson allied himself with Brown and Root, Bush also looked to a major Texas corporation, Enron, to bankroll his early campaigns in exchange for political favors later on. The corporate money served both men well in their bids to vanquish opponents with more immediate and obvious popular appeal, enabling them to wage lavish media campaigns even as they resorted to more underhand campaign tactics. The outrageous distortions that Bush and Rove used against Ann Richards in the 1994 Texas governor's race and against John McCain in the 2000 Republican primary were not all that different from the unstinting smear campaign Johnson waged against Coke Stevenson in 1948.

Johnson is certainly not George W.'s only role model. As we shall see, the Bush political style also bears strong traces of Jacksonian nationalism, as well as the front-porch corporate hucksterism of William McKinley's Rovian campaign manager, Mark Hanna. Something of Johnson's electoral ruthlessness was unmistakably at play, though, during the 2000 presidential recount, as the Republicans seized the initiative at the first possible opportunity and quickly sought to shut down all challenges. Rove has to be the first politician or consultant since Johnson to demonstrate a comparable appetite for victory at any cost. Rove's friend and mentor Lee Atwater certainly stooped to some low campaign tricks of his own, especially during George Bush Senior's trouncing of Michael Dukakis in the 1988 presidential campaign. But Atwater never had a Florida—or, for that matter, an unprovoked and calamitous Middle Eastern war to sell to the American public.

Rove, like Johnson, learned to play rough very early in his career, almost ripping the heart out of the College Republican movement as he concocted a bogus slate of alternate delegates to get himself elected chairman in 1973. The experience left him with no sense of remorse, only euphoria. Even in the thick of the Watergate scandal, Rove had been teaching the dark arts of political espionage and negative campaigning to College Republican weekend seminars, his message being not that dirty tricks were wrong, but that it was important not to get caught. When Rove's adversary for the chairmanship, Robert Edgeworth, leaked details of the seminars to the media in a last-ditch attempt to wrest back the post he felt was rightfully his, the head of the Republican National Committee (RNC) reacted not with shock at Rove's behavior, but with fury at Edgeworth for airing the party's dirty linen in public. The RNC head at the time was none other than Poppy Bush, George the Father, who not only endorsed Rove's fraudulent election but invited him into the family inner circle as a trusted confidant, a position he never relinquished. This Republican embrace of dirty electioneering, and the dirty politics behind it, was to become a recurring feature of the sustained rightward shift in American politics over the next three decades. And as the conservative revolution progressed, Rove and the Bushes were among its prime beneficiaries.

2

THE ANTIDEMOCRATIC TRADITION AND THE NEW RIGHT

★ ☆ ★ ☆ ★ ☆ ★ ☆ ★ ☆ ★ ☆ ★ ☆ ★

You gotta remember the smartest thing the Congress did was to limit the voters in this country. Out of three and a half to four million people, two hundred thousand voted. And that was true for a helluva long time, and the republic would never have survived if all the dummies had voted along with the intelligent people.
—Richard Nixon, to John Ehrlichman on the White House tapes (1971)

If this were a dictatorship, it'd be a heck of a lot easier, just so long as I'm the dictator.
—George W. Bush, six days after the Supreme Court made him president

NOBODY GOES FAR in American public life without professing to love democracy. It is the closest thing the country has to an established religion; disavow democracy, and you might as well disavow America itself. That does not mean there is anything close to unanimity on what that democracy should look like. One might think government "of the people, by the people, for the people" implied the greatest possible participation of the largest possible number of citizens in the management of their own affairs. But there are those, in both major parties, for whom this Lincolnian ideal inspires anxiety and discomfort, even horror. Some of them are in prominent positions of power—as they have been, to a greater or lesser extent, since the dawn of the republic. They genuflect before the altar of representative democracy, as everyone must, but really what they do is take the language of America's civic religion and appropriate it to denote something quite different—giving tax cuts and regulatory windfalls to the corporations who sponsored their campaigns, say, even if this perpetuates middle-class economic insecurity and an ever-widening income gap between the very rich and everyone else; or defending America's commercial and strategic interests overseas, even if this means upholding ugly dictatorships and colluding in the suppression of popular opposition to them. In short, they redefine the public interest as their own interest and see elections not as a celebratory expression of popular will, but rather as an exercise in salesmanship and obfuscation, the province of slithery strategists and borderline crooks, in which half the electorate is deterred from coming to the polls at all and the other half is bombarded with deceptions and personalized attacks on the other candidates. Under such circumstances, voters themselves can sometimes come to look like the enemy.

A week before the 2004 presidential election, conservative newspaper columnist Mona Charen wrote an irascible piece for the *Washington Times* asserting that it was indeed the voters who posed the gravest threat to the American political system. The problem, she explained, was that at least a quarter of them were too ignorant to be trusted, a fact the chattering classes chose to overlook out of a misplaced sense of political correctness. "If a person is utterly ignorant about matters of public policy," she argued," then he or she has a solemn obligation to refrain from voting." Curiously, she didn't think it was the media's responsibility to provide more substantive coverage of the issues, or the government's responsibility to improve the quality of public education. If the voters were ignorant it was their own fault—their "choice," as she put it—and they should have the courtesy to butt out of the political process altogether.

It was probably no coincidence that Charen's piece appeared on the eve of a keenly anticipated presidential election in which all forecasts correctly pointed to the highest voter turnout in a generation. Bush partisans like herself were understandably nervous that a rush of new voters might translate into more support for John Kerry. (Many leading Democrats made the same erroneous supposition.) But Charen's sentiments were informed by ideology as well as partisan interest. Since the country's foundation, similarly reactionary voices have warned about the dangers of excessive democracy and the questionable desirability of universal suffrage. When these voices have been in the ascendant politically, they have also taken direct action—orchestrating, for example, the deliberate disenfranchisement of the black South and much of the industrial working class in the first half of the twentieth century. Overt expressions of antidemocratic thought were largely drummed out of public discourse in the wake of the civil rights movement and the Voting Rights Act, but the underlying political sentiment never went away. Periodically, a newspaper commentator or think-tank analyst will revive the old arguments that excessive deference to the will of the people is an invitation to social and political chaos, that power is best left in the hands of those who understand and wield it best, that opening the process to the poor, the ignorant and—by implication—the dark-skinned can lead only to corruption, fraud, stagnation, or worse.

In the wake of the Vietnam War, for example, it became fashionable in certain conservative circles to blame the American defeat on an excess of meddling in the policy debate by both the media and the grassroots antiwar movement. In 1975, the year Saigon fell, Michel Crozier, Samuel Huntington, and Joji Watanuki wrote a notorious book to that effect for the Trilateral Commission. Called *The Crisis of Democracy*, it argued that popular participation in government had gone too far, that there was in fact an "excess of democracy," and that if leaders wanted to be more effective they needed to counter the trend through greater authoritarianism, the cultivation of a more pliant media, and a general encouragement of apathy and political disengagement. The philosophy underpinning these arguments was very much of a piece with the late-nineteenth-century opponents of universal suffrage: essentially, a belief in a natural ruling order, which should be left alone to exercise its power for the greater good of everyone.

No politician or writer for a mainstream publication has dared be quite so forthright. George Will came close in a 1983 *Newsweek* column in which he said people were not owed the right to vote per se, merely the right to good government. Again, the implication was that some Americans were better placed than others to decide what that good government should be. High voter turnout was not necessarily an indication of a robust democracy, Will added; just look at Weimar Germany and where it led.

The flaw in such arguments is that they suggest the problem lies with democracy itself—that greater popular representation will invariably turn order into chaos. It is certainly true that moments of political instability can be marked by high electoral turnout, but that is because voters respond all the more strongly when they feel issues of vital importance are at stake. Sometimes democracy will prevail over the threat of tyranny, and sometimes, as in Germany in the 1930s, it will not. But it seems churlish to blame the failures on the very political movements working hardest to prevent them. Conservatives in the United States—and by conservatives I mean some of the more entrenched interests of both major parties, not just Republicans—have an abiding belief that an outwardly calm environment is by definition a symptom of political well-being. Robert Kaplan wrote an essay for the *Atlantic Monthly* in 1997 in which he said voter apathy troubled him less than the idea of a volatile political system with a hyperactive, out-of-control electorate. "The last thing America needs," he wrote, "is more voters—particularly badly educated and alienated ones—with a passion for politics."

Yet this belief is surely misplaced. Democracy is a messy, rowdy, unpredictable business, as it should be. There was nothing neat or tidy about the crowning achievements of American democracy: the Revolutionary War, the movement to abolish slavery, or even the relatively civilized battle for women's suffrage. Order and tranquility are either indicative of a homogeneous, contented, largely static society—Liechtenstein, not Louisiana—or else they betoken some crucial missing democratic element. Where they are not the chilly consequence of jack-booted authoritarianism, they are achieved through widespread alienation, disengagement from the political process, and deep conformism in public discourse.

The United States is of course notorious for poor voter turnout. As of early 2005, an ongoing study by the International Institute for Democracy and Electoral Assistance (IDEA) placed it 139th out of 172 countries for national elections since 1945, lower than any other industrialized country and roughly on a par with the likes of Bangladesh, Gambia, and Kyrgyzstan. In reality things probably aren't quite that bad, because IDEA's numbers are based on voting-age population, not the narrower and more accurate gauge of voter eligibility, but they are still quite bad enough. The figures for local elections, where interest can be low and meaningful competition scant, are even more shameful. Turnout rates from some of the most spectacularly ill-attended races of the 1990s include 5 percent for a mayoral election in Dallas, 7 percent for a congressional primary in Tennessee, 6 percent for a gubernatorial primary in Kentucky, and barely 1 percent for a handful of school board elections in suburban Detroit. The United States certainly does not want for electoral contests: no other country asks its voters for their opinion on quite so many judges, school board members, or parks commissioners, much less solicit permission to issue bonds for local building projects or rewrite city tax codes. The problem is, too many voters either do not care one way or the other about these issues, feel overwhelmed by the expertise they must acquire to pronounce on them, or else see little point in adding their voices to what can often be a done deal deprived of meaningful electoral competition. Is this contentment, or a system ripe for takeover by unscrupulous power brokers who have understood how to manipulate the widespread apathy for their own ends?

Oddly, the ills of the system are routinely ignored by the two major parties, and almost all debate on the topic is drowned out by near-constant affirmation of the country's greatness and strength. In their book *Why Americans Don't Vote and Why Politicians Want It That Way*, Frances Fox Piven and Richard Cloward describe this mind-set as America's "democratic hubris," the illusory notion that the United States still leads the world in its commitment to mass political participation, just as it did in the 1830s and 1840s. Not only is this clearly not the case, but the practice of modern politics is in fact a betrayal of many of the principles that the Jacksonians, and before them the Jeffersonians, saw as key to the health of the American democratic experiment. In those early days, expanding the franchise was regarded as a bulwark against the accumulation of power by "the aristocracy of our monied corporations," as Thomas Jefferson put it. Political leaders were supposed to be free of corporate influence as a precondition of their effectiveness and accountability. Decision making was supposed to be devolved as far down to the local level as possible. Fat chance of much of that these days. It was also hoped that political parties, to the extent that their development was inevitable, could remain dynamic and flexible. Narrowing the field to the Tweedledum and Tweedledee of modern-day Republicans and Democrats, with each acting as a foil for the other's disinterest in broader political engagement, was never the idea at all.

There are good reasons to question the founding fathers' attachment to democracy—many were deeply skeptical—just as there are reasons to wonder how representative the Jacksonian system really was. Still, the collective memory has become suffused with an almost religious reverence and nostalgia for the early life of the republic, from the drafting of the Constitution to the first explorations of the untamed West. Not only is the present justified by false analogy with the past, to which it is linked along a supposedly unbroken continuum, but the past itself has taken on mythological overtones, placing it beyond criticism and, in a certain sense, beyond history. This idealization has been going on for a long time and, paradoxically, has been invoked most forcefully when American democracy has been at its weakest. Woodrow Wilson's administration loved to talk about rediscovering America's lost values of freedom and individual enterprise—this at a time when the White House itself was segregated, race-baiting and lynching were becoming common currency in the South, and voter participation everywhere was plummeting because of literacy tests, registration requirements, and overt official hostility to immigrants and blacks. Yale historians Charles Seymour and Donald Paige Frary perhaps captured the truer spirit of the age when they wrote in 1918: "The theory that every man has a natural right to vote no longer commands the support of students of political science."

Nostalgia has always been a potent weapon for America's anti-democrats. Folk memories of a pseudo-Jeffersonian rural idyll, in which landowners administered their own affairs wisely and equitably, were invoked with insistent regularity in the mid-nineteenth century as a way of denouncing the vices of urban political machines and, later, the rowdy effrontery of the radical farmers' and Populist movements. The premise was that certain citizens (white rural Protestant landowners, for the most part) were "real" Americans deserving of full voting rights, while the rest (industrial workers, agricultural laborers, foreigners, and former slaves) were of questionable legitimacy and should be vigorously challenged at the polls, if not barred outright. The appeal to an idealized past was a convenient foil for the underlying political agenda, which was to limit the power of the cities in state and national politics, to strangle any popular labor movement capable of challenging the capitalist class, and to find a workable settlement of grievances between Southern states and the North in the wake of the Civil War. In the end, all questions of race, civil rights, suffrage, and state-versus-federal control were made subordinate to the generation of wealth, which was used to placate the political elites even as it came to hang a large chunk of the electorate out to dry.

From the defeat of the Confederates in 1865 to the end of the First World War, and particularly during the pivotal decade of the 1890s, the great advances in voting rights that had marked the first half of the nineteenth century were systematically and drastically checked. All aspects of voting, from registration to polling-place access to the intelligibility of the ballot itself, were made as arduous and as obstacle-ridden as possible for voting groups regarded as undesirable. If they were not hamstrung by poll taxes or quizzes on the contents of their state constitutions, they might find that voter registration in their county was restricted to an impossibly few hours a month, or that their precinct location was moved thirty or forty miles away without warning on the eve of the election. The restrictions greatly empowered the two major parties, which found it convenient, after they had established their near-exclusive duopoly, to sponsor the voters they wanted and ignore the rest. Even those who did make it to the polls were given precious little to decide. With the Democrats firmly in control in the South from the mid-to-late 1890s and the Republicans dominant almost everywhere else at the state and national levels, party competition collapsed and voter participation shriveled right along with it.

Although the cause of voting rights made significant strides in the twentieth century, with women getting the vote in 1920, blacks winning full rights in 1965, registration tests and other restrictions abolished, and the franchise expanded to include eighteen- to twenty-one-year-olds, the damage wrought during the Gilded Age and its aftermath has never been fully mended. Other industrialized countries have experienced problems with voter apathy in recent years, but only in the United States has there been an almost exact correlation between participation and socioeconomic status. In other words, it is the bottom half of the heap that fails to show up time after time. And the parties seem to like it that way, preferring to control the electorate they know than to try to grow themselves a new one. The 2004 presidential election was a little unusual because of the intense competition and the correspondingly high passions on both sides. Liberal groups inspired by Howard Dean's insurgent candidacy for the Democratic nomination found new ways to raise money and expand grassroots activity through the Internet—though still, overwhelmingly, in the top half of the electorate—while conservatives expertly marshaled by Karl Rove and the Republican National Committee did much the same, to even greater effect, through churches and community groups. The result was a sharp uptick in turnout, with 17 million more voters flocking to the polls than in 2000. But that outburst of energy, typical of watershed elections throughout U.S. history if rarely sustained over time, did not have more than an incidental impact on lower-order races for Congress, state, and local office. The system as a whole remained largely moribund because of the absurd number of safe seats reserved for incumbents and the dearth of substantive discussion of the issues at stake. The political class appeared, for the most part, to be conducting a conversation with itself, offering little to alleviate a long-standing but rarely expressed anxiety that government in America might not, after all, rest on the consent of the governed.

In the past decade or so, much of the political mainstream, both Democrat and Republican, has gone beyond simply ignoring the problem of growing electoral disengagement and begun to rationalize it by somehow equating deregulated market forces and a robust economy with giving people what they want. As Thomas Frank has written with characteristic verve about the Clinton era:

> From Deadheads to Nobel-laureate economists, from paleo-conservatives to New Democrats, American leaders in the nineties came to believe that markets were a popular system, a far more democratic form of organization than (democratically elected) governments . . . Markets expressed the popular will more articulately and more meaningfully than did mere elections. Markets conferred democratic legitimacy . . . ; markets looked out for our interests.

Only the progressive wing of the Democratic Party, along with libertarian third parties and the non-Democratic left, has continued to plead a more or less conventional case for voting rights: greater ease of registration, better education on the issues, longer and more worker-friendly polling hours, and so on. On the Republican right, meanwhile, some influential voices have taken a radically different tack and questioned the utility of voting at all. Benjamin Ginsberg, a prominent Republican Party election lawyer in the forefront of the Bush-Gore battle in Florida, has been writing books for years in which he has questioned the electoral system's capacity to promote effective government and traced the outlines of what he calls a "postelectoral era." "The era of the citizen is now coming to an end," he declared in 2002. Ginsberg does not opine whether he sees this change as beneficial. That, after all, might constitute a violation of America's sacrosanct adherence to democracy worship. But he does argue that government has found ways to circumvent the mass electorate, relying on the courts, its own bureaucracy, and "weapons of institutional combat" such as congressional investigations, media revelations, and alliances with foreign governments to further its agenda. Politics has thus been reduced to a personal, not a collective, experience for the individual voter and needs to be tailored as such.

A Cato Institute report published a few weeks ahead of the 2004 presidential election took Ginsberg's argument a step further, envisioning a future in which the individual citizen's primary tool of political expression would no longer be the ballot box but rather "foot-voting," that is, staying in a community if its leadership was acceptable and leaving for somewhere more amenable if it was not. The author of the report, George Mason law professor Ilya Somin, did not quite dare advocate the abolition of voting—he left that ambiguous—but suggested voter ignorance had reached heights that sharply circumscribed its usefulness. Instead, he proposed a system of radically "decentralized federalism" in which cities and townships would compete in a sort of civic free market for the custom of their inhabitants. The argument was bizarre, almost laughably so, since the foot-voting he described has always existed and in no way precludes the continuation of electoral democracy. It was also uncomfortably reminiscent of the venom with which hot-blooded Republican partisans shouted down certain Hollywood liberals and other Bush administration critics in the wake of September 11. What Somin was saying, albeit dressed up in polite professorial language, was, *Hey buddy, this is America, and if you don't like the way we run things, just get the hell out.*

Such reactionary nonsense might not be worth noting but for the resonance with similarly antidemocratic thinking in the corridors of power. Institutionally, the biggest culprit has been the Supreme Court, which not only struck a blow against the principle of counting all the votes in its election-ending *Bush v. Gore* decision in 2000, but also chose to throw into doubt, as no Supreme Court had in over a century, the very notion that citizens have a right to vote at all. Both in oral argument and in the final majority ruling, it was pointed out that the Constitution grants no rights of suffrage in presidential elections, and that state legislatures are entitled to withdraw the vote at any time and issue their own slates of presidential electors. Justice Antonin Scalia was particularly vehement on this point, appearing quite unbothered by more than a century and a half of established voting practices, and making only tangential reference in his remarks to the—admittedly incomplete—voting rights provisions of the Fourteenth and Fifteenth Amendments.

Antidemocratic thought has also had a direct influence on the Bush administration. On the edges of policy making (but absolutely central to the Republican grassroots) are the Christian fundamentalists, who reject the separation of church and state and believe God, not the people, should be the ultimate arbiter of governmental power. One thinks of General William "Jerry" Boykin, the deputy undersecretary of defense for intelligence, who acknowledged Bush was not the choice of "the majority of America" in 2000 but argued that his lack of democratic legitimacy only proved he had been chosen directly by God. Even closer to the heart of the administration are a number of key defense and national security players, the hard core who pushed for the 2003 invasion of Iraq, whose driving ideology is not religious but stems from their admiration for the late University of Chicago philosopher Leo Strauss. Strauss, a German Jew who fled the Nazis but did not think persecuting Jews was, in itself, entirely illegitimate, was a confirmed antimodernist who saw liberal democracy as a recipe for weak, flabby, decadent societies. He reserved his greatest admiration for tyrants in the classical sense—leaders who could keep their people lean and dynamic through fear, judicious management of social conflict, and national solidarity against an external enemy, real or invented. He believed power was too important to be entrusted to the vulgar masses, preferring the establishment of an elite who could be relied upon to invoke religion, nationalism, and a world divided into good and evil to rein in the population's essential wickedness and keep it happy with the opiate of "consoling lies."

Among the administration's leading Straussians were Paul Wolfowitz, the deputy secretary of defense, who eventually admitted that the drumbeat of alarm about Saddam Hussein's nonexistent weapons of mass destruction was never more than a convenient publicity hook for war; Adam Schulsky, who headed up the Pentagon's disinformation operation and was thus a sort of deception peddler-in-chief; Richard Perle, of the National Defense Policy Board; Stephen Cambone, undersecretary of intelligence; and Elliott Abrams, Iran-Contra scandal veteran and member of the National Security Council. Other influential acolytes and former students of Strauss's included both Irving Kristol, the father of the neoconservative movement, and his son William Kristol, editor of the *Weekly Standard*; cultural warrior and former education secretary William Bennett; and Supreme Court Justice Clarence Thomas.

It seems extraordinary that a single university professor should attract such a loftily placed following outside the academy. Indeed, the very suggestion that the administration had fallen into the hands of a Straussian cabal prompted Wolfowitz to scoff at one point about the ravings of "fevered minds." Some of Strauss's academic defenders have insisted he was a pedagogue, first and foremost, and would have been horrified to be associated with anything as crude as a political movement. But there is no doubt that his neoconservative students and admirers developed a kinship over a very long period, starting in the Reagan administration and continuing through the Republican drought of the Clinton years, when they formulated their Project for a New American Century, including "regime change"—a specifically Straussian term—in Iraq. One hesitates to call them fascists, even if an ideal form of fascism is what Strauss outlined. It is certainly safe to say that their intellectual training taught them to be contemptuous of democracy and its traditions. Perhaps the best way to understand their ambitions in the American context is to set them against the president Strauss himself admired most, Abraham Lincoln. From the Straussian perspective, Lincoln did two things worthy of admiration: he set aside the Constitution when he felt it served a higher national interest, and, in his efforts to stitch a divided country back together, he laid special emphasis on creating a national mythology centered on the enduring wisdom of the founding fathers. The Civil War is a rich stew all around for the Straussian imagination: the renewal of a country and a national purpose through bloodshed and heroic sacrifice. There was more to Lincoln than that, of course, not least his idealistic vision of a true people's democracy. One supposes the Straussians would dismiss that as just another consoling lie.

When George W. Bush was elevated to the presidency by a partisan Supreme Court at the end of the battle over Florida, it was widely suggested that the reason people didn't take to the streets in fury was that the political stakes just weren't high enough. The country was essentially prosperous, stable and happy—a "hotbed of rest" in the witty formulation of CNN commentator Jeff Greenfield—so why rock the boat? The election *was* awfully close and, heck, someone had to come out the winner.

With a little hindsight, one can appreciate how flawed this thinking was, and not just because it was premised, once again, on the illusory notion that calm in the streets must be a mark of political well-being. The Bush administration embarked on a far more radical path than any of the soothing media pundits predicted, and Bush's campaign pledges—to be a "uniter, not a divider," to keep the federal budget in the black, to keep the United States out of the nation-building business—proved little more than consoling lies in themselves. All early assumptions that Bush would want to govern from the center, in acknowledgment of the bizarre fashion by which he rose to power, were likewise blown out of the water. None of this, though, came out of the blue, nor should it have elicited such widespread surprise. The Republicans had spent a generation planning their return to political supremacy, developing something that they and the Democrats had studiously avoided for most of their history —a dominant, driving ideology. It was, as it turned out, an ideology more extreme than anything seen since the 1920s: a plutocratic vision of U.S. leadership at home and unilateralist military supremacy abroad, a systematic demolition of the institutions and programs established by the New Deal as well as radical corporate deregulation, especially in the energy sector. In its very conception this program was hostile to the economic interests of the great mass of the electorate, who were to be co-opted through concealment of the degree of radicalism being contemplated, and also through the perpetuation of culture wars full of fake outrage that pitted mainstream America against a supposedly all-powerful, arrogant liberal elite. The new Republican ideology was not an ideology in the sense commonly applied to political parties in a democracy, because it was a creed shared only by the leadership, not by the party's supporters, who were fed little morsels about "family values" and "standing up for America" but otherwise kept almost completely in the dark, if not also actively deceived about what the party was up to.

The Republican sweep of the House of Representatives in 1994 marked one high-water mark of this new radicalism, as Newt Gingrich notoriously described President Clinton as "the enemy of normal Americans" and the neoconservative stalwart Kenneth Starr went sniffing through the dirty laundry of a White House intern who didn't know when to keep her mouth shut. The 2000 campaign, wrapped though it was in the mantle of moderation, was another pivotal moment. Even during primary season Karl Rove made clear that the model he was emulating was the 1896 McKinley campaign, which had transformed the political landscape, bringing the Populist rebellion to an abrupt halt and heralding an entire generation of Republican dominance in Washington. Political journalists were either disinclined to believe Rove could bring about such a sea change, or else they were not historically savvy enough to understand what he was talking about. Either way, most of them failed to appreciate the scope of his and Bush's ambition.

Warning signs had also long since started flashing, for those willing to see them, about how dirtily the Republicans were prepared to
play—more dirtily than anything they had attempted when their
ideological edge was blunter and both they and the Democrats still
abided by a few rudimentary limits on the rules they dared bend and
break. (Among other things, the new Republican ideology ripped up
the rules of bipartisan engagement, during elections and at every
other time; bipartisanship was now defined, by Grover Norquist, as
"another name for date rape.") The new hardball tactics were
defined, first and foremost, by resentment. For most of the previous
half-century, starting with the Roosevelt administration, the
Republicans had been the minority party in Congress and felt they
had swallowed more than enough humiliation. They were particularly outraged, and rightly so, by an episode in 1984 in which the
Democratic leadership in the House voted to reseat an incumbent
Democrat from Indiana's Eighth District even though he had not
actually won reelection. The incumbent, Frank McCloskey, had
come out narrowly ahead on election night, only to fall several hundred votes behind his Republican challenger, Richard McIntyre,
after a recount. The Indiana secretary of state certified McIntyre as
the winner, but the Democrats, in an extraordinary act of lordly pre-
sumption, refused to acknowledge his victory. Dick Cheney, then a
congressman from Wyoming, vowed on the spot to take revenge. "I
think we ought to go to war," he said. "There's unanimity. We need
bold and dramatic action."

To seize their chance, the Republicans needed an identifiable
enemy, and they found the ideal one in Bill Clinton. On the very
evening of his election in 1992, Bob Dole, then the Senate minority
leader, argued he didn't have a proper mandate since the presidential vote had been split three ways (with Bush Sr. and Ross Perot),
leaving Clinton without a popular majority. And it only went down-
hill from there: "Not My President" T-shirts, interminable investigations into pseudoscandals, conspiracy theories about Vince
Foster's suicide, and on and on. When the Republicans took control
of the House in 1994, they weren't content just to bask in their upset

victory. They accused the Democrats of misusing the just-passed National Voter Registration Act, also known as the "motor voter" law, to register untold numbers of ineligible felons, noncitizens, children, and dead people, as well as a particularly eye-catching Lhasa Apso dog from California, all the better to steal as many congressional races as possible. A flurry of dead-end legal actions suggested that the accusations had little, if any, merit. But that, perhaps, was not the point. A decade after the Indiana incident, the Democrats were on notice that the boot was now on the other foot and they had better watch out who was going to get stomped on next.

The Republicans were not above playing their own electoral tricks when the stakes seemed high enough. One play that went wrong—and thus came to public attention—was an attempt in a crucial 1995 California legislature race to place a dummy Democratic candidate on the ballot to split the opposition in a competitive Orange County assembly district. The dummy candidate turned out to be a friend of the Republican aspirant, Scott Baugh, and was unceremoniously thrown back off the ballot by a federal judge after the real Democrat figured out what was going on. Six people wound up facing vote fraud charges, including the wife of the local Republican congressman and a senior adviser to the Republican speaker of the state assembly.

Mostly, though, the Republicans were interested in waging non-electoral warfare of the kinds outlined in Benjamin Ginsberg's books. These methods were scarcely more honest or ethical than fiddling elections, but they had the inarguable advantage of staying on the right side of the law. The effort to impeach Clinton was, of course, the centerpiece. It might not have paid immediate dividends— Clinton was too smart and too popular, and the Republican leadership too hypocritically tangled in its own nexus of extramarital affairs. But it helped create an enduring image of Democrats as slippery, equivocal, moral degenerates and Republicans as upstanding defenders of rectitude in public life. The language of Christian conservatism was especially significant here, at a time when the religious right was taking over the Republican Party in one heartland state after another, including Bush's Texas. When the 2000 election battle erupted, the Republicans' repeated invocations of morality made a crucial difference in public perceptions as the Bush campaign, turning reality at least 140 degrees on its head, painted the Gore camp as the real frauds and cheats and themselves as the aggrieved defenders of a victory rightfully earned.

The real wonder of the past decade is that in a country split almost exactly evenly between the two major parties, the Republicans have contrived to win control of almost everything. It is important not to underestimate the brilliance of party strategists like Karl Rove in persuading lower-income voters to go against their own pocketbooks and still find compelling reasons to vote GOP. One cannot overstate, either, the Democrats' repeated failure to grasp who exactly they are supposed to be representing, or why— their failure, in other words, to counter the Republicans' hard-charging ideology with one of their own. But the system has also been skewed in the Republicans' favor in ways that clearly do not reflect the will of the people. Sometimes this has been the doing of the Republicans themselves, sometimes it has been a matter of two-party collusion, and sometimes it has been an accident of broader rightward-flowing political currents. If America is in danger of solidifying into a one-party state at the national level, it is because of three major distorting effects: the majoritarian system, particularly some of the more recent aggressive bouts of gerrymandering of congressional and state legislative districts; the drastic increase in the prison population, due to the war on drugs and other factors, and the devastating effect it has had on voter eligibility; and finally, that old thorn in the side of progressive political thinking, the Electoral College.

The electoral system, first of all, has become so sclerotic, especially when it comes to House and state assembly races, that holding elections at all can sometimes seem like a waste of time. For the past few election cycles, around 99 percent of House incumbents have been reliably reelected, and the margins by which they have cruised to victory have steadily grown. It is unusual for congressional races to go entirely uncontested, but at the state legislative level more than one-third of winning candidates routinely face no major-party opposition at all. (In 2000, the figure was 41 percent; in 2004 it was 36.9 percent.) There are a handful of reasons for this trend, but chief among them is the insidious effect of gerrymandering—the periodic redrawing of district boundaries, based on the decennial U.S. Census—which is unwisely but irresistibly overseen in all but a handful of states by the politicians themselves.

Already in the 1991 round of redistricting, incumbents were shameless about making their own districts safer, and dominant parties in state legislatures were equally shameless about screwing their opponents. But the 2001 round was worse still, partly because the level of rancor between the two major parties had reached record heights, and partly because computer technology made it possible to process previously unimaginable quantities of voter data and redraw boundaries with forensic precision to achieve any desired outcome. The geographical contortions involved can be bewildering. The salamander-shaped district in Elbridge Gerry's 1790s Massachusetts that gave rise to the term "gerrymander" in the first place has nothing on the primal squiggles and stretchings that now sully the electoral map, sometimes crossing mountains, deep canyons, or hundreds of miles of wilderness as they go. One notorious gerrymandering effort in California was nicknamed the "Jesus district" because you had to walk over water to get from one side to the other.

Politicians are often refreshingly candid in admitting what this is all about. "We are in the business of rigging elections," North Carolina state senator Mark McDaniel said bluntly after the 2001 round. "This . . . basically does away with the need for elections," concurred Tony Quinn, a Republican redistricting consultant in California. And they were not exaggerating. The 2004 House of Representatives elections were "the least competitive in history," according to Rob Richie of the nonpartisan Center for Voting and Democracy, because the number of marginal races plummeted to less than one in twenty, a record low, and only three incumbents outside Texas lost their seats. Texas was a special case, because of an aggressive and utterly anomalous extra round of gerrymandering orchestrated by the House's Texan majority leader Tom DeLay in 2003, which was designed solely to tip the balance of Texas's congressional delegation from Democratic to Republican control. (And so it came to pass.) In California, the most populous state in the union, not one of the 153 congressional and legislative seats up for grabs changed party hands. "What kind of democracy is that?" California's unorthodox movie-star governor Arnold Schwarzenegger asked as he proposed moving the redistricting process back into the hands of an independent, nonpartisan panel at the beginning of 2005. There were grounds to wonder whether Schwarzenegger's interest in this issue was to enhance democracy itself, or merely to create more Republican districts in an overwhelmingly Democratic state. Still, his analysis of the problem was spot-on, and all too rare among politicians in the corrupted two-party landscape.

There is nothing about gerrymandering that inherently favors one party or the other, of course, but the net effect of the last rounds of redistricting nationwide has been a decisive Republican advance, which the Democrats, because of the concomitant collapse of electoral competition, have little chance of recouping in the foreseeable future. In 2000, a particularly anomalous year, the Democrats actually won more House votes than the Republicans in the 371 districts where the race was even remotely competitive. But the Republicans picked up 191 of these districts, and the Democrats only 179. In 2004 the Republicans at least won a majority of the votes as well as a majority of the seats, but their performance still received a crucial extra boost. With 50.1 percent of the vote, they picked up 53.3 percent of the seats, while the Democrats won 47.5 percent of the vote and only 46.4 percent of the seats. The Senate tells a similar story, although there the gerrymander is hardwired into the federal system because every state gets two Senate seats regardless of size. Since the Republicans tend to dominate the less populous states, they need markedly fewer votes than the Democrats to win a majority on Capitol Hill. In 2004, for example, Democratic Senate candidates won roughly three million more votes than Republicans, but the Republicans still picked up four extra seats. There is something almost Soviet about these races, where the results are predetermined to the point where the side with fewer votes actually ends up ahead. What is being created is a system where politicians no longer have to worry about public accountability, because they know no matter how much they cheat, steal, or screw up, they will almost certainly get reelected anyway. Instead of the people electing the government, it is as if Brecht's famous poem about the 1953 uprising in East Berlin had become reality, and the government, thanks to the manipulations of gerry-mandering, was electing the people instead.

Not every distortion is of equal concern. The whole point of a majoritarian system, after all, is to reward small victories with deci-sive margins in the interests of strong government. It is certainly true that much of the pro-Republican gerrymandering would not have taken place without Republican gains in various statehouses over the past fifteen years, just as pro-Democratic gerrymandering in California, an exception to the overall trend, was made possible by the Golden State's shifting to the center-left in the mid-1990s. But winning decisive majorities is one thing; locking in those majorities so they become permanent is quite another. Look at Florida, a state where voter registration tilts slightly in the Democrats' favor, but where the governor's office, both houses of the legislature, and an overwhelming majority of county governments are all in Republican hands. The only competitive elections left in Florida are statewide ones, and even there the Democrats face daunting disadvantages so long as the administration of elections remains, as it has been for years, in partisan Republican hands.

Chief among those disadvantages is the blanket disqualification of felons and ex-felons. It is not, as Republicans sometimes enjoy arguing, that criminals are automatically attracted to the Democratic Party. But it is a fact that African Americans tend to vote Democrat by a nine-to-one margin. And it is also a fact that African Americans are imprisoned in numbers way out of proportion to their represen-tation in the overall population. The situation is particularly acute in

Florida, because African Americans are pursued there more zealously than anywhere else in the country—a staggering one in three black Floridian men has a criminal record—and because Florida is one of just seven states that denies felons the automatic restoration of their voting rights once they have completed their sentences, a tradition originating in the vote-suppression laws of the Jim Crow era. In all, between four hundred thousand and six hundred thousand adults in Florida have lost their suffrage rights because of a criminal history. Even allowing for the likelihood of low turnout, this group represents a lost bloc of tens of thousands of potential votes, more than enough to sway the outcome of a close race.

As Florida goes, so goes the nation. A sixfold increase in U.S. incarceration rates since the 1970s, fueled notably by a surge in drug-related prosecutions carrying ever more draconian penalties, has translated into the disenfranchisement of almost five million voting-age Americans. That's well over 2 percent of the voting-age population, compared with less than 1 percent in 1976. (The incidence of violent crime, meanwhile, has remained roughly stable over the same period.) Of these, around 1.5 million have completed their sentences. There is nothing automatic about denying convicted criminals the vote, and indeed two states, Maine and Vermont, allow their prison inmates to participate fully in the election process. But in many states, especially Republican-controlled ones, the case for disenfranchisement carries very concrete political benefits. Christopher Uggen of the University of Minnesota has calculated that because of the exclusion of felons and ex-felons, Republicans have won at least seven Senate races over the past twenty years that would otherwise have gone to their Democratic opponents. If ex-felons had been allowed to vote in 2000, Al Gore would have carried Florida by about sixty thousand votes, and with it the presidency. Conversely, if today's incarceration rates had existed in 1960, Richard Nixon would have won the popular vote against John F. Kennedy and very possibly prevailed in the Electoral College, too. The South is the region where the felon disenfranchisement issue resonates the strongest, not least because it is where the question of race remains most explosive. In 2001, South Carolina's Republican-controlled House of Representatives seriously considered a bill to disenfranchise felons for fifteen years beyond the completion of their sentences. When it was suggested to one of the bill's sponsors, John Graham Altman, that such a law would adversely affect African Americans, he replied: "If it's blacks losing the right to vote, then they have to quit committing crimes."

A whiff of the bad old days of slavery and segregation also pervades the presidential Electoral College. Not only was its inception the result of an accommodation with the Southern states, allowing them to include their slave populations in the state-by-state weighting of the college, even though the slaves themselves had no right of suffrage, but it also continues to discriminate against African Americans, since the votes of overwhelmingly Democratic black minorities in the South are drowned out and effectively annulled by white Republican majorities in those states. And that is only one shortcoming of the college system. Because each state gets one electoral vote per senator, regardless of population, the system automatically works against larger, more populous states in favor of smaller, rural ones. These days, that means a built-in advantage for the Republicans—Bush took eleven of the seventeen smallest states in both 2000 and 2004. Reliably Democratic California, for example, has roughly seventy times the population of reliably Republican Wyoming, but in 2004 it had fifty-five electoral votes against Wyoming's three, a ratio of just over 18:1. A Wyoming vote, in other words, carries almost four times the weight of a California vote. Before the Civil War, Southern plantation owners effectively voted on behalf of their slaves; now the sparse populations of the Great Plains and the West effectively cast votes on behalf of elk, buffalo, and longhorn sheep.

There are no good arguments in favor of the Electoral College, only bad ones. And even these boil down, essentially, to just two. There is the traditionalist argument, which, like the country-music patriarch in Robert Altman's movie *Nashville,* suggests "we must be doing something right to last two hundred years." And there is the federalism argument, which says that without the Electoral College the smaller states would lose what little visibility they retain in Washington. Both are disingenuous, if not antidemocratic and blatantly partisan in the current context. Contrary to received wisdom, the Electoral College has in fact been a factor of great instability, either sparking or threatening to spark crises on a regular basis throughout America's history. The 1800 election was a mess because of an Electoral College tie between the front-runners. In 1824 and 1876 the system sowed sufficient confusion for the rightful winner of the presidency to be robbed of his prize. In 1888 and again in 2000 the popular vote and the Electoral College tally were at variance. One can argue the college played a role in starting the Civil War, because it elevated Abraham Lincoln to the presidency in 1860 with just 39 percent of the vote, which happened to be concentrated strategically in the North. Every presidential election between 1872 and 1892 was close enough to fall prey to the college's arcana; the country can consider itself lucky that only two of the six contests were adversely affected. In the twentieth century, there were near misses in 1948, when Dewey was just a few thousand votes shy of winning the Electoral College, even though he lagged more than two million votes behind Truman; in 1960, when Kennedy's razor-thin official margin in the popular vote was probably the only thing that saved the country from a protracted Florida-style dispute over fraud and the wavering allegiance of twenty-six Dixiecrat electors in the South; in 1968, when Nixon was sufficiently worried about a meltdown that he called Hubert Humphrey before the election and tried to get him to agree that the popular vote winner should be awarded the presidency in the event of an Electoral College tie (Humphrey told him to get lost); and 1976, when very modest swings in Ohio and Hawaii would have been enough to give Ford the Electoral College, even though Carter was decisively, if narrowly ahead in the popular vote.

The federalism argument is almost entirely hollow, because the smaller states already punch well above their weight in the Senate and receive attention from presidential campaigns only if, like New

Hampshire or New Mexico, they happen to be battlegrounds. Preserving a state-by-state presidential primary system, which has nothing to do with the Electoral College, is a much more effective way of letting the voters of Iowa, or South Carolina, have their moment in the limelight. Proponents of the federalism argument are often just a whisker a way from outright hostility to representative democracy. Like the architects of Jim Crow, they believe there is a part of the country that represents the "real" America, whose voices deserve to be heeded, and another part, made up of degenerate city-dwellers, smarty-pants intellectuals, and the wrong sort of immigrant, who do not. Shortly before the 2004 election, Gary Gregg of the University of Louisville wrote a series of pro–Electoral College pieces for *National Review Online* that at least had the merit of being admirably frank about all this. He characterized Al Gore's supporters in 2000 as "a narrow band of the electorate"—an odd way to describe Gore's 48.4 percent plurality—which was "heavily secular, single, and concentrated in cities." The Electoral College, by contrast, stood up, like the Republican Party, for "the values of traditional America." The underlying thrust of Gregg's argument could not have been clearer: Republican votes have more integrity than Democratic votes, and given the choice he'd rather get his kind of president into the White House than the person who actually won. A democratic position this is not.

Even when the popular vote and the Electoral College are in alignment, there are other aspects of the system that betray the cause of representative democracy. For a start, supporters of the minority party in nonbattleground states are as good as disenfranchised and their motivation for voting severely curtailed. Without the Electoral College, one can imagine a progressive revival taking root in the South, or for that matter a revival of more diverse conservative voices in California. Minority party supporters in any given state would have a way of expressing themselves and participating in the process. As it is, the Electoral College system offers minimal incentive even to majority party supporters in nonbattleground states, since turnout has no effect on the outcome. The winning candidate takes every last electoral vote, whether 20 percent turns out or 90 percent. A direct election would make every vote instantly more valuable, including votes for third-party candidates. It would also greatly broaden national political debate, because the candidates would no longer be addressing wedge issues relevant to the most closely contested states. They would have to tailor their messages to the country as a whole.

One can fantasize endlessly about the abolition of the Electoral College, but in practice—barring a meltdown more spectacular than any the system has thrown up so far—the prospects of its demise are remote. The states most disproportionately overrepresented in presidential elections are sufficiently numerous to block ratification of any constitutional amendment put forward to change the rules. It would be a mistake, though, to see small states as the only obstacle to reform, or even to view the issue as another Republican-versus-Democrat impasse. The Democrats, it is true, have a glimmer of extra awareness about the desirability of abolishing the Electoral College, if only because they stand to gain more in the short term. Yet it is the Republicans, paradoxically, who in the last couple of election cycles have shown more inclination to organize and fight over potential new voters. The bottom line is that conservative opinion in both parties is nervous about the implications of electing the president directly. Strategists would fret about the unknown consequences of unleashing new political forces they might not be able to control. They would be forced to rewrite the already complicated and expensive rules of presidential campaigning. And the cozy duopoly the parties have enjoyed for more than a hundred years could just be upset because direct election would ease the path for third- or even fourth-party candidates. In other words, it is not just reactionaries like Gary Gregg who love the Electoral College. The entire system has become addicted to its own paucity of democratic accountability, even as it persists in congratulating itself with clockwork regularity on being the greatest democracy on the planet.

★ PART ONE ★

Voting in the Age before Mechanization

3

SLAVERY AND THE SYSTEM

★ ☆ ★ ☆ ★ ☆ ★ ☆ ★ ☆ ★ ☆ ★ ☆ ★

Let it stand as a principle that government originates from the people,
but let the people be taught . . . that they are not able to govern themselves.
—New England historian and clergyman Jeremy Belknap

Democracy as we now understand it has been superimposed on an old governmental
structure which was inhospitable to the idea. —E. E. Schattschneider

THE FOUNDATIONS OF the American political system were
not laid, as is often supposed, by semimystical sages working in
beatific harmony to extend their wisdom across the ages. The
framers of the U.S. Constitution were politicians, and as politicians
they bickered, schemed, clashed, cut deals, broke promises, and
even walked out on each other before reaching an ineluctably messy
compromise. For three months over the course of a swelteringly hot
Philadelphia summer, from May to September 1787, delegates from
twelve of the thirteen independent American states sat behind
closed doors at the Pennsylvania State House and sweated out the

details of their nascent republic. Their only relief was to repair from time to time to Benjamin Franklin's garden, where smaller groups sought refuge from the sultry heat of the negotiations beneath a shady mulberry tree. The "miracle" later hailed by Washington, Madison, and others derived not so much from the republican architecture they devised as from the fact that they reached any agreement at all. That agreement, endorsed by the signatures of thirty-nine of the original fifty-five delegates, with no active opposition from the others, was indeed a remarkable achievement. But it also had its price. The big states capitulated to the smaller states, and Northern states capitulated to the South. Key issues, most notably the manner of choosing a president, were ducked, deferred, or otherwise left in a state of confusion. Others were omitted altogether, not least the Bill of Rights, which was submitted separately to the states as a list of ten constitutional amendments and ratified on a greatly decelerated timetable. (Georgia and Connecticut did not give final approval until 1939.) Every one of these concessions and accommodations took the young country a step or two further away from the ideals of the Declaration of Independence, which had proclaimed all men to be created equal and vested legitimate political authority in the "consent of the governed." Put more bluntly, America's democratic aspirations, as we now understand them, were hobbled from the very beginning.

These days the Constitution is revered as the keystone of American democracy, but democracy was the issue perhaps furthest from the minds of a majority of the framers. Indeed, the very concept scared most of them rigid. Edmund Randolph, who was Thomas Jefferson's law partner in Virginia and went on to serve as attorney general and secretary of state, saw "the turbulence and follies of democracy" as the root cause of every problem besetting the country. Alexander Hamilton was careful to point out that what the framers were creating was a republic, not a democracy, and that an excess of popular participation could only precipitate a backslide into monarchy or some other form of tyranny. James Madison and Gouverneur Morris of Pennsylvania argued in similar terms that giving the franchise to the poor would induce them to sell their votes to the rich and turn the House of Representatives into a new aristocracy. John Adams, who did not attend the convention because he was ambassador to London at the time, worried that universal suffrage would stifle the American spirit of enterprise, since it tended "to confound and destroy all distinctions, and prostrate all ranks to one common level." Elbridge Gerry of Massachusetts, originator of that ingenious manipulation of the popular will, the gerrymander, dismissed democracy as "the worst . . . of all political evils."

When the framers talked about liberty, what they generally meant was the protection of property rights, not democracy. At its founding, the United States was primarily a country of landowners, farmers, and small-scale entrepreneurs who wanted nothing more than to tend to their interests without interference or challenge. They didn't want to see the emergence of a ruling nobility, but equally they did not want to grant the slightest indulgence to the agrarian classes or, in the South, to the slaves working their plantations. With very few exceptions, states accorded voting rights on the basis of property owned by male citizens of European ancestry. Blacks, Native Americans, women, and the nonpropertied classes were almost universally excluded. For many political leaders of the time, this arrangement was a matter of more than self-interest. It was also the key to maintaining social and political order. As Chancellor James Kent of New York put it, in terms that were to find resonance in every power center in the Western world over the next century: "Universal suffrage jeopardizes property and puts it into the power of the poor and the profligate to control the affluent . . . Universal suffrage, once granted, is granted forever, and never can be recalled . . . but by the strength of the bayonet." With Britain still recovering from the Gordon Riots of 1780 and France on the threshold of its own regicidal revolution, a little nervousness on the part of the ruling classes was perhaps understandable.

The paradox of the American experience was that the newly independent country could not decide whether it wanted to embark on a revolutionary experiment in political leadership or whether it was content simply to adapt existing structures to its own circumstances. During the Revolutionary War and for quite a while after, the anticolonialist rhetoric certainly pointed to a new, meritocratic form of government. The British had been thrown out under a banner of no taxation without representation, and most of the early state constitutions took the notion of representative democracy seriously enough to recognize voting as a fundamental right. When push came to shove, though, the framers proved far more inclined to follow the example of Britain's political institutions than they were to rebel against it. They were heavily influenced by the writings of Sir William Blackstone, whose six-volume *Commentaries on the Laws of England* (1765–1769) they cannibalized wherever they felt applicable. Much of their distaste for universal suffrage no doubt originated with Blackstone's view that poor people cannot be trusted with the vote because "they would be tempted to dispose of them under some undue influence or other." Deference to Blackstone may also explain why the framers rejected a parliamentary system and invested the presidency with many of the powers associated with a monarch—an "elective monarchy," Thomas Jefferson later called it. Although the framers denied ever considering the reestablishment of an actual king, the monarchical example cannot have been far from their thoughts during that long Philadelphia summer. John Adams suggested the president should be commonly addressed as His Highness, and Washington himself initially fancied being known as His High Mightiness.

As is now widely appreciated, no aspect of the Constitution was a greater or more enduring betrayal of the ideals of the Declaration of Independence than its indulgence of the perpetuation of slavery. What is less well understood is how slavery and the slaveholder culture profoundly affected the organization of key institutions, including both Houses of Congress and the presidency. The decision to give each state two Senate seats irrespective of size or population was not, as conventional wisdom would have it, the product of high-minded idealism about federal checks and balances and the need to protect minority interests. Rather, it was the result of a negotiated concession that the Southern and smaller Eastern states successfully wrested as their price for participating in the Union. The bald fact was that many minorities remained entirely unprotected—most glaringly, Native Americans and blacks—while one group, the slave-holders, enjoyed gross overrepresentation in the new body, and thence throughout the political system. As Michael Lind of the New America Foundation has written: "The Senate has always functioned as the last bastion of white supremacy. The balance of slave states and free states in the Senate permitted the South to preserve slavery and weaken the federal government for a generation after its population had been surpassed by that of the North." It did not help that until the Constitution was changed in 1913, senators were generally appointed by state legislatures, not elected. Hence the observation of Yale historian Robert Dahl that the Senate's real raison d'être was not as a democratic check on the rest of the system, but rather as a bulwark against "too much democracy."

The disproportionate weight accorded to slaveholders was even more glaring in the apportionment of congressional seats and, by extension, in the design of the presidential Electoral College. One of the biggest sticking points for Southern states was the possibility that their slave populations, who were of course automatically barred from voting, might count against them when it came to cal-culating the size and number of their congressional districts. So they pressed for, and obtained, a deal allowing them to have it both ways: including slaves in the population base for the purposes of carving up the political map, but continuing to grant the vote to whites only. The North might not have liked this blatant piece of political knavery, but it also felt unable to reject it out of hand, since the country's economic fortunes relied on the South for its ports and the income from its sugar and cotton crops. The upshot was an ugly compromise, whereby slaves were each counted as three-fifths of a person in overall population weighting, even as they continued to count as zero-fifths of a person in almost every other respect. The arrangement, known as the "federal ratio," was not just an endorse-ment of slaveholding in a country nominally committed to the equality of all men. It was also a clear violation of the principle of "one person, one vote," since plantation owners were effectively permitted to cast ballots on behalf of their human chattel as well as themselves. It did no honor to Washington, Jefferson, Madison, and other Southern notables that they were personal beneficiaries of this shameful system.

The adoption of the Electoral College only compounded the outrage. Admittedly, this was not undertaken lightly, or particularly willingly. Deciding how to elect the president was the single biggest sticking point at the Philadelphia convention, the lone outstanding issue forcing the delegates into a fourth month of deliberations. The matter was put to a vote no fewer than sixty times, encompassing every conceivable permutation from direct election by the people, to appointment by Congress, to the involvement on one level or another of the individual state legislatures. None of these possibilities satisfied the convention entirely, and indeed the concept of an Electoral College, in which the number of electors in any given state was equal to the size of its congressional delegation, was rejected in the early going before being put back on the agenda and reconsidered in the desperate final days when everyone just wanted to make a deal and go home. The convention, in other words, voted against the Electoral College before voting for it. Under the circumstances, the final deal was notable more for what it did *not* achieve than for what it did. It did not establish a constitutional right to vote, an omission that has never been fully corrected, even in the sobering wake of the Civil War, the collapse of Reconstruction, and more than half a century of racial segregation in the South. It did not establish any single method for selecting presidential electors, delegating that decision to the state legislatures. And it left the appropriate procedures in the event of a tie or a disputed outcome maddeningly vague, a miscalculation destined to expose the country to serious risk of a constitutional crisis on at least four occasions.

Naturally, there were reasons for all these flaws, some of them merely misguided as opposed to plain wrong. Opposition to the popular election of the president, for example, was not solely motivated by antidemocratic sentiment. Madison worried that the country was too large to produce a reliable roster of candidates of true national stature, and that in their absence only candidates hailing from the largest states could hope to prevail. He was mistaken about that—even in his own time, America did not want for political celebrities—but the point was not an unreasonable one. If the convention had wanted to cut the people out of presidential elections altogether, it would have opted for appointment by Congress. Five times a majority of delegates plumped for just that, but they could not muster the votes to make the plan stick. The one good thing about the Electoral College, then, was that it left open the possibility of greater democratic accountability in future presidential contests on a state-by-state basis. But everything else about it was thoroughly indefensible, and for constitutional boosters to claim, as they have for the past two centuries, that it was an inherently democratic instrument somehow protecting the interests of the smaller states is manifestly absurd. As designed at Philadelphia, the presidency, House, and Senate were all creatures of slavery, not democracy.

It is difficult to overstate the insidious effect slavery had on the young life of the republic. As the historian Leonard Richards has documented, in the sixty-two years from George Washington's first election as president until 1850, slaveholders—especially Virginians—controlled the White House for fifty years, the Speaker's chair in the House for forty-one years, and the chairmanship of the purse-string-holding House Ways and Means Committee for forty-two. Without the federal ratio, Missouri would have become a nonslave state and Andrew Jackson's Indian removal policy would have been voted down, while the Wilmot Proviso would have passed, outlawing slavery in territories won from Mexico. The Senate, for its part, rejected countless antislavery provisions.

The Electoral College was not put to the test during Washington's two terms. But as soon as the revered general retired to Mount Vernon, it fell victim to political scheming only incidentall related to the will of the voters. Because of the confusion left in the wake of the Philadelphia convention, the presidential electors of 1796 ended up being selected in any one of three ways: popular election of a statewide slate of electors (the method most familiar now), popular election of individual electors by congressional district, and appointment by the state legislature. The candidates for president and vice president did not run in teams, but vied separately for Electoral College votes on the understanding that the man who came in second, regardless of party affiliation, would become vice president. On top of all that, Alexander Hamilton came up with an extra wrinkle, giving each elector two votes to select a first and second choice, in a failed attempt to derail Washington's heir apparent, John Adams, and promote the South Carolina Federalist Thomas Pinckney in his place. The result was an unseemly grab for electoral votes between Adams and the man who turned out to be his closest rival, Thomas Jefferson. Adams won the election only because he plucked one vote each from Virginia and North Carolina, where electors were chosen by district. Had those states had a single slate of electors, Jefferson, not Adams, would have been declared the winner.

Chaotic as it was, 1796 was just a warm-up for the Adams-Jefferson rematch of 1800, when the system melted down altogether and exposed for the first time the undue influence of the slave states. Jefferson and the man intended as his running mate, Aaron Burr of New York, ended up with the exact same number of electoral votes, a scenario the framers had not properly considered. The election was thrown into the House of Representatives, as the rules dictated, where once again it fell prey to intense political intrigue. The will of the people was no longer a consideration, since the Constitution did not require the House to pay the slightest attention to it. Had the members done so, they might have noticed that at least twelve of Jefferson's seventy-three electoral votes were based not on voter numbers but on the distorting effect of the federal ratio. Without the ratio, he would have fallen not only behind Burr, but also behind Adams, who trailed the two front-runners by just eight electoral votes. As it was, the race came down to a straight competition for the loyalties of the state delegations in Congress, now numbering sixteen. Jefferson could count on eight of them, but needed one more to clinch the race. He found his extra support in the form of James Bayard, the lone congressman from Delaware, who had approached both leading candidates but received no response from the Burr camp. The House, which had stayed in continuous session for six days, declared Jefferson the winner on the thirty-sixth ballot.

The 1800 election was to prove decisive for many reasons. It was the undoing of the Federalists and the beginning of a more representative phase in the life of the republic. Jefferson, who embodied many of the ideals of the suffrage movement, called it a new revolution. But the awkward fact of the matter was that he didn't actually win in a meaningful, democratic sense. As John Quincy Adams later commented: "The election of Mr. Jefferson to the presidency was, upon sectional feelings, the triumph of the South over the North—of the slave representation over the purely free." Federalist critics, starting with Timothy Pickering, who had served as secretary of state under both Washington and Adams, took to calling him the "Negro president." They did not mean it as a compliment.

The structural problem of electing the vice president was fixed easily enough by the Twelfth Amendment, which was passed in time for the 1804 election and formalized the idea of a single ticket for each presidential candidate and his deputy. Not everyone was thrilled with the change, because it shifted the balance of power between the two posts decisively toward the top of the ticket. As Leonard Richards has written: "That office had some stature before 1800, but after 1800 the Virginians turned it into a dead-end job, and made sure that it always went to a political has-been." One can make the argument that the diminished powers of the vice presidency had something to do with slavery, too, since it became standard practice to place colorless Northerners in the number two spot as a way of justifying the predominance of Southerners vying for the presidency. Timothy Pickering, for his part, never stopped campaigning to repeal the Twelfth Amendment, arguing that it served only to elevate fools to the second most powerful office in the land.

• • •

It is not usually considered polite, outside the confines of university political science departments, to point out the shortcomings of the Constitution or indeed to engage critically with it at all. In the popular imagination it has come to be seen as almost divine in inspiration, an expression of America's national aspirations so pure that to question it is to attack the very marrow of the country's being. This mythology of the Constitution is, in some respects, as old as the document itself. In a letter to his fellow ambassador, John Adams, Jefferson described the delegates to the Philadelphia convention as "an assembly of demi-gods." But much of the contemporary wonderment had to do with the exhausting and genuinely impressive task of bringing together states otherwise disinclined to find common ground, much less embark on the creation of a new country. There were certainly political benefits in talking up the framers' achievements. Indeed, *The Federalist Papers* were essentially a form of propaganda designed to help secure the Constitution's ratification by the individual states.

Constitution worship, per se, did not take full flight until after the Civil War, when the manifest fragility of the country thrust new significance on the document laying out the terms of its union. George Bancroft's six-volume *History of the United States,* published in the mid-1880s, portrayed the country's foundation as nothing less than providential and the Constitution as a text as inspired as the Bible. Later, as the United States took an ever more commanding role on the world stage, the Constitution acquired what historian Michael Schudson has described as a sacred aura and the "trappings of a religious cult." America the superpower no longer regarded it as a mere foundational law—and one written for very different historical times—but rather as a timeless national creed. We still see plenty of that today, not least on the Supreme Court, where the more conservative justices do not talk about adapting the Constitution's eighteenth-century provisions to contemporary circumstances but seek instead to determine the intent of the founders as if Madison, Franklin, et al had plainly foreseen the era of high-speed Internet access, corporate campaign financing, and gay marriage. Conservative ideologues call this attitude "strict constructionism." Gore

Vidal was perhaps closer to the mark when he derided the Rehnquist court's approach as deliberation by Ouija board.

In the mythologized interpretation, the Constitution is seen as a robustly forward-looking document that raised the United States above the ranks of ordinary nations and made its future greatness possible. This is not an entirely indefensible position, but it does overlook some of the most interesting theoretical work of the past sixty years, some of it produced by historians who are themselves quite conservative. In a fascinating analysis published in the late 1960s, Samuel P. Huntington argued that the Constitution was in fact a strikingly reactionary document that overlooked a century and a half of reformist political thinking in Western Europe and had more in common with England under the Tudors than it did with contemporary systems of government. The centralization of power—the signal modernizing trait of the seventeenth and eighteenth centuries, which had taken place in England through the evolution of a parliamentary system and in France under the technocratic influence of Colbert and his followers—was entirely missing from the American model. In Europe, governmental power had been consolidated in reaction to the persistence of feudal social structures and the increasingly inefficient distribution of power between Crown, Church, and aristocracy. In America, however, there was no aristocracy to react against and, given the abundance of land and other resources, no immediate need for aggressive government intervention to manage public affairs. Huntington wrote:

> Political modernization in America has thus been strangely attenuated and incomplete. In institutional terms, the American polity has never been underdeveloped, but it has also never been wholly modern. In an age of rationalized authority, centralized bureaucracy and totalitarian dictatorship, the American political system remains a curious anachronism. In today's world, America's political institutions are unique, if only because they are so antique.

The constitutional separation of powers, often cited as the corner-stone of the American democratic system, was much more an adap-tation of the Tudor model than it was a blueprint for streamlined public administration. It wasn't the power that was separated, in fact, so much as the institutions of government, which overlapped and competed with each other and quickly became bogged down in inefficiency—one enduring reason why Americans are so suspicious of governmental authority. The question of who exactly held sover-eignty over American affairs remained ill-defined beyond the rhetor-ical insistence that it lay with "the people." As we have seen, and shall continue to see throughout this book, the governing institu-tions created by the Constitution have been less than perfect arbiters of this popular will. Huntington argued that the very idea of government by the people is vague, if not meaningless, since it does not address the question of who is in charge, and within what limi-tations. "Popular sovereignty," he wrote, "is as nebulous a concept as divine sovereignty. The voice of the people can be about as readily identified as the voice of God. It is thus a latent, passive, and ulti-mate authority, not a positive and active one."

As a rhetorical trope, however, popular sovereignty has never ceased to exert its fascination. With the rise of Andrew Jackson, America's first truly populist politician, it became the rallying cry and catchall for every government initiative, the cover behind which every abomination and outright betrayal of "the people" could con-veniently lurk. Curiously, it came to fruition through yet another botched election.

America in 1824 was in a state of political flux, largely because the outgoing president, James Monroe, had neglected to groom a suc-cessor. There were no parties, since everyone, following the collapse of the Federalists, now claimed to be a Jeffersonian Republican, and thus no obstacles to naked factionalism between the candidates for the White House. John Quincy Adams was regarded as the best-qualified contender, having served as minister to the Russian Court and secretary of state. Henry Clay, the Speaker of the House, was considered the most ambitious. Jackson, with his track record as an army general who had beaten back the British at New Orleans and conquered the Florida swamps, was the one with the most flamboyant popular appeal. But he was also regarded with alarm in elite circles, where he came across as brutish, unlearned, singularly unqualified, and barely literate. The elite, however, did not fully appreciate the impact of the 1812 war against Britain, which had brought Jackson to public prominence. Not only did the war heighten the sense that the United States had embarked on a bold experiment in representative government, posing a direct threat to the old continent, but it also prompted a significant acceleration in the growth of the voter base, since it did not seem fair to force unpropertied Americans to take up arms for their country while denying them the vote. Most white men were now eligible for the franchise, regardless of class, even if blacks, Native Americans, and women remained firmly excluded.

The upshot was that Jackson won ninety-nine electoral votes, ahead of Adams, with eighty-four, and William H. Crawford, the secretary of the treasury recently paralyzed by a stroke, with forty-one. Clay came in fourth, with thirty-seven votes. The election was not over, since Jackson had won only a plurality, not a majority, of the Electoral College, and the whole thing was thrown, as it had been in 1800, into the House of Representatives. Jackson appeared to have a much stronger lock on the White House than his forebears twenty-four years earlier, not only because he had come out clearly ahead—no ties this time—but also because he could much more easily claim a popular mandate. In 1824 only six states out of twenty-four still appointed presidential electors through their legislatures, and their number would soon dwindle down to just two, Delaware and South Carolina. As in 1800, however, the rules dictated that popular will need not have anything to do with the selection of a new president by the House. And Jackson ended up royally shafted. Clay, who had been eliminated from consideration for the White House because he lagged so far behind, took full advantage of his Speakership to assume the role of kingmaker instead. He presided over furious negotiations, deals, and at least some instances of attempted bribery, at the end of which Adams was declared the winner, with the support of thirteen state delegations to Jackson's seven.

A furious Jackson took advantage of the public's newfound appetite for accountability as he sought to stir up outrage for his own misfortune. On his way home from Capitol Hill to Tennessee he made one strident speech after another. "The people have been cheated," he thundered in Frankfort, Kentucky. "Corruption and intrigues at Washington . . . defeated the will of the people." When Adams appointed Henry Clay his secretary of state, Jackson and his followers immediately cried foul at what they saw as a "corrupt bargain" between the two men. Jackson was so successful in his campaign for sympathy that even Adams's vice president, John Calhoun, declared himself incensed by the deal with Clay, saying it was the most dangerous blow the liberty of the country had yet sustained.

There is no doubting the authenticity of the anger and frustration felt by Jackson, but what those emotions spurred him to do was entirely new in the annals of politics in the United States, or indeed anywhere: a candidate reacting to defeat by going straight back out on the campaign trail for the next election. Before Jackson, it had been regarded as sacrosanct that presidential aspirants should remain silent on their own behalf. Not only did he break that rule with impunity, he did it with unalloyed glee. Nobody had ever run a populist campaign before, and Jackson more or less made it up as he went along. He avoided debates and lofty forums, preferring to organize barbecues, tree plantings, parades, public rallies, and dinners. He and his supporters encouraged the expansion of the burgeoning newspaper trade and courted many titles for their endorsement. His campaign lavished funds on flyers and printed advertisements— the 1828 campaign was the first to hit the one-million-dollar spending mark—and put the personality of the candidate front and center, complete with his very own symbol, a sprig of hickory. The Jacksonians also gave their cause a party identification, calling themselves "Democrats" and plugging into the burgeoning political machine in New York State, the Albany Regency, to supplement their base of support in the South and West.

Above all, Jackson made sure that his opponent was subject to a steady drip of negative commentary, a tactic later taken up by politicians as disparate as Lyndon Johnson and George W. Bush, whose win-at-all-costs campaigning styles, if not necessarily their political philosophies, put them firmly in the Jacksonian tradition. Jackson used the language of democratic accountability to portray Adams as an oligarch and a snob, denouncing "the kingly pomp and splendor that is displayed by the present incumbent" and arguing that America should not be "palsied by the will of our constituents." As the election drew nearer, so did the nastiness of the campaign. Adams was accused, with no apparent justification, of pimping for Tsar Alexander I while he was minister to Russia. Jackson was accused, equally fancifully, of being the offspring of a "common prostitute" and a mulatto, while his wife, Rachel, was denounced as an adulteress and a bigamist. The strain of the campaign probably pushed Rachel into an early grave—she died of a heart attack shortly before Jackson took office. The year 1828 also marked the first presidential election with known instances of ballot fraud. Wagonloads of Jackson supporters, many of them from his native Tennessee, spilled over state lines to Kentucky and Ohio to cast votes in the names of citizens who had died—a technique that would become all too familiar in years to come. When the ballots were counted, Jackson had a crushing majority in the Electoral College—178 to Adams's 83—and his 56 percent score in the popular vote was the strongest of any presidential candidate's throughout the fractious nineteenth century.

Jackson certainly campaigned as a populist, and over his eight years in the White House he continued to inspire a surge of democratic political fervor that made the United States truly exceptional among nations. Turnout more than doubled, from 27 percent to 56 percent, between his defeat in the 1824 election and his victory four years later, and it continued to climb steeply throughout the 1830s. Suffrage might have been restricted to white males, but that alone put America far out in front of its European counterparts. It was the intense degree of participation in local, state, and national affairs throughout the union that so impressed, and unnerved, Alexis de Tocqueville on his travels in 1831. "It is hard to explain the place filled by political concerns in the life of an American," he wrote in *Democracy in America.* "To take a hand in the government of society and to talk about it is his most important business and, so to say, the only pleasure he knows." Mass political movements in most countries were a phenomenon that emerged in reaction to the industrial revolution; only in the United States did mass participation largely *precede* industrialization.

Whether Jackson governed with the popular interest in mind is quite another matter. He might have roused the new class of unpropertied voters by depicting Adams as an aristocratic bogeyman, but he did so by appealing to the same anti-intellectual, antielitist sensibilities that attracted them to Protestant fundamentalist religion, then gaining its first significant foothold on American society. He was never much of a champion of the workingman in his rhetoric, and he certainly wasn't in practice. He defended the rights of property owners against the emerging industrial working class, most notably when he sent federal troops to break up a strike on the Chesapeake and Ohio Canal at Williamsport, Maryland, in 1834. His battle to destroy the Bank of the United States, which he sold as a grand populist showdown, probably did more harm than good to the average American, since the bank was a guarantor of middle-class economic stability, and its collapse precipitated a sharp recession. "Only the speculators and those so rich that they could not be hurt profited," Thomas P. Govan wrote in his biography of the head of the bank, Nicholas Biddle, "as the nation moved through unrestrained cycles of 'boom and bust' to the financial injury of those who engaged in productive enterprises: farmers, merchants, manufacturers, shippers, bankers and investors."

At the same time, the ideology of Jacksonian democracy was blatantly racist, exclusionary, and aggressively expansionist. It led directly to the Cherokee "Trail of Tears" and other bouts of Native

American ethnic cleansing and then, under later presidents cast from the Jacksonian mold, the fulfillment of Manifest Destiny and war with Mexico. It was Jackson who elevated Roger Taney, later responsible for the notorious Dred Scott decision in defense of slavery, to the chief justice's seat, a move that prompted the *New York American* to comment at the time that "the pure ermine of the Supreme Court is sullied by the appointment of that political hack." Jackson's was an ideology that celebrated "toughness, maleness, and whiteness," as Michael Kazin has written, and did so largely by scapegoating blacks and Native Americans.

Whatever one ultimately thinks of Jackson's political legacy, there was clearly a disconnect between his campaigning rhetoric and the results he produced in office. He claimed to be the champion of the common man, even as he ushered in an industrial era that would corral those same common men into mills, factories, and railroad companies with few protections. Nationalist expansionism was less an answer to these problems than it was a distraction. (Again, the parallels with George W. Bush are closer than one might at first imagine.) James Parton, Jackson's first biographer, who seems to have been appalled by his subject's vulgarity, deplored "this most lamentable divorce between the people and those who ought to have been worthy to lead them." Thomas P. Abernethy, in his 1955 biography, was even more scathing: "Not only was Jackson not a consistent politician, he was not even a real leader of democracy . . . Democracy was good talk with which to win the favor of the people and thereby accomplish ulterior objectives. Jackson never really championed the cause of the people; he only invited them to champion his."

In terms of absolute numbers, the Jacksonian era was a high point of participatory democracy, an outpouring of energy and enthusiasm that was later emulated but never entirely recaptured. Voters would gladly travel for hours to reach their polling places, glowing with the "feverish excitement" noted by Tocqueville. Turnout was little short of stunning, climbing to a high point of 80 percent of eligible voters in the 1840 presidential election and staying at much the same level for the next forty years. None of that, however, translated into meaningful popular representation in Washington. The blame for that failure rests largely with the framers of the Constitution and the distortions they foisted onto a young country, even as its idealistic citizens dreamed of leading the world into an uncharted democratic future.

4

PATRONAGE, LIQUOR, AND GRAFT: THE ASCENT OF MACHINE POLITICS

★ ☆ ★ ☆ ★ ☆ ★ ☆ ★ ☆ ★ ☆ ★ ☆ ★

A big city like New York or Philadelphia or Chicago might be compared to a sort of Garden of Eden, from a political point of view. It's an orchard full of beautiful apple trees. One of them has got a big sign on it, marked: "Penal Code Tree—Poison." . . . I never had any temptation to touch the Penal Code Tree. The other apples are good enough for me, and O Lord! How many of them there are in a big city!
—George Washington Plunkitt, Plunkitt of Tammany Hall

I don't think there was ever a fair or honest election in the City of New York.
—William Marcy "Boss" Tweed

EARLY IN THE morning of the November 1868 election in New York City, armed gangs poured out of saloons, flophouses, and gambling dens and flocked to the polls to do their worst on behalf of the Tammany Hall political machine. Armed with brass knuckles, slingshots, clubs, and the occasional firearm, they paraded exuberantly through the streets, chanting war whoops as they went. Some were under instruction to stuff ballot boxes with fraudulent votes, or to oversee the count so the result would correspond to a predetermined outcome. Others were simply wreckers out to vandalize polling places favored by the Republican opposition and beat up the other side's election officials. The third, and largest, contingent were "repeaters," each of whom had been given five dollars, as much liquor as they could hold, and a list of the recently deceased whose names they were to use to cast as many ballots as possible. "Vote early and often" was Tammany's much vaunted maxim, and that is exactly what these men intended to do.

Many of the repeaters were known criminals—"thieves who had several aliases," according to a police patrolman in the Seventh Precinct who disapproved of what he saw but knew better than to go up against the power of Tammany and its all-powerful figurehead, William Marcy Tweed. Their ringleader was a certain Henry J. Lawrence, an Englishman who went by the street name "Nibbs" or "Nibbsey," a celebrated pickpocket who, according to a subsequent report, "has stolen fortunes, but somehow or other always slips through and is never prosecuted." The repeaters carried changes of clothing, including several sets of coats and hats, so they could plausibly come forward a second or third or fourth time in the guise of an entirely new person. They presented themselves as young men and grandfathers, new immigrants and third-generation New Yorkers, workingmen and affluent merchants. One particularly scruffy repeater tried to pass himself off as a well-known Episcopalian clergyman. When a poll worker told him, "You ain't Bishop Doane," he responded, "The hell I ain't," and threatened to punch his lights out. Many of the repeaters sported full beards at the beginning of the day, only to end it clean-shaven. A Tammany tough called Big Tim Sullivan later explained:

> When you've voted 'em with their whiskers on, you take 'em
> to a barber and scrape off the chin fringe. Then you vote 'em
> again with the side lilacs and a mustache. Then to a barber
> again, off comes the sides and you vote 'em a third time with
> the mustache. If that ain't enough and the box can stand a few

more ballots, clean off the mustache and vote 'em plain face. That makes every one of 'em good for four votes.

This was a crucial election for Boss Tweed and the Tammany machine, an opportunity to achieve something close to a monopoly on power at both city and state level. Tweed's handpicked New York mayor, John Hoffman, was running for governor, and his right-hand man, "Elegant" Oakey Hall, was running for mayor in Hoffman's place. Tweed already had full control of the Tammany machine itself (he held the figurehead title of Grand Sachem and also the chairmanship of the general committee, the key executive position). He also had the run of several state committees, including the all-important finance committee (of which he was chair), many of the state and municipal courts, the New York public schools, and the city's highly lucrative public works commission. The Tweed Ring was at the absolute apogee of its power, and it had every intention of maintaining and extending it by any means necessary.

The groundwork was laid several months in advance, notably through the fraudulent naturalization of tens of thousands of Irish immigrants who could be counted on to vote for the Democratic Party ticket. New York had been acquiring new citizens at a rate of about nine thousand per year during the 1860s, but Tammany put in a request for an initial forty thousand application forms as it opened a dedicated naturalization office in a saloon bar in late September. By the end of October, the office had sent almost sixty thousand names to the New York Superior Court, which approved them, in the words of the *New York Tribune*, "with no more solemnity than the converting of swine into pork in a Cincinnati packing house." Tammany had witnesses on hand to vouch for each of the applicants. One such witness, a certain James Goff, attested to the good character of no fewer than 669 immigrants, only to be caught stealing a gold watch and two diamond rings less than forty-eight hours after the end of his court appearance.

Naturally, Boss Tweed won his election, but the triumph turned unexpectedly sour on him, proving to be the beginning of the end of his remarkable career. The sheer brazen excess of his henchmen's tactics, together with the greed of the cronies he had catapulted into power, became political liabilities that inspired first betrayal, then official investigation, and ultimately imprisonment and disgrace. Tammany became a nationally reviled byword for election fraud and strong-arm political tactics of all stripes. To a large degree, the reputation was richly deserved; there was absolutely nothing pretty about the way the Tammany machine set about acquiring and clinging to power. Already ten years before the 1868 election, when Boss Tweed was just beginning his ascent of the slippery New York political ladder, a select committee of the state assembly reported: "Of late years, fraud and simulation at the ballot-box have become extensive and enormous. No sane man will deny this; no man can controvert this fact; the evidence of its existence is as manifest and notorious as any well-known truth."

But the demonization was also a highly political maneuver propagated and encouraged by a wide array of Tammany's enemies—the "hayseeds" of upstate New York who resented the power of the metropolis, Republicans who felt unfairly excluded from the affairs of the country's most vibrant big city, Protestant nativists threatened by the public mores of urban Catholics, and antidemocratic reactionaries, dressed up as righteous reformers, who saw nothing but corruption and danger as a consequence of immigrants and the working class being given the right to vote. Yes, Tweed's boys played dirty at election time, often very dirty. But they were hardly the only ones. New York in the 1850s and 1860s saw furious battles pitting Tammany politicians against one another, Tammany against the statewide Democratic Party, and Democrats against Whigs, Know-Nothings, and the city reform movement. Sometimes those battles were purely political, and sometimes they led to bloodshed in the streets. Elections were elemental struggles between rival factions and parties, each determined to prevail over the other at any cost. Tammany's opponents also employed toughs and street gangs, played games with the vote count, and resorted to intimidation and violence. Both sides used repeaters, and both brought in illegal voters from other states, nicknaming them "pipe-layers" because they were instructed to say, if challenged, that they were recently arrived contract workers in town to lay some pipes. The mentality on all sides was to steal the other guys' votes before they stole yours. The Tweed Ring's only distinction, in the end, was to be better at this than anybody else. And that was a matter of organization as much as corruption. To the extent that the Tammany machine sought to represent the working class of the city and encouraged mass political participation, it was in fact a positive influence on the country's democratic well-being. The deeper problem was that the system as a whole was rotten to the core, and had been for some time.

The voting practices established by colonial America were never designed to cope with a democracy of the masses. Instead of evolving and adapting to their times, however, election administration set a pattern destined to replicate itself right up to the present day: changing too little, too late, and, as often as not, for all the wrong reasons. The gentleman voters of seventeenth-century New England foresaw no need for ballot security. Indeed, most of the colonies conducted their votes by an open show of hands, a tradition that persisted in some parts of the South well into the nineteenth century and was not abandoned in Kentucky until 1890. Massachusetts was the first territory to introduce the notion of a rudimentary ballot box—a hat into which voters dropped either strips of paper or colored beans. By 1647 the system had evolved to the point where the names of favored candidates were written on open papers "not twisted nor rouled up, that they may be the sooner perused." By the time the United States was founded, most ballots were still being written out by hand, with little or no thought given to the possibility of manipulation or fraud. Printed ballots did not become common until a Supreme Court decision authorizing them in 1829, the year after Andrew Jackson's election. And even that reform proved woefully inadequate. Ballot production was left in the hands of political parties, which used different paper sizes and colors to distinguish themselves, obliterating any hope of secrecy at the polls. Even in states that passed laws insisting on plain paper ballots, such as Maine, the parties adopted different shades of white and different paperweights to keep themselves apart. Theoretically, this was meant to help illiterate voters, but in practice it also allowed party poll watchers to exercise near-total control over each precinct.

The first formal complaint of vote fraud occurred as early as 1789, in the wake of a congressional race in Georgia between two generals from the Revolutionary War. Anthony Wayne was initially declared the winner, but his opponent, James Jackson, pointed out that there were more votes than voters in one county, that a crooked judge had suppressed votes in another, and that the election was marred by other "undue and corrupt practices" such as the recording of voters who later said they had not shown up on election day at all. Congress, which in those days still had the capacity to be shocked by such practices, voted to throw General Wayne out of the House and left the seat vacant until the next election.

The problems were greatly compounded as the franchise expanded and the electoral process was taken over by the political parties. In the absence of a professional class of public administrators, party involvement was perhaps inevitable. But it was also a poison denying even the possibility of a fair system, since those put in charge were the very people whose futures depended on the outcome of any given vote. The best that could be hoped for was that competing parties would police each other, on the principle that it takes a thief to watch a thief. But as Joseph P. Harris noted a century later in his survey of election administration, thieves are apt to make bargains. With rival parties quickly staking out their own swaths of territory in city wards and county precincts, the thieves were not always that evenly matched in any case. In very short order, party operatives came to view vote rigging not as an abomination but as a solemn duty. By the 1830s, in certain parts of Philadelphia election officers were sworn in on a city directory instead of a Bible and vowed, above all else, to "do justice by their party." In the 1844 presidential election, New York City had a turnout of fifty-five thousand but only forty-one thousand eligible voters.

These problems were by no means restricted to the cities, but it was in the cities that they were most visible, especially as industrialization took hold and America's urban populations began to mushroom. In New York the signal event was the opening of the Erie Canal in 1825, transforming what had been a sleepy Dutch village into a hard-living, hard-drinking, faction-ridden metropolis in which slums rubbed up against fine rows of brownstones, and rowdy Irish Catholic immigrants overturned the sober, orderly existence of the original Protestant settlers who had previously cordoned off the cobblestone streets every Sunday to prevent the circulation of traffic on the Sabbath. In less than twenty years the city's population jumped from one hundred thousand to half a million, creating a sociopolitical climate rife with opportunity but also teetering on the brink of chaos. By 1841 both the Whigs and the Democrats were hiring street toughs to press for partisan advantage on election day. Within a few years, convicts who promised loyalty to one party or the other were routinely being let out of prison to enable them to cast a ballot. No longer could America live the Jeffersonian dream of a nation of small freeholders tilling their lands in a state of equality, economic security, and moral probity. In fact, Jefferson himself had warned that "when we get piled upon one another in large cities, as in Europe, we shall become corrupt as in Europe, and go to eating one another as they do there." The challenge of America's rapidly growing cities was to find a way to manage the chaos and somehow maintain the country's economic dynamism, even as the blights of poverty, disease, drunkenness, and violence took hold.

The answer was the creation of political machines capable of offering the working-class masses jobs, urban infrastructure, shortcuts through municipal red tape, and a helping hand with the byzantine complexities of a less than tender criminal justice system. The interest of the machines in providing all these things was the promise of votes and the perpetuation of their own power structures. In other words, theirs was a classic patronage system typical of any society lacking full economic or political maturity. The most immediate antecedent was eighteenth-century Britain, which was equally notorious for gin, corruption, and rotten elections. But the cities also established patterns later replicated in many other transitional societies, from Italy or Greece after the Second World War to post-Communist Eastern Europe. Early- to mid-nineteenth-century America did not possess a civil service capable of taking on the social and political problems of the cities and fixing them by bureaucratic fiat. Nor did it have an established social safety net outside the volunteer efforts of private religious charities. It operated instead on the spoils system, which had the undeniable virtue of creating political structures that perpetuated themselves instead of relying on the public purse or the sponsorship of the rich. Everyone had a personal stake in the system, and politics was conducted on an intensely local, highly personalized scale. Granted, the tendency was for public morality and the law to be treated as the stuff of political horse-trading. But at its best the machine model was more efficient than any bureaucratic system could hope to be. Participants frequently expressed deep professional pride in their unique ability to tend to the problems of the city and sign up new political recruits while they were at it. Nobody has ever explained this more memorably than George Washington Plunkitt, a Tammany Hall stalwart who outlined his "regular system" in a famous oral history:

> If there's a fire on Ninth, Tenth or Eleventh Avenue, for example, any hour of the day or night, I'm usually there with some of my election district captains as soon as the fire-engines. If a family is burned out I don't ask whether they are Republicans or Democrats, and I don't refer them to the Charity Organization Society, which would investigate their case in a month or two and decide they were worthy of help about the time they are dead from starvation. I just get quarters for them, buy clothes for them if their clothes were burned up, and fix them up till they get things runnin' again. It's philanthropy, but it's politics, too—mighty good politics. Who can tell how many votes one of these fires brings me? The poor are the most grateful people in the world, and, let me tell you, they have more friends in their

neighborhoods than the rich have in theirs. . . . The consequence is that the poor look up to George W. Plunkitt as a father, come to him in trouble—and don't forget him on election day.

Reformers later in the century professed themselves shocked at the naked influence-peddling, corruption, fraud, and embezzlement that such a system inevitably spawned. The excesses were very real and at times threatened to undermine what dynamism the system had created. But it is also doubtful another model could have functioned better without alienating, starving, or otherwise repressing the mass of the population to the point of anarchy and mass violence. Politics was an inescapably vicious business when people were engaged in a daily struggle for survival, and party rivalry was frequently expressed in terms of gang warfare. The rich, who had the most to fear from outright insurrection, understood better than anyone the price to be paid for a modicum of political and social peace. Plunder was something one could choose to accept or deplore, but it was also a fact of life, the venal juice that kept the whole system circulating. Boss Tweed himself explained it with characteristic bluntness after his fall from grace: "A politician in coming forward takes things as they are. This population is too hopelessly split up into races and factions to govern it under universal suffrage, except by the bribery of patronage, or corruption." Subsequent historians have not entirely disagreed with him. D. W. Brogan wrote in 1954 that political machines like Tammany Hall "gave some kind of coherence to a society in perpetual flux, in which even the natives were bewildered by the new problems of urban life in cities growing like the prophet's gourd." To the poor the system gave both bread, in the form of favors big and small, and circuses, in the form of parades, excursions, and stirring rhetoric about the people versus the powerful. Some of this, naturally, was a sham, but some of it was entirely genuine. Getting the balance right, between demagoguery and delivering the goods, between ripping off the people and giving them just enough sense of democratic empowerment, was what the delicate art of big-city politics was all about.

Such was the precarious world the young Bill Tweed set out to conquer when he first entered New York politics in the early 1850s. It was not his venality that put him on the map, although that would certainly bring him notoriety in due course. Rather, it was his organizational skills, establishing him as the first of the big-city bosses. Tweed was in many ways an outsider, a Scottish Protestant in a city increasingly dominated by Irish Catholics. But he also had an instinctive feel for the street-level politics on which city machines were built. Trained as a bookkeeper, a skill that would never cease to pay dividends, he began his career as a firefighter in the Seventh Ward, leading a company of seventy-five men he gave the name Americus Engine Company Number Six. Their emblem, a snarling red tiger, was later appropriated by the cartoonist Thomas Nast in his anti-Tweed drawings and became an enduring political symbol. The firefighters were Tweed's loyal troupe, happy to vote the way he told them and lend their muscle to the cause in any way he deemed necessary. Not that they, on their own, were enough: he narrowly lost his first run at public office, for the position of assistant alderman in 1850. The following year he was back, running for alderman, and this time he was cunning enough to put up a straw-man candidate to split the Whig vote and guarantee his own victory. Very quickly, Tweed was in his element. He joined the Common Council of New York, a group of political opportunists who came to be known as the Forty Thieves because of their singular talent for graft. They earned thousands of dollars in kickbacks from the sale of franchises for the Third Avenue Railroad, the Gansevoort Market, and the Broadway streetcar line. They even made money from the city's Fourth of July fireworks display and from the flags and bunting ordered for Henry Clay's funeral in 1852.

The popular legends surrounding Boss Tweed and his cronies often suggest they took shameless advantage of Democratic Party dominance in New York City to line their pockets and trample on the rights of their political adversaries. In reality, the system was nowhere near so dictatorial. Tammany Hall and the Democrats did not assert full control over the city until the Civil War. They faced stiff competition, first from the Whigs and then, after the first big wave of Irish immigration, from the nativist Know-Nothings. The working-class vote was never a foregone conclusion for the Democrats. In fact, in the 1830s and 1840s splinter groups such as the Locofocos and the Barn-burners had railed against Tammany's "aristocratic" aloofness and its toeing of the Democratic Party's pro-slavery line. Elections were an orgy of cheating and intimidation not because Tammany Hall ran a tyrannical one-party system that was forever seeking to expand its authority, but rather because the competition for power was ferocious and left no room for magnanimity. The greed of the Tweed ring was ultimately an expression of its insecurity. It never controlled a majority of voters in the city and was keenly aware that its grip on power could slip at any moment. Tweed's career itself almost ended before it had begun. In 1852 he was elected to Congress and spent two unhappy years in Washington. By the time he returned, he had lost control of the Seventh Ward to the Know-Nothings and failed to regain his alderman's seat in the 1854 elections.

It was by exploiting the cracks in the city's various political façades that Tweed engineered his comeback. First, he got himself elected to the city board of supervisors, which had been set up as a bipartisan reform body with a mandate to stamp out corruption. Once there, Tweed made sure he took personal control of the key spending and planning committees. He also proved highly adept at bribing the board's Republican members, never more so than when he induced Peter Voorhis, a Republican coal merchant, to stay away from a meeting in 1859 at which the supervisors were set to appoint the city's 600 election inspectors. Without Voorhis, who received a twenty-five-hundred-dollar pay-off, the Democrats enjoyed a six to five majority on the board. By the time Tweed was through, party sup-porters—including a generous smattering of barkeepers, gamblers, and street thugs—had been nominated to 550 of the open positions.

Tweed's next move was to outmaneuver his archrival and fellow Tammany man, Fernando Wood. Wood, who served several terms as mayor, had proved highly adept at staking out multiple positions, some of them contradictory, in an effort to forge a viable majority. In his campaign for the 1859 mayoral election, for example, he made a big play for the Know-Nothing vote and came out strongly in favor of slavery. At the same time, though, he hastened the naturalization of four thousand new immigrants. Tweed jumped on these contradictions and made sure that they would prove Wood's undoing, especially after the Civil War broke out and New York erupted in rioting over the draft. By 1863 Wood had been thrown out of Tammany Hall, his rival organization Mozart Hall had been crushed, he was personally exposed for fleecing a quarter of a million dollars from the city coffers, and he was kicked upstairs to a congressional seat in Washington, effectively exiling him from New York forever.

Tweed was now in full control, but he preferred to pull the strings from behind the scenes instead of taking center stage. He was not much of a public speaker, and he knew it. His real strength was in the committee room, where his imposing bulk and outsize personality were both arresting and intimidating. A contemporary writer, Francis Fairfield, said he "looked like something that God hacked out with a dull axe," with his large head topped with scraggly strands of reddish-brown hair, his vast nose, broad shoulders, and bony fists. A glittering diamond reliably shone on his lapel pin. When anyone accused him of dishonesty, he insisted that he was a man of his word at all times. (His secretary later commented that he was "not an honest politician, but a level one.") When anyone accused him of playing fast and loose with electoral rules, he responded: "Well, what are you going to do about it?" The Tammany men appointed to public jobs throughout the city bureaucracy acted as the bedrock of his political organization. Numbering twelve thousand at the height of his powers, they were known as the Shiny Hat Brigade. Everything, even his rapidly accumulating personal wealth, was a matter of politics. He took the profits of his graft and sunk them in the New York Printing Company, which promptly took over all municipal printing contracts and also served the needs of his personal stable of city newspapers. That in turn provided jobs for his organization, tightened his grip on the flow of information, and also generated new profits. After his election victories in 1868, he moved to amend the New York city charter, giving the mayor the power to appoint city department heads for fixed terms of four years or longer, a move designed to make it much more difficult for a rival political organization to challenge the power of Tammany on the strength of a single election victory.

The eight years when the Tweed Ring had the run of things, from 1863 to 1871, were not entirely bad ones for New York, as it shed its last vestiges of provincialism and asserted itself as a major metropolis. During this period Central Park was completed, the Metropolitan Museum of Art was incorporated, and Broadway became a boulevard. Thieves of all dimensions thrived, from the grafters at city hall to the con men and pickpockets out on the streets, but violent crime was notably kept in check. Call it social and political equilibrium, of a kind. The weak link, in the end, was no more and no less than Tweed's own cupidity. Before he took over, the standard kickback on city contracts was 10 percent. Once he asserted control, however, the rate shot up to 35 percent, with Tweed taking 25 percent for himself. The system simply could not sustain itself at that level. Grand public works projects no longer made financial sense except as tools for the personal enrichment of the participants. There are no hard figures on the extent of the Tweed Ring's looting of the public purse, ledger manipulation being one of its hallmarks, but estimates range anywhere from $20 million to $200 million. Nothing symbolized the brazen greed more than the New York County Courthouse building, which had been budgeted at $250,000 in the late 1850s but ended up costing more than $6 million, not least because the stone supplier was a Massachusetts quarry belonging to Tweed himself. The city was gouged all over again with the interior decoration—$2.5 million for plastering, $4.8 million for carpets, and on and on. Roscoe Conkling, then a local Republican congressman, complained that New York spent more furnishing the county courthouse than the Grant administration did running the U.S. Postal Service.

The greed, naturally, became infectious. When the New York County sheriff, Jimmy O'Brien, asked Tweed for a large payoff and was turned down, he took revenge by leaking the city's bookkeeping records to the *New York Times*. The *Times* editor, George Jones, was himself offered a fabulous five-million-dollar bribe to keep the story out of the paper, but he demurred. The head of the state Democratic Party, Samuel

Tilden, spearheaded an official investigation, leading to Tweed's arrest and his eventual indictment on 120 counts of forgery, grand larceny, false pretenses, and conspiracy to defraud (but largely letting the corrupt businessmen and non-Tammany politicians Tweed dealt with off the hook). After a brief interlude spent on the run in California, Tweed faced two separate trials, conviction, and imprisonment. The master of graft managed to wriggle his way out of prison in 1875—he later said the escape cost him sixty thousand dollars—and fled first to Florida, then to Cuba, and finally to Spain. At length, he was apprehended again and extradited back home, where he died behind bars in 1878.

The downfall of the Tweed Ring was a genuine scandal, but it also became a public spectacle from which a number of individuals and interest groups sought profit. Among these was the popular press, then coming into its own not least because of Thomas Nast's satirical anti-Tammany cartoons in *Harper's Weekly*. ("Thou Shalt Steal As Much As Thou Canst" was the legend Nast had placed atop the county courthouse.) Tilden, for his part, took full advantage of the publicity generated by his Tweed investigations to catapult himself into the New York governor's office and from there, in 1876, to make an ill-fated run for the presidency. The scandals were also a godsend to politicians of all stripes who did not happen to have a base of support in the cities and who looked on the organizational power of the urban machines with alarm. To them, the fall of Tweed was a golden opportunity to initiate a full-blown suppression of the urban vote under the banner of electoral reform, and they set about the task with gusto, as we shall see in the next few chapters. Nobody, admittedly, gave this last group more ammunition than Boss Tweed himself, who was hauled before New York's board of aldermen in 1875 and proved strikingly candid in his answers about the operation of his election machine:

Q: Now, Mr. Tweed, with regard to elections—to the management of the elections for the city and county officers—and generally, the elections for the city and county: When you were in office, did the Ring control the elections in this city at that time?

A: They did, sir; absolutely.

Q: Please tell me what the modus operandi of that was. How did you control the election?

A: Well, each ward had a representative man, who would control matters in his own ward, and whom the various members of the general committee were to look up to for advice how to control the elections.

[. . .]

Q: What were they to do, in case you wanted a particular man elected over another?

A: Count the ballots in bulk, or without counting them announce the result in bulk, or change from one to the other, as the case may have been.

Q: Then these elections really were no elections at all? The ballots were made to bring about any result that you determined upon beforehand?

A: The ballots made no result; the counters made the result . . .

Q: Mr. Tweed, did you ever give any directions to any persons to fal-sify or change the result of the actual bona fide ballots cast in any election?

A: More in the nature of a request than a direction.

In truth, the picture painted by this testimony of democracy perverted could have applied to rural areas just as well as cities like New York. In the wake of the Civil War, the distribution of veterans' pensions throughout the Northern states had become a grand opportunity for corruption and cronyism, especially at election time. "From New England to Minnesota," historian Lawrence Goodwyn wrote, "hundreds of small towns, as well as broad swaths of rural America, became virtual rotten boroughs of Republicanism." Vote purchasing was rampant in all parts of the country, especially in districts where money was a more pressing material need than political loyalty. The going rate was, if anything, higher in rural areas, because it was more difficult to make wholesale purchases of blocks of votes in the sparsely populated countryside. In upcountry Tennessee it might take no more than a glass of whiskey, a plug of tobacco, or a pound of coffee to win over a voter. But in other areas the prices were considerably steeper. One contemporary writer, J. L. Gordon, wrote of his experience in rural districts: "Men of standing in the community have openly sold their votes at prices ranging from fifteen to thirty dollars, and that for securing the more disreputable elements—the 'floaters,' as they are termed—new two-dollar bills have been scattered abroad with a prodigality that would seem incredible but for the magnitude of the object to be obtained." Floaters, or repeat voters traveling from precinct to precinct, were also the subject of a notorious letter written by the treasurer of the Republican National Committee to an operative in Indiana in 1888 and intercepted by a Democratic Party spy. The treasurer, Colonel William W. Dudley, gave the go-ahead to his correspondent to finance floaters up and down the state in blocks of five in the interests of achieving a plurality of ten thousand votes or more in the presidential election. Colonel Dudley—"two-dollar Dudley," as he became known—was threatened with a full-blown criminal trial, but got off on a technicality after he threatened to reveal the entire inside workings of the RNC in court.

Within a few years of the Tweed scandal, several states would confront the problem of vote stuffing, especially the use of tissue-paper ballots that could be folded one inside the other. Many of them passed laws requiring that when the number of votes exceeded the number of eligible voters, the excess should simply be discarded—a process that was also prone to manipulation and corruption. In the 1870s, however, the focus of almost all the commentary was on lurid stories from the cities. As a matter of straight news judgment by the popular press, one can understand why. It was only in the cities, after all, that the topic of elections could be spiced up with tales of extortion and unholy collusion involving politicians, policemen, whores, gamblers, saloonkeepers, and back-street abortionists. As the reformist journalist Lincoln Steffens chose to put it a generation later, this was "government of the people, by the rascals, for the rich." Every city seemingly had, or was about to acquire, its own larger-than-life machine boss: Blind Boss Buckley in San Francisco, Doc Ames in Minneapolis, Chris Magee in Pittsburgh, James McManes and the Gas Ring in Philadelphia.

Philly was, in fact, a worthy rival to New York when it came to the sheer degree of venality, which perhaps explains why the tower of its city hall rose higher than the Great Pyramid of Egypt or St. Peter's in Rome. Even the inimitable Plunkitt of Tammany Hall reeled in horror at the shenanigans of the Republican Party machine there. "The Philadelphians ain't satisfied with robbin' the bank of all its gold and paper money," he said. "They stay to pick up the nickels and pennies . . . Why I remember, about fifteen or twenty years ago, a Republican superintendent of the Philadelphia almshouse stole the zinc roof off the buildin' and sold it for junk. That was carryin' things to excess." Everyone was registered to vote in Philadelphia—dead dogs, children, fictional characters, even the founding fathers. As a Gas Ring notable once said, invoking the names of the framers of the Constitution in a speech in Independence Hall: "These men, these fathers of American liberty, voted down here once. And they vote here yet." Elections in Philadelphia were run by division assessors, who were in turn political appointees of the city machine. In one notorious court case, it was shown that a city assessor was running elections out of his house, which also happened to be a brothel and also the address at which two of his election officers were registered. Indeed, as the official complaint said, "the major part of more than 200 names on the assessor's list were registered from brothels, badger houses, gaming houses and other places of revolting wickedness."

It was easy to forget, with so many irresistible stories in circulation, that there was more going on in the cities than bribery and corruption. The urban machines of the nineteenth century also produced the highest voter turnout rates in American history. Nothing before or since has ever touched their efficiency in bringing people, especially the working classes, to the polls. One can of course be cynical about numbers when the voter rolls were padded, the ballots themselves were routinely fiddled, and the official tally bore only an incidental relationship to the actual vote totals. Not every election was subject to the same degree of manipulation, though, while the turnout rate stood constant at 80 percent or higher from the 1840s until the 1890s. Something about this deeply flawed system was clearly working right. Not that it was widely recognized at the time: the prevailing mood was one of impatience and refusal to distinguish the good from the bad. As a consequence, the city machine model of politics soon found itself under siege from all sides. When calls for reform reached fever pitch and reaction began in earnest, the effect was precisely the opposite of the one the liberals, Mugwumps, and assorted civic-minded reformers claimed to be lobbying for. As we shall see, much of the corruption, graft, and indeed election fraud that most concerned them remained intact, while voter participation—the one indicator of democratic robustness worth preserving—plummeted dramatically, never to recover.

5

THE THEFT OF THE CENTURY

★ ☆ ★ ☆ ★ ☆ ★ ☆ ★ ☆ ★ ☆ ★ ☆ ★

[N]o amendment or statute has yet solved the central problems that bedeviled the
election of 1876. Irregularities in the selection of electors can still occur in the states.
The Negro voter can still be intimidated and defrauded of his right to vote. A
"minority President" like Hayes, who receives a majority of the electoral vote but
not of the popular vote, can still be elected. These disquieting possibilities, which
were at the bottom of the trouble in 1876, could arise to haunt us again.
—Louis W. Koenig, The Election That Got Away (*1960*)

SAMUEL TILDEN WENT to bed on the night of November 7,
1876, convinced he was the first Democrat in twenty years to be
elected president of the United States. Nationally, he had chalked
up about a quarter of a million votes more than his Republican challenger, Rutherford B. Hayes. He was leading handily in his home
state of New York, had a lock on most of the South, and appeared
to be leading even in the three states—Florida, Louisiana, and South
Carolina—still controlled by Republican "carpetbag" governments
with the support of federal troops. By late evening Tilden was
assured of 184 Electoral College votes, just one shy of the magic

number needed for victory, with every prospect of pushing the total over the 200 mark by the time the count was complete.

He was not the only one to think the race was in the bag. Almost every major newspaper in the land called it for Tilden in their head-lines for the following morning's editions. The mood at Republican Party offices across the land was glum. Zachariah Chandler, the chair of the Republican National Committee, drowned his sorrows with a bottle of whiskey and passed out before midnight. Hayes himself, sitting at home in Columbus, Ohio, spent the evening con-soling his wife. According to his journal, he "soon fell into a fresh-ing sleep and the affair seemed over."

Some people were not quite so ready to give up, however. In New York, a one-legged Civil War general and disreputable former diplomat, "Devil Dan" Sickles, stopped by Republican Party head-quarters on his way back from a consolatory outing to the theater and realized, as he checked through the returns, that Hayes could still squeak home in the Electoral College if the vote in the three closely contested Southern states went his way. The point about Florida, Louisiana, and South Carolina was not that the Republican numbers looked good there—they did not—but that all three were under Republican control and therefore in a position to delay, massage, or otherwise manipulate the figures to the party's advantage. General Sickles knew time was of the essence. So, after trying in vain to rouse Zachariah Chandler, he simply fired off telegrams in the chairman's name telling party operatives in the key Southern constituencies: "With your state sure for Hayes, he is elected. Hold your state." A few hours later, a telegram from South Carolina's Republican governor, Daniel Chamberlain, came back with the words: "All right. South Carolina is for Hayes. Need more troops."

Across town at the offices of the *New York Times*, the ardently pro-Republican editor, John C. Reid, was having thoughts similar to Sickles's. Late in the evening he received repeated inquiries from the Democratic Party leadership asking him for the *Times's* latest vote esti-mates. The inquiries made him suspect that the Democrats were not as confident of victory as their public statements suggested. So he ordered the headline "Results Still Uncertain" for his first edition and sent off his own volley of telegrams to Republican friends in the South. "Can you hold your state? Answer immediately," he wrote. By the time the *Times'* second edition went out, Reid had put Louisiana and South Carolina in the Hayes column, leaving only Florida's four electoral votes in doubt. The provisional tally, according to the *Times:* 184 for Tilden, 181 for Hayes.

At 6:00 AM on November 8, Reid hastened to Republican Party headquarters, where he bumped into Senator William Chandler of New Hampshire. Together, they shook Zachariah Chandler awake and resolved that from then on the party would base its estimates not on reports coming in from the field, but from the figures put out by the *New York Times*. Almost immediately they released a statement claiming victory: "Hayes has 185 votes and is elected." The plot to steal the presidency was in full swing.

It was no surprise, perhaps, that this election should stir such strong passions. The Republicans had invented themselves from scratch as the natural party of government, fought and won the Civil War, freed the Negro slaves, and made strenuous attempts to hold the fractious Union together through a combination of economic incentive, political coercion, and military occupation. They were not about to throw all that away. Although the decadelong attempt at Reconstruction was manifestly falling apart, with federal garrisons in the South tumbling like ninepins, black emancipation running smack into a wall of white supremacist bigotry, and carpetbagger governments being "redeemed" one after the other by the indigenous plantation-owning class, the Republicans were determined to cling to what they could. Much of their campaign rhetoric was about invoking the "bloody shirt"—the personal sacrifices that soldiers like Devil Dan Sickles, who lost a leg at Gettysburg, had made to keep the country together. Many genuinely feared that a Democratic Party victory would lead to the reintroduction of slavery, the creation of a new wedge between North and South, and perhaps even a second Civil War.

The Democrats, for their part, were anxious to return to power after a sixteen-year absence from the White House. The Southern wing of the party was of course seething with bitterness over the Confederate defeat and thirsty for revenge. They felt oppressed by the presence of federal troops, especially outside polling stations, and believed Negro rights were being promoted ahead of the interests of poor whites in the region. But even moderate Democrats believed the Republican experiment had failed, seeing their own unorthodox patchwork coalition of liberal Northerners, Southern whites, and the industrial working class as the best hope for preserving the Union. Moreover, they sensed that the country was sickened by the corruption scandals that had emptied out a good portion of President Grant's cabinet over the previous four years, and by the Wall Street panic of 1873 that accompanied them, and they positioned themselves accordingly as the dependable alternative for voters who were anxious to close down the "carnival of thieves." Tilden's reputation as the man who bagged Boss Tweed was therefore the single most important factor behind his nomination to the top of the Democratic ticket.

He didn't, as it turned out, have a whole lot else to go on. Tilden was a thoroughly uninspiring candidate: bookish, pedantic, uncharismatic either in private or at the speaking podium, devoid of all outward signs of passion, secretive, and indecisive. He had made his fortune rescuing and restructuring bankrupt railroad companies, hence his less than alluring nickname, the Great Forecloser. He had the ear of Wall Street, a notable asset in the North against an increasingly business-minded Republican Party, but he could count on the sympathy of almost nobody. Not that Hayes was any more attractive. The Ohio governor was, in the words of Henry Adams, a "third-rate nonentity" whose chief attraction at the nominating convention was that he had no disagreement with any of the party's hotly competitive factions. Under other circumstances the Republicans might have gone with James G. Blaine, the more obviously talented Maine senator and former House Speaker, but Blaine had fallen victim to a railroad financing scandal and lost vital support among convention delegates. In retrospect it seems odd that so crucial an election should have thrown up such colossally dull candidates. Their colorlessness and lack of ego was, paradoxically, one of the main reasons why the country did not lapse into widespread violence either during their protracted election dispute or after. Tilden was prepared to accept defeat gracefully, and Hayes was willing to govern as the compromise victor that he was. At the same time, the pusillanimity of the candidates was a symptom of just how broke both major parties were—and alongside them, the entire machinery of American democracy. The glaring inadequacies of the presidential electoral system and the way it laid itself open to gross manipulation were merely the surface manifestations of a much deeper malaise.

Whatever the strength of Tilden's claim to the presidency, it is important to remember that the Democrats were far from blameless in the murky intrigues of 1876. In all three contested states in the South, party supporters embarked on campaigns to intimidate, threaten, and cause physical harm to black voters. In Louisiana, where a riot by White Leaguers in New Orleans had been heavy-handedly put down by federal troops two years earlier, Democrats went on an anti-Republican rampage so brutal it "would have disgraced Turks in Bulgaria," according to an account in *Harper's Weekly.* Armed gangs burst in on Republican Party meetings and murdered a number of elected officials. In Florida, black sharecroppers were warned that anyone suspected of voting for Hayes would be subject to a 25 percent surtax by local shopkeepers, landlords, doctors, and lawyers. In one incident outside Lake City, a white gang forced a group of black men to endure a mock hanging, making them promise not to vote Republican before letting them go. Throughout the state on election day, illiterate blacks in some precincts were given Democratic ballots misleadingly decorated with Republican symbols.

In South Carolina, which had a majority black population, such tactics did not just tarnish the election. They may well have had a decisive impact on the outcome, raising questions not only about Tilden's claims to a narrow lead in the presidential race, but also about the state governor's election, in which the Republican incumbent, Daniel Chamberlain, found it so hard to believe he could have been beaten by the former Confederate general Wade Hampton that he refused to concede for five months. Violence in South Carolina exploded as early as July 4, when centennial celebrations in the small black-majority town of Hamburg, on the Georgia state line, were interrupted by a standoff between two white farmers and the commander of the local militia. The farmers collected as many white friends as they could muster and returned for an orgy of looting and violence, killing six people, including the town marshal, and capturing two dozen others. The Hamburg Massacre, as it became known, had a chilling effect on the turnout of black voters throughout the western part of the state. At the same time, it energized the white population, including many purportedly moderate Democrats who had previously supported Governor Chamberlain but parted company with him after he condemned the bloodshed. Although the violence was not entirely one-sided—black Republicans were later responsible for a spate of murderous incidents in and around Charleston—the unapologetic use of terror as a political organizing tool certainly was. The Republicans had nobody to match Martin Gary, another former Confederate general, who orchestrated a vicious campaign on behalf of the Democrats to drive freed slaves from their homes, have them whipped, and, in some instances, murdered. Gary gloated that he didn't believe in issuing threats to individuals. "If he deserves to be threatened," he said, "the necessities of the times require that he should die. A dead Radical [Republican] is very harmless." By the time election day rolled around, Democratic repeaters and ballot-box stuffers were out in strength, especially in the western counties of Edgefield and Laurens, where they racked up large enough majorities to offset record Republican turnout and decisive Republican margins elsewhere in the state.

In the face of such outrages, the Republicans did little or nothing. The disintegration of the Reconstruction effort—especially after President Grant chose to withhold sending federal troops to Mississippi to help the floundering Republican governor Adelbert Ames—appears to have dampened their appetite for the political fight. Indeed, representatives of the national party scarcely set foot south of the Potomac during the summer and fall of 1876. In October, Grant sent troop reinforcements to South Carolina because of concerns about escalating violence, but in electoral terms the decision backfired because the Republicans exposed themselves —not for the first time—to the accusation that they were trying to politicize the army.

The uncomfortable truth, not given public expression at the time, was that the Republicans were losing interest in the South, not only because their prospects of holding on to power were diminishing, but also because the cause of black emancipation was beginning to look like too much trouble for too little reward. Partly this was a matter of political priorities, in a party rapidly turning into a flagship for business, not the rural poor. Partly it was the result of a waning commitment to the very notion of universal suffrage. The corruption of America's cities was becoming legendary in the wake of the Tweed scandals, and with it came a heightened nervousness among business owners and capitalist entrepreneurs—the new Republican constituency—about the wisdom of empowering the very social class they hoped to exploit as a malleable and, if necessary, expendable labor force. For similar reasons, the party of Lincoln was now prepared, without a twinge of conscience, to abandon Southern blacks to their fate. The Indiana newspaper proprietor and Republican partisan John Defrees wrote a revealing private letter to Benjamin Harrison during the election campaign in which he opined: "The truth is, the Negroes are ignorant, many of them not more than half civilized . . . [and] no match for the whites." Northern Republicans like Senator Roscoe Conkling of New York bristled at the fact that the end of slavery had expanded the South's voting population and given the region extra weight in Congress and in the Electoral College. He did not think blacks had the intelligence or the independence to vote for themselves, and assumed they would continue to do the bidding of their former white owners. "Shall one white man have as much share in the Government as three other white men merely because he lives where blacks outnumber whites two to one?" he thundered. "No sir; not if I can help it." He was, of course, flat wrong about the pliancy of black voters, but the attitude was widely shared by his congressional colleagues.

The dwindling faith in democracy on both sides of the political fence was the crucial context in which the cynicism and tawdry negotiation of the postelection battle took root and flourished. Lousy elections invariably stem from lousy politics, and in 1876 the political atmosphere was little short of putrid. Neither party had the remotest faith in the system's essential fairness, so both relied on the tactic they knew best: a brute display of partisan strength. The Republicans controlled the election canvassing boards in the three contested states and so ensured that all three came out for Hayes. This they achieved by throwing out votes for one flimsy reason or another until Tilden's initial advantage had been erased and reversed. In Louisiana, they rejected 13,000 Democratic ballots and only 2,500 Republican ones—enough to give the state's eight presidential votes to Hayes. In Florida they noted the large Democratic majorities in Jackson County and promptly disqualified the lot on a technicality. The Democrats, meanwhile, took advantage of the victories they were claiming in the three states' gubernatorial elections, as well as their emerging majorities in the state legislatures, to reject the conclusions of the canvassing boards and prepare rival slates of electors proclaiming Tilden the victor.

Corruption flourished at every stage of this bizarre process. In Florida, Republican senator William Chandler showed up in mid-November with ten thousand dollars in cash stuffed into a carpetbag. The lone Democrat on the three-man canvassing board, Samuel B. McLin, was subsequently induced to side with the majority, with assurances that he would be "taken care of" in a Hayes administration. (He died before he could take up his sinecure, as associate justice of the New Mexico Supreme Court.) The Louisiana canvassing board, described by the House Speaker and future president, James Garfield, as "a graceless set of scamps," let it be known it was for sale to the highest bidder, even though it was composed entirely of Republicans. The board chairman, Madison Wells, first tried to squeeze his own party, demanding two hundred thousand dollars for each of his two white board members, and, in the words of the federal treasury agent who acted as his go-between, "a smaller amount for the niggers." When that deal was rejected, Wells approached Tilden and the head of the Democratic Party, Abram Hewitt, with an offer to give all four board votes to Tilden for a million dollars. Again, he was turned down, although Tilden's nephew, Colonel William Pelton, was later found to have conducted further secret negotiations by means of intriguingly coded telegrams. Phil Sheridan, the Northern general who had put down the White League rebellion, called Wells "a political trickster and a dishonest man [whose] conduct has been as sinuous as the mark left in the dust by the movement of a snake." When the Republican slate of electors was finally sent to Washington, two of the eight signatures turned out to be forgeries—a fraud that came to light only as a result of a congressional investigation two years later, by which time it was too late to remedy.

To any reasonable person it was evident from the outset that Tilden, even accounting for intimidation and outright cheating, had carried Louisiana, had almost certainly carried Florida, and with them the presidency. Only South Carolina could be described as too close, or too dirty, to call. That was what Hayes himself wrote in his diary on November 12, five days after the election—although he was later persuaded to change his mind. It was also the view that was privately taken by President Grant and a number of senior Republicans, including Senators Blaine and Conkling. None of them felt that a Tilden administration would spell the end of civilization as they knew it. On the contrary, Grant had sent a telegram to General Sherman three days after the election stating unequivocally: "Either party can afford to be disappointed in the result, but the country can not afford to have the result tainted by the suspicion of illegal or false returns." None, however, dared express such sentiments in public, and within weeks, if not days, it became plain the situation was anything but reasonable. Rank-and-file Republicans thought there was nothing wrong with crying fraud even as they set about shamelessly stealing as many of their own votes as possible.

Indeed, they thought the one entirely justified the other. Everyone looked to Congress to decide which of the rival slates of electors to accept, but it was uncertain whether this duty should fall to the president of the Senate, whose constitutional task was to open the returns from the states, or to the House of Representatives, designated under Article II of the Constitution as the ultimate arbiter of presidential election disputes. Since the president of the Senate was a Republican, and the House was under Democratic control, there was no prospect of reaching bipartisan consensus to resolve the crisis. As had happened in 1800, when Thomas Jefferson and Aaron Burr finished with the exact same number of Electoral College votes, a presidential election had sprung a surprise outcome for which there was no precedent and no clear remedy established by the Constitution or any of its amendments.

Meanwhile, the contest grew progressively madder. Tilden refused to lobby publicly for his own cause, and when Congress reconvened in December he withdrew altogether, spending hours each day in his private study in Albany to write, incredibly, a book-length study of the previous twenty-two presidential elections. His purpose—to determine whether the head of the Senate had any discretionary power over the outcome of a disputed race (his unsurprising conclusion: no)—may have been pleasing to certain constitutional scholars, but it drove Hewitt, his party boss and campaign manager, to distraction. "It was absurd for the head of the party to labor on it to the neglect of more vital tasks," he complained. In the popular press and in the streets, Democratic partisans were beginning to rally under the slogan "Tilden or War!" but Tilden himself was about as belligerent as a feather bedspread.

Not that that stopped his fellow Democrats. With the South seemingly slipping away, they cast around other states for any glimmer of a possibility of an extra Electoral College vote. To their delight, they found one in Oregon, a state carried handily by Hayes, after they discovered that one of the Republican electors was a federally appointed official and therefore susceptible to disqualification under the Constitution's rules prohibiting "persons holding an office of trust or profit." The fact that the elector, John W. Watts, had never been more than a fourth-class postmaster, drawing the less than princely salary of $268 a year, did not deter the Democrats. Nor did the fact that he had resigned his commission on receiving his appointment as elector. Oregon's Democratic governor, L. F. Grover, removed him, even though he had no authority to do so under state law, and replaced him with a loyal Democrat (who, incidentally, received the considerably more princely sum of $3,000 from the Democratic National Committee for his pains). Naturally, the Republicans cried foul. The upshot: Oregon became the fourth state to offer rival slates of electors for Congress to tussle over.

For most of December and almost all of January, the impasse persisted with little sign of a solution. At length, a compromise between the two chambers of Congress was reached with the creation of an extraordinary electoral commission made up of five House members, five senators, and five justices from the Supreme Court who were to decide the election on Congress's behalf. Politically, the commission was composed of seven Republicans, seven Democrats, and one Independent. When the House and Senate convened to vote the commission into existence, the understanding was that the Independent would be Supreme Court Justice David Davis, who had started his political career as Abraham Lincoln's presidential campaign manager but had drifted away from the Republican mainstream and was now as close to neutral as anybody. To almost universal surprise, however, the Illinois legislature chose the very moment of the commission's formation to elect Davis to the Senate. This was a straight power play by Illinois' dominant Democrat-Greenback coalition, encouraged by Tilden's meddling nephew Colonel Pelton (acting, once again, without the knowledge or approval of his uncle). The hope was that the Senate appointment would pressure Davis into feeling sufficiently beholden to the Democrats to side with Tilden. But the play backfired. Davis did not feel beholden so much as compromised and promptly resigned from the commission. His replacement, Justice Joseph P. Bradley of New Jersey, was a Grant Republican and thus much more likely to side with Hayes.

And so it worked out. Bradley and the rest of the commission essentially had three choices: award all the contested states to Hayes, award one or more of them to Tilden, or throw out the contested electoral votes and give the election to Tilden by default. The night before the commission was to render its decision, the Democratic National Committee chair, Abram Hewitt, sent a surrogate to Bradley's house to see which way he was leaning. According to Hewitt, Bradley read his decision aloud and made clear he was siding with the Democrats. But that was before he was visited by New Jersey senator Fred Frelinghuysen, who, together with Bradley's outspoken wife, spent half the night talking him into changing his opinion. By morning, the election belonged to Hayes, the Republicans were jubilant, and the Democrats erupted in indignation at what they called the bullying of "eight villains to seven patriots." They had every right to be furious. As Jeremiah Black of Pennsylvania, a former secretary of state, put it: "If this thing stands accepted and the law you have made for this occasion shall be the law for all occasions, we can never expect such a thing as an honest election again. If you want to know who will be president . . . [y]ou need only to know what kind of scoundrels constitute the returning boards, and how much it will take to buy them."

A handful of Democrats threatened to filibuster the final vote on the House floor and so postpone the election past the expiration of President Grant's term on March 4—creating a whole new constitutional headache—but they abandoned the plan under a compromise hashed out between four Southern Democrats and five Republicans at the Wormley House Hotel in Washington in late February. Under the deal, Hayes would assume the presidency, but he would also withdraw all remaining federal troops from state houses in the South and allow the contested Democratic gubernatorial candidates to take office. This was the Compromise of 1877, which formally ended Reconstruction and, at the same time, averted the risk of a second Civil War. Congress ratified the election with less than forty-eight hours of Grant's term still to run. Hayes was secretly sworn in as soon as the vote was completed, just to make sure nothing else could go wrong. Two days later, at his public inauguration, he took the oath of office all over again. As Roy Morris Jr. concluded in his history of the centennial election: "It was all a sham—he was already President—but perhaps, given the circumstances, it was only fitting."

The compromise was seen at the time as the key element to the resolution of the drama, but there are reasons to question just how important it really was. After all, the Democrats' big concession at Wormley House, letting Hayes enter the White House, had already been decided by the electoral commission. And the Republicans' big concession, withdrawing federal troops from the South, was already well on the way to becoming reality in the final phase of the Grant administration. Even the filibuster was no more than a delaying tactic. It was, perhaps, less a compromise than a recognition of reality. Given the madness that had overtaken the country in the course of the four-month election dispute, reality wasn't a bad place to come back to. But it would be a mistake to see the outcome as remotely honorable. True, war was averted, but not the violence, bloodshed, and misery heaped on Southern blacks now that their political protectors were abandoning them. The bargain was a shabby one, shredding the country's ideals of democratic fairness and replacing them with a new political calculus based, first and foremost, on economic opportunity. Zebulon Vance, the ultimately successful Democratic candidate for governor in North Carolina, remarked glumly in a private letter written in the middle of the dispute that constitutional government was being destroyed, that the South was powerless to stop it, and the North was "too busy making money" to care. James Garfield, writing to Hayes at the same time, concurred: "The Democratic businessmen of the country are more anxious for quiet than for Tilden." At the Wormley House negotiations, the question of a land grant for the Texas Pacific Railroad, one of the bargaining chips the Republicans conceded in exchange for acceptance of a Hayes presidency, occupied rather more of the delegates' energy than the integrity of the electoral process. The will of the people was no longer a priority. This was America's Gilded Age, and the rights of the majority, alongside those of the country's vulnerable minorities, only stood in the way of the true national mission, which was for capitalist entrepreneurs to accumulate as much wealth as humanly possible.

One hundred and twenty-eight years later, an eccentric little book sought to argue that the 1876 election was not at all the low point of American presidential democracy, but rather its finest hour. By far the most significant thing about *Centennial Crisis: The Disputed Election of 1876* was that it was written by William Rehnquist, the chief justice who was responsible for putting George W. Bush in the White House in similarly controversial circumstances in 2000. In seeking to rehabilitate one of the darkest chapters of U.S. history, Rehnquist seemingly hoped to go some way toward rehabilitating himself. But his book goes beyond mining the past for self-justification. He finds genuine inspiration in the work of the electoral commission, admiring its decision to put Hayes in the White House, because it allowed America to go on "about its business." "This outcome," he writes, "was a testament to the ability of the American system of government to improvise solutions to even the most difficult and important problems," which is a bit like asserting that a group of penniless men who rob a bank and get away with it are to be commended for their initiative. Are chief justices really supposed to say things like that?

Rehnquist's hero, naturally, is Justice Joseph P. Bradley, a man "placed in an almost impossible position" because he knew he would be criticized by the losing party, whoever he picked as president. As it happens, Rehnquist thinks Bradley made the right decision, not because it reflected the will of the voters—he more or less admits it did not—but because it was the speediest, most effective way to shut down debate and prevent overeager advocates of democracy from getting in the way of the continuity of government. "Perhaps a truly independent commission could, in due time, have produced satisfactory proof that, at least in Louisiana, Tilden had received a majority of the vote," he acknowledges. "But at what cost in terms of future challenges in close presidential elections?" This is a mind-boggling argument—that democracy, in a pinch, is just too darn messy to be convenient—and comes perilously close to suggesting we are better off without any democracy at all. Given Rehnquist's long personal history of skepticism about the usefulness of voting rights, going back to his documented efforts to prevent Mexican Americans from voting in Phoenix in 1962, his position is not entirely surprising. He's the kind of conservative who will always get nervous when the machinery of state breaks down and previously well-hidden flaws start to surface. His is the impulse of any power elite: to stop the rot as quickly as possible and lock society's demons back in the cupboard where they belong. In the end, his book only reinforces what we already learned from the majority ruling in *Bush v. Gore*—that sometimes the people have to be saved from themselves.

Rehnquist has an intriguing way of defending the Bradley decision that is not unlike the contorted reasoning of *Bush v. Gore*. Since it was the Republicans who were in control of the three disputed Southern states in 1876, he argues, it was their slate of electors that had the greater stamp of authenticity. For sure, their election results may not have been accurate, but it was not the role of the federal government or the courts to "go behind" the certifications they provided. Not only was Justice Bradley correct in upholding a Hayes victory; he was actually demonstrating an admirable impartiality. "One need not choose between the Democratic and Republican arguments to say that the position accepted by Bradley was a reasonable one," Rehnquist concludes. Again, his logic is deeply troubling— better to validate fraud, so long as it is officially sanctioned, than to denounce it. Conveniently, he chooses to ignore the fact that the Republican governments in Florida, South Carolina, and Louisiana were installed by force at the end of the Civil War and only persisted through the presence of federal troops. He says nothing about the mounting opposition to Northern "carpetbaggers," nothing about the incendiary issue of race, and fails entirely to mention Tilden's quarter-million margin in the popular vote.

His argument only fully makes sense, in fact, in the light of the 2000 election, when the Supreme Court majority he led chose to accept the returns provided by a blatantly partisan Republican state government in Florida instead of insisting that the votes be counted properly and completely. Why worry about the suppression of black votes in 1876 when his own court made so light of the problem in 2000? How can Tilden's lead in the popular vote seem relevant when Al Gore's substantial edge over Bush was so roundly ignored? At the beginning of this chapter, I quote Louis Koenig's warning that the bedevilments of the Tilden-Hayes race risk recurring at any time because they have never been fully confronted and resolved. The events of 2000, and the Rehnquist court's reaction to them, demonstrate exactly what he was warning against.

6

THE 1896 WATERSHED AND THE PARADOX OF REFORM

★ ☆ ★ ☆ ★ ☆ ★ ☆ ★ ☆ ★ ☆ ★ ☆ ★

We are all pots, and our bottoms are all sooty —Mark Hanna

IN 1878 THE historian Francis Parkman published a highly
influential essay lamenting the corruption of American democracy
and the takeover of the country's largest and most powerful cities
by "blackguards . . . abject flatterers, vicious counselors and greedy
plunderers." The blame for this lamentable state of affairs, Parkman
wrote, lay not in the venality of the emerging capitalist system, nor
even primarily in the moral turpitude of the city bosses themselves.
The problem lay, rather, with the voters, who had become too
numerous, too disparate, too unreliable, and, above all, too ignorant
to be trusted. Parkman's essay was called "The Failure of Universal
Suffrage," and in it he unleashed a torrent of grandiloquent invective
against a system that, he said, allowed "the weakest and most
worthless" to be counted as equals with "the wisest and best." In the
wake of the Tweed scandals in New York, his condemnation was
categorical:

It is in the cities that the diseases of the body politic are gathered to a head, and it is here that the need of attacking them is most urgent. Here the dangerous classes are most numerous and strong, and the effects of flinging the suffrage to the mob are most disastrous. Here the barbarism that we have armed and organized stands ready to overwhelm us. Our cities have become a prey. Where the carcass is, the vultures gather together. The industrious are taxed to feed the idle, and offices are distributed to perpetuate abuses and keep knaves in power.

This was red-meat rhetoric, but it also resonated widely in a country that was queasily aware of the degree to which its democratic ideals had been distorted and challenged by industrialization, mass immigration, the bitter legacy of the Civil War, the Negro question, and graft on an epidemic scale at every level of public office. Not so long ago, Jefferson and his heirs had imagined good government as a consensus of country landholders, and America itself as a land of limitless space, opportunity, and natural plenty far from the chaos and corruption of Europe's capitals. Now, cities like New York and Philadelphia had taken on the same sprawling, overcrowded, diseased, violent, liquor-soaked aspect as eighteenth-century London—the epitome of everything the heroes of the American Revolution had fought against. Parkman's essay is infused with nostalgia for the "wholesome traditions" of an idyllic Jeffersonian past:

A New England village of the olden time—that is to say, of some forty years ago—would have been safely and well governed by the votes of every man in it; but now that the village has grown into a populous city, with its factories and workshops, its acres of tenement houses, and thousands and ten thousands of restless workmen, foreigners for the most part, to whom liberty means license and politics means plunder, to whom the public good is nothing and their own most trivial interests everything, who love the country for what they can get out of it, and whose ears are open to the promptings of every rascally agitator, the case is completely changed, and universal suffrage becomes a questionable blessing.

But Parkman wasn't merely nostalgic. His vision was also explicitly exclusionary, filled with deep disdain for foreigners, blacks, and "the masses," which is to say the entire industrial working class. He denounced the "monstrosities of Negro rule in South Carolina" just as vehemently as the corruptions of New York, and returned again and again to animal imagery when talking about the lower orders, suggesting at one point that differences of class and education among humans were "incomparably greater" than the differences between man and beast. Echoing Tocqueville's tyranny of the major-ity, he characterized democracy as the new despotism in a country where "no royalty is left to fear, except the many-headed one that bears the name of Demos, with its portentous concourse of courtiers, sycophants and panders." The old tyranny of kings and aristocrats was, if anything, preferable to the prospect of rule by a dirty, unruly, and ignorant mob. "If we are to be oppressed," he declared, "we would rather the oppressor were clean, and if we are to be robbed, we like to be robbed with civility."

In part, Parkman was giving expression to the archetypal impulse of the white Anglo-Saxon Protestant: the conviction that he was part of a natural ruling order in America and that everyone else was worthy only of disparagement and disavowal. Certainly, snobbery and paternalism were salient features of both his essay and a similar one that appeared a few years later by the prominent University of Michigan geologist Alexander Winchell. Parkman argued that giving up the franchise was a small price for the lower orders to pay for the promise of good government—an arrangement whose mechanics he did not see the need to explain. Winchell said there was nothing more natural than to "seek to lodge political influence in the wisest and safest hands," much as a passenger on an ocean liner "gladly relegates command to the best captain and the best engineer" (as for example, on the *Titanic*.)

But the antisuffrage argument also appealed to something baser and more enduringly elemental, the sense first cultivated by the Jacksonians that the white religious rural heartland was the real America, and that everything else—cities, foreigners, Catholics, intellectual ideas, black emancipation, Native American rights, secularism, and multiculturalism—was a dangerous aberration to be resisted as a matter of national pride and even of national security. This has been a powerful, and insidious, idea throughout American history, justifying, among other things, the South's Jim Crow laws, the anti-Communist witch hunts of the 1950s, and the evangelical nationalism of George W. Bush. At the time Parkman and Winchell were writing, it offered a catchall explanation for corruption, vote fraud, the shock of industrial-era alienation, the collapse of Reconstruction, the cowboy justice of the West, and Custer's last stand at Little Big Horn. Why not blame *everything* on universal suffrage, especially when so many unlearned, unwanted voters weren't even proper Americans?

It was, of course, entirely irrational to heap the shortcomings of American democracy at the feet of the very people the system was designed to serve. But rationality was not nearly as persuasive in 1870s America as fear and confusion, both of which abounded across the political spectrum. In 1875 Governor Tilden of New York responded to the Tweed scandals he had helped to expose with a proposal to restrict the franchise in municipal elections to taxpayers and rent payers. His measure failed, but the issue remained insistent enough for the *New York Times* to write a couple of years later: "It would be a great gain if people could be made to understand distinctly that the right to life, liberty and the pursuit of happiness involves, to be sure, the right to good government, but not the right to take part, either immediately or indirectly, in the management of the state." John Davenport, who investigated the city's immigration frauds under Boss Tweed, concurred that democracy could be successful only when its participants were "free, unprejudiced, sober and educated" (in other words, white, Protestant, and middle-class). In 1878 Justice Joseph P. Bradley, the man who had denied Tilden the presidency and thrown it to his Republican rival, Rutherford B.

ANDREW GUMBEL

Hayes, wrote a Supreme Court opinion invalidating the 1875 Civil Rights Act on the grounds that blacks—then facing a torrent of discriminatory laws, an attempt by plantation owners to yoke them into a neofeudal agricultural labor system, and the wrath of the Ku Klux Klan—must cease "to be the special favorite of the laws."

Much of the opposition to universal suffrage was fueled by industrialists and large-scale entrepreneurs, who saw the will of the people as a dangerously unpredictable obstacle to their business ambitions and became increasingly cynical about manipulating it to suit their needs. In the more rapidly industrialized East, factory owners understood that with a little organizational savvy they could control the votes of their employees. A Senate report from the 1880s showed that workers at New England textile mills were routinely marched to the polls or transported in their employers' carriages, given their ballots in advance, and instructed to hold up the papers in full view at all times. Workers who went against the mill owner's political wishes risked losing both their jobs and their company housing. The *Boston Herald* commented: "It is very improper to intimidate voters, but there is a way of giving advice that is most convincing." In the South newspapers reported that a "job-lash" was used in Augusta, Georgia, to force mill employees, both white and black, to vote "regular." In the West, where new communities were sprouting and foreigners were hired en masse to pick fruit and work on the railroads, the techniques were scrappier but substantially similar. In 1872 the leadership of Los Angeles overcame popular opposition to a bond issue and land grant it needed to lure the Southern Pacific Railroad line into their city by buying up the votes of hundreds of Mexican Americans. As Henry O'Melveny, founder of one of Los Angeles's most powerful law firms, wrote in his memoirs: "[They] not only did not understand the questions submitted at the election, but they did not care. It was just the common, ordinary practice to buy their votes." And it was not only the city that sought to cheat. The antibond forces also offered the Latinos money in exchange for their support, but they were outbid.

111

If there was confusion about the true sources of electoral corruption, it was largely due to the abiding belief, also going back to the Jacksonian era, that the interests of democracy and the interests of capitalism were one and the same. Jackson himself had inadvertently disproved that theory when he found it necessary to use federal troops to break up a strike on the C & O canal in Maryland in 1834. Even more graphically, the popular revolutions that had punctuated European political life throughout the nineteenth century were illustrations of the antagonism between capital and labor in industrialized societies. America, however, persisted for an improbably long time in the belief that it was immune from such pressures. As late as the 1950s, the historian Louis Hartz insisted that "the mass of the people . . . are bound to be capitalistic, and capitalism, with its spirit disseminated widely, is bound to be democratic." Hartz admitted that nineteenth-century America offered plentiful examples to the contrary, but these he described as ironic, not indications that his fundamental faith was misplaced.

In truth, American democracy was at its most dynamic when the capitalist system was beset by flaws and divisions, especially when those flaws led to vigorous competition between political parties and a keen solicitation of the popular vote. City machines worked best when their power was an even match for the industrial interests who were anxious to do business with them. Likewise, they were at their least corrupt when they were forced to fight for their survival in the court of public opinion. As Frances Fox Piven and Richard A. Cloward have written: "So long as machine control was contested, turnout of working-class voters remained crucial to machine success, and the machines exerted themselves to enlist voters and help them hurdle whatever barriers they confronted." It was when the machines became too comfortably entrenched that they started to gorge themselves at the expense of the public and their business clients, and corruption reached intolerable levels.

All of this, along with growing antagonism to the very notion of universal suffrage, was imperfectly understood by the movement which clamored for wide-ranging public sector reform in the wake of President James Garfield's assassination by a disgruntled office-seeker in 1881. The reformers, most notably a group of liberal Republicans who came to be known as Mugwumps, believed fervently that a prosperous, capitalistic society run in the public interest was both desirable and possible. Some of them, admittedly, believed that the only way to achieve this was to kick the uneducated classes out of the political process. Others were willing to a lesser or greater degree to accept the exclusion of the lower orders as the price to be paid for moving society forward. (In 1883 the laissez-faire guru and prominent Mugwump William Graham Sumner wrote a book pondering *What Social Classes Owe to Each Other*. His answer: precisely nothing.) To the reformers' credit, they made considerable headway as the spoils system gave way to the formation of a professional civil service under the presidencies of Chester Arthur and Grover Cleveland and later inspired some of the most heartening changes of the Progressive Era. When it came to the management of elections, however, they learned the hard way what every reformist American generation has found out and then seemingly forgotten: that changing the mechanics of voting, on its own, does nothing to clean up the system and can, under the wrong political circumstances, undermine the reformers' good intentions and make things significantly worse. No period has been more disastrous for American democracy, in fact, than the last two decades of the nineteenth century.

The reformers' central idea, the introduction of a secret ballot, was, on the face of it, an unimpeachable harbinger of progress. Across the industrialized world, it was understood that party-printed ballots, with their identifying shapes and colors, were an invitation to coercion, bribery, and outright theft. They also made it difficult, if not impossible, for voters to pick members of different parties for different offices. In 1856 Australia became the first country to enact the switch to a uniform ballot, printed at public expense, in which all candidates and all parties were listed together. That in turn made it possible to enact secret balloting procedures, everything from curtained voting booths to the sealing of ballot boxes until after the close of the polls. The so-called Australian ballot was adopted in Britain in 1872 and in Canada two years later. In the United States it was first proposed by the Philadelphia Civil Service Reform League in 1882 and introduced on an experimental basis in Louisville, Kentucky, in 1888. Within a year it had been adopted in seven states, and by the time of the 1896 presidential election it was being used in thirty-nine. By 1916 only two states, Georgia and South Carolina, had not adopted it, but since they were under de facto one-party rule by then, the motivation for the switch was negligible.

At first the Australian ballot was greeted with derision, its introduction mocked in the popular press as a "penal-colony reform" and "kangaroo voting." But then its more underhand possibilities began to be appreciated, and the complexion of the debate changed entirely. The realization soon dawned that if ballots were under the control of city or county authorities, not political parties, then they could also be subject to all manner of official controls and qualifications. Political leaders who were troubled by the voting of new immigrants, say, could simply write their own registration rules for newly naturalized citizens. Literacy tests, education tests, good character requirements, and other such restrictions were gleefully written into state laws. Indeed, many observers thought suffrage restriction was the whole point of the Australian ballot. As the labor reformer George Gunton summarized: "So obvious is the evil of ignorant voting that more stringent naturalization laws are being demanded, because too many of our foreign-born citizens vote ignorantly. It is to remedy this that the Australian ballot system has been adopted in so many states."

A rather less approving spin was applied by the *New York Sun* in May 1889, when the state's own Australian ballot law, the Saxton bill, was going through the Albany legislature. "Whatever tends to increase the number of legal voters and to make citizens more active participants in the affairs of government is wise and salutary," the paper wrote presciently. "Whatever tends to impair or restrict the rights of franchise, to limit the number of voters, or to vex and harass them in the exercise of this most important duty is pernicious and dangerous. The Saxton bill would make it harder for the citizen to vote. That is its aim. Its tendency is to gradual disfranchisement." In the New York context it was clear that Albany was taking aim at the Tammany Hall machine in an effort to restrict its statewide influence. Later, in 1898, the state redrew the municipal boundaries of New York City to include the outer boroughs in a further attempt to dilute the power of the Manhattan-based machine. It also launched a series of graft investigations and passed a flurry of laws, all of them ostensibly designed to regulate the relationship between business and politics, but really intended only to muzzle the urban Democratic Party. Explicitly anti–city machine reforms were passed in other states, too, none more blatant than a measure cooked up by New Jersey Republicans that severely restricted the days on which prospective voters could register and stipulated that they must show up at the registrar's office in person. Revealingly, the law applied only to the state's seven largest cities. (When the Democrats got back into power in New Jersey, they modified the law so party representatives could register on individual voters' behalf, thus reasserting the power of machine politics at the expense of third-party candidates and independents.)

One problem inherent in the Australian ballot, even without the additional hurdle of qualifying tests, was that it made voting much more difficult for the illiterate, who were still a significant proportion of the adult population, especially in the rural South. The old party ballots were coded by size or color and required no word recognition skills. But the new ballots, printed in black ink on a white background, offered no such assistance, except in cases where the local authorities put party symbols next to the candidates' names. This occurred in the more conscientious jurisdictions, but in many others officials found it preferable to deter the illiterate from voting altogether. In Florida the entire state abandoned party designations, either symbols or words, and made sure the Democratic Party candidates were always listed first. Anyone wishing to vote Populist or Republican had to count down five, ten, or even fifteen names, and even then the voter had to be familiar with the names to avoid mistakes. Even when the ballot layout was not deliberately confusing, the multiplicity of candidate names and races often made it inadvertently so, prompting an Ohio court to issue a nonbinding dictum in 1909 questioning whether the state's ballot laws were not tantamount to an unconstitutional, backdoor education test.

Many political leaders loved the Australian ballot precisely because of its manipulative possibilities, especially in the South, where, as we shall see in the next chapter, it fit snugly into the architecture of segregation and mass disenfranchisement being erected in all eleven states of the old Confederacy. The president of the Alabama State Senate welcomed the new ballot's introduction with delight, because, he said, "the ignorant"—meaning Negroes and poor whites—"are practically disfranchised." Each state passed its particular restrictions in the full knowledge that they would be applied selectively, for specific political purposes. When the head of Alabama's state constitutional convention was asked if even Jesus Christ would qualify under a particularly stringent good-character clause, he replied: "That would depend entirely on which way he was going to vote." In Louisiana, which was slower than some of its neighbors in enacting a new segregationist constitution, the Democratic Party had to insist on the introduction of the Australian ballot ahead of the 1896 presidential election, warning that without it William McKinley, the Republican nominee, might win enough black votes to carry the state. The Republicans later estimated that passage of the new law cut the black vote in half.

The Australian ballot had one big advantage for election administrators, which was to purge polling stations of many of the outward signs of corruption and chaos. Drunkenness, violence, and direct intimidation diminished markedly, to the point where Big Dick Butler, a New York bruiser who had worked to undermine the Tammany Hall machine, complained: "Elections nowadays are sissy affairs. Nobody gets killed any more and the ambulances and patrol wagons stay in their garages." But the abuses were far from eradicated. They were merely more difficult to spot, a circumstance that might have satisfied bureaucrats concerned with appearances, but did absolutely nothing to improve the quality or reliability of the voting process. Ballot stuffing became harder, and the use of tissue ballots was effectively eradicated. But repeating remained common, especially in precincts where the poll workers were corruptible, as they often were. At the turn of the century in St. Louis, the Democratic Party boss, Colonel Ed Butler, was notorious for calling out across police lines on election day and asking, "Are there any repeaters out here that want to vote again?" Later, many party precinct captains found it simpler to infiltrate the local election board and get them, as insiders, to write down the names of bogus voters in the register and fill out ballots on their behalf. Eldon Evans, one of the earliest and best historians of the Australian ballot in the United States, commented: "It is of course obvious that the selection of honest officials is an essential of the Australian system or any other system for that matter. The trouble with all of the foregoing methods of defeating the Australian ballot is with the officials and not with the system itself."

Other corruptions abounded. In Chicago precinct officers would stick a pencil lead under their thumbnail—the so-called "short pencil" technique—and use it to spoil ballots cast for unfavored candidates. In Atlantic City, Louis Kuehnle handed out carbon paper so he could later verify how his cohorts had voted. Once satisfied, he paid them two dollars each. In Arkansas the carbon paper was part of official electoral procedure, with voters taking home a signed receipt in case the election should be contested. This was, of course, an invitation to bribery. In many cities, chain voting, also known as the "Tasmanian dodge," became common. Someone would obtain a blank ballot, usually from a corrupt poll worker. The local boss would fill it out and hand it to a voter. The voter would then drop the completed ballot in the box and bring the one he was given inside the polling station back out untouched for the boss to fill out again and give to the next voter in line. All of these transactions involved either the paying of personal favors or, quite often, the exchange of hard cash. In 1892 one independent study estimated that about one in six of Connecticut's votes were purchasable. A decade later a judge in Ohio found that 26 percent of the voters in Adams County had been routinely selling their votes, and that as many as 85 percent of the local electorate had done so at some point in their lives. One woman who pleaded guilty of vote fraud on behalf of herself, her husband, and son told the court: "We thought it was the law to pay us for our votes."

Why was the introduction of the Australian ballot such a disaster for democracy in the United States—a failure on its own terms as a tool against corruption, as well as a cover for a broader suppression of the vote—when it was so resoundingly successful just about everywhere else? The answer had a lot to do with the kind of themes we have examined throughout this book—the intensely local nature of party politics in the United States, the fluidity of what those parties stood for other than meticulous control of their own supporters, and the ability of the parties to find ways to manipulate whatever voting system it was confronted with. In other words, even a laudable reform like secret balloting became the plaything of a corrupted political environment.

Many of the flaws in the late-nineteenth-century system dated back to the immediate aftermath of the Civil War, when Congress and the states wrestled with the question of securing voting rights for Negroes and fell short in ways that were to have devastating repercussions. On paper, at least, passage of the Fourteenth and Fifteenth Amendments in the late 1860s had much to recommend them. For the first time, they introduced into the Constitution the concept of a right to vote—no small feat in itself. They made it impossible for the former slave states to deny blacks the vote in a systematic and blatant way. And they introduced the idea that racial discrimination could no longer be an overt instrument of public policy. All this, though, was not enough. Henry Adams said at the time that the Fifteenth Amendment was "more remarkable for what it does not than for what it does contain." With just a half-dozen more votes in the Senate, the amendment would have outlawed forever the very possibility of restrictions or qualifications for voters and aspirants to public office. That was the intent of Henry Wilson of Massachusetts, whose version of the amendment would have abolished all discrimination on the grounds of "race, color, nativity, property, education or religious belief." In other words, no literacy tests, no good-character tests, and no restrictions on recently naturalized immigrants. Wilson's amendment, however, was defeated, and in its place came a much more tentative form of words—that "the right of citizens of the United States to vote shall not be denied or abridged . . . by reason of race, color, previous condition of servitude." The amendment, as passed, certainly prevented wholesale disenfranchisement through explicitly discriminatory election laws, but it also left open the possibility of penalizing blacks—and other unfavored social groups—through other, more circuitous means.

The problem, even in the first flush of victory for the Union and the abolition of slavery, was that Northern politicians could not muster sufficient enthusiasm for Negro voting rights. Not only was their support of the amendments halfhearted, it was also motivated more by political expediency than by principle. The Fourteenth Amendment was supposed to force the South to give its black population the vote, but it didn't quite. It gave Southern states the option of continuing to disenfranchise their former slaves as long as they were willing to have their congressional districts and their weight in the presidential Electoral College shrunk accordingly. The dirty truth was that for all the fine rhetoric about freedom from slavery and the rights of man, many Northern states and territories, including New York, Connecticut, and almost all of the upper Midwest, did not want to accord their own black population full voting rights or allow them to run for office.

The Fifteenth Amendment, meanwhile, came about not so much as a corrective to the shortcomings of its predecessor as an acknowledgment by the Republican Party that, like it or not, it needed the Negro vote to guarantee its future political survival. The Republicans thought they could not lose the 1868 presidential election after they drafted a universally admired war hero, Ulysses S. Grant, as their candidate. But lose it they almost did. Grant barely squeaked home in nine battleground states, from Connecticut to

California, and could thank his stars that three former Confederate states, Mississippi, Texas, and Virginia, had not yet rejoined the Union. Key to his narrow victory were the 450,000 Negroes who gave him his slight plurality in the overall popular vote. Clearly, this constituency needed to be cultivated, and its numbers increased, if the Republicans wanted to remain the natural party of government into the 1870s and beyond. After the Fifteenth Amendment was drafted, its passage, paradoxically, was much smoother in the South—whose white elites regarded black suffrage as regrettable, but inevitable—than in the North. Thomas Carlyle, the great British historian, summarized the divergent attitudes admirably. The message that Negroes received from the South, he said, was "God bless you! and be a slave," while the message from the North was "God damn you! and be free." This ambivalence, motivated by racism but also by the general misgivings about universal suffrage, set the stage for the many abuses to follow.

One of the reasons the United States felt so insecure about suffrage rights was that it started out unnervingly ahead of the rest of the industrialized world. In Europe the secret ballot was introduced as part and parcel of an incremental expansion of voting rights in reaction to social and political unrest, or at least the threat of it. In the United States, where the industrial working class came into existence with the franchise already in place, the undeniable merits of the Australian ballot were ignored or swallowed up in a wave of anxiety that voting rights had gone way too far, and that social and political unrest would be the inevitable consequence. In Europe the tendency in the late nineteenth century was to appease the restive working class with ever greater rights, culminating in the creation of a broad-based union movement and the establishment of full-fledged parties of labor. In the United States in the same period, similar calls for empowerment of both the industrial and agricultural working classes were frustrated, and eventually overwhelmed, by a broad-based capitalist ethic whose proponents believed democratic rights needed to be curbed, not extended, because they fueled only turpitude and chaos and stood in the way of the expansion of wealth and national prosperity.

For thirty years after the end of the Civil War, the confrontation between capitalism and popular democracy raged inconclusively and along multiple, crisscrossing battle lines. The antisuffragists and laissez-faire capitalists were countered by the rise of the Populists, who seethed with fury at the abandonment of rural America in favor of the new industrial cities and believed bedrock America was being betrayed by the coastal elites. The nativists and rural Puritans whose own loathing for the corruptions of the metropolis was more viscerally moral or religious in character, were countered, meanwhile, by the increasingly powerful cultural magnet of America the melting-pot—the America of Emma Lazarus, Ellis Island, and penniless immigrants dreaming big dreams in the land of opportunity. Reformers straddled all sides of these various fences, either taking the Mugwump position that politics needed to be orderly to be effective, or siding with the Populists in an effort to create an urban-rural alliance of working people against the capitalists, or, as a third variant, believing that industry and the labor movement should make common cause in the interests of both wealth creation and protection of the common man. Amid such confusion, the country wavered between razor-thin pluralities for Republican presidents and razor-thin pluralities for Democrats, and even in Congress, then more powerful than at any time before or since, the parties yo-yoed between progressive and reactionary prescriptions. In 1888 Benjamin Harrison captured the White House for the Republicans without winning the popular vote—the last time that would happen until 2000—and eked out a majority in the Electoral College only with the help of massive vote-buying operations in Indiana and Pennsylvania.

All these contradictions finally came to a head in the 1896 presidential election, in which the Populists and the Democrats joined forces behind Nebraska's William Jennings Bryan, the golden-tongued "Boy Orator of the Platte," while the Republicans threw their all behind William McKinley, the amiable but taciturn figurehead candidate backed by the first significant outpouring of corporate money in the country's history. It was as important a presidential contest as any the United States has held. McKinley's victory and the collapse of the Populist movement ushered in an era of national Republican rule lasting almost uninterrupted until the Great Depression. It introduced a broad bipartisan consensus on the primacy of the capitalist ethic—flawed and overreaching though much of the political class, McKinley included, thought it was—and the scuppering of any possibility of creating a European-style social democracy. It marked the Republican Party's final abandonment of Southern blacks and removed the last obstacles to segregation and Jim Crow, to which the Populists, at least in some places, had been the last significant line of resistance. At almost every level, from the presidency to Congress to state government, it heralded the collapse of meaningful two-party competition, as the Democrats consolidated their grip on the South but abandoned their leadership ambitions virtually everywhere else. It reduced the country to a patchwork of uncontested political fiefdoms where rival factions within the party in power could, and did, argue furiously about policy and reform, but where the individual voter held little or no sway. It was, in short, a disaster for the cause of representative democracy.

This is not, admittedly, the way the story is usually told. The standard textbooks point out that McKinley ushered in the Progressive Era, lasting until America's entry into the First World War, in which the robber barons were reined in by regulation of the railroads and the food industry, by laws clamping down on child labor and sweatshops, by the Sherman Anti-Trust Act, by the introduction of an income tax, initially levied only on the richest 10 percent, and by the explosive growth of public education. All of this is true, but one of the great paradoxes of the era is that none of these important reforms happened as a result of popular participation in the political process—in fact, quite the contrary. By 1904 only one in seven American voters lived in a state where presidential elections were remotely competitive. By 1920 that proportion had dropped even further to around one in nine. Voter participation collapsed from 79 percent in the 1896 election to just 49 percent in 1920. Turnout in the Southern states tumbled from 57 percent in the

McKinley-Bryan election to less than 20 percent in the 1920s. The evisceration of black voting rights was responsible for a large part of that, but not all. The decline was across the board and correlated closely to socioeconomic status. The bottom half of the population, whites as well as blacks, simply vanished from the process.

One of the great puzzles of the Progressive Era was that it owed its successes to forces that were almost entirely removed from the electoral cycle. Its dynamism lay chiefly in the factional struggles within the Republican Party once it attained its post-1896 dominance, and also in an outpouring of civic activism, notably muckraking journalism. Progressivism was, in essence, the Mugwump dream come to fruition: the achievement of good works without the distraction and chaos of mass popular participation. Some of the reforms impinged directly on the electoral process, most notably the Seventeenth Amendment, mandating the direct election of senators; various innovations, including party primaries, ballot initiatives, and the recall of underperforming officeholders; and finally, in 1920, the culmination of a seventy-year struggle for women's suffrage. All but the last of these was conceived, though, not to empower the electorate but rather to circumscribe the power of corporations and their legislative lobbyists. The party primary system was, if anything, used to disenfranchise voters further, particularly in the South, where the Democrats used it as one more tool to keep blacks away from the polls. The attainment of women's suffrage was a little different, largely due to the leverage the female workforce obtained in the wartime armament factories. But it, too, had only a muted effect on the overall shape of American politics, since women's voting patterns, at that time, tended to mirror men's.

The Progressive Era was very much a middle-class phenomenon, while to the largely disenfranchised working classes its benefits were far from clear-cut. Prices in the early years of the twentieth century went up faster than wages, after running behind them for the previous quarter-century, and the income gap between rich and poor widened appreciably. This was a reflection of the fact that political leaders had made a fundamental decision to accept the capitalist system as an essential component of democracy as they saw it. Mostly they sought only to moderate capitalism, not to challenge it head-on. The captains of industry and commerce, for their part, were forever seeking to co-opt the politicians one way or another. The Roosevelt White House, for example, was certainly capable of showing sympathy to striking workers, riling the industrial bosses, or staring down the power of the trusts. But when Roosevelt broke from the Republicans to run on the Progressive Party ticket in 1912, his insurgent movement found funding from none other than his old Wall Street nemesis, J. P. Morgan.

At the root of all these developments was a generational shift in the Republican Party, away from invocations of the "bloody shirt" of the Civil War toward a more broadly nationalist program reflecting America's growing economic power and its first major forays into adventurism on the world stage, starting with the Spanish-American War and the occupation of the Philippines. The McKinley campaign of 1896 successfully painted itself as the face of America's future— urban, industrial, modern, diverse, committed to the fast-track prosperity of hard money—in contrast to Bryan, who scared even his Populist allies with his seemingly backward evangelical pieties and his depiction of cities as the nemesis of the American heartland. McKinley's success can be measured by the breadth of his support, reaching as far to the left as socially conscious reformers like Robert La Follette and Lincoln Steffens, and including the most influential union leader of the day, Sam Gompers of the American Federation of Labor. In truth, though, both campaigns were riven with contradictions, in McKinley's case because of a clash between his own personal instinct for reform and the unapologetic business-first agenda of his campaign manager, Mark Hanna. Hanna was an Ohioan, like McKinley, and a phenomenally successful magnate from Cleveland who applied the ethos of the marketplace to the political world in ways that had never been attempted before, but were to become an enduring model for the campaigns of the future. Indeed, a century later Hanna became the hero and role model for George W. Bush's equally canny campaign manager, Karl Rove, who harbored, and largely realized, his own ambitions for a wholesale realignment of American politics.

Just as Bush spent the initial phase of his campaign in Texas receiving the attentions of campaign contributors and corporate leaders, McKinley, who was not overly fond of traveling or public speaking, was kept at home in Canton for what became known as his "front-porch campaign." Rather than going out to drum up support around the country, he let the country come to him, especially business leaders and assorted influence-seekers who flooded into Ohio by the thousands. At the same time, Hanna solicited hefty campaign contributions, extracting a quarter of a million dollars each from Standard Oil and J. P. Morgan. "All questions of government in a democracy are questions of money," Hanna once said, directly contradicting Thomas Jefferson's warnings about the dangers of creating an "aristocracy of our monied corporations."

With his money and the influence it bought him, Hanna set about bringing every major newspaper into the McKinley camp. He also pioneered a new, aggressive approach to campaigning by mail, spending sixty thousand dollars a week on postage and sending out at least three hundred million pieces of literature over the course of the campaign. In all of them, he hammered home the single powerful message that McKinley was the "advance agent of prosperity" and that he alone could keep America's economic engines running smoothly. As Lawrence Goodwyn explained in his history of the Populist movement, this was the "first concentrated mass advertising campaign aimed at organizing the minds of the American people on the subject of political power, who should have it, and why."

The Bryan campaign was simply steamrollered. Its single biggest vulnerability was its rejection of hard money and its embrace of silver, the subject of Bryan's rousingly memorable "Cross of Gold" speech at the Democratic convention, because it gave the Republicans an opening to accuse its opponents of jeopardizing the country's future, even of hating prosperity itself. But the Democrat-Populist alliance was also torn apart by its own contradictions. It was deeply split on the question of race, in the South and beyond. The agricultural interests of the Farmers' Alliance felt not the slightest commonality with the urban industrialists in the Democratic Party, for reasons of class as well as political culture. There was a rural versus urban divide, a Protestant versus Catholic divide, an evangelical versus liberal-intellectual divide. Many Populists understood how the differences between their disparate constituencies were being exploited by their opponents—and perhaps also by their allies—but realized they were powerless to stop them. The Populist leader Tom Watson of Georgia (later to become a startlingly caustic racist) valiantly told one audience of blacks and poor whites during the 1896 campaign: "You are made to hate each other because upon that hatred is rested the keystone of the arch of financial despotism which enslaves you both." In the end, McKinley and the Republicans projected coherence, the Democrat-Populist alliance only incoherence. The result, which became clear only over time, was that representative democracy sustained a hit from which it never fully recovered, the cause of reform was attenuated and eventually ran into the deregulatory orgy of the go-go 1920s, and the South was condemned to darkest night for two generations.

7

THE LONG AGONY OF THE DISENFRANCHISED SOUTH

★ ☆ ★ ☆ ★ ☆ ★ ☆ ★ ☆ ★ ☆ ★ ☆ ★

The slave went free; stood a brief moment in the sun; then moved back again toward slavery. —W. E. B. Du Bois

We have done our level best. We have scratched our heads how we could elimi-nate every last one of them. We stuffed ballot boxes. We shot them. We are not ashamed of it. —Senator "Pitchfork Ben" Tillman

ON THE MORNING of November 10, 1898, a highly disci-plined troupe of two thousand white vigilantes gathered in the streets of Wilmington, North Carolina, with the express intent of murdering as many Negroes as they could find and seizing control of the city. They were not ordinary hooligans, not "plug uglies," as one of their number later explained, but rather "men of property . . . clergymen, lawyers, bankers, merchants . . . asserting a sacred privi-lege and a right." Two days earlier, through ballot-box fraud and a well-orchestrated campaign of terror that scared most black voters into staying home, they helped engineer a resounding statewide electoral victory for the Democratic Party over the "Fusionist" coalition of white Populists and black Republicans that had run North Carolina for the previous four years. In Wilmington itself the mob was frustrated, since no municipal elections were due until 1900 and the Fusionist mayor, council of aldermen, and chief of police all remained in office. So, after a stop at the city armory to load up on repeating rifles and rapid-fire guns, they marched on the printing press of the city's only black-owned newspaper—a particular object of their fury—and methodically smashed every window, ripped apart every fixture, and knocked down every hanging kerosene-powered lamp. As they retreated, someone threw a match onto the fuel that was spilling out over the wooden floor, and the place went up in smoke and flames.

Next, they advanced to a black-majority neighborhood called Brooklyn, where they opened fire on all they encountered. Meeting only a handful of poorly armed resisters, they left behind a trail of dead and dying bodies. Wilmington's black coroner later took delivery of fourteen corpses, although the death toll was almost certainly higher because some of the bodies were buried in secret. One of the men unlucky enough to be caught in the mob's fury was a local black politician named Daniel Wright. At first the vigilantes threatened to string him up on a lamppost, then decided instead to turn him loose. "Run, nigger, run!" they shouted, before opening fire and cutting him down in a hail of at least forty rounds. Wright lay bleeding for ninety minutes—"like a pigeon thrown from a trap," according to a local newspaper account—before anyone dared pick him up and carry him to the city hospital, where he died the next day.

From Brooklyn a handful of the vigilantes stormed city hall, where they forced Silas Wright, the mayor, to resign at gunpoint along with his board of aldermen and the entire police department. Every last black officeholder, including a justice of the peace, the deputy clerk of the municipal court, and the superintendent of streets, was removed and run out of town, along with the cream of the city's black professional class. Most fled of their own accord, while others were frog-marched to the railroad station, loaded on a northbound train, and placed in a special car where they were held under armed guard until the train had crossed the state line into Virginia. The black women and children left behind were expelled from their homes and forced to huddle in the swamps on the city's edge before they, too, embarked on their own reluctant exodus. Within a month fourteen hundred people, almost 15 percent of Wilmington's black population, had abandoned the city for good. Colonel Alfred Moore Waddell, a former three-term Democratic congressman, who had led the armed uprising, became the new mayor, while other prize city positions were distributed among his cohorts. "We have taken a city," one of the ringleaders, the Reverend Peyton H. Hoge of the First Presbyterian Church, said from the pulpit on the Sunday after the slaughter. "To God be the praise."

Never in the history of the United States has there been so outright a subversion of democracy and the rule of law, certainly not one where the perpetrators were so richly rewarded and the victims denied the satisfaction of even a single criminal prosecution for their loss and suffering. Historians have variously referred to the events of November 1898 as a race riot, an uprising, a rebellion, a pogrom, or a coup. But none of these words, on its own, carries the full weight or significance of what took place. The killings and subsequent seizure of power signaled not only the end of any possibility of populist, biracial government in the American South. It also ushered in a period of one-party rule so absolute that it amounted to a checkerboard of white supremacist dictatorships across the eleven states that had seceded from the Union at the start of the Civil War. The fact that North Carolina was the breaking point was no coincidence. It was the only state where the Fusionists had gained control of both the governor's office and the legislature and had begun to lay out a progressive agenda based on greater devolution of power and regulation of the excesses of monopoly capitalism. As such, it posed a threat not only to the traditional white plantation-owning class, but also to the industrial interests supported and sponsored, at a national level, by both major parties. Wilmington, an attractive city lying thirty miles up the Cape Fear River from the Atlantic coast, was always likely to be a focal point of trouble. It was one of a number of Fusionist-controlled, black-majority cities where the fury of the white property-owning classes could have exploded at any moment. What made it stand out from the rest was that it also played host to an ugly debate going right to the heart of the cultural differences between whites and blacks in the South—the vexed question of interracial sex and its explosive power to move otherwise mild-mannered citizens to rage and violence.

In the summer of 1898 Wilmington's white newspaper, the *Messenger*, reproduced an inflammatory year-old speech by the Georgia feminist Rebecca Felton, in which she resorted to shameless race-baiting to advance the cause of women's suffrage. Accusing white men of ignoring the physical threats their womenfolk supposedly endured at the hands of depraved black males, she opined: "If it requires lynching to protect woman's dearest possession from ravening, drunken human beasts, then I say lynch a thousand negroes a week." This sort of material was not untypical for the *Messenger*, which, like other Democratic newspapers across North Carolina, was by then reporting breathless accounts of "Negro atrocities" on a daily basis. The Democratic political leader Daniel Schenck had given fair warning from the start that the 1898 campaign would be "the meanest, vilest, dirtiest campaign since 1876" and that the party's slogan would be "but one word . . . nigger." But on this occasion the provocation was too much for the publisher of Wilmington's only black newspaper, the *Daily Record*, who felt compelled to respond. In a scathing editorial addressed directly to white women, Alex Manly asserted that most reports of rape by black men were untrue and motivated by flagrant racism. In many cases, as he said the women well knew, the couplings were consensual and were characterized as rape only after the woman's family discovered them. Manly dismissed many of the most vocal accusers as "carping hypocrites" because they chased after black women themselves. "Tell your men," he wrote, "that it is no worse for a black man to be intimate with a white woman than for a white man to be intimate with a colored woman."

Not one word of the editorial was untrue, but Manly touched so many cultural raw nerves that he was accused from one end of the state to the other of besmirching the honor and good name of white women. It was as if he had committed a symbolic act of rape himself. "The impudent nigger ought to be horsewhipped and run out of town," one Wilmingtonian told his friends. Others gave serious thought to organizing a lynching, but they were urged by South Carolina senator "Pitchfork Ben" Tillman to wait until after the election. Manly, as it turned out, was already in the sights of the white supremacists because of his prominence as a black businessman, and because he was of biracial parentage. His grandfather, in fact, had been Charles Manly, North Carolina's governor from 1849 to 1851, who had sired two families, one with his white wife and one with a black slave. By his very existence, therefore, Manly bore witness to one of the most glaring inconsistencies between the white supremacists' public words and private deeds. The fact that he was prepared to air further home truths about the sexual interaction of the races in his newspaper was too much for many white North Carolinians. By the time Manly's printing press was torched, he had long since fled to Washington.

The Manly controversy fed right into the Democrats' near-messianic campaign to wrest control of the state back from the "race traitors." The Democratic mayor of Durham, William A. Guthrie, assured his supporters: "The Anglo-Saxon planted civilization on this continent and wherever this race has been in conflict with another race, it has asserted its supremacy and either conquered or exterminated its foe. This great race has carried the Bible in one hand and the sword [in the other]." The Red Shirts, a militia under Democrat control, appeared in town after town, including Wilmington, breaking up political meetings and threatening violence against any dark-skinned citizen who dared show his face at the polls. The *Raleigh News and Observer*, another Democratic paper, published this incendiary ditty:

> *Shall low-born scum and quondam slaves*
> *Give laws to those who own the soil?*
> *No! by our gransires' bloody graves,*
> *No! by our homesteads bought with toil.*

Colonel Waddell, the leader of the vigilantes, was part of a committee calling itself the Secret Nine, which made meticulous preparations to ensure a Democratic victory in November, including
the drafting of a Wilmington Declaration of Independence, which
repudiated the constitutional rights of "an ignorant population of
African origin." In one campaign address Waddell told a cheering
crowd: "We will never surrender to a ragged raffle of Negroes, even
if we have to choke the current of the Cape Fear with carcasses." On
the night before the election, he told his followers: "If you find the
Negro out voting, tell him to leave the polls, and if he refuses, kill
him, shoot him down in his tracks. We shall win tomorrow if we
have to do it with guns."

In the end, simple intimidation and a little judicious ballot-stuffing
were enough. On election day the *Messenger* published one last
provocation urging the "sons of Carolina, proud Caucasians, one
and all" to rise up and protect the "spotless virtue" of their women
with "strong and manly arms." The Red Shirts were all over the city,
standing guard outside polling stations with their Winchester rifles,
from which they released the occasional warning volley. The police
were nowhere to be seen. The hairiest moment occurred when a
train bringing North Carolina's Fusionist governor, Daniel L. Russell,
to Wilmington to vote was intercepted and attacked by a raging
mob who vowed to lynch him on the spot. He was bundled out of
the train to safety by good luck more than judgment, and never
made it to the polls. Neither did many of his terrified supporters.

Wilmington's five-thousand-strong Republican majority of 1896
was transformed into a six-thousand-vote margin for the Democrats—
in a city of just twenty thousand. As the ensuing violence erupted, the
most astonishing thing was that no authority, at state or national level,
thought to intervene. Three days after the killings, one Wilmington
woman wrote an anonymous, and unanswered, letter to President
McKinley asking him why he hadn't sent federal troops to prevent
black citizens from dying "like rats in a trap." Some of the white Populist leaders who had been forced to flee the city made separate repre-
sentations to the White House, but received no greater satisfaction.

The McKinley administration had no intention of being dragged into a new and, probably, futile Reconstruction effort. The Justice Department later indicated it had given some thought to mounting a prosecution, but backed off after concluding that any trial before a Southern jury was more than likely to end in acquittal. Thus did the abandonment of the South, under way for more than twenty years, reach its shockingly heartless climax.

The Wilmington events were exceptional, even set against the beatings, whippings, and lynchings that regularly punctuated life in the South in the last decade of the nineteenth century. But they also fit into a pattern of deepening democratic repression going back to the end of the Civil War. Violence was never the principal instrument of that repression; rather, it was the means by which the squashing of the black vote and the Populist movement was jolted along to the next level. The preferred method of control was through discriminatory suffrage laws and domination of the electoral process, which, once established, avoided unpleasant headlines and gave the appearance of political respectability and order. As the journalist and historian W. A. Dunning wrote in a report on the collapse of Reconstruction for the *Atlantic Monthly*: "It penetrated gradually to the consciousness of the most brutal white politicians that the whipping or murder of a Negro, no matter for what cause, was likely to become at once the occasion of a great outcry in the North, while by an unobtrusive manipulation of the balloting or the count very encouraging results could be obtained with little or no commotion."

The governments of the old Confederacy had to tread carefully, however, especially after the passage of the Fifteenth Amendment, which outlawed overt forms of discrimination. While Reconstruction was still formally under way, the Southern white elites did not want to invite the attentions of federal troop garrisons. After 1877 they did not want to run the risk of Reconstruction being revived. When the leadership's pace became too slow for the tastes of the more hotheaded white supremacists, or indeed when it appeared that the repression of the old slave class was sliding into reverse, violence was the invariable result. In the 1870s the chief perpetrators were white militias such as the Ku Klux Klan. By the 1890s the paramilitary forces were more starkly integrated into the structure of the Democratic Party—Red Shirts in North Carolina, Mason Guards in Tennessee, and so on. The spasms of violence were undeniably effective, since they concentrated the minds of the politicians and emboldened them to pass ever more stringent anti-suffrage laws. At first this was a matter of excluding broader categories of felons from the vote, say, and making sure, via a white-dominated police force, that as many ex-slaves as possible acquired a criminal record. By the 1890s and the early 1900s the machinery of repression had been codified in new, more explicit state constitutions that endorsed the whole evolving apparatus of Jim Crow—poll taxes, educational tests, understanding clauses, and the rest. It certainly helped, as this repressive architecture was being established, that the whole country, North and South, was racked with misgivings about the desirability of universal suffrage and was bent on eliminating both fraud and "ignorant" voting. The worst outrages against democracy may have taken place in the South, but the process involved the collusion of the entire political system and the tacit blessing of both major parties.

The primary motivation for the old Confederacy was straightforward revenge for the humiliations of the Civil War. A perception quickly took hold during Reconstruction that the civil rights of the ex-slaves were being promoted ahead of those of poor whites, and that Northern carpetbagger governments were, more generally, being propped up by fraud and foul play of all kinds. This perceived injustice became a useful pretext when the political boot switched to the other foot, and the restored white elites resolved to put the Negroes and their political sponsors back in their place. As the chair of Tennessee's Senate redistricting committee said with refreshing frankness in the early 1880s as he carved up the state to ensure that no Republican could be elected for the next ten years: "I believe in the law of revenge. The Radicals disfranchised us, and now we intend to disfranchise them."

The first felony restrictions targeted at black voters cropped up as early as 1868, which was when Florida instituted the laws that continued to keep many African Americans away from the polls in the 2000 presidential election and beyond. The first "redeemed" state to up the ante, though, was Georgia, which had wriggled free of Reconstructionist rule as early as 1871 and wasted no time purging itself of all Radical Republican influence. "Give us a convention," the Confederate veteran Bob Toombs said in 1876, "and I will fix it so that the people shall rule and the Negro shall never be heard from." The following year a state convention duly took place, and the result was the introduction of a particularly onerous poll tax obliging citizens to pay an ongoing annual tribute for the right to vote. Georgia had had a poll tax before Reconstruction, but voters—then restricted to whites—had previously paid only for the year in which the election took place. The cumulative poll tax paid immediate dividends and ushered in perhaps the most repressive of all the one-party Southern regimes.

Elsewhere, the new all-white governments resorted to gerrymandering and strict state control of the electoral process to strangle the voting rights of their black populations. One widespread technique was to pack black voters into the smallest possible number of legislative districts. One constituency in Mississippi was nicknamed the "shoestring" because it was three hundred miles long and no more than twenty miles wide. Another technique was to restrict the number of polling places in black-majority areas, put them twenty or even forty miles away from the densest population centers, change their locations without warning, disrupt transportation services such as river ferries on election day, and then run out the clock on those who made the long and uncertain journey by having Democratic Party poll watchers endlessly challenge their eligibility. Yet another technique was to abrogate the power of counties to appoint their own officials and place all appointments at the discretion of the governor. Across the South, black-majority counties were thus subjected to the minority rule of harshly reactionary local whites or, in some cases, administration by outsiders on a quasi-colonial basis.

As the Farmers' Alliance and Populist movements took off in the 1880s, a second wave of restrictions came in the form of tighter registration criteria. Alabama conducted its registration process in May, one of the year's busiest farming months. In North Carolina voters were required to prove "as near as may be" their age, place of birth, and place of residency—requirements all but guaranteed to suppress the turnout of former slaves, since many did not know exactly where or when they were born, and their addresses frequently had no street names or house numbers. Naturally, the restrictions were applied unevenly, depending on race and income level, and were open to all manner of abuses. In Louisiana, already well known for its sharp political practices, the number of registered white males exceeded 100 percent of the population, even as actual participation slumped from 160,000 in 1876 to 108,000 in 1884. The state's leadership made no bones about what it was seeking to achieve. Senator Samuel McEnery said of Louisiana's 1882 election law that it was "intended to make it the duty of the governor to treat the law as a formality and count in the Democrats."

All these measures were not enough for South Carolina, which felt especially vulnerable to the risks of universal suffrage, because it alone among the Southern states continued to have a black-majority population. The *Columbia Daily Register* dismissed the very notion of majority rule in 1880 as "a mere count of noses." Two years later the state pioneered the so-called eight-box law, a voting precinct rule that called for a separate ballot box for each race being contested. If illiterate voters wanted to participate, they needed to memorize the position of the boxes in advance or risk having their vote thrown out. It was a simple matter for poll workers to get the better of even the best-prepared voters, however: they needed only to rearrange the boxes into new configurations over the course of election day. The resulting diminution in turnout among poor blacks and whites alike in turn opened the door to further abuses. For example, party workers could draw up lists of voters who were unlikely to come to the polls and then cast fraudulent ballots on their behalf.

Some combination of all these restrictions—poll taxes, gerrymandering, eight-box laws—was in place in every Southern state by the time the Populist revolt reached its zenith. In some states, it was enough. Florida, for example, saw voter participation plummet from 75 percent of its adult male population in 1888, just before the institution of voting reforms, to barely more than 30 percent in 1892. The Republicans were wiped out in the 1890 election, and the Populists were crushed two years later. In Tennessee, where the Democrats had to resort to uncomfortably blatant vote-stealing and intimidation tactics to overturn a solid black Republican majority in Memphis in 1888, the passage of a new election law inspired the *Memphis Daily Appeal* to note in the wake of the 1890 election that "the enemy is completely annihilated." Turnout shriveled dramatically, while the margins of Democratic victory jumped roughly fourfold across the state. Tennessee, incidentally, was the first former Confederate state to experiment with the Australian ballot, a move immediately hailed as an unqualified success by Democratic partisans. The party newspaper, the *Memphis Daily Avalanche*, commented: "It is certain that many years will elapse before the bulk of the Negroes will reawaken to an interest in elections, if relegated to their proper sphere, the corn and cotton fields."

In states where the Populist movement scored its greatest successes, however, it became clear that even more robust measures were called for. Thus it was that Mississippi, a stronghold of the Farmers' Alliance, became the first state to rewrite its constitution in the hope of achieving what its governor, Robert Lowry, ominously described as "the quiet . . . so desirable and important for the public welfare." The 1890 document was a blueprint for circumventing the Fifteenth Amendment, which was admired and copied across the region. Indeed, a later governor, James Kimble Vardaman, subsequently admitted that the state's revised constitution had "no other purpose than to eliminate the nigger from politics." Among its provisions were a residency requirement of two years in the state and one year in the district (a safeguard against "vagrancy"—also known as being poor, most likely dark-skinned, and constantly on the move in search of work); proof of poll tax payment over two consecutive years; an "understanding" clause requiring voters to be able to read and "give a reasonable interpretation" of the state constitution; and a long list of disqualifications for crimes as nebulous as bribery, forgery, embezzlement, and bigamy. It was so blindingly obvious that these provisions were aimed at suppressing the black vote that the constitution's authors felt obliged to add this paragraph, which might have been funny if its consequences were not so tragic:

> Every provision in the Mississippi Constitution applies equally, and without discrimination whatever, to both the white and Negro races. Any assumption, therefore, that the purpose of the framers of the Constitution was ulterior, and dishonest, is gratuitous and cannot be sustained.

Within a few years, other states were following Mississippi's example and adding their own wrinkles and innovations. South Carolina's constitution, passed in 1895, exempted voters from taking a literacy or understanding test if they could show they owned and had paid taxes on property assessed at three hundred dollars or more. Louisiana's constitution (1898) instituted the "Grandfather clause," which said that any son or grandson of a voter deemed eligible to vote before 1867 had an automatic right to the franchise. Since blacks were all slaves before 1867 and automatically excluded, this was a backdoor way of readmitting illiterate or semiliterate whites to a process that otherwise risked excluding them. With every new constitutional convention, the participants became more confident and also more brazen about their intentions. Senator Tillman said of South Carolina's understanding clause: "Some poisons in small doses are very salutary and valuable medicines." When Virginia assembled its convention in 1901, one participant, state senator Carter Glass, was moved to exclaim, in response to an objection about possible discrimination: "Discrimination! Why, that is precisely what we propose; that exactly is what this convention was elected for."

If the constitutions remained ambiguous in their wording, there was no doubting the racial abuses that went on in their name. In

Alabama black voters soon realized they stood no chance of passing the literacy and understanding tests, no matter how well educated they were. One Birmingham teacher who was asked to recite the preamble to the state constitution from memory was told she had failed because she accidentally skipped a word. Another would-be voter, when asked for the meaning of the term "habeas corpus," responded: "Habeas corpus—that means this black man ain't gonna register today." In much of the South the process did not even get as far as testing. Once Democratic Party domination was established, a new form of exclusion was cooked up—the all-white primary. The Fifteenth Amendment, of course, prohibited the systematic exclusion of blacks from general elections, but it was not seen as applying to primaries, which were strictly intraparty affairs and could therefore be conducted as the leadership saw fit. Primaries in general were a relatively new phenomenon, which, paradoxically, had been sold to the general public as a democratizing tool that would end the practice of nominating candidates behind closed doors. As with so many ostensibly progressive democratic reforms, however, this one was subject to immediate abuse. Since the South was now a one-party fiefdom, the primary was the only election that counted, and restricting it to whites effectively cut democratic participation down to a small club of good ol' boys. The proverbial smoke-filled room might have become a smoke-filled hall, but the political makeup of the nominating committee was substantially unchanged.

It is important to stress that lower-income whites were victims of this system as well as blacks. As the Democrats grew more powerful, they also became more conservative and more inclined to bow to corporate interests at the expense of the broader public, white or black. In many states, taxes on the rich were cut and incentives were lavished on developers and corporations, while employment opportunities for the poor were sharply restricted. Some Democrats, such as William A. Handley of Alabama, even saw an economic interest in restricting suffrage, making the point that fraud and its associated expenses become unnecessary when the electorate itself is selected in advance. "We want to be relieved of purchasing the Negroes to carry elections," Handley said. "I want cheaper votes." All this was cheered on by the pro-Democratic press. As early as 1898 the New Orleans *Daily Picayune* denounced universal suffrage as the "most unwise, unreasonable and illogical notion that was ever connected with any system of government," and said it was as important to shut "every unworthy white man" out of the electoral process as it was to exclude "every unworthy Negro." Even with the introduction of the Grandfather clause, Louisiana's white voter registration figures fell from 164,000 in 1897 to less than 92,000 in 1904. Black registration shrank from 130,000 to barely over 1,000 in the same period.

The response of the federal authorities to this blatant thievery of Southern democracy was nothing short of disgraceful. Congress, which had vigorously upheld the rights of black voters during Reconstruction, simply gave up the effort, and by 1894 the last vestiges of federal supervision of state and local elections were scrapped. The Supreme Court, which had a lousy record of defending civil rights going back at least as far as the *Dred Scott* decision of 1857, and which kept repeating—accurately, but undemocratically—that the Constitution conferred the right of suffrage on no one, was downright insidious in its contributions to the unfolding disaster. The *Plessy v. Ferguson* ruling of 1896 endorsed the notion of "separate but equal" status for the races and became the template for more than half a century of segregation. *Williams v. Mississippi* in 1898 pointedly refused to recognize that Mississippi's new constitution was discriminatory to black voters. *Giles v. Harris* (1903), concerning the voting rights of thousands of Alabaman blacks who alleged their names were being improperly kept off the registers, effectively removed the courts from any role in policing the fairness of elections.

Soon it was open season for demagogues, oligarchs, and dictators, against a backdrop of continuing repression and eye-popping violence. The political culture varied from state to state, and the degree of repression depended in large measure on the success of single politicians in overcoming Democratic Party factional infighting. Most restrictive was Virginia, where an elitist attitude to leadership had long obtained. Between 1925 and 1945—the heyday of Governor, then Senator Harry Byrd—turnout in Democratic gubernatorial primaries rarely scraped much above 11 percent, a strikingly dismal showing even for the South. Most authoritarian, meanwhile, was Georgia, where lynching was tantamount to a local specialty and segregation laws became so tight that the only place Atlantans of different races were allowed to consort together in public was the Grant Park Zoo. The long governorships of Eugene Talmadge and his son, Herman, were spectacular in their lackadaisical corruption. The historian V. O. Key reported in 1949 that local Democratic leaders didn't even bother to muster support among the voting faithful, because they knew they could just as easily fiddle with the count instead. (The *Atlanta Journal* would win a Pulitzer prize after it proved theft in the 1946 election, which Herman claimed on the basis of write-in votes following the sudden death of his father.)

During the segregationist period itself, the word "dictator" was most commonly attached to Huey Long, the outsize King of Louisiana, but the epithet was probably undeserved. Yes, Long resorted to strong-arm tactics and the power of patronage to impose his will on just about every area of public life in the state. Yes, he was corrupt and self-serving. But he also smashed the cozy, bigoted network of parish sheriffs who had previously held sway in the state; greatly expanded voter participation among poorer Louisianans, thanks in part to the 1934 abolition of the poll tax; talked the populist talk even if he didn't always walk the populist walk; and held the segregationists and Klansmen in deep contempt. (Of one Klan leader, he famously said: "When I call him a son of a bitch I am not using profanity, but am referring to the circumstances of his birth.") What made him threatening, in fact, was not his authoritarianism but his fearless populism. His detractors may have called him a "tin-pot Napoleon," but Long presented white Louisianans, at least, with something the rest of the South scarcely knew during this darkest period of American history: a real choice at the ballot box, which they embraced gratefully, defects be damned.

• • •

141

In 1946 the Evers brothers, Charles and Medgar, rolled up at the courthouse in Decatur, Mississippi, to register to vote. Both were keenly aware of the general contempt in which young black men like them were held by the white majority. Having just returned from combat in the Second World War, however, they believed they were owed a modicum of respect. The state of Mississippi did not entirely disagree. For once, its deeply ingrained loathing of the black man was trumped by the swell of its patriotic breast, and the legislature decided to exempt returning soldiers, black as well as white, from payment of the poll tax for two years. The National Association for the Advancement of Colored People (NAACP), of which both brothers would become prominent spokesmen, was organizing hard to bring out the black vote all over the South. It escaped nobody's attention that the U.S. Army had gone to Europe to oppose a racial ideology dividing the world into natural-born masters and slaves. If it was right to fight the Nazis, why on earth should the white supremacists back home get away with anything?

The Evers's white neighbors followed them incredulously to the courthouse, where at length one of them snarled: "Who you niggers think you are?" Charles responded: "We've grown up here. We've fought for this country and we should register." Their applications were received in stunned silence, and the brothers went on their way. Later, when Charles tried to vote he was turned away from his polling place by a gang of white men brandishing guns. Some kind of point, however, had been made, and the campaign to restore black voting rights in the U.S. South was firmly under way.

Largely because of the war, men like Eugene Talmadge in Georgia or Theodore G. Bilbo, a powerful Mississippi senator now running for reelection, came to look less like the unassailable autocrats they once were than desperate old reactionaries clinging to power even as the tide of the times was turning around them. Talmadge warned during the 1946 campaign that "wise Negroes will stay away from the white man's ballot boxes." Bilbo railed furiously against Mississippi's poll tax repealers, calling them "Negro lovers" and telling them to go "straight to hell." In speech after speech he made his positions crystal clear. "I want to make it absolutely impossible for the Negro to vote," he said. "America cannot be saved from the fate of mongrelism except by the physical separation of the races." He wasn't shy even to invoke the spirit of the Klan. "You know and I know what's the best way to keep the nigger from voting," he told one rally. "You do it the night before the election. I don't have to tell you any more than that. Red-blooded men know what I mean."

It proved to be the final campaign for both men. Talmadge died before election day and was replaced on the ballot by his son, whose narrow victory relied, among other things, on him purging thousands of hostile voters from the rolls to counter a surge in black turnout. As for Bilbo, he almost failed to be seated because of a revolt by Senate Republicans who were appalled by his openly racist views. Only illness averted the humiliation of rejection by his peers. He was diagnosed with cancer of the jaw, headed to the hospital instead of Capitol Hill, and died within a few months.

The tide had in fact been slowly changing for some time, starting with some very modest nudges toward reform under Franklin Roosevelt's presidency. Roosevelt did not feel he had a great deal of room for maneuver, since he relied on the South as a bedrock of Democratic support. He certainly did himself no honor by refusing to sign an antilynching law. But he did make sure that government aid during the Great Depression reached the black population, and he instituted a system of annual crop-restriction referenda across the South, which he opened up to cotton operators, tenants, and sharecroppers irrespective of race. His Fair Employment Practices Committee took advantage of the national wartime emergency to ensure that armaments factories hired all races on an equal basis— causing a social revolution in white supremacist bastions everywhere from South Carolina to Long Beach, California. Roosevelt also quietly backed moves to abolish the poll tax, which disappeared in Florida in 1937 and in Georgia in 1945, having previously been scrapped in Louisiana and North Carolina. The biggest reform of his tenure, however, was undertaken by the U.S. Supreme Court, which at last woke up from its century-long slumber on racial issues and, in a landmark ruling in 1944, declared the white primary to be unconstitutional. The most conservative states, such as Georgia and South Carolina, responded furiously to the ruling by threatening to do away with primaries altogether, but their efforts quickly became bogged down in legal complications, and they were gradually forced to admit defeat.

Harry Truman proved considerably bolder than his predecessor, initiating integration of the navy in 1946 and extending it to the rest of the armed forces two years later. His 1946 Commission on Higher Education recommended repealing segregation, as did the nascent U.S. Commission on Civil Rights, which he founded, in a landmark report titled *To Secure These Rights*. Truman was consciously breaking a taboo in a party that had come to rely on the electoral power of the Solid South, and indeed he almost lost the 1948 election as the Dixiecrats split from the Northern Democrats. He did see some political dividends, as black voter registration quadrupled over his six-year White House tenure. But the numbers remained disappointingly low—more than three-quarters of Southern blacks remained unregistered—because of continuing intimidation and violence, and also because many Southern blacks needed convincing after decades of systematic repression that there was any point in even trying to vote.

America's changing role in the world was a decisive factor in the shift in attitudes. The Second World War gave black Americans a new sense of empowerment, and the Korean War helped erase any lingering resistance to the integration of military ranks. The establishment of the United Nations and the decision to station its headquarters on U.S. soil—not to mention the publication of its own Universal Declaration of Human Rights—put an international spotlight on the South like never before. The deepening standoff with the Soviet Union made it especially urgent to get rid of this direct domestic contradiction to America's international mantra of democracy and freedom. As a 1952 brief filed by the attorney general's office on the issue of segregation in public schools argued: "It is in the context of the present world struggle between freedom and tyranny that the problem of racial discrimination must be viewed . . . Racial discrimination furnishes grist for the Communist propaganda mills, and it raises doubt even among friendly nations as to the intensity of our devotion to the democratic faith."

It was not just Northern liberals who felt this way. A certain hotly anti-Communist congressman and rising Republican star by the name of Richard Nixon agreed wholeheartedly. It might have been in the two major parties' interest to ignore the South for the past fifty years, but now it behooved both to foster reform as quickly as possible. Aside from the fine talk about principles and moral values, there were new votes to be had and international prestige at stake. When the school district in Little Rock, Arkansas, refused to abide by the Supreme Court's *Brown v. Board of Education* desegregation ruling and blocked nine black students from entering Central High School in 1957, President Eisenhower and Nixon, now his vice president, ended up sending federal troops south of the Mason-Dixon line for the first time in eighty years. Thereafter, the Republican Eisenhower administration and the Democratic Senate, led by Lyndon Johnson, cajoled each other into enacting incremental rounds of civil rights legislation. The Republicans wanted to regain the black vote it once took for granted, while the Democrats— especially wily Southerners like Johnson—wanted to demonstrate that they were now Roosevelt's party of the working man, not the cabal of regional bigots personified by Talmadge, Bilbo, and the Dixiecrats.

This is not the place to give an account of the U.S. civil rights movement. Suffice to say that during the upheavals of the early 1960s—from the civil disobedience campaigns, to the Birmingham church bombings, to the March on Washington—the incentive to enact political reform in the South only increased. The violence in Alabama, Mississippi, and elsewhere not only gave the Kennedy and Johnson administrations moral imperative to sweep away the legal apparatus of segregation and accord full electoral rights to all eligible adults regardless of race, education, or literacy. It also made these things politically possible—and desirable. Even before passage of the Voting Rights Act (VRA) in 1965, black voter registration had swelled from around 20 percent in 1952 to 35 percent. Thus President Johnson had concrete figures in front of him as he made the decision to buy the allegiance of America's black voters and spurn the Southern conservative wing of his own party.

Initially, Johnson's calculations appeared to pay off splendidly as registration soared ever higher and electoral turnout, encouraged by the dispatch of federal examiners to Southern states, hit its highest point in decades. In Alabama the VRA spurred a jump in black registration from 19 percent to 52 percent. In Mississippi it went from 7 percent to 60 percent. Culturally, there was an undeniable sea change, as every last vestige of legal segregation was dismantled, poll taxes were formally outlawed under the Twenty-fourth Amendment, and the language of racism became taboo in American politics for the first time since the country's foundation. Any hopes that the race issue would simply fade away and vanish were quickly dashed, however. Five days after Johnson signed the VRA, riots broke out in the black Los Angeles suburb of Watts, and further violence followed in other non-Southern cities, most notably in Detroit in 1967. Clearly, voting rights alone were not enough. As C. Vann Woodward wrote in his book *The Strange Career of Jim Crow*, whatever legal restrictions had been in place in the South were mirrored by "de facto segregation of residence and schools in the North." The stage was thus set for the continuing political misfortunes of African Americans in all parts of the country, including persistent problems of access to both the ballot box and to elective office.

In the South, state governments reacted to the VRA in much the same way as they had to Reconstruction almost a century earlier. They gerrymandered districts either to pack the black voters into the smallest possible number of constituencies or to disperse them so their influence on election results would dwindle to insignificance. Thus it was that Arkansas, a state where blacks made up just under half the population, managed to avoid sending any black candidates to Congress for several decades. At the state and county level, single-member district systems were replaced in many states with at-large elections, making it much more difficult for black-majority wards or counties to be represented by black elected officials. Offices that looked likely to fall into the hands of African Americans were simply abolished, or switched from elective to appointive status. A handful of states also saw a revival of runoff elections, a tactic already employed after the collapse of Reconstruction to block the path of black or progressive candidates who came out ahead on the first round. Since runoffs usually saw a precipitous decline in turnout, they were also an effective vote-suppression mechanism.

Such techniques ebbed and flowed over the forty years or more. Conservative Southern Democrats slowly lost ground to a Republican Party that was more obviously in tune with an increasingly traditionalist, increasingly evangelical white electorate. By the early 1990s many black Southerners had come to believe that the concentrated "safe" districts they had been handed through redistricting in Georgia, North Carolina, and other states were probably the best representation they could hope for. A flurry of lawsuits, however, challenged the legality of these packed districts, which were denounced as "racial gerrymandering." A sympathetic majority on the Rehnquist Supreme Court handed down two rulings, *Shaw v. Hunt* and *Shaw v. Reno*, giving voters the right to challenge any redistricting plan they can show to have been decided "predominantly" on racial grounds. Black activists saw this as one more attempt to circumscribe their political effectiveness, a sign that 130 years after the abolition of slavery, the white power elite was still concocting stratagems to prevent them from taking their rightful seat at the democratic table.

Across the country, rising incarceration rates from 1980 onward adversely affected African Americans and, because of felony voting restrictions, disproportionately denied them the right to vote, as we saw in chapter 2. Diversionary tactics and intimidation have continued to plague black precincts, both north and south of the Mason-Dixon line. It is rare for an election to go by without the appearance of postcards or flyers disseminating inaccurate information about polling hours, precinct locations, or even the date of the election. In 1981 New Jersey Republicans formed a "ballot security task force" composed of off-duty police officers who made it their business to intimidate minority voters as they were trying to reach the polls. In 1990 Senator Jesse Helms's reelection campaign in North Carolina sent out 125,000 postcards to African Americans telling them, incorrectly, that if they hadn't been at their current address for more than thirty days they were ineligible to vote and risked criminal penalties if they tried to cheat the system. Both incidents were the subject of federal lawsuits and settlements under which the defendants promised not to engage in such dishonest practices again. In 2003 anonymous flyers in some of Baltimore's African American neighborhoods warned that anyone with outstanding parking tickets or unpaid rent would not be allowed to vote. In Philadelphia that same year, threatening men driving sedans with magnetic signs resembling police insignia systematically challenged black voters and took down their details on clipboards.

The net effect of these incidents has been to keep black voters wary and disinclined to feel part of the system. And that in turn has created a generation of elected officials who are disinclined to pay attention to their interests, or to the more general interest of protecting voting rights and encouraging democratic participation. By 2004, with much of the South deemed to be solid Republican terrain, 47 percent of eligible African Africans in Florida and 34 percent in Georgia remained unregistered. Another big chunk of the black population—in Florida the rate was one adult male in three—had lost the right to vote altogether because of a criminal conviction. African Americans may no longer be slaves, or subjected to openly discriminatory segregation laws or voting restrictions, but they have yet to find their political voice, especially in Southern states, where the political structure, if not necessarily society at large, remains deeply wedded to the divisive, antimodern values of the old Confederacy.

8
CHICAGO: THE *OTHER* KIND
OF MOB RULE

★ ☆ ★ ☆ ★ ☆ ★ ☆ ★ ☆ ★ ☆ ★ ☆ ★

There was no doubt in the minds of any of us, after the sort of testimony we heard in Chicago, that organized crime and political corruption go hand in hand, and that in fact there could be no big-time organized crime without a firm and profitable alliance between those who run the rackets and those in political control.
—*Tennessee Senator Estes Kefauver,* Crime in America *(1951)*

Mr. President, with a little bit of luck and the help of a few close friends, you're going to carry Illinois. —*Chicago's Mayor Daley to John F. Kennedy on election night, 1960*

ON THE NIGHT of September 28, 1920, alderman Johnny Powers of Chicago's Nineteenth Ward was shaken out of bed by the explosion of a bomb left on his front porch. Someone wanted to let him know that after forty-two years as the undisputed boss of the Nineteenth, he might want to think twice about running for reelection. That someone was almost certainly Tony D'Andrea, the Sicilian sewer-diggers' union leader, macaroni manufacturers' agent,

149

and president of the secretive Unione Siciliana, also known as the Black Hand, who had gone up against Powers in the past and made clear he didn't care how many laws he had to break to muscle in on his turf. The Nineteenth had been a predominantly Irish area at the start of Powers's career, but now it was 80 percent Italian. With Prohibition just under way, the Italians wanted in on Powers's gambling and bootlegging rackets every bit as badly as his political fiefdom. Shortly afterward, D'Andrea announced he would challenge Powers for the position of alderman the following February. Then things got truly nasty.

Eleven days before the election, a dynamite bomb exploded at a crowded D'Andrea rally, punching a three-foot hole in the brick wall of the auditorium and injuring seventeen people. A week later D'Andrea's campaign headquarters were leveled in another detonation, and the home of one of his lieutenants was also bombed. Throughout the Nineteenth Ward, gunmen patrolled the streets and stood guard outside their bosses' homes. Both campaigns received death threats. Campaign workers were ambushed and beaten. The Powers campaign accused D'Andrea of bombing his own side to bring out the sympathy vote, but produced no supporting evidence. D'Andrea appealed to the Cook County state's attorney, Robert Crowe, who proposed tougher sentencing guidelines for acts of political violence, but did absolutely nothing to track down the perpetrators.

On election day itself, three of Powers's campaign workers, including an election judge and a precinct captain, were kidnapped and held until the vote was over. The police, who were out in force across the ward, arrested fifty people before lunchtime and found two hundred pounds of dynamite stashed in an abandoned building. When the counting was done, Powers was declared the winner by the wafer-thin margin of 435 votes—not that anybody believed this was the real figure. Still the violence did not let up. In March two of Powers's precinct captains were gunned down. By April, D'Andrea was carrying a firearm wherever he went. In May he was hit by thirteen shotgun blasts on his way home from dinner at the Bella Napoli restaurant, which belonged to his friend and fellow politician, Diamond Joe Esposito. The gunmen had rented the apartment across the hall from D'Andrea's, which they vacated as soon as the job was done. Police later recovered a freshly sawed-off shotgun and a hat with a twenty-dollar bill stuffed into the band. "For flowers," said the hastily scribbled note.

Such was the opening act of an extraordinary decade of political violence in Chicago, in which the machinery of democratic elections, along with everything else, fell prey to gangsterism and the law of the gun. D'Andrea died with vengeance on his lips, although the hit man he urged to kill Powers on his behalf, Two-Gun Johnny Guardino, was himself felled before he could carry out the deed. The Roaring Twenties were in full gear, and the machine guns hardly stopped rattling, in the Nineteenth Ward or anywhere else. Diamond Joe Esposito, who had been a pallbearer at D'Andrea's lavish funeral, sought to forge a more cautious path via the patronage of the moderate Republican senator Charles Deneen and managed, for a while, to be almost respectable. But he, too, came to a grisly end, as we shall see, after Al Capone's boys decided he had crossed them and their friends at city hall.

Chicago's political leadership thought at first that it could do business with the bootleggers and racketeers, which is why neither Crowe, the state's attorney, nor Big Bill Thompson, Chicago's larger-than-life mayor, chose to offer more than token intervention in the burgeoning war in the Nineteenth. Thompson, a Republican with ties to some of the most corrupt business interests in Illinois, was unseated in 1923 by William Dever, a Democrat, who took the opposite tack and launched an aggressive police onslaught on speakeasies, gambling dens, and brothels. In his first year in office alone, Dever padlocked four thousand saloons, including many so-called black-and-tan bars, where patrons of different races socialized together on the South Side, and revoked sixteen thousand business licenses. His approach, however, only made things worse. Cut loose from city hall, the bootleggers built up their own organizations free of the slightest regulatory restraint. The big fish swallowed the little fish, until every last racket had been consolidated into a single crime syndicate that was too powerful, and too well armed, for anyone to touch it. As James Merriner wrote in his history of corruption in Chicago, the Mob graduated from being a joint venture of city hall's to being its parent company.

When it came to elections, Chicagoans were well used to acts of casual corruption, vote buying, ballot stuffing, and the rest. In the early years of the century, the colorful aldermen of the First Ward, John "Bathhouse" Coughlin and Michael "Hinky Dink" Kenna, had perfected the art of rounding up vagrants on election day, offering them food, lodging, and limitless booze, and shuttling them from precinct to precinct to cast multiple ballots at fifty cents a shot. The irregularities had inspired the creation of reformist movements like the Bureau of Public Efficiency and the Citizens' Association, which reported in 1919: "It has been a matter of common knowledge in Chicago during recent years that thousands of fraudulent votes have been counted in each election in certain wards." Chicago even developed its own fraud vocabulary. Repeaters were known locally as "stingers." Padding the registers with the names of the deceased was known as "ghost voting." Accompanying voters into the booth to make sure they did as they were told—an increasingly common practice—was called "four-legged voting."

The Prohibition era, though, with its killings, kidnappings and *omertà*, the Sicilian Mafia's code of silence, took things to an entirely different level. The roles of ward boss and crime boss merged, which meant that the furious political struggles of the period came increasingly to resemble the settling of scores between criminal gangs. There was no lack of conflict. The Republicans were split between loyalists of Big Bill Thompson and reformist protégés of Senator Deneen, a feckless but essentially honest former prosecutor and Illinois governor. The Democrats, reflecting broader national trends, were split between populists, who embraced Chicago's thick goulash of immigrant constituencies, and conservatives, who found deference to blacks and recently arrived foreigners corrosive to the moral good of the community. There were cross-party fault lines between supporters of Prohibition and anti-Prohibitionist "wets," and also between political reformers and apologists for the machine model. Each one of these confrontations manifested itself primarily at ward level, where the fights were waged the hardest and with the most personal venom.

The violence shaking the Nineteenth Ward had spread citywide by the time of the 1926 Republican primary, a contest so badly marked by violence and fraud that it prompted an official investigation. Gangs of armed men roved from precinct to precinct on the day of the election, slugging poll workers who got in their way and bundling campaign rivals into the backseats of limousines for safe-keeping until the vote was over. An audit of the books in the Twentieth Ward, which was rapidly eclipsing the Nineteenth as the city's most troublesome, revealed close to three thousand votes that had been cast in the names of nonresidents, nonvoters, children, the dead, or people who had filled more than one ballot. Ballot stuffing had, in fact, been rampant in many parts of the city. In the Sixteenth Precinct of the Forty-second Ward, already notorious for its crooked election workers, the Citizens' Association reported:

> When there were not voters in the polling place [ward heeler John] Sherry would walk to the back door and holler "all right." Then men would come in from the rear room and from the second floor with bunches of ballots that they had marked, and Sherry would open the ballot box and the men would drop the ballots in the box. At intervals during the day Sherry and O'Malley (an official who has never been appre-hended) would take about ten ballots at a time and go into a polling booth and mark them and put them in the ballot box.

The reformers demanded, and obtained, a partial recount, the results of which were so out of kilter with the original returns they could only conclude the first set of tallies had been plucked out of thin air. A reformist judge named Edmund Jarecki was soon hearing dozens upon dozens of electoral fraud cases, at one point canceling his summer vacation so he could get through the caseload. By September

1927 he had presided over 169 trials, in which twenty-three defendants—many of them election workers—had been found guilty and fifteen sentenced to prison. The pace of prosecutions was unprecedented, in Chicago or anywhere else. But his efforts did not meet universal approval. When a legal technicality threatened to invalidate his first eleven sentences, Jarecki appealed to Crowe, the state's attorney, to iron out the glitch with a simple writ of mandamus. Crowe declined.

The reformers' efforts could not halt the epidemic of violence, which produced a new murder every three days in 1926 and almost three times that many after Big Bill Thompson returned to the mayor's office in 1927. The single biggest orgy of explosions and killings took place in the run-up to the Republican primary of April 1928, thereafter known as the Pineapple Primary because of the more than sixty bombings that bloodied the campaign trail. That election was to prove pivotal in a city increasingly sickened by the daily gunplay and by the mounting evidence of collusion between the Republican machine running city hall and Al Capone's outfit. The Bureau of Internal Revenue would later estimate that in 1927 alone, the Capone gang spent $30 million paying off politicians and the police, including a contribution of at least $150,000 to Thompson's reelection campaign. Even without those figures in front of them, though, Chicagoans knew something was badly amiss. Locally, the power elite was known as the Big Fix. Nationally, the city was a disgrace. Much of the popular anger was directed at Crowe, who in seven years as state's attorney had somehow failed to secure a single conviction for a gangland killing and had not managed so much as an indictment following the murder of his own deputy, William McSwiggan, outside a Capone-controlled speakeasy in Cicero in 1926. Since Crowe was now up for reelection, against a judge backed by Senator Deneen, he was also, in the opening months of 1928, at the very center of political attention.

The first major bombings took place at the homes of two Thompson loyalists, city comptroller Charles Fitzmorris and adviser William H. Reid. Then, less than three weeks before election day,

Diamond Joe Esposito was riddled with fifty-eight bullet holes on a Nineteenth Ward sidewalk even as bodyguards stood on either side of him. The word on the street was that Esposito had failed to deliver the political protection that the Capone mob expected in exchange for a contribution to Senator Deneen's campaign fund. On the night of Esposito's funeral, the homes of Deneen and Crowe's challenger, Judge John Swanson, were both firebombed. Nobody was hurt, but Swanson subsequently gave a tearful account of how his wife and two small grandchildren narrowly escaped serious harm. The pressure was on Crowe to deliver some culprits, but as usual he came up empty. And he provoked outrage by suggesting that Deneen and Swanson had arranged the bombings themselves to discredit his campaign. Such insensitivity was probably his undoing. Before the bombings, Crowe secured the endorsement of the Chicago Bar Association and the city's crime commission. But both turned against him as public fury boiled over.

The election itself saw a heavy deployment of what the *Chicago Daily News* described as "names to be reckoned with in games where pistols are trumps." A precinct captain in the Fifth Ward, Arthur Robert Taylor, was bludgeoned by six men armed with shotguns and thrown into the back of a green sedan whose windows were plastered with campaign posters for a rival candidate. When he was tossed onto a street corner a few hours later, he was bleeding profusely from the head. Elsewhere, poll workers were beaten, threatened and, in one case, shot and seriously wounded. Late in the day a black candidate for Republican ward committeeman in the Bloody Twentieth, Octavius Granady, was chased down a street by a limo filled with gangsters, pinned to the sidewalk as the vehicle swerved onto the curb and machine-gunned to death. Four policemen and three street thugs were later tried for his murder, but all were acquitted.

All this violence did not, in the end, have the desired intimidatory effect. Turnout across the city reached an unassailable seven hundred thousand, more than had gone to the polls at the previous presidential election, and the voters unequivocally tossed out Crowe and a slew of other candidates riding Big Bill Thompson's coattails. Public demands for a cleanup were now irresistible. The septuagenarian head of the Chicago Crime Commission, Frank J. Loesch, was appointed special assistant state's attorney general, with a mandate to investigate and prosecute the violence surrounding the Pineapple Primary. He indicted twenty people on charges of assault, kidnapping, conspiracy to murder, and vote fraud, of whom seventeen went to trial and sixteen were convicted, among them a state senator and other officeholders as well as saloon owners, gamblers, and brothel keepers.

The reputation of the Thompson administration never recovered. In 1929 the St. Valentine's Day Massacre marked the final loss of public patience with the Capone mob and its political protectors. That same year, a report by the Chicago Employers' Association titled *It's a Racket!* reeled off a catalogue of urban horrors—for example, the fact that in a single month fifty thousand business employees who had refused to pay protection money to the Midwest Garage Owners Association had their tires slashed where they had parked. In 1930 citizens' groups petitioned for the removal of the chair of the city board of election commissioners after an investigation of fifteen of the city's most notorious wards revealed that more than three hundred precinct officers had police records for crimes ranging from murder, assault and battery, armed robbery, and bombing to burglary, rape, gambling, prostitution, and embezzlement. By 1931 Thompson was out of office and out of politics for good. The *Chicago Tribune* commented somewhat luridly on the end of his career: "For Chicago Thompson has meant filth, corruption, idiocy and bankruptcy. He has given our city an international reputation for moronic buffoonery, barbaric crime, triumphant hoodlumism, unchecked graft and a dejected citizenship . . . He made Chicago a byword for the collapse of American civilization."

Not that his replacement was exactly hell-bent on cleaning up. Anton "Tough Tony" Cermak was not interested in reform, only in replacing the old, worn-out Republican machine with an equally ruthless but more effective Democratic one. A Czech immigrant himself, he pieced together a winning coalition largely by bringing

Chicago's disparate immigrant communities and labor unions together under the Democratic banner. Rather than indulge the criminal subculture of Prohibition, he swept into office with a strong mandate to oppose Prohibition altogether—which meant, in practice, spreading the wealth of the rackets rather than eliminating them, as Mayor Dever had tried to do. The level of violence may have abated under Mayor Cermak's tenure, but corruption certainly did not. A 1934 report by the Women's Civic Council complained that large numbers of convicted criminals were being hired to serve as election judges and clerks, and that votes were still being sold for fifty cents each, as they had been in the days of Hinky Dink Kenna. In 1935 a follow-up investigation into vote fraud led to the conviction of ninety-nine defendants, thirty-seven of whom were sent to prison for crimes, including copying the signatures of drunks and vagrants off flophouse registration books to pad out the rolls, casting ballots for noncitizens and the dead, and fiddling with election-day vote counts either to "run up the count"—add votes to one side—or "level the count"—take them away from the other side.

Cermak himself did not live to see the trials. He developed dysentery from a leaking sewage pipe at the South Michigan Avenue hotel where he was living, went to Miami Beach to recuperate, and ended up on the wrong end of a couple of assassin's bullets during a meeting with the newly elected Franklin Roosevelt. It was widely assumed that the gunman, an Italian immigrant named Giuseppe Zangara, was aiming for the president and missed. But in Chicago plenty of people became convinced that Cermak was the intended target. Why else would he have two holes so perfectly inscribed on his chest? That kind of marksmanship doesn't happen by accident. One widely circulated story had a ward boss back in Chicago asking an aide whether Cermak had died yet. When the aide said he didn't know, the boss retorted: "Well, put a hunnert under his nose, and if he doesn't twitch, then you know he's gone."

Something clearly went awry with all those late-nineteenth-century efforts to smash the big-city machines. Not only did the machines not die, but they were actually strengthened, first by the inanities of Prohibition and later by the election of Roosevelt, who used at least some of them to disburse federal aid during the Great Depression and so shore up support the Democrats badly needed outside of the South. Tammany Hall flourished through the early part of the century, suffering only when Roosevelt, a New Yorker with a direct interest in his home state's political intrigues, threw his support to the reformist Fiorello La Guardia in 1934. The setback was only temporary, however, and Tammany's braves were back as soon as La Guardia left office in 1945. Elsewhere, the 1920s and 1930s saw thriving, if deeply corrupted, machines in Jersey City, under Frank Hague; Boston, under James Michael Curley; and Kansas City, under the Pendergasts. Kansas City was, in many ways, a miniature Chicago with its own bootleggers, gun-toting gangsters, and freewheeling underground jazz clubs. Its police force was so corrupt it was eventually taken over by the state, its city payroll was stuffed with three thousand people who didn't actually have jobs, and there was enough electoral fraud in the wake of the 1936 general election to generate 278 criminal cases and 259 convictions. The Mugwumps must have been turning in their neatly kept graves.

The truth was that voting restrictions and charter reforms introduced alongside the Australian ballot served not to eliminate the machines but only to entrench them deeper, and in many cases make them more conservative. In cities where one party enjoyed uncontested dominance—which was most of them—the suffrage restrictions were more helpful than not to the ward bosses, because they made it easier to keep tabs on the size and makeup of the electorate. Chicago was a bit of a departure from the norm, for a couple of reasons. First was because of the lightning speed with which it had developed as an economic powerhouse and a major population center. As Charles Edward Merriam, a valiant but failed reformer up to 1930, observed, it is highly unusual for a city to go from scratch to four million people in less than a century. What was barely a village in 1833 was incorporated as a city in 1838, by which time the first voting fraud scandal had already erupted. In the 1890s the visiting British author and church minister William Stead regarded Chicago's rapidly multiplying corruptions as positively satanic and speculated what a new Jesus Christ would have to do to clean it up. Rudyard Kipling, visiting around the same time, concluded it was inhabited by savages. In 1911 a vice commission report, considered so scandalous that it was withheld from the public for two years, calculated that the annual economic value of a prostitute—of which there were four thousand within the city limits—was four and a half times greater than that of a store clerk. No wonder Chicago was regarded as a wonderland by racketeers, enterprising ward bosses, and robber barons like Charles Yerkes, the streetcar entrepreneur and "Goliath of graft" so venal he was eventually run out of the country. When Big Bill Thompson first became mayor in 1915, the spoils system "swept over the city like a noxious blight," as Merriam later wrote, and Chicago became perhaps the "only completely corrupt city in America." It was Thompson's Chicago that witnessed the throwing of the 1919 World Series and whose elected officials took shameless advantage of the anti-immigrant Palmer raids the same year to eavesdrop on federal wiretaps and earn a little blackmail money on the side.

The other thing that made Chicago different was that it was a place of genuine political competition, in a country with precious little of that commodity to go around. Not only were Democrats and Republicans evenly matched in the city, but also Illinois was one of the few toss-up states in presidential elections. No vote could be taken for granted, and theft, given the prevailing political atmosphere, was rampant on all sides. Nothing was considered a more precious political asset than control of the city's electoral bureaucracy, which Merriam estimated was worth anywhere between fifty thousand and one hundred thousand votes in either a primary or a general election. Political victories almost always translated into greater influence inside the voting precincts, in part because of a city rule stipulating that election judges and clerks had to serve in the ward where they lived, at the pleasure of the local ward committees. The intention might have been to make it easier to check the identity and eligibility of prospective voters, but it was also an invitation to corruption. Election judges appointed by the machine served the machine; those from the opposing party were either bought off or otherwise induced to remain silent. The bloody battles of the 1920s were, in one sense, a fight to establish a workable political machine that could assert definitive control over the voting apparatus and thus perpetuate itself indefinitely. Once Tony Cermak and the Democrats created just such a machine, it remained in place, with only the briefest of interruptions, until the tail end of the Daley era almost half a century later. With armed gangsters roving the streets, crooks manning the precincts, and racketeers in cahoots with the political parties, the reformers never stood a chance.

Corruption remained a steady feature of Chicago life throughout the Kelly-Nash years of the 1930s and 1940s (popularly known as Nelly-Cash). In fact, corruption was worn almost as a badge of pride. Just like Plunkitt of Tammany Hall, Chicago ward bosses took professional satisfaction in their ability to win allies through simple acts of consideration and cutting of bureaucratic red tape. They ran a city-wide patronage machine worth as many as three hundred thousand votes at election time, so it was natural for precinct captains to help spring the faithful from jail, order ambulances to take their pregnant wives to hospital, or offer short-term loans to the hard-up. For elections, the machine provided as much as twenty thousand dollars per ward to get out the vote, either in the form of straight bribery or, more commonly, as payment for poll workers whose loyalty could be vouchsafed. Bosses like Vito Marzullo of the Twenty-fifth Ward found it faintly ridiculous to think of playing the game any other way, deriding reformers as "goo-goos" (short for "good government"), who were all talk and no action. "While reformers want to build a new city, a new church and a new country," Marzullo told the author Edmund F. Kallina Jr., "if you give them ten dollars they could not get a dog out of the pound."

The machine ethos, and the corruption that went with it, had hardly abated by the time the Kefauver Committee visited in 1950 as part of its nationwide investigation into organized crime. Senator

Kefauver later concluded that "every example of rottenness which we found anywhere in the United States was duplicated, in some form or another, in the capital of the Capone mob." Famously, he subpoenaed Mob luminaries, who insisted, straight-faced, that they had never heard of the Mafia and had no idea even what it was. But he also talked to Daniel Gilbert, an improbably affluent police captain, who told the committee he had taken bets on every city election since 1921 and never lost. In some races, his winnings were as high as ten thousand dollars. "Is that legal?" Kefauver asked him. "Well, I would say it was legal if a fellow wants to make a bet on an election," came the disingenuous reply. "There is nothing illegal about it. No violation of the law."

Gilbert ran for sheriff that same year and lost, partly as a result of the negative publicity from his testimony. But the Chicago machine soon proved it was unafraid of anything Kefauver or anyone else could throw at it. In 1955, after an eight-year hiatus in which a non-machine Democrat occupied the mayor's office, a certain Richard Daley, chair of the Cook County Democratic Party, revived the old network of alliances that had served the party so well in the past, especially in the notoriously dirty "river wards," and handily defeated his reformist challenger, Robert Merriam. Merriam, whose father, Charles Edward, had run an equally unsuccessful reform campaign for mayor in 1911, denounced Daley as "the front man for a pack of jackals who have been feeding off the city for the past twenty-four years." But Daley wasn't bothered. He so reveled in his election victory that he turned his election-night vote tally, 708,222, into his vanity license plate.

Outside Chicago, Mayor Daley is known for two things: letting his notoriously brutal police force loose on the antiwar demonstrators outside the Democratic National Convention in 1968, and stealing the 1960 presidential election for John F. Kennedy. Whether he actually *did* steal the election or *how* he did it are not questions that receive a lot of attention these days. That's partly because the shock of JFK's assassination made such matters distasteful for the better part of a generation, and partly because his frustrated challenger, Richard Nixon, was reckoned to have got his due—perhaps more than his due, in the light of subsequent events—when he ran for the White House again in 1968 and won. Much of the opprobrium felt by Republican partisans at the time has thus faded to no more than a gentle buzz of curiosity. Americans don't generally like to entertain the possibility that the world's most powerful office has been stolen, and skeptics down the years have found plenty of reasons to pooh-pooh the idea. Did Kennedy really need Illinois anyway? Didn't various recounts and court challenges prove the essential veracity of the Chicago count? Would Nixon really have backed down, dogged fighter that he was, if he thought he was the rightful winner?

These are all valid questions, of course, but they do not alter the fact that back in 1960, while the election was actually in progress, the situation stank to highest heaven. Kennedy came out on top by the slimmest of pluralities in the national popular vote—just 118,000 ahead of Nixon, out of 68 million cast. In a dozen states or more the result was a toss-up, or close to it. Without Illinois, Kennedy might have become dangerously dependent on the Deep South, where twenty-six segregationist electors were threatening to bolt the Democratic ticket if they did not receive significant concessions on federal civil rights policy. (Fourteen of them ended up choosing Harry Byrd, the veteran Dixiecrat senator from Virginia, instead of Kennedy.) Certainly, without Illinois or Texas, which Kennedy also clung to by his fingernails on election night, there was a risk that a presidential election would be thrown into the House of Representatives for the first time in 136 years.

Under the circumstances, the figures from Illinois looked just too good to be true. Kennedy was said to have squeaked home in the state by just 9,400 votes. In Chicago his margin was 456,000, on a reported turnout of 89.3 percent. Those were near-mythical figures, even by the standards of a city with notoriously broad shoulders. Daley had won reelection the year before with a margin of almost 470,000, but that was against a token opponent in a race nobody seriously expected him to lose. Four years earlier, against Merriam,

Daley's edge had been just 120,000. Could Chicago's Republican voters really have switched allegiance so wholeheartedly, or so casually, in a presidential election where their state was the pivot on which the outcome would more than likely rest?

To many Chicagoans it just didn't seem believable. Already in early October the *Daily News* had begun running pieces about thousands of invalid names showing up on registration lists. The paper also took a look at the city's board of election commissioners and discovered that of 180 appointees, all but four were Democrats. Certain wards remained almost as dirty as they had been in the 1920s, none more so than the Twenty-fourth, where an election judge by the name of Benjamin "Short Pencil" Lewis was notorious for filling in blank ballots and spoiling unfavorable ones with a piece of lead wedged into a fingernail. (Three years later, on the night of a local election in which he himself ran and won, Lewis was found handcuffed and shot to death under his desk, a cigarette symbolically burned down to his short-pencil finger.) With such stories circulating freely ahead of the Nixon-Kennedy vote, an outfit called the Committee for Honest Elections put in a request to send observers into polling stations. But Mayor Daley accused the committee chairman, David Brill, of partisan Republican bias and turned him down.

Sensing the chance to bust open the scandal of the century, a *New York Herald Tribune* reporter, Earl Mazo, who also happened to be a friend of Nixon's, began publishing as many accounts as he could lay hands on pointing to manipulation or fraud. One Chicago precinct, he wrote a few weeks after the election, had returned 397 votes from just 376 voters. Others recorded the votes of the dead, allowed people to cast more than one ballot, or were caught engaging in ballot stuffing. Mazo did not limit his ambitions to Chicago. In Texas, where he suspected Kennedy's running mate, Lyndon Johnson, of resorting to at least some of the old tricks that had got him elected to the Senate in 1948, he alleged that Democratic Party operatives had paid off the poll tax of poor Mexican Americans and dragged them less than willingly to the polls. The problem with Mazo's anecdotes, though, is that they were no more than that—just anecdotes, unsupported by much in the way of corroborating evidence. Even if they were all true, they did not add up to more than a few dozen extra votes for Kennedy, nowhere near enough to overturn the result.

There is little doubt that election-day fraud took place, and on quite some scale. A special prosecutor later brought voting-related criminal charges against 677 people across the city, although he never got as far as prosecuting them, because their cases were moved out of Chicago to the court of a Daley crony in East Saint Louis who promptly squashed the lot. Several years later a Pulitzer prize–winning series in the *Chicago Tribune* uncovered hard evidence that the Daley machine habitually registered vagrants for the purposes of stealing their votes, intimidated Republican election judges to the point of holding them in police custody on election day, and threatened to "vise" ward bosses—that is, have them thrown out of office—if they couldn't come up with the vote totals expected of them. That said, it was always going to be too much for Nixon's friends to hope that the Chicago machine was capable of manufacturing nonexistent votes by the tens of thousands. Even Big Bill Thompson and his Prohibition goons had not pulled off anything so spectacular. Nixon must have understood this as he made his decision to concede instead of pushing for recounts or other legal challenges. A recount did take place in a sharply contested lower-order race for Cook County state's attorney, but only a few hundred extra votes were found for the unsuccessful Republican candidate, not enough to alter the outcome. One can only assume a presidential recount would have proved equally underwhelming.

The problem with Mazo and the other fraud seekers was that they were looking in the wrong place. The Daley machine was too smart simply to invent vote tallies and be caught by anything as obvious as a recount. For a start, the brand-new lever voting machines installed in Cook County in time for the 1960 election made meaningful recounts impossible, and were open to certain abuses, as will be explored more thoroughly in the next chapter. But the votes were clearly there—or most of them, anyway. The key question was how they were generated. More than forty years later, we still don't know the precise answer to that question, but we have a pretty good idea. Take as a starting point the evidence of Robert J. McDonnell, a leading Chicago defense attorney specializing in organized crime cases, who revealed a few years ago that he had helped set up a meeting between Joseph Kennedy, the future president's father, and the Mob leader Sam Giancana. McDonnell told investigative reporter Seymour Hersh that he was asked to make contact with Giancana by a circuit court judge and acquaintance of Kennedy's named William J. Tuohy. " Tuohy asked me to his chambers," McDonnell recounted. "I went. We chatted. He said, 'I don't know how to pose this question. Do you know Mooney Giancana?' I said yes. He said, 'How do you suggest that I arrange a meeting between Mr. Giancana and Joseph Kennedy?'"

McDonnell believed that Giancana mobilized the Mob, and the Mob, by hook or by crook, dragged out the required numbers of voters to deliver Illinois to Kennedy. Chicago was certainly a town that knew all the tricks: padding the rolls and casting votes on behalf of the departed and the dead, registering vagrants and transients and inducing them to stay away so their names could be used by the party, accompanying voters into the booth to make sure they did what they were told, and so on. "They just worked—totally went all out," McDonnell said. "[Kennedy] won it squarely, but he got the vote because of what Mooney had done." He was not the only one to think so. According to Tina Sinatra, her brother, Frank, also met Giancana and talked him into backing Kennedy. It was not an easy sell, because of Bobby Kennedy's tough stance on organized crime in general, and Giancana in particular, in his work for the Senate Select Committee on Improper Activities in the Labor or Management Field, better known as the "rackets committee." But as an FBI special agent in Chicago, William F. Roemer Jr., wrote in his memoirs, Giancana was later heard on a wiretap offering his support to Kennedy in return for a commitment "to back off from the FBI investigation." FBI wiretaps also revealed that Mafia money was funneled into the Kennedy campaign in Chicago. Some people believe JFK himself met Giancana and even played golf with him. Judith Campbell Exner, who shared a bed with both Kennedy and

Giancana at different points, wrote in her own memoirs that the Mob leader once told her: "Listen, honey, if it wasn't for me your boyfriend wouldn't even be in the White House."

One thing we don't know is the extent to which Mayor Daley was personally involved in election rigging. It would be naïve to suppose he was unaware of it. The quote at the head of this chapter (which was handed down via Kennedy to the *Washington Post* executive editor Benjamin Bradlee) indicates that Daley knew about the "few close friends" even if he wasn't totally on top of their activities. Daley's interest in Kennedy, as it turned out, had less to do with electing a Democrat to the White House than it did with using the charismatic young senator as an asset in the race he really cared about, the fight for Cook County state's attorney. All politics is local, as Tip O'Neill liked to say, and nowhere more so than Chicago, where the machine preferred to keep its faithful safely within city limits and reserve statewide or national office for those, like Adlai Stevenson, who displayed disturbingly reformist tendencies or were otherwise disloyal. The Republican who was running for state's attorney in 1960, Benjamin Adamowski, had been one of Daley's challengers in the 1955 mayoral election and risked becoming a serious threat to both the machine and Daley's own political future if he was allowed to become the county's chief prosecuting attorney. Thanks to the Kennedy wind in the Democratic Party's sails, plus the unspecified contribution of Giancana's boys, Adamowski was defeated by more than twenty thousand votes. The recount that Adamowski requested, and obtained, made no substantive difference, because his race, like the presidency, wasn't entirely fought and won on election day. Mostly, it was sewn up in advance. Or as the *Chicago Tribune* put it at the time, once an election in Cook County has been stolen, it stays stolen.

That's not to say there wasn't considerable maneuvering and jockeying on election night itself. Over and above the question of inflated figures favoring the Democrats in Chicago, there was the distinct possibility of shifting totals downstate favoring the Republicans. The result was an extraordinary game of chicken, not unlike the big Senate races in Texas in the 1940s, in which one side dared the other to release more of its returns so it could adjust the rest of its figures accordingly. According to Kennedy campaign staffer Kenneth O'Donnell, Daley was quite open about this. "We're trying to hold back our returns," the mayor told him, according to Adam Cohen and Elizabeth Taylor's book on Daley, *American Pharaoh*. "Every time we announce two hundred more votes for Kennedy in Chicago, they come up out of nowhere downstate with another three hundred votes for Nixon." This tit-for-tat cheating may have been a key reason why the court cases alleging fraud went nowhere. The Republicans did not want to push the issue for fear of being given a dose of their own medicine.

What did that medicine consist of? One place the Daley machine might have played fast and loose was with so-called D&O ballots, short for "defective and objected to"—the area of Short Pencil Lewis's expertise. When these ballots were reexamined after the election—a relatively small proportion after the introduction of the lever machines across most of the county—they showed a moderate but unmistakable pattern of errors favoring the Democrats. Some informed insiders believe these strategems made the crucial difference. G. Robert Blakey, a former special prosecutor, told Seymour Hersh in the mid-1990s that to judge from FBI wiretaps he had heard, "enough votes were stolen—let me repeat that—stolen in Chicago to give Kennedy a sufficient margin that he carried the state of Illinois."

Even if the public at large was induced into thinking all was well with the 1960 election, many Republican loyalists refused to forgive or forget. When Mayor Daley's son Bill flew to Florida to head Al Gore's postelection committee in the agonizing 2000 contest, it prompted fury from the likes of Curt Weldon, a Republican House member from Pennsylvania, who vowed publicly he would "use every ounce of energy I have to deny the electors being seated if I believe the political will of the people was thwarted by the son of Mayor Daley of Chicago." Someone else who appears to have borne a permanent grudge was Nixon himself. For all his public utterances about national unity and respect for the process, he was overheard telling several people at a Christmas party a few weeks after the election: "We won, but they stole it from us." From then on, he had it in for the Kennedy clan in a very personal and vindictive way. When it looked like his Democratic opponent in the 1968 race would be Bobby Kennedy, Nixon told his speechwriter Richard Whalen: "We can beat the little S.O.B." To make sure he wouldn't be the Daley machine's fool twice, Nixon set up a fraud squad in Illinois called Operation Eagle Eye. And when Illinois once again failed to report its results the morning after the election, he tried to pressure his opponent, Hubert Humphrey, into conceding anyway. Nixon eventually took the state 43.4 percent to 42.72.

It seems likely that Nixon's obsession with being cheated in Chicago in 1960 was a direct motivation for the Watergate break-in and other underhanded plots of the 1972 campaign season. These days most people think of Watergate as a scandal about the abuse of executive power. But it was, at its heart, part of a concerted effort to steal a presidential election. The fact that Nixon coasted to a second term against George McGovern does not alter the fact that he planned the campaign as if he could hold on to the White House only through dirt and dishonesty. And the fact that McGovern won the Democratic nomination was not in itself entirely divorced from the intrigues being cooked up in the Oval Office. As early as May 1971, Nixon's chief of staff, Bob Haldeman, wrote in his diary, the president was thinking "that we should put permanent tails on Teddy [Kennedy] and [Maine senator Edmund] Muskie and Hubert [Humphrey] on all the personal stuff, to cover the kinds of things they hit us on in '62: personal finances, family and so forth." Nixon's gang sent an undercover agent to Chappaquiddick to pose as a newspaper reporter and try to dig up dirt on Kennedy—specifically, to "catch him in the sack with one of his babes," which the agent couldn't manage. They reduced Muskie to a quivering wreck after spreading smear stories about his wife ahead of the New Hampshire primary and sending out bogus Muskie campaign literature accusing Humphrey and another Democratic candidate, Henry "Scoop" Jackson, of sexual indiscretions. Some CIA operatives came to suspect that one of Nixon's "plumbers" had also fed a sophisticated form of LSD to Muskie to make him paranoid and unstable.

Aside from the break-in at the Democratic National Committee's headquarters in the Watergate building, the plumbers planned burglaries at the Brookings Institution and the U.S. National Archives. As many as one hundred premises may have been targeted in all. The Nixon White House was also determined to destroy George Wallace, Alabama's segregationist governor and presidential candidate, who threatened the Nixonian Southern strategy by splitting the conservative vote. It set the IRS on Wallace's state administration and leaked a preliminary audit indicating widespread corruption. It channeled four hundred thousand dollars to Wallace's opponent in the 1970 governor's race. And there is some evidence it might have had a hand in the 1972 shooting that came close to ending Wallace's life. G. Gordon Liddy and Howard Hunt certainly discussed the possible murder of newspaper columnist Jack Anderson, a plan that was rejected. They also concocted plans—never executed—to mug antiwar demonstrators heading to the 1972 Republican National Convention in Miami and to abduct leaders like Abbie Hoffman and Jerry Rubin to Mexico.

Nixon appeared to believe he could get away with all this because the public retained a touching faith in the system and would regard the very thought of executive malfeasance on this scale as preposterous. Back in December 1960 he had talked Earl Mazo into discontinuing his series on fraud in the Kennedy race, telling him: "Earl, those are interesting articles you are writing, but no one steals the presidency of the United States." On that, he and Mayor Daley could have found a rare point of agreement.

★ **PART TWO** ★

Voting in the Machine Age

9

LEVERS, PUNCH CARDS, AND THE FALLACY OF THE TECHNOLOGICAL FIX

★ ☆ ★ ☆ ★ ☆ ★ ☆ ★ ☆ ★ ☆ ★ ☆ ★

The perpetual rush to novelty that characterizes the modern marketplace, with its escalating promise of technological transcendence, is matched by the persistence of pre-formed patterns of life which promise merely more of the same . . . Every new, seemingly bold departure ends by following an already familiar path.
—David F. Noble, America by Design (1977)

Technology alone does not eliminate the possibility of corruption and incompetence in elections; it merely changes the platform on which they may occur.
—Rebecca Mercuri

TAMPA, 1970. A crazy rumor is circulating that the chair of the county election board has a lever-operated voting machine worth thousands of taxpayer dollars sitting in his backyard. An even crazier rumor says he's using it to smoke fish. At the election supervisor's office, a local straggly bearded eccentric named Jim Fair—the scion of a respected Tampa family whose countercultural thrift store, the Salvation Navy, is a haven for vagrants, Vietnam vets, and discount shoppers—is running the show and driving his experienced staff crazy by hiring temporary workers he refers to as "students and hippies with educated minds." The hippies drink on the job, leaving wine bottles in desk drawers, and filch loose change from their colleagues' purses. When five of the permanent employees complain, they are not merely ignored. They are fired.

Everyone knows something strange is going on, but it takes a while to work out exactly what. For the past nine years, Hillsborough County has been buying lever machines from the Shoup Voting Machine Company of upstate New York—great clunky behemoths full of gear-toothed mechanical counters that are said to be both fraud- and foolproof, not to mention indestructible. Once Fair gets into office, though, it is announced that the county's $1.5 million investment might not have been so solid after all. About two hundred of the machines are declared obsolete, and Hillsborough feels compelled to replace them at a further cost of $530,000. Shoup takes the old machines off the county's hands for $30 a pop, refurbishes them, and sells them to Harris County, Texas, for $1,500, a dizzying mark-up of 5,000 percent. They seem to work fine.

A grand jury is convened, but somehow it can't identify any crimes or anyone to indict. The governor of Florida, Claude Kirk, preempts the court system and removes Fair from office for "misfeasance and malfeasance." Fair promptly goes into hiding, along with his faithful Weimaraner, Smokey, and does not reappear until his official removal hearing in the state Senate, where he is voted down 46-0. Fair claims he is not running from the law, only from the threat of being locked in a mental asylum (which is where, for a while, he ends up). Only when the feds intervene does the whole scheme unravel, with President Nixon's attorney general, John Mitchell, taking personal charge of the operation. One of the first places the feds look is county election board chair Ron Budd's backyard, where, indeed, they find he has converted the giant metal frame of a lever machine, supplied courtesy of Shoup and friends, into a mullet-smoking rack.

Such was the plotline of the first really juicy scandal of the voting machine age. Truly, you could not make this stuff up. The "obsolete" machines, of course, were part of an elaborate kickback scam, whereby Shoup, or at least Shoup's agents, milked the Hillsborough taxpayers twice over, then profited all over again by reselling the first batch to Houston. It was the new machines, meanwhile, that turned out to be the defective ones, breaking down so calamitously in the 1971 Tampa city elections that the outcome of one council race could not be determined at all. Naturally, there was something for the politicians in this arrangement. Shoup wrote out checks for tens of thousands of dollars to a certain Arturo Garcia—who did not exist—which were then taken to an obliging bank in Tampa and converted into cash for distribution among key city and county officials. Soon, indictments were flying in all directions, and a half-dozen officials and Shoup company employees were convicted of bribery and election fraud. At trial Ron Budd emerged as the linchpin, since in addition to his election board duties he worked for the agent who both bought back the county's lever machines and negotiated the sale of the new ones. He was sentenced to ten years behind bars.

All around, the 1970s were to the voting machine business what the Lincoln County wars had been to the Wild West. Not only was the Shoup Voting Machine Company locked in a fierce competitive battle with its perennial lever machine rival, the Automatic Voting Machine Company (AVM) of Jamestown, New York, but both now had to contend with a new player on the scene, the maker of the Votomatic punch-card machine, which was eating up market share in state after state and threatening to edge both companies out of business. Not only was the Votomatic far cheaper, it was also vastly lighter—18 pounds, compared with at least 700 pounds for the lever-operated device—and could be stored in one-eightieth of the space. On top of that, it had the allure of novelty, a computer system for a computer age. (The fact that it didn't work reliably was not widely noticed until much later.) Where the lever machine manufacturers couldn't maintain their competitive advantage by arguing the merits of their product, they did so through political influence-peddling and bribery, finding plenty of willing recipients of their largesse in county election offices, especially on the East Coast. "The further east you went, the more corrupt it was," said Bob Varni, the founding chairman of the Votomatic company, Computer Election Systems (CES), who retains fond memories of watching his rivals glad-hand themselves into near-oblivion and profiting handsomely from their misfortunes.

AVM almost went belly-up in 1973 after a concatenation of disasters. The chairman of the board, Lloyd Dixon Sr., dropped dead a month after signing the biggest contract in the company's history, a $19 million deal to deliver ten thousand machines to Venezuela. Then the Venezuelans reneged on the contract, lumbering AVM with $13 million in out-of-pocket expenses. Finally Lloyd Dixon Jr., the new chief executive, was indicted for bribing election officials in Buffalo, New York, and was forced to resign in disgrace. He was eventually acquitted, getting away with only a minor sanction for violating Securities and Exchange Commission rules on unauthorized payments to company officers. But by then AVM's name was well and truly tarnished, not least because of lesser bribery scandals for which it received punishment in Arkansas and Texas. The company's voting machine assets were spun off from its other interests and left to fend for themselves, eventually reemerging as a major force in the late 1990s under the new name of Sequoia Pacific.

Shoup skirted just as close to the edge of disaster, if not closer. Its great strength was the cultivation of political contacts in county election offices, who could be counted on—much like the gang in Tampa—to stick by its interests through thick and thin. It had pioneered the approach in Louisiana in the 1950s, when it took advantage of a power struggle between Governor Earl Long and his would-be rival, Secretary of State Wade O. Martin, to clean up the state's entire voting machine market. By the early 1970s, though, it wasn't so easy to stay one step ahead of the law, and Shoup and its election official clients racked up bribery convictions in Texas, Kentucky, and Illinois. In Philadelphia one Shoup-associated voting official skipped town rather than face trial, while another, city com-missioner Maurice Osser, was acquitted of soliciting bribes from Shoup only to be convicted of accepting one hundred thousand dol-lars in a brown envelope from a ballot-printing company.

Bob Varni remembers noting that at one point Shoup had lost almost its entire customer service department to the criminal justice system. So he suggested, with considerable chutzpah, that his own company do the job for them. "At first we were rejected," he recounted. "But three or four months later, we got the phone call." One of Shoup's top salesmen, Irving Meyers, had himself been con-victed on bribery charges and knew he needed a pro to mind the shop while he served his six-month sentence at a low-security facil-ity on a military base in Florida. Meyers told Varni: "I will give you all the help I can. I'll be at Eglund Air Force Base. Come and meet me any time you like."

It didn't take Varni long to realize that the more the feds cracked down on the questionable business relationships between the older voting machine companies and county election offices, the more markets it opened up for him and the Votomatic. CES was never caught in a bribery scandal, and Varni and his fellow directors made sure to keep it that way. "We all came out of IBM, and nobody at IBM would have thought of passing money over. It didn't enter our minds," he said. "We got solicited for 'campaign contributions' from time to time by county supervisors. They wouldn't ask blatantly, but we knew what they were saying. And we just laughed them off. We became the boy scouts of the industry. When the feds cracked down, it worked in our favor. When the Shoup people started going to jail, everyone loved us." And when the CES customer service team made its temporary home at Shoup's headquarters, then located in Cherry Hill, New Jersey, they stuck the knife in even deeper. "We called the FBI," Varni said with relish, "and gave them a green light to investigate whatever they wanted."

This sly piece of competitive one-upmanship was particularly galling to members of the original Shoup family, who had been rea-sonably successful up to that point in warding off the Votomatic threat, at least on the East Coast, by demonstrating how easy it was to rig the punch-card ballots. Ransom Shoup Sr. and his son, Ransom II, talked themselves into an invitation to address Congress and showed how, with the help of a doctored master punch card, the vote totals in any given race could be adjusted to a predetermined outcome. The Shoups also demonstrated how a thumbtack concealed in a shirt cuff could be used to punch extra holes to invalidate ballots, a variant on the old short-pencil trick, and also how prepunched ballots could be distributed outside polling stations in a modified version of chain voting. Their criticisms of the Votomatic were spot-on, but at the time most observers saw them as just canny business showmanship. When the Tampa scandal erupted, any credence the Shoups might—and should—have enjoyed disappeared in an instant.

Ransom Shoup II has since argued that the scandals of the early 1970s were the fault of rogue salesmen, and of shareholders who took advantage of the company's precarious financial position to dictate management practices of their choosing. "It was those kinds of shenanigans that led my father and me to break off and start our own company, and sue to get the family name back," Ransom told *Philadelphia* magazine in 2001. Sure enough, he and his father left the Shoup Voting Machine Company behind and founded the R. F. Shoup Company instead. Soon, though, they were getting into trouble all their own.

In 1978 Philadelphia experienced a major breakdown of its Shoup lever machines during a contentious special election to determine whether Mayor Frank Rizzo should be allowed to run for a third term in contravention of the usual term-limit rules. Federal prosecutors became suspicious because more than three-quarters of the machine failures occurred in predominantly black districts, whose residents were known to be vehemently against extending Rizzo's tenure. (He lost anyway.) The U.S. Attorney's Office, perhaps a little too trustingly, asked Ransom Shoup II to come in and investigate with a team of experts. And they—perhaps unsurprisingly, given how much of their business relied on the supposed impregnability of their products—concluded that the machines had not been tampered with at all. Rather, they said, they were old and poorly maintained, more so in poorer black districts than in the rest of the city.

Before he submitted his report, Shoup had a little idea, one he was later to regret deeply. It dawned on him that the person most likely to be embarrassed by his findings was Margaret Tartaglione, the city commissioner responsible for administering elections. And Tartaglione, a staunch Rizzo supporter, was already in trouble—she had been arrested on election day on charges of interference after she made a last-minute change in the location of a politically sensitive polling station. So Shoup offered her a deal. If she gave him the maintenance contract on Philadelphia's voting machines, he would, prosecutors later alleged, give her an opportunity to sanitize the report to cast herself in the best possible light. Tartaglione told an intermediary she would meet Shoup over lunch to talk the deal over. Unfortunately for Shoup, she also went to the FBI and got herself wired. As a consequence, he was prosecuted and convicted on fraud and obstruction of justice charges, and received a three-year suspended sentence.

That was the end of Shoup's career in Philadelphia, but it didn't stop him from exploiting his political contacts in other cities and, in due course, introducing one of the very first direct recording electronic, or DRE machines, known as the Shouptronic. In 1990 Shoup stunned everyone when he somehow managed to get hold of a confidential assessment report on his own and rival bids for a $50 million voting machine purchase by New York City. He insisted that the report, considered so sensitive it was farmed out to a private research company and kept secret even from certain members of the city's board of elections, magically turned up on his desk one day in a plain envelope. Nobody ever managed to disprove his account. And anyway, by the time news of the leak became public, Shoup had already won the contract.

The company was also active overseas, where, according to Shoup's longtime overseas marketing director, Ron Lawyer, the first question was almost invariably: "Can the things be rigged?" In Nigeria in the early 1980s, President Alhaji Shehu Shagari told Lawyer he had four specifications: the machines had to be able to travel by canoe, to be strapped on a camel, to be nailed to a tree, and, finally, to be foolproof and tamperproof. The fourth specification, however, was not to be fulfilled until Shagari had contested and won the next election. When Lawyer told the story to the *Chicago Tribune* in 1993, he did not say whether these terms were accepted or not. But it became a moot point, because Shagari was overthrown before an election could so much as take place.

In 1957 AVM put out an intriguing promotional film for lever machines that oozed with the period's curious mix of techno-optimism and Cold War paranoia. The title says it all: *Behind the Freedom Curtain*. So too does the opening declaration of its narrator, purportedly a small-town newspaper reporter who feels duty-bound to trumpet the wonders of fully automated voting and, by inference, the importance of lever machines in the struggle against Communism, corruption, and other evils. "We announce without apology this is going to be a flag-waving production," he says. Paper ballots, we are told in no uncertain terms, are complicated to use, prone to voter and clerical error, and open to all manner of mischief, from intimidation to fraud, because of the number of human hands they pass through. Machines, by contrast, guarantee ballot secrecy, accurate counting, and speedy delivery of the results. "You will register and count your own vote," the narrator reports excitedly. "It's already counted the moment you leave. Nor can the machine make a mistake . . . Mechanical counters cannot get tired, cannot get cranky, cannot forget." The film shows repeated images of oversized paper ballots being ripped, filled in incorrectly, and stamped VOID by indifferent clerical workers lost in a fog of coffee fumes and cigarette smoke. Voting on paper, our reporter-narrator suggests, is quaint, behind the times, almost antique—as absurd as riding a horse and buggy in the age of the automobile. He asks: "Can democracy compete with his right hand tied to a hitching post?"

Throughout the film—indeed, throughout the history of voting machines—it is the individual voter who is touted as the real consumer, the person uppermost in the mind of the inventors and vendors of the latest wonder-mechanism. But it is not, of course, the voter who selects the machines for purchase. And it is not, primarily, to the voters' needs that the machines are tailored. Rather, they are designed to appeal to the city precinct workers or county election board members who have to struggle through the logistical nightmare of multirace elections on an annual or biannual basis. Beyond the blather about freedom and consumer convenience, *Behind the Freedom Curtain* also makes sure it hits the real selling points: that after the initial capital outlay, counties can make considerable savings by cutting down on temporary staff and consolidating precincts and, at the end of election night, produce quick and easy results that, as a bonus, cannot be second-guessed or lead to extra work, because there are no paper ballots to recount.

In truth, lever machines were never particularly user-friendly, for either voters or election administrators. Because of their bulk and the profusion of intricate parts—thousands upon thousands of cogs and switches and counters—they were also irritatingly difficult to store, transport, and maintain. In the Louisiana bayous they had to be dragged by barge from warehouse to polling station. Worst of all, contrary to their reputation, they were far from immune to mistakes, or to mischief. Almost forty years after their introduction in Lockport, New York, in 1892, Joseph P. Harris reported for the Brookings Institution: "It is significant that the machines have never been able to succeed if the voter is given his preference between voting the machine and voting a paper ballot."

The first switch-and-lever machine was pioneered by Thomas Edison shortly after the end of the Civil War, but at that time nobody was interested. Because ballots were still issued by political parties, not election officials, there was no mileage in shelling out good money for a machine premised on fairness and accuracy; the parties were much more interested in spending money on buying votes for their own side. Once the Australian ballot was introduced, though, and elections were removed from direct party control, it was a different story. An inventor and safe-maker named Jacob Myers came up with the first commercially viable model, and it was a Mugwump's democratic dream: shiny, new, and giving all outward appearances of tidiness, efficiency, and protection from rascaldom. Appearance, not reality, was the great seduction. As Lewis Mumford was to write a few decades later, modern societies have "the careless habit of attributing to mechanical improvements a direct role as instruments of culture and civilization," an expectation machines themselves are in no position to live up to. The lever devices were no exception.

City after city spent tens of thousands of dollars on United States Standard Voting Machines (the precursor to AVMs), only to suffer buyer's remorse almost immediately. By 1929 lever machines had been purchased in twenty-four states, only to be discarded again in fifteen of them. County officials found them either too unwieldy, too tricky for the voter, too expensive to buy in sufficient numbers, or too problematic to keep in good working order. In Chicago, true to that city's venal reputation, the machines were also the object of a bribery scandal that infuriated the reformers of the Chicago Bureau of Public Efficiency. A few hundred machines were delivered to the Windy City in 1912, but were never used because of protracted legal action leading to court injunctions and a fraud and bribery investigation by the Illinois state legislature. As a result, Chicago voters stuck with paper until 1959.

The Shoups were in the voting machine game almost from the start. Samuel Shoup, the family patriarch, whose other claim to fame was to have invented the paper napkin dispenser, studied Myers's invention and sought to improve on it, wheeling out his own prototype in 1895. As the desire to beat back the corruptions of city machines continued apace through the first half of the twentieth century, Shoup and AVM became market leaders. Most of the early misgivings about their products gave way to an almost limitless faith in the power of technology, and they never lacked for work or new customers. The Shoups, in particular, took care to cultivate a public image as operators who were savvy enough to outsmart the rascals, selling a machine they said was well-nigh indestructible. Over the years, they boasted that Shoup products had survived being shot at in Kentucky and dynamited in Tennessee. Even card sharks and FBI agents, they claimed, had tried to find a way to cheat the system, only to fail at every turn.

The bravado was all very compelling, but the machines were nowhere near as indestructible as the Shoups or their clients fancied. Like modern DREs, lever machines worked on trust. They were flawless only if you chose to believe they were; in the absence of physical ballots to go back and check, there was no way to be sure. If one or more of the internal counters malfunctioned, who was to know? If a problem was suspected, how was a technician supposed to locate it in the sea of cogs and gears in the machine's innards? Mechanical breakdown became a particular problem over time, especially because the machines were so unwieldy to shift in and out of storage between elections. "We had one once that fell onto the hood of a Buick," a New York voting machine technician told the *Los Angeles Times* in 2000. "An automobile has 5,000 parts; a voting machine has 27,000 parts. If a guy drops it from a moving truck, it goes out of alignment. If it's put out of alignment enough, it won't work."

As for cheating, it was undeniably more difficult with a lever machine than with paper ballots—chain voting was out, for a start— but hardly a stretch for the kind of corrupt precinct captains who could always find a way around any technological challenge. There was nothing to stop poll workers and election judges from continuing their practice of gathering the names of nonvoters, especially those they had paid to stay away, forging their signatures on the registry and casting ballots on their behalf. In Louisiana this procedure was popularly known as "ringing the bell," because the Shoup machines would tinkle every time voters pulled the lever to indicate that they had made their final choices. Theoretically, at least, it was also possible for a technician of moderate skill to preprogram the machines and manipulate the vote totals. Michael Ian Shamos, a voting equipment inspector for the state of Pennsylvania, wrote in 1993 that lever machines "can be subtly altered so that a fraction of votes for a particular candidate will not register." There was also a way to override this alteration, Shamos added, so that it could not be detected in preelection testing.

As the scandals of the early 1970s raged, a number of concerned public officials took a closer look at the machines and detected various ways to alter the count, either while an election was still in progress or right after it had ended. In Tampa the supervisor of elections sent in to clean up the mess left by Jim Fair and friends, an insurance salesman named Jim Sebesta, spent time with a technically savvy deputy in the warehouse where the Shoups were stored and found a way to switch vote totals between rival candidates using little more than a large paper clip. "In a very short period of time—maybe ten seconds—in a particular race in a particular precinct, you could rig it," recalled Sebesta, who was later elected a Florida state senator. "When we confronted Shoup with that, they went ballistic."

Louisiana offered an even more dramatic demonstration of tampering possibilities in the wake of the 1979 governor's race, in which one candidate, Louis Lambert, appeared to have advanced past the first round through fraudulent means. Lambert, the choice of the ruling Democratic Party establishment, only squeaked into the runoff, thanks to fourteen providential Shoup machines whose vote totals magically shifted in his favor well after the polls closed. Nobody believed for an instant this could have happened by accident, and an angry electorate punished Lambert by rejecting him and electing the state's first Republican governor since Reconstruction instead. What nobody could figure out was how Lambert's men had done it—until a state representative by the name of Peppi Bruneau got up and showed them. Bruneau hauled a Shoup 1023 lever machine into a public legislative hearing, walked over to it, and pulled out just two tools—a screwdriver and a wooden cuticle stick. With the screwdriver, he plucked off a long strip of Plexiglas where the candidates' names were displayed. With the cuticle stick, he poked into the innards of the machine, exposed the counters to clear public view, and, with a simple maneuver, reversed the vote totals for two candidates running for the same office. "It was incredibly simple to do," he said. "Clearly, somebody knew you could do that. In fact, there was a wide-standing allegation you could do that."

The man who taught Bruneau the fix was a well-intentioned voting machine technician named Jerome Sauer. At first Bruneau thought Sauer should conduct the public demonstration himself, since he was the one who had identified the problem, but Sauer had been warned by Louisiana's commissioner of elections, Douglas Fowler, that if he so much as touched a Shoup machine he would be arrested. So Bruneau stepped in, using his position as an elected official to have the Shoup machine subpoenaed and thus placed beyond Fowler's reach. After the hearing it was agreed that Shoup would now fit its machines with thicker, wider, longer Plexiglas. There were no hard feelings toward the company, which was not suspected of involvement in the scam. Even Bruneau said: "I have no problem with the Shoup machine per se if it's engineered right."

What is striking, more than twenty-five years later, is not the fallibility of the machinery—someone was bound to figure out something, sooner or later—so much as the parallels between the intransigent behavior of election administrators then and now. Computer scientists, voting rights activists, lawyers, and losing candidates who have challenged the integrity of electronic touchscreen machines in recent years have found themselves rebuffed and threatened in their requests for access to source codes and audit trails just like Jerome Sauer. In Louisiana, up to 1999 they were actually rebuffed by another man named Fowler—Douglas's son Jerry, who followed his father into the commissioner of elections' office only to be undone by a spectacular corruption scandal, which will be described in chapter 11.

When Votomatic punch-card machines were first deployed in 1964, an official in DeKalb County, outside Atlanta, reported excitedly that using them was "as simple as stirring coffee with a spoon." Administrators in all three states where the Votomatic made its debut—California, Oregon, and Georgia—allowed themselves, like so many others before and since, to be blinded by the technology and by the fact that the technology now involved computers. It didn't even occur to them to ask the tough questions about reliability, transparency, and security. The Votomatic was a thirty-year dream come true for its inventor, Joseph P. Harris, whom we have encountered at various points in this book as the foremost chronicler of America's dysfunctional administration of elections up to the first phase of the machine age. And if it was good enough for Harris, a reformer with unassailable credentials, they figured it had to be good enough for them. Harris had studied at the University of Chicago under Charles Edward Merriam, the ultimate well-intentioned "goo-goo," and he spent the bulk of his career as a political science professor arguing in favor of greater professionalism in the civil service and greater public accountability. There was one glaring flaw in his thinking, however. He, too, believed technology alone held the answer to the problems of election management.

Already in the 1930s Harris had tinkered with the idea of a miracle machine to end fraud and error once and for all. In those days he didn't give much consideration to the computer, then in its infancy, but imagined a giant sorting machine a bit like a player piano. He even took out a patent on the concept. Then the war intervened, and he moved from one academic job to another before settling at the University of California at Berkeley. His voting machine remained no more than a pipe dream until about 1960, when a student asked him if he'd ever considered adapting an IBM PortaPunch machine. He hadn't, but he soon did, not least because the PortaPunch was a delightfully cheap device, costing about seven dollars at the time. Harris approached Bill Rouverol, who taught mechanical engineering at Berkeley, and together they came up with a prototype. The basic idea was very simple: to place a punch card, or series of punch cards, beneath a standard paper ballot and use a metal stylus to push out perforated paper squares corresponding to the voter's choices. Originally, Harris imagined putting the stylus on a long rod that could reach all the way across a full-sized ballot.

Then, in 1962 he underwent cataract surgery, which in those days required the patient to remain immobile for several days after the operation, and he had the time to come up with something better. With his head wedged between sandbags, Harris developed the idea of chopping the ballot into pages and placing them on a displaced axis so voters could index their way across the card as they flipped the pages over from one race to the next.

Once he was out of the hospital, Harris put in a phone call to Bob Varni, then a West Coast IBM executive, and asked him if he might be interested in going into business with him. Varni said yes. After trying and failing to sell the idea directly to IBM, Varni chipped in five thousand dollars, as did a number of his colleagues. That was enough to build some prototypes, which were successfully tested in five California counties. By the time 1964 rolled around, IBM had reorganized its supplies division, took another look through its pile of rejected business ideas, and decided the Votomatic was worth investing in after all. Thus the Harris Votomatic Company became Computer Election Services, manufacturing forty thousand machines on IBM's behalf for the handsome sum of $16 million. Varni took on responsibility for selling the new machine in the Western United States, and business boomed. Counties particularly loved the fact that results came so fast and so painlessly. Unlike lever machines, whose cumulative vote totals still needed to be totted up by hand, the punch-card system did all the tabulation work itself, spitting out the tallies as soon as ballots from the Votomatic terminals had been fed into the high-speed card reader.

Like lever machines, though, the convenience favored the county officials much more than it did individual voters, who had to struggle to align the punch card correctly between the template and the index points, struggle all over again to push the card all the way in, and then punch cleanly enough to detach the cardboard square, or chad, cleanly from the rest. The four corner points of each chad were known in technical jargon as "frangible connections," a description more apt than anyone realized at the time. As we now know, punch-card voting turned out to be just a little too frangible all around.

The first big setback came with the California primary of June 1968, when bad luck conspired to compound the technical shortcomings. To collect votes from the city of Los Angeles, which then had seven thousand precincts, CES set up two tabulation centers, one of which happened to be right next door to the Ambassador Hotel, where Bobby Kennedy was shot shortly after midnight. The police swarmed the area and cordoned off ten square blocks, making it impossible for election officials to bring ballots in from their precincts. The delay was hardly disastrous—the count was completed by 6:00 AM—and, under the circumstances, should have been perfectly understandable. But a handful of media commentators, notably the syndicated columnist Jack Anderson, decided this was an unmissable opportunity to have a go at almighty IBM. Soon, a certain conventional wisdom began to spread that Votomatics were not all they were cracked up to be. In some quarters they were ridiculed for being downright slow. In much the same way that touch-screen manufacturer Diebold's political agenda came to be questioned thirty-five years later, fingers were also pointed at IBM's chief executive, Thomas Watson, who was thought to harbor presidential ambitions. Had he bought himself a voting machine company, people wondered, to count himself into high office? One imagines that Shoup, with its rock-solid connections to the power elites on the East Coast, might have had a hand in this torrent of negative publicity. Whoever was responsible, IBM quickly decided to get out of the elections game before a bigger scandal could hit and do real damage to its core business interests. By 1969 CES was an independent company again, and IBM gave every indication of wanting to forget it had ever been associated with them.

Curiously, IBM's gun-shy attitude has turned out to be the rule, not the exception, among major corporations considering whether to get involved in the technology of elections. Few big-name companies have ever shown much interest, and of those that have, none has stuck around for long. Hewlett Packard was involved in developing an optical-scan system in the early 1970s, and Dell put in a pitch to design an electronic voting machine in the wake of the 2000 election, but both quickly faded away again. Ask voting systems professionals why this should be, and they will tell you it is because the business is just too fraught with risk—to the bottom line, and also to people's reputations. "It's such a big expense to make and market the equipment," Kimberlee Shoup, daughter of Ransom, explained to me. "It's a big country, but counties don't tend to upgrade their equipment very often. The 2000 election and after was an exception, obviously. But mostly, you only get sales here and there, which all the other companies are trying to grab as much as you. Frankly, some of the smaller counties aren't even worth our while. You have to develop and manufacture the equipment up front and then spend another $100,000 just to get it through the federal testing process. Then you have to get certified in each state. And that's before you can even make your first sale."

When I spoke to Kimberlee in early 2005, she had been in the business twenty years, overseeing the marketing of the Shouptronic DRE before it was spun off to another company, then getting into the electronic touch-screen business through a new Texas-based company called Advanced Voting Solutions (AVS), which took over the Shoup name and what was left of its product line. (AVS's delightfully ambiguous slogan: "Helping shape American history for over one hundred years.") Kimberlee's career trajectory illustrates some home truths about the elections business: that people rarely survive the cutthroat competition very long; that companies are forever hitting hard times, merging or getting taken over; and that the only way to make it at all is by forging close personal relationships with county supervisors and election officials—a frequent recipe, as we have seen, for corruptions both casual and spectacular. No Fortune 500 company is going to want to put a foot in that nest of vipers.

IBM certainly missed out on a handy little earner by walking away from CES. By 1977, when the original CES shareholders decided to cash out, the Votomatic enjoyed a 20 percent market share and a presence in twenty-nine states, representing 21.5 million registered voters. In terms of defending its technical reputation, however, IBM probably got out just in time. Following a smattering of problems reported up and down the West Coast in the late 1960s, Los Angeles suffered a major meltdown in a 1970 primary election as ballot cards jammed, candidates' names were either misaligned or left off the ballot altogether, and more than five hundred precincts failed to have their votes counted because of multiple computer malfunctions. At the same time, computer scientists and public officials began expressing serious qualms about the integrity of the Votomatic's tabulation software. A study commissioned by the city of St. Louis found that punch-card balloting was "more easily subject to abuse" than lever machines, because there was no way of making sure the counters had been set to read the cards correctly. "It is possible to write a program in such a way that no test can be made to assure that the program works the way it is supposed to work," said the 1970 report by the accounting firm Price Waterhouse. "It is possible to have instructions in computer memory to call in special procedures from core, tape, or disk files to create results other than those anticipated."

Breakdowns big and small continued to be reported throughout the 1970s—in Detroit, Houston, and, in almost every election, Los Angeles. A tortuous 1976 recount in LA introduced the world to the problem of hanging and pregnant chad, although nobody outside Southern California paid much attention at the time. In San Antonio the official canvass of a 1980 election reported that sixteen-hundredths of a percent fewer votes had been cast than reported on election night. No explanation was ever forthcoming to account for the anomaly, leading the *San Antonio Express* to suggest a new slogan for the universal suffrage movement: "One man, 0.9984 vote."

The single most withering critique of the Votomatic was penned in 1980 by Michael Shamos, the Pennsylvania voting equipment examiner, who ripped the entire system to shreds without even mentioning the chad problem. Not only were punch cards laughably passé in the computer industry, he wrote, but the machinery was cumbersome, easily prone to tampering, and a security "nightmare." Shamos showed how arbitrary numbers could be entered into the machines' counters and how, with just a little practice and no tools of any kind, a voter could disassemble the ballot-page mechanism and rearrange or substitute pages in less than a minute. As the Shoups had during their presentation to Congress, Shamos explained how easy it was for an election fixer to change the vote totals by slipping a rogue programming card into the system.

Shamos also pinpointed an enduring problem with the way computer voting equipment was bought and sold: the fact that systems are certified for use without any public authority having access to the programming software. "It is a complete mystery to me how a program can be 'submitted' for certification unless the examiners are permitted to inspect it," Shamos wrote. But in the 1980s there was no requirement even to submit the software to a private testing lab, much less make it available to county and state authorities in case of operational controversy. Deborah Seiler, the head of California's election division, who would later become a sales rep for Diebold, told the *New York Times* in 1985 that she had certified a number of systems without inspecting anything. "At this point," she said, "we don't have the capability or the standards to certify software, and I am not aware of any state that does."

Already at this early stage, voting rights campaigners began to fret about the degree of control being signed away to vendor companies, an issue that remains equally pressing today. Not only did the manufacturers shroud their products in secrecy, but they also became actively involved in running elections, because technophobic administrators in many places thought having them around would help prevent mistakes. That did not change when the Federal Election Commission (FEC) finally published some minimal standards for electronic voting in 1990. As Mae Churchill of the Urban Policy Research Institute in California wrote to the FEC at the time: "The proprietary interests of voting system vendors have been allowed to drive the standards drafting procedure . . . The privatizing of elections is taking place without the consent or knowledge of the governed."

On three particularly arresting occasions during the 1980s, the volatilities and unauditable quirks of punch-card voting collided with incendiary state or local politics, leading to the strong suspicion that an election had been stolen. The first case arose in 1980 in Kanawha County, West Virginia, where a powerful incumbent Democratic congressman, John Hutchinson, had been expected to trounce his Republican opponent by a double-digit margin. The Republican, Mick Staton, was oddly confident, though, that the polls were wrong and that he would finish ahead by five points. There was an inherent conflict of interest in the management of the race, since the county clerk was not only a Republican but was also married to Staton's single largest campaign contributor. Then, on election night a young Republican state legislator named Walter Price saw some very odd things going on in the count room. According to an account he later gave under oath, Peggy Miller, the county clerk, got down on her knees four times during the night and, as she consulted notes on a clipboard, turned a key on the master computer, flipped some switches, and turned the key back again. Price also saw Miller's husband, Steve, enter the computer "cage," pull a pack of what looked like computer punch cards out of his suit jacket, and hand them to his wife. Peggy Miller ran these through the card reader, retrieved them, then handed them back to her husband. This looked an awful lot like the reprogramming maneuver described by Shamos and the Shoups.

When Staton was declared the winner by a five-point margin, exactly as he had predicted, Price became convinced he had been a witness to vote fraud and, despite his party affiliation, resolved to denounce it publicly. The Millers denied everything and, despite the legal challenge filed almost immediately against Staton, arranged for all materials relating to the election to be destroyed as soon as the West Virginia statutes allowed. The case dragged on for years, stirring enough disquiet for the state to introduce a mandatory manual recount of 5 percent of ballots in all elections. In the absence of physical evidence, though, the prosecution never stood much chance, and the charges were eventually thrown out.

Spotty record-keeping may also have saved the bacon of election officials in Dallas in the wake of a bruising mayoral election in 1985. Shortly after 8:00 PM on election night, Mayor Starke Taylor was trailing one of his opponents, Max Goldblatt, when the central computer processing the ballots suffered a power failure. When the power came back up a few minutes later, Taylor was unaccountably in the lead, and stayed there for the rest of the night. He ended just 472 votes above the 50 percent threshold required to avoid a runoff, a margin later reduced to 448 after a machine recount. The strange thing was that while Taylor's lead remained relatively constant, the overall number of ballots counted in the election yo-yoed wildly. At 10:55 PM on election night, 78,398 votes were counted as being in, but less than an hour later the figure shot up to 80,208. Two days later it was down to 79,783 and then, after the recount, back up to 80,149. Odd things also appeared to be happening at the precinct level. In one district, 425 Goldblatt ballots recorded at 10:55 PM on election night simply vanished. In another area known to favor Mayor Taylor, the number of ballots reported jumped from an initial 295 to 547. Max Goldblatt's campaign manager, Terry Elkins, asked later, in an interview with the *New York Times:* "If the county is unable to count ballots, how in the world can we trust its count of the votes for each candidate?"

Elkins spent the next eighteen months trying to pinpoint exactly what had happened and persuaded the Texas attorney general to open an official investigation. She and Goldblatt were both convinced the election had been stolen, or at least that they had been wrongly denied a chance to face Taylor in a runoff. Their biggest problem in substantiating this belief was that when they put in a request to examine the ballots and other auditing documents, they learned that many of the records were too incomplete to be usable, while others had been destroyed altogether. The Dallas County election administrator at the time was Conny McCormack, later to become a big cheerleader for Diebold touch-screen machines as registrar-recorder of Los Angeles County. She offered a number of explanations to reconcile the discrepancies. The overall ballot count was inconsistent, she said, because certain precincts were split between voters who lived within the Dallas city limits, and were therefore eligible to vote for mayor, and those who did not. The lower of the two counts on election night accounted only for Dallas city voters, while the higher count included ineligible voters who happened to live in split precincts. As for the changing figures at precinct level, those were due, she said, to ballot-reader malfunctions.

The attorney general's office gave the investigation to the Dallas County district attorney—not, perhaps, the most objective of choices—which bought every one of McCormack's explanations and asserted, more than two years later, that no fraud or manipulation had taken place. One has to wonder, though, how the DA's office could be so sure. As an accountant with Arthur Andersen told a Texas House investigation into the same election: "The audit trail should consist of everything from the ballots themselves to the console log being printed by the computer on election night. The present laws don't identify what the minimum requirements are . . . So you really couldn't tell if there was fact to these allegations or not. That has been one of our problems. Records aren't available; there are no auditable results." The attorney general's office agreed, writing in July 1986 to the state director of elections that while there was insufficient evidence to establish proof of fraud, this was not in itself grounds for comfort. "[T]he electronic voting system in use lacks adequate security features to provide any assurances of the absence of fraud," Assistant Attorney General Robert L. Lemens wrote. "As a result, this office has found that it will be difficult to demonstrate to the complainants that Texas elections are free from fraud and, thereby, free local election officials from suspicion."

It was clear to everyone that the system needed overhauling, and in 1987 Texas passed a new election law requiring an audit trail, a compulsory manual recount of 1 percent of the vote in at least three precincts, and a requirement that computer program codes be deposited with the secretary of state. Other states came to understand the importance of similar action. The California attorney general's office conducted a study into the Votomatic and concluded that all electronic vote-tallying systems should have "reliable tamper-proof audit trails." Even with this widespread acknowledgment of the problem, however, it proved almost impossible to induce politicians to take the appropriate action. Even where new laws were passed, as in Texas, they fell victim, either immediately or over time, to interpretations favoring the secretive status quo between vendors and county election officials. *New York Times* reporter David Burnham, who did an outstanding job of covering election-related issues during the 1980s, offered perhaps the most compelling reason for this foot-dragging. "One of the key problems," he wrote in a 1987 letter to a computer science professor at George Washington University, "is that the people who have been elected, who have been placed in power by a possibly shaky system, are understandably, and perhaps unconsciously, reluctant to look at the process that put them there."

The third very dubious election of the decade took place in Florida in 1988, where the Democratic candidate for Senate, Buddy MacKay, was projected on election night to be the winner but ended up trailing his Republican rival, Connie Mack, by 34,500 votes out of more than 4 million. The odd thing here was that in four of the state's most heavily populated, most Democratic counties—covering Miami, Tampa, West Palm Beach, and Sarasota—the drop-off between the number of people recording a vote for president and those voting for the Senate was a staggering, and utterly anomalous, 20 percent. Translated into voter numbers, that meant as many as 200,000 votes entrusted to Votomatic punch-card machines vanished into the ether, votes that most likely would have broken heavily in MacKay's favor. Election officials, including David Leahy in Miami (later to play a prominent role in the 2000 presidential election fiasco), suggested that voters overlooked the Senate race because it was squeezed onto the bottom of the first page, beneath the list of candidates for president. That explanation did not hold, however, because a number of counties had the same ballot design but not the same problem. While Tampa had a drop-off rate of 25 percent between the presidential and Senate race, next-door St. Petersburg's drop-off rate, with the same ballot, was just 1 percent.

MacKay, for one, became convinced the election had been stolen and even did some research to figure out how. "What could have happened," he said in a television appearance during the 2000 imbroglio, "was that the machines could have been programmed so that in my big precincts, every tenth vote got counted wrong." One leading computer scientist, Peter Neumann of SRI International in California, confirmed that MacKay's hunch was entirely plausible. "Remembering that these computer systems reportedly permit operators to turn off the audit trails and to change arbitrary memory locations on the fly," he wrote about the Mack-MacKay race in the journal *Risks Digest*, "it seems natural to wonder whether anything fishy went on." MacKay pressed to have the ballots examined and recounted, but under Florida law at the time recounts were left to the discretion of county canvassing boards. They all turned him down flat, on the grounds that he had no concrete evidence to establish a pattern of foul play. "It's a real Catch-22 situation," MacKay told the *Los Angeles Times* at the time. "You've got to show fraud to get a manual recount, but without a manual recount you can't prove fraud."

The election of 1988 was in many ways a trial run for 2000. Among other things, it prompted calls for the abolition of "old" technologies—everything from paper to lever machines and punch cards—and their replacement with DRE systems. A report that year by a private technical evaluation group called ECRI fell right into the fallacy of the technological fix by arguing that while paper was inherently unreliable, computer voting was only unreliable if it was poorly managed. (In truth, of course, management is everything, regardless of the medium.) Picking up on this theme, the ever-canny Shoup wrote to the FEC's Voting Equipment Standards Advisory Committee barely a month after the disasters of the Mack-MacKay election and announced that the Shouptronic source code was henceforth available for outside review. "The public interest served by securing public confidence in direct electronic voting systems takes precedence over the remote possibility that some competitor might gain access to our source code and thereby enhance their product's marketability," Shoup's chief engineer, Robert Boram, wrote with uncommon graciousness. "We would hope all vendors of all election systems using any form of computers would now open their source codes to outside review. Let's put to rest the concerns raised as to the degree of reliability and integrity of computerized voting systems." It's a pity Boram's sentiments weren't echoed a decade later, when the DRE craze really took off. Back in the late 1980s the technology was still too new, and the motivation to switch systems too lackluster, for his idea to take hold.

Boram was refreshingly honest all around when it came to the realities of computer voting. He told *New York Newsday* in 1992 exactly why it was a mistake to rely on the internal audit mechanism of a DRE as opposed to an independently verifiable paper trail. "I could write a routine inside the system that not only changes the election outcome," he said, "but also changes the images to conform to it."

Not that the Shouptronic escaped its own share of controversy. It had been deployed in New Hampshire during the 1988 Republican primary, when George Bush Sr. trounced Bob Dole by fifteen points, having trailed in the opinion polls by eight or nine. At the time, political commentators attributed the dramatic swing to a series of last-minute television ads by the Bush campaign accusing Dole of wanting to raise taxes. But Dole, for one, couldn't figure out how he lost. (He later said he had lost many nights' sleep over it.) Bush certainly received considerable political help from New Hampshire's governor, John Sununu, who supported his candidacy from the outset and was later elevated to White House chief of staff for his pains. But did Bush also receive more sinister forms of support? Conspiracy theorists have hovered over this one for years, but Dole never issued a formal challenge, and there is simply no evidence to substantiate the suspicion of miscounted votes. The most one can say is that the machines certainly made foul play possible, whether or not Shoup and New Hampshire's election officials were in on it. Another prominent computer scientist, Ken Thompson, delivered a famous lecture a few years before the Dole-Bush primary in which he demonstrated that a bug could be introduced into computer software independent of the source code. "The moral is obvious," he concluded. "You can't trust code that you did not totally create yourself . . . No amount of source-level verification or scrutiny will protect you from using untrusted code . . . A well installed microcode bug will be almost impossible to detect."

By the mid- to late-1990s, it was not just the Votomatic's technological specifications that were cause for concern. In many jurisdictions the machines were getting old and, without the proper maintenance, becoming ever more susceptible to the now-infamous chad problem. A 1988 report written by Roy Saltman of the National Bureau of Standards had noted the myriad risks of chad either failing to detach themselves when punched, or falling out in places the voter did not intend. As the systems aged, the stylus became blunter, the plastic template guiding the stylus to the center of the chad eroded, and the plastic runners holding the mechanism in place began to fray. Saltman had thought one answer might be to devise a spring-loaded puncher, but designers and engineers who grappled with this idea subsequently said they could not make it work. After the 2000 debacle, Bob Varni—who continued to take a passing interest in voting systems—became convinced that much of Florida's chad problem was caused by poor maintenance. "The holes in the plastic template slope inwards in a conical shape, but after heavy use they start to hollow out," he said. "We're talking about a three-dollar part. We used to recommend counties buy new [templates] every six to eight years. If they'd done that in Florida, it would never have got to hanging chads. For lack of a three-dollar part, they blew this whole thing."

Not everyone agrees the problem was quite that simple. When Rebecca Mercuri, a computer scientist who has studied voting systems longer than just about anyone, was presented with Varni's thesis, she reeled off a long list of other reasons why the Votomatics malfunctioned. For a start, she said, the stylus was poorly designed and was neither big nor wide nor square enough. Second, the paper used to make the punch cards was of variable quality. Third, the knives used to prescore the punch cards tended to dull over the course of a factory pressing, so not all chad detached with equal ease. Fourth, it was common for loose chad to be sucked back into its holes, leading to misreadings by the machine. Fifth, many counties didn't bother to clean the detached chad from the machine between elections, leading to growing congestion. "The bottom line is, the Votomatic is just a badly designed piece of equipment," she said. "I bought one on eBay after the 2000 election, and the first thing that happened after I opened it up was that years' worth of chad flew out all over the place."

One man who felt personally wounded by the meltdown in Florida was Bill Rouverol, the Berkeley engineer who had partnered with Joe Harris on the original design of the Votomatic. By the time of the 2000 election Harris was long dead, but Rouverol was still in fine fettle and spent part of his eighty-third birthday on a plane from San Francisco to West Palm Beach, Florida, where he met election officials and sought to give his own explanation of what had gone wrong. Essentially, Rouverol thought the machine needed more light. In fact, he'd thought that ever since 1962, when he suggested installing a backlight so voters could know by the beam shining out at them that they had successfully detached the chad. Joe Harris scotched the idea at the time, thinking it too complicated, but Rouverol couldn't help thinking he had been right all along. Indeed, as soon as he got back home from Florida, he set about examining every one of the Votomatic's design flaws and seeing if he couldn't come up with something better.

It was a largely futile exercise, but it was also a labor of love for a man who was determined not to let the late-night comics, with their endless stream of chad jokes, have the last word on his career and his legacy. Rouverol not only installed a light, he also enlarged the size of the hole so that the beam shooting out at the voter would be unmistakable, like something from *Close Encounters of the Third Kind.* To avoid the problem of incorrectly inserted ballots, he made the card itself the light-switch mechanism, so voters would know not to start punching until they saw the bulb begin to glow. Finally,

Rouverol dispensed with prescored ballots and all those troublesome frangible connections, designing a new puncher in the shape of a helical scissor that was both durable and user-friendly. It took Rouverol four years to develop his new invention, the new, improved—dare one say perfect—punch-card machine. When he showed it to me in the living room of his one-bedroom apartment in Berkeley, he had high hopes it might still find favor in some county somewhere. "My machine would cost around $400 retail, which is a lot less than the $4,000 it costs to buy a DRE with a printer attached," he said. "Could that be attractive to the poorer counties?"

In an ideal world, perhaps. One can admire Rouverol's dedication and good intentions. One can, and should, be deeply skeptical of the new generation of voting machines. But the age of the punch card, surely, is gone forever. Like so many other miracle machines in the history of American elections, the Votomatic arrived with high hopes only to reap bitter disappointment. One suspects it will be missed by nobody.

10
DEMOCRACY'S FRANGIBLE
CONNECTIONS: FLORIDA 2000

★ ☆ ★ ☆ ★ ☆ ★ ☆ ★ ☆ ★ ☆ ★ ☆ ★

There is probably a Chernobyl or a [Three Mile Island] waiting to happen in
some election, just as a Richter-8 earthquake is waiting to happen in California.
—Willis H. Ware of the Rand Corporation, 1987

You know why we never paid attention to this until now? I'll tell you: because
we don't want to know that our democracy isn't so sacred.
—Indiana Elections Division codirector Candy Marendt, December 2000

ON THE MORNING OF November 8, 2000, two candidates
locked in a tight contest for a strategically vital national office woke
up after a few snatched hours of sleep to discover, like Al Gore and
George W. Bush, that their race was too close to call. Slade Gorton,
the veteran Republican senator from Washington State, found himself leading by a margin of less than two-tenths of a percentage
point against his Democratic challenger, Maria Cantwell, with hundreds of thousands of absentee ballots still to be accounted for. As
results poured in from the rest of the country, it became clear that

this was going to be the pivotal race for control of the upper house. If Gorton prevailed, the Republicans would have a 51-49 majority. And if Cantwell won, the chamber would be evenly divided 50-50, leaving the deciding vote in the hands of the new vice president—whoever that might be.

Undaunted by the stakes, or by the prospect of protracted uncertainty, Gorton and Cantwell hit upon what would come to be regarded as a radical, even eccentric notion: they agreed to sit out the race until all the votes had been counted as accurately as possible and one of them was declared the winner. For two weeks Gorton maintained a slim lead, although his initial 3,000-vote margin gradually dwindled as more conservative eastern counties finished counting and the more heavily populated, more liberal western ones kept going. On the very last day, Cantwell pulled into the lead for the first time, thanks to an unexpectedly high volume of absentee ballots from Seattle. She finished the provisional final count with a margin of 1,953 votes.

Gorton offered not a murmur of complaint, saying only that he had shifted from a position of cautious optimism to one of cautious pessimism. State law required an automatic machine recount, because the two candidates were separated by less than half a percentage point, and the recount duly went ahead, giving Cantwell a final margin of 2,426 votes out of roughly 2.5 million cast. On December 1, three and a half weeks after election day, she finally celebrated her election as Washington's next senator. There were no lawsuits. No procedural objections were raised about the state's punch-card voting machines—or anything else. It would be reassuring to think that the two candidates' calm adherence to the principle of counting every vote might have held at least some sway over the brutal presidential contest being waged at the opposite end of the country. But of course it didn't work out that way.

It is hard to think back on the thirty-six-day fight for the presidency in Florida without being overcome by a deep queasiness. For those with no personal memory of previous presidential election controversies—and that was most people, since there had been none for forty years—the night of November 7, 2000, was like a long wait at a railway station for an express that hurtled toward its appointed stop without ever quite managing to arrive. Was it just late, or had it derailed? Was this an accident, or the result of foul play?

The media portrayed the 2000 election as a low-stakes contest in a country enjoying unparalleled peace and prosperity. But that was not how it felt in Austin, where the Republican faithful from across Texas descended in keen anticipation of taking back the country after eight years of usurpation and moral turpitude under Bill Clinton. Those not fortunate enough to be invited to the Bushes' private election-watching reception at the Four Seasons Hotel gathered across Congress Avenue at the Driskill, where the heavy drinking turned as ugly as the rapidly deteriorating political mood of the early part of the evening. As the key dominoes fell one by one to Gore—Michigan, Pennsylvania, and, it seemed, Florida—there was rank disbelief, even talk of insurrection. "If Gore and Hillary both win, I'm leaving the country!" one man shouted. When Hillary Clinton duly clinched her New York Senate seat, his jaw dropped open and he slugged down what must have been the third or fourth whiskey of the night. "I hate her!" someone else called from the crowd. An elegantly dressed Houston socialite passed out from the shock and the booze and had to be carried into the street to await a paramedics' truck. Across the street the Bushes slipped away from their reception, the gala dinner untouched, and retreated to the homier comforts of the governor's mansion. Television footage later showed them sitting grim-faced in armchairs. "We haven't been up this late in years," said an appalled Barbara Bush, the candidate's mother. And the night was just beginning.

The first bombshell arrived when Florida was taken out of the Gore column and deemed too close to call. Then, for four hours, nothing. Rain beat down on the outdoor crowds in both Austin and Nashville, dampening efforts to keep the faithful buoyed with second-rate music acts. At 1:15 AM central standard time came bombshell number two: Fox News called Florida for Bush, and the other networks quickly followed suit. In Austin the crowd went wild—jumping, hugging their neighbors, raising three fingers in a "W" salute. A montage of images from the campaign flashed up on a giant video screen before the sea of shivering bodies under ponchos and umbrellas, to the musical accompaniment of Stevie Wonder's "Signed, Sealed, Delivered"—a premature but carefully calculated declaration of victory. In Nashville, Gore called Bush to congratulate him and was seconds away from stepping onto the podium in Legislative Plaza to make his concession speech when he was intercepted and told the vote totals in Florida were narrowing dramatically. Gore called Bush back to make his now celebrated unconcession, and the country was thrown into renewed suspense, where it remained for the next thirty-six days.

It soon became apparent just how weird the Florida election was. Throughout the campaign, Bush had made jabs at the "fuzzy math" of Gore's spending plans, but they were nothing compared with the fuzzy math coming out of the Sunshine State. The networks' original call for Gore was based on an exit poll from the Voter News Service (VNS), a media consortium, which gave the vice president a seemingly unassailable 7.3-point advantage. Obviously, the VNS estimate was riddled with errors, including double counting of some counties and wild overestimations of Gore's margin in others. The networks made their call fifty minutes after the polls closed in Miami, Tampa, and Jacksonville, but ten minutes before voting ended in the Panhandle, which is one hour behind the rest of Florida. The effect on voters in those predominantly conservative northwestern counties remains unknown.

At the other end of the night, the initial determination in Bush's favor was made by none other than the Republican candidate's cousin, John Ellis, who was monitoring returns for Fox News. Ellis in turn was in close phone contact with both George W. and his brother Jeb, the Florida governor. The other networks, naïvely mistaking Fox's naked partisanship for a good, old-fashioned journalistic scoop, blindly followed Ellis's call—a misjudgment that was to give the Bush campaign a key psychological advantage in the days and weeks to come.

Within hours, complaints began pouring in about irregularities, obstruction, and possible foul play. Florida's black voters had turned out in record numbers—16 percent of the electorate, compared with 10 percent four years earlier—only to encounter problems with police roadblocks outside polling stations, unhelpful or overtly intimidating poll workers, voter rolls that omitted the names of valid voters, confusing ballot designs, and faulty machinery. Many African Americans were furious with Governor Bush for dismantling the state's affirmative action policies and came out specifically to show their displeasure at a man they nicknamed "Jeb Crow." They voted for Al Gore by a margin of nine to one, but their votes, as the U.S. Commission on Civil Rights later estimated, were up to ten times more likely to be disqualified than those of nonblacks, for a variety of reasons largely to do with income levels and the availability of voting machinery in poorer neighborhoods. At Miami-Dade County's Precinct 255, housed inside the Lillie C. Evans Elementary School, the punch-card machines failed preliminary testing and subsequently missed 13 percent of the votes cast on election day. In both Miami and Tampa, election officials sent out emergency supplies of laptop computers to help verify voter eligibility in crowded polling stations, but attended disproportionately to more affluent areas. Anyone in a precinct without access to a laptop was forced to seek confirmation of eligibility by telephone. (Florida had no system of provisional balloting in 2000.) Lines to county election supervisors' offices were invariably jammed.

Voter inexperience, combined with confusing or contradictory instructions, also played a role. Gadsden County, the only black-majority county in the state near the Georgia state line, registered the single highest spoilage rate—a staggering 12.33 percent. Voters there were instructed to "Vote for ONE" in the U.S. Senate race, but to "Vote for Group" in the presidential election. Many voters opted for more than one presidential candidate. Some filled in every circle except Gore's. Others opted for all ten presidential candidates and then wrote in Gore's name for good measure. In Duval County, the names of the presidential candidates were laid out over two pages even though the instructions of the sample ballot told voters to "Vote Each Page." Some twenty-two thousand ballots were thrown out because of double voting, the bulk of them in four predominantly African American city council districts in Jacksonville.

It was not only African Americans who cried foul. In Palm Beach County, thousands of distraught Jewish voters—some of them Holocaust survivors—reeled in horror at the realization that they might have accidentally voted for the right-wing, explicitly anti–Jewish Reform Party candidate, Pat Buchanan. Their undoing was the soon-to-be-infamous "butterfly" ballot layout, with its confusing alignment of candidates' names on either side of a central bar of punch holes. The butterfly ballot had caused problems everywhere it had previously been used, but was nevertheless favored by Palm Beach County's miserably incapable election supervisor, Theresa LePore, who thought the county's disproportionately elderly voting population would like the larger type made possible by spreading the presidential ballot over two pages. Buchanan won an improbable 3,424 votes in Palm Beach, way out of line with his dismal percentages elsewhere in the state. A political scientist from Berkeley subsequently calculated that at least 2,000 of these must have been meant for Gore.

The final contributory factor in the great Florida train wreck, the one that attracted by far the greatest attention, was the general inadequacy of the Votomatic machines that were used in almost all the large urban counties and, following a trend familiar to election professionals but almost nobody else, slid ever further toward total decrepitude. Overall, Florida lost 2.93 percent of its vote total in 2000, representing a steady increase from 2.5 percent in the 1996 presidential election and 2.3 percent in 1992. The Votomatics' discard rate was 3.93 percent, although in some of the big urban counties it was considerably higher—4.37 percent in Miami-Dade, 6.39 percent in Palm Beach, 9.23 percent in Duval. One of the Gore campaign's great misfortunes was that some of the counties most favorable to the Democratic Party thus had the highest incidence of lost votes, while those using an optical-scan system, where the discard rate hovered just above 1 percent, leaned heavily to the Republicans. The Bush campaign enjoyed other advantages, too: some Florida counties had systems to notify voters if they had cast an invalid ballot and offered them a second chance. But only 26 percent of eligible black voters lived in those counties in 2000, compared with 34 percent of nonblack voters.

Conventional wisdom, as it has evolved since 2000, would have us believe that the punch-card ballots were *the* key obstacle to resolving the election, an impression bolstered by the hordes of lawyers who descended on Florida and focused almost exclusively on whether, and how, the votes should be recounted. The media also played a role in the pop-culture demonization of pregnant, hanging, and swinging chad, especially after canvassing board members in the Southern Florida counties were paraded on national television staring cluelessly at near-indecipherable 12 x 26–hole cards with the help of flashlights and giant magnifying glasses. A great deal of the opprobrium was justified, since the system had clearly been rotten for years and nobody, in the absence of a major electoral crisis, had thought to do anything about it.

The fact is, though, it wasn't the Votomatics that ultimately turned Florida into such a mess. Whatever the flaws in the machinery, it should have been possible to agree on standards for counting and recounting the ballots and to continue to do so until the job was done. The Gorton-Cantwell race in Washington State demonstrated how to do that. But the battle over Florida was about something much more elemental and vicious than the niceties of recount procedure. It was, essentially, a *political* fight, one in which the win-at-any-cost mentality so prevalent at key moments in America's electoral history, as we have seen, became visible in ways almost entirely unfamiliar to modern electorates. Some of that visibility took on the form of actual physical symptoms, such as the angry boil that erupted on George W.'s face, or the coronary that sent Dick Cheney to the emergency room for the fourth time in his checkered cardiac career. This was a battle fought primarily by politicians, who found it convenient to heap blame on election officials and voting machine manufacturers but were really only deflecting attention from their own machinations. It happened because one side, the Republicans, had an entrenched advantage in the state and chose to exploit it well beyond the usually understood rules of fair play. And it happened because neither camp, in the end, was interested in transparency and democratic accountability as much as it was in winning by any and all means available.

The shameless grab for power was so unnerving, so out of kilter with commonly held notions of the spirit of American democracy, that many people sought to rationalize it as an isolated event or to pretend it was not happening at all. The media, which admittedly had a direct interest in spinning out the drama for as long as possible, was notably reticent in calling the race—mathematically, politically, or morally—for one side or the other. One of the first authors to rush an account of the Florida battle into the nation's bookstores, Jake Tapper of the online magazine *Salon*, was more outspoken than most about naming heroes and villains, but even he asserted it was impossible to tell who had really won. Others took refuge in statistics to reach the same conclusion. "Whatever happens," wrote mathematician John Allen Paulos as the struggle was reaching its climax in the Supreme Court, "the margin of error is greater than the margin of victory or defeat." In a perfect mathematical universe, of course, he would be right. Florida's voting machines missed almost 3 percent of the electorate, while the 537 margin by which Bush was eventually declared the victor represented less than one ten-thousandth, or 0.01 percent, of the vote. But this was an election about much more than mathematics, and it seems safe to assert that from almost any standpoint, it was Gore who should have carried Florida, not Bush.

How do we know this? Let's start with the narrow, technical question of how the count would have gone if the votes had been assessed as accurately as possible. We have a trove of information on this, because two different media consortia gained access to the ballots under Florida's so-called Sunshine Law and conducted their own recounts. Their conclusion: in a full manual recount of the entire state, incontrovertibly the fairest and fullest approach even though it was spurned by both major parties, Gore would have come out ahead. Ironically, the four Democrat-leaning South Florida counties at the heart of the lawsuits were not, on their own, enough to guarantee Gore a decisive margin. The four counties (Miami-Dade, Brown, Palm Beach, and Volusia) would have put him over the top only using the laxest standards for recounting the "under-votes"—those recorded the first time around as having shown no vote for president. In a statistical quirk that could hardly have been pre dicted, least of all by Democratic Party lawyers, Gore in fact made up the decisive ground in eighteen predominantly Republican-leaning counties, representing 1.58 million votes, which buckled to heavy pressure from Tallahassee and chose not to conduct machine recounts the day after the election—a fact made public only after Bush was safely certified as the winner. In Lake County alone Gore registered a net gain of 130 votes. The vice president also fell unfair-ly short in the count of overseas military ballots, a source of great con-tention for a few days in mid-November. Those ballots were even-tually counted under standards so lax the *New York Times* subsequently concluded that 680 of them, cast for Bush, should never have been included. That factor alone could have overturned the official 537-vote Bush margin.

One can quibble that such number crunching remains statistically unsatisfactory, since we're still talking about a difference of just a few hundred votes. So let's ask a slightly broader question. Which candi-date did Floridians who turned out on election day *intend* to vote for in greater numbers? Again, the evidence overwhelmingly favors Gore. An unknown number of African American voters, probably some-where in the low tens of thousands, either spoiled their ballots, were wrongly turned away at the polls, or were intimidated before they even got there. Most would have voted Democrat. In Palm Beach County, confusion over the butterfly ballot did not just lead around 2,000 Gore supporters to cast their vote mistakenly for Buchanan. It was also responsible for a statistically anomalous rash of 19,000 "overvotes," ballots spoiled because more than one vote was cast for president. The *Palm Beach Post* went through these overvotes one by one and concluded that they represented a lost trove of about 6,600 net votes for Gore. (Ballots double-marked for Gore and Buchanan were counted by the paper for Gore; ballots marked for Bush and Buchanan were counted for Bush.)

On the other side of the equation, the only possible source of unfairly lost Bush votes was the Panhandle, because of the networks' premature declaration that the election was over before the voting had been completed. There is no way to quantify these, however, or even to say for certain that they were lost at all. So we are left with the deduction that in a more smoothly and more honestly managed election, Gore could have taken Florida by a margin of, say, 30,000. That's 0.5 percent of Florida's six million votes—still a slim difference, but one that begins to look statistically defensible. If we throw in a couple of other considerations—Gore's half-million vote lead in the popular vote, and the fact that, Florida aside, he was ahead in the Electoral College—the evidence starts to point toward only one logical conclusion: Al Gore won the 2000 presidential election.

That being so, can we say the election was actually stolen? The Republicans certainly indulged in enough dishonesty, underhandedness, and foul play to make it look that way. Once the Supreme Court got involved, simply pulling the plug on the manual recounts to hand Bush the election, the case started to look compelling. Before that, though, the picture was a little more complicated—too confused and messy, perhaps, to qualify as outright, premeditated theft. The Republican Party operatives who swooped on the Sunshine State for the postelection battle were as discombobulated by the shortcomings of Florida's voting machinery as anyone. At the time, they had no way of knowing which candidate deserved to prevail. The point, though, is that they never troubled themselves with the question. All they saw was that Bush had a slim lead in the provisional count on the morning of November 8, and they resolved to move heaven and earth to keep it that way. In other words, they did not steal the election so much as grab hold of it while they had the chance and refuse to let go.

Their efforts were helped considerably by the groundwork

already laid by the Florida Republican Party. It didn't hurt, of course, that Bush's brother Jeb was governor, or that the cochair of his state election campaign, Katherine Harris, was also secretary of state, the official responsible for overseeing and certifying the vote. Neither was exactly shy about displaying a strong partisan interest before, during, or after the election. Harris had campaigned for Bush in New Hampshire and drafted the retired Gulf War commander Norman Schwarzkopf, a known Bush supporter, to record a series of get-out-the-vote public service announcements. Despite the supposed "firewall" that existed between the secretary of state's and the governor's offices, public records requests made by the *Miami Herald* demonstrated that Harris and Jeb Bush were in regular e-mail contact during the recount. (What those e-mails said we will never know, because the operating system on Harris's office computers was hastily changed, erasing the messages. Intriguingly, the substitute operating system was *older* than the one it replaced.)

It didn't hurt, either, that the Republicans were in charge of a majority of Florida's sixty-seven counties. In Seminole and Martin Counties, election supervisors permitted Republican Party operatives, and Republicans only, to come into the office, go through absentee ballot applications, and make sure the paperwork for registered party members was shipshape. This not only gave the Republicans a partisan advantage; it was also a clear violation of Florida election law. In Martin County the GOP representative was even authorized to take the application forms home with him—a security lapse no election administrator should have countenanced.

Most egregious, however, was Katherine Harris's endorsement of a contentious, error-ridden voter purge list that later became the subject of a lawsuit by the NAACP. Ostensibly, the list was intended to help counties rid their electoral rolls of known felons. In practice, however, it was a scattershot disenfranchisement mechanism aimed disproportionately at African Americans. Not only did it have the effect of depressing the Democratic Party vote, but it was also a distasteful throwback to the days of Jim Crow, in a state that had elected its first black member of Congress only eight years earlier.

The purge list had its origins in a contested 1997 election for mayor of Miami, in which the apparently defeated incumbent, "Crazy Joe" Carollo, managed to convince a judge that his rival, Xavier Suarez, had stolen the race through massive absentee-ballot fraud. Carollo's lawyer, Kendall Coffey—later employed by the Gore campaign—produced evidence of voters who had no idea they had voted, voters who did not live within the Miami city limits, voters who were paid ten dollars apiece to cast their votes for Suarez, and, inevitably, voters who were stone-cold dead. The case had many eye-popping elements, not least the determination of the U.S. Third District Court of Appeals that absentee voting was a privilege, not a right, and that the entire block of absentee ballots, fraudulent or not, could therefore be discarded with a clear conscience. For Florida's state election officials, however, the key alarm that the case sounded was the manifestly chaotic state of county voter registration rolls. If urban counties with highly mobile populations had voter rolls filled with dead people, nonresidents, and felons, then that was an open invitation to fraud in all elections, not just local ones. Naturally, the Republicans in Tallahassee were much more worried about fraudulent Democratic votes than they were about fraud in general. The problem with purging the rolls of nonresidents and the dead was that it might put unwelcome heat on the majority-Republican Cuban exiles in Miami's Little Havana, which is where the Carollo-Suarez contest largely played out. By focusing exclusively on the felon question, the state leadership could largely side-step the Cuban problem and target African Americans, the Democratic Party's most reliable constituency, instead.

The felon purge list was initiated by Katherine Harris's predecessor, Sandra Mortham, who subcontracted the job to a private Atlanta firm called DBT/ChoicePoint. DBT/ChoicePoint in turn made a spectacular botch of it by failing to cross-check names with other identifying data, and by including names of ex-felons who had done their time in other states and had their voting rights restored. As a result, the list became riddled with inaccuracies and injustices of all kinds. Black Floridians saw this as a continuation of an openly discriminatory public policy spanning the eras of slavery, Reconstruction, and segregation. Even before the list's introduction, Florida was one of just seven states to deny its ex-convicts the automatic restoration of their voting rights on completion of their sentences—a law dating back to 1868 when white plantation owners were urgently looking for ways to repress newly freed Negro slaves. To this day, the criminal justice system handles a disproportionate number of African Americans; one in three black men in the state is barred from voting because of run-ins with the law.

The secretary of state's office was inundated with complaints about the felon list by the time Katherine Harris took over, but she pursued it anyway. For the 2000 election the Florida Division of Elections sent the counties a list of 173,142 names, equivalent to almost one-third of the total number of felons and ex-felons in the state. That was when some of the most glaring errors came to light. Those who were listed as convicted criminals included Linda Howell, the election supervisor of Madison County on the Georgia state line, and a smattering of local government employees from around the state well known to the very officials being asked to scrub them from the rolls. None had criminal histories. In Tallahassee, Leon County election supervisor Ion Sancho conducted a thorough check of all 694 people on his list and found that only 33 were convicted criminals—an error rate of 95 percent. One of those wrongfully listed, a local church minister named Willie Whiting, said he felt "slingshotted into slavery." Sancho and a handful of other county supervisors dropped the list, but an unknown number of others chose to implement it, resulting in thousands, possibly tens of thousands, of would-be voters losing their rights.

So much for the groundwork. As soon as the election was over, the Republicans moved with remarkable speed to shore up the slim lead Bush held in the provisional count. One of Florida's savviest political operators, lobbyist and lawyer Mac Stipanovich, effectively moved into Katherine Harris's office and directed her every move. His oft-repeated mantra, as Jeffrey Toobin related in his book *Too Close to Call*, was to "bring this election in for a landing." That meant, in essence, resisting all efforts to recount votes and enforcing the strictest possible certification deadlines. It was Harris's office, with Stipanovich in the background, that persuaded eighteen of the sixty-seven counties not to conduct machine recounts the day after the election and to keep the move quiet so the Democrats would not find out about it. It was also Harris's office that chose to mess with the rules for overseas military ballots. In theory, these needed to be postmarked by election day to be considered valid, but her staff put out a series of statements in the days immediately following the election suggesting it was enough for the signature on the ballot application *inside* the envelope to be dated November 7 or sooner. Whether coincidentally or not, the number of military ballots from overseas suddenly swelled in the wake of these declarations. Just 446 were received between election day and November 13. By November 16 the number had reached 2,575, and by November 17 it was 3,733. The decision on what to do with these fell to the lone Democrat holding statewide office in Florida, Attorney General Bob Butterworth, who responded to the intense pressure piling in on him from all sides by seeking out a weaselly compromise. Late postmarks, he decreed, would not be acceptable, but missing or illegible postmarks would be, so long as the date accompanying the signature was in order. The issue was subject to litigation all the way to the end of the postelection battle, not least because the Florida statutes were genuinely ambiguous. But enough military votes slipped through in the wake of the Butterworth ruling to give Bush a net gain of 176 votes. One Republican operative described these as "Thanksgiving stuffing."

The Republicans were particularly adept at whipping up outrage among their supporters with the suggestion that it was the Democrats, not them, doing the stealing. The party stayed relentlessly on-message, as it was to continue to do during the Bush presidency, delivering one aggressive set of talking points after another that managed to make right look like left and up like down. "Make no mistake," said Tom DeLay, the House chief whip, "we are witnessing nothing less than a theft in progress, and the American people, the

Constitution and the rule of law are all potential victims." (Had he been talking about his own side, he wouldn't have been far off the mark.) David Horowitz, the consultant and commentator, accused the Gore camp of launching "an ill-advised and reckless post-election coup." Antitax campaigner Grover Norquist threw in a telling reference to the earlier battle over President Clinton's impeachment—another Republican power grab that was twisted into a blanket condemnation of their opponents. "If we learned anything then," he said, " it was that the rule of law means nothing to these people." George Will, the bow-tied columnist and noted skeptic about the usefulness of mass political participation, formulated the phrase most often repeated to denounce the Democrats' recount demands: "slow-motion grand larceny."

On the ground in Florida, the overseas military ballots became a subject of particular potency. As one Bush lawyer, Jim Smith, argued: " The man who would be their commander-in-chief is fighting to take away the votes from the people that he would command." The fact that Smith had argued for a strict application of the postmark rule just one day earlier was quietly forgotten in the mounting foment against "Sore Loserman," as the Democratic ticket was rapidly renamed. The Republicans also sent in Montana governor Marc Racicot, a former military prosecutor, to act as chief public-relations man, a job at which he proved witheringly efficient. Racicot reeled off whole lists of irregularities allegedly marring the recount process in Palm Beach and Broward Counties and asked: "What in the name of God is going on here?" Soon, stories were circulating of Democrats pushing pieces of chad out of punch cards, taping others back on, and even stuffing the little squares in their mouths. All of this was pot-stirring, nothing more. There were, for example, cases of loose chad taped onto ballots, but in every known instance it was the voters who had done the taping to rectify a mistake.

The factual niceties made no difference to hard-core Republican partisans, whose ugliest stunt was to burst into the recount room at the Miami-Dade government center the day before Thanksgiving and reduce the election supervisor's office to a state of such turmoil that the ongoing recount was abandoned for good. The so-called Brooks Brothers riot was spun by the Republicans as a spontaneous expression of disgust by citizens who were fearful for the future of their democracy. In reality it was a carefully planned exercise in intimidation, staged by elected Republican officials with the backing of paid party sympathizers, and designed expressly to prevent any new Gore votes from surfacing.

Such was the Republican interpretation of defending democratic values. The Democrats liked to think of themselves as more principled. They argued more than once that their postelection strategy was based on taking the moral high ground and fighting for small-*d* democracy. In truth, though, their ground was not quite as high as they fancied. They certainly played fairer than the Republicans, often seeming hurt as well as stunned by the ruthlessness of their opponents. But they also suffered from the perennial Democratic affliction of chronic indecisiveness. For much of the thirty-six-day battle, they yo-yoed between the equally indefensible positions of trying too hard to win at all costs and not trying nearly hard enough.

The trouble began, as it often does, with the lawyers. It's not that Democratic lawyers are worse than Republican ones, as the Republicans like to argue. Nor is the opposite true, as some Democrats suggested after the Republicans became the first to file a court brief just four days after the election in an attempt to stymie the recount process from the outset. The point, in the context of a contested election, is that all lawyers are equally bad, because they shift the emphasis away from figuring out who really won and reduce the contest to a tug-of-war in which the so-called will of the people is yanked this way and that for partisan advantage. Moreover, these lawyers all know one another from previous stand-offs and are much more alike than their party labels would suggest. Sometimes they take the side that says counting all the votes is the only way to serve democracy; sometimes they argue that reexamining the ballots would be a grotesque exercise in selective vote-hunting after the fact. It all depends on whose side comes out ahead in the initial count. David Boies, the Gore lawyer who argued in favor of manual recounts in Tallahassee and before the Supreme Court, was not nearly so liberal-minded when he defended Congresswoman Jane Harman of California against allegations of absentee-ballot fraud in a 1994 House race. Then, he just wanted to get the whole thing over with. The Republican chair of the House Oversight Committee who adjudicated Harman's fitness to be seated, meanwhile, was a prominent Miami Cuban named Lincoln Diaz-Balart. He happily allowed that case to drag on for eight months before agreeing Harman had won—very different from the role he played in 2000 as the chief instigator and cheerleader of the Brooks Brothers riot, arguing that no good could come of allowing the Bush-Gore election to go on even one day longer.

The gospel of the Democratic lawyers in Florida was a manual called *The Recount Primer,* which three party operatives with plentiful experience of contested elections had written in 1994. Anyone pondering the purity of the Democrats' motives need only read this passage to understand what was really going on:

> The posture a campaign takes with regard to punch card problems will depend on whether the candidate is ahead or behind . . . If a candidate is ahead, the scope of the recount should be as narrow as possible, and the rules and procedures for the recount should be the same as those used election night . . . If a candidate is behind, the scope should be as broad as possible, and the rules for the recount should be different from those used election night.

In other words, all is fair in love, war, and elections. It was Gore's lawyers who came up with the idea of requesting manual recounts in four counties, not the whole state, in the belief that this was the most efficient way to find the votes they needed to wrest back the lead. After the Republicans filed suit to challenge this, Gore briefly considered backing off from the selective recounts in exchange for a bipartisan commitment to recount the whole state by hand. Had he gone through with this, not only would he have served the cause of democracy, but he also would have stood a much better chance of winning. His decision to chicken out and take the lower, seemingly more expedient route was his single worst move of the entire election, condemning him to a moral and political hell entirely of his own making. Gore himself seemed to realize his mistake, because on November 15, four days after deciding to press ahead with the selective recounts, he tried to backtrack. By that stage, though, his offer of a statewide recount as a possible Plan B looked pusillanimous and insincere, an afterthought more than a strategy, and the Bush campaign turned him down flat. From that moment on, the Gore campaign was crucially stripped of any moral authority it might otherwise have claimed. When the candidate argued, toward the end of November, that ignoring votes meant "ignoring democracy itself," the Republicans were not stung, but, rather, elated to have such an easy opportunity to take him down. "Al Gore is not interested in counting every vote," they said, "he's simply interested in selectively recounting the votes he thinks will help him overturn the results of this election." Intriguingly, the Florida State Supreme Court indicated as late as December 7 that it would entertain the idea of a statewide hand recount. But by that time, neither side was remotely interested.

The adviser who ultimately talked Gore out of pressing for a statewide recount was his running mate, Joe Lieberman, who played a curiously ambivalent role throughout the thirty-six days in Florida. Lieberman had pointedly refused to drop his Senate reelection campaign when he became the vice-presidential candidate, making him look from the get-go like a man hedging his bets. Once the election was over, there were occasions when he seemed just a bit too willing to countenance defeat. At the height of the overseas military ballot controversy, he went on NBC's *Meet the Press* and promptly conceded the entire issue. "We ought to do everything we can to count the votes of our military personnel overseas," he said. "I would give the benefit of the doubt to ballots coming in from military personnel." That statement alone cost the ticket hundreds of votes. In early December Lieberman was at it again, telling a group of congressional

Democrats that he was "proud of the race we ran," as if it were now in the past. This might have been a verbal slip, but it also added to the very thing the Republicans were trying to establish—an aura of inevitability.

Bush's final triumph was, of course, sealed not in Florida but in the Supreme Court. The *Bush v. Gore* decision that ended the election has rightly been condemned as a scandalously partisan intervention that robbed the voters of the very notion of democratic accountability. The five justices who formed the deciding majority concluded that the possibility of "irreparable harm to the petitioner"—that is, Bush losing the election—was of greater legal consequence than counting votes. It may be, as some constitutional scholars have argued, that the decision will come to be regarded as a "self-inflicted wound" every bit as damaging as the Dred Scott decision of 1857. Certainly, that was the fear of Justice John Paul Stevens when he wrote in his final dissent that the loser in the election was "the Nation's confidence in the judge as an impartial guardian of the rule of law."

From a voting rights' standpoint, the most alarming aspect of the Supreme Court decision was the suggestion, made in oral argument and again in the majority opinion, that voters are not the final arbiters of presidential elections. From a purely technical standpoint, of course, Justice Antonin Scalia was correct when he asserted that "there is no right of suffrage under Article II [of the Constitution]." Article II was the tortured compromise the framers hashed out in the final days of the Constitutional Convention of 1787 to determine how to elect presidents. As we have seen, the framers, fearful as they were of an excess of democracy, left it up to individual state legislatures to decide how to pick their electors. In the early years of the Republic, some states did indeed prefer to appoint their electors instead of consulting the people. But we are talking about the preindustrial age, when universal suffrage was still viewed as an eccentricity, not the norm of civilized societies. Since the Jacksonian era it has been an article of faith that U.S. democracy is founded on the will of the people. The right to vote might have been restricted, manipulated, and abused, but the fundamental notion that political leaders should be elected, not appointed, has never been questioned. Or at least it wasn't until the meltdown in Florida.

The first person to suggest taking the decision out of the hands of the voters was not a Supreme Court judge but Tom Feeney, the Republican speaker of Florida's lower house, who reread Article II sometime in November and noted the power it accords to state legislatures. Feeney was first and foremost playing a game of political brinksmanship, warning the Florida Supreme Court, six of whose seven members were appointed by Democratic governors, that if they leaned too far in Gore's direction he had the means to retaliate. This was dangerous enough ground to be treading—"playing with fire," in the words of President Nixon's White House counsel Leonard Garment. Even Feeney, though, must have been surprised that the U.S. Supreme Court backed him up so vigorously. "The individual citizen has no federal constitutional right to vote for electors for the President of the United States," the majority opinion read, "unless and until the state legislature chooses a statewide election as the means to implement its power to appoint members of the Electoral College. The state . . . after granting the franchise in the special context of Article II, can take back the power to appoint electors." Presumably, this was the sort of close literal reading of the Constitution President Bush had in mind when he expressed a preference for "strict constructionists" as judicial nominees. If so, the *Bush v. Gore* decision sets an ominous precedent for future close elections.

Florida may be where the 2000 election was fought most vigorously, but it was far from the only state to witness problems or near-catastrophic breakdowns. Had the Electoral College arithmetic outside Florida been closer, we could have seen knockdown legal fights in as many as half a dozen states. The Sunshine State was one of four where the official margin of victory was slimmer than the number of ballots discarded as undervotes. Two others, New Mexico and Oregon, were carried by the slimmest of margins by Gore, while the fourth, New Hampshire, slunk narrowly into the Bush column.

In Oregon, which voted entirely by mail, a pilot study conducted shortly after the election suggested that as many as 36,000 ballots statewide were filled in by someone other than the signatory. That alone could have been grounds for a debilitating lawsuit, since Gore's margin in the state was just 6,765. Other states were spared machine-related problems only because the outcome happened to be decisive. Several, including Georgia, Idaho, Illinois, South Carolina, and Wyoming, had higher rates of rejected or uncounted ballots than Florida. When the Democratic staff of the House Judiciary Committee, led by Representative John Conyers of Michigan, looked into the irregularities, they established that more than 1.2 million ballots in thirty-one states, plus the District of Columbia, had been rejected as undervotes. (The other nineteen states kept no records of their discarded ballots.) Since it seems unlikely that more than a tiny fraction of the electorate would have deliberately left the presidential ballot blank—exit polls and other data suggest that figure should have been somewhere around 0.5 percent—we can say with some certainty that the number of uncounted votes was at least twice as large as Al Gore's 500,000 official margin in the popular vote.

A 2001 report by the Voting Technology Project, a joint venture of Cal Tech and the Massachusetts Institute of Technology, painted an even gloomier picture. It estimated that somewhere between four and six million presidential votes were lost. Roughly two million of these were rejected as overvotes or undervotes. Somewhere between one and a half and three million were never cast because of bureaucratic difficulties with the registration process. Another million or so were lost because of problems at polling stations, either because voters could not locate the correct precinct, or because the hours were inconvenient, or because the lines were too long. The Cal Tech/MIT report did not even attempt to quantify the number of absentee and overseas ballots that went missing. But we know many of them did, sometimes in strange and mystifying ways. The votes of Steven and Barbara Forrest of Bellevue, Washington, turned up several days after the election in the Danish city of Odense. They had somehow been slipped into an envelope containing navigational charts sent to a Danish couple by a company on Shaw Island, fifty miles north of Seattle. The Danes, Brian and Helle Kain, called the U.S. Embassy in Copenhagen to flag their discovery, only to be told that it was too late for the stray votes to be counted. Quite how the Forrests' votes ended up in that envelope remains a mystery.

Other, more brazen forms of electoral chicanery were alive and well in 2000, especially in local races. The *Los Angeles Times* sent a reporter to Alice, Texas, origin of the infamous Box 13 that gave Lyndon Johnson his decisive last two hundred votes in the stolen 1948 Texas Senate race. What the paper uncovered was a thriving vote-buying business in which women openly known as "vote whores" were paid by the political parties to talk people into abdicating control of their absentee ballots in exchange for monetary or other favors. In what remained a poor part of the country, vote whoring represented an opportunity to earn a precious few thousand dollars a year. "Last I heard," the town's police chief told the *Times*, "it was $20 a vote." Some vote whores handed out dollar bills or glasses of beer to gain access to the absentee ballots. Others simply stole freshly dispatched ballots out of mailboxes, unsealed the envelopes by sticking them in the microwave for a few seconds, and then filled them out as they saw fit with a forged signature matching the name on the envelope.

At the presidential level, perhaps no state outside of Florida was more questionable than New Mexico, a state with its own tarnished tradition of electoral malfeasance. The director of the state election bureau, Denise Lamb, gave some idea of the culture when, in 2003, she explained her rationale for triple-audit canvassing of every vote cast in the state, regardless of the machinery in use. "If we voted with black and white marbles, someone would figure out a way to cheat," she said. The 2000 election was rife with stories of boxes of votes mysteriously disappearing and others suddenly popping up again. In Rio Arriba County, a sparsely populated area in the north that had a reputation for being the dirtiest county of all, one precinct registered 203 voters but 0 votes for president, Senate, or the House. The

glitch was later ascribed to an electronic voting machine malfunction that was not spotted until it was too late. In Bernalillo County,
encompassing Albuquerque, the vote count went on for several days,
slowly transforming a narrow statewide lead for Gore into a tantalizingly thin 134-vote edge for Bush. Then, six days after the election, an extra 500 Gore votes materialized out of nowhere in Doña
Ana County in the south, turning his 134-vote deficit into a 366-
vote victory.

The Republicans were deeply suspicious of the miracle five hundred, particularly since the county clerk, Rita Torres, was a
Democrat in the staunchly Democratic city of Las Cruces. Their suspicions only deepened two years later when Torres's successor was
prosecuted and convicted on five criminal charges of violating state
election laws. Among the complaints against the clerk's office was
the allegation that it had deliberately supplied too few voting
machines to Republican-leaning precincts in order to depress
turnout. (Admittedly, Republicans were accused of doing exactly the
same thing in the counties they controlled, especially on the barren
eastern side of the state.)

So were the five hundred votes Box 13 all over again? Actually,
no. Or not quite. Both sides now agree it was a Republican volunteer, not a Democrat, who noticed the discrepancy during the vote-
canvassing process and joked about it with his Democratic counter-
part, who then pounced on it and reported it to a higher authority.
At some point during the counting process, a precinct worker had
scribbled down the number 620 on a sheet of paper to denote the
running vote total for Gore. The problem was, the six looked just
like a one, resulting in the number being transcribed into the provisional results as 120—five hundred lower than it should have been.
After years of grumbling and dropping dark hints, the Republicans
came around and acknowledged the transcription error. The party's
local vote fraud expert, Bill Wheeler, told me it was an "honest mistake." The Democrats, however, had their own qualms about what
happened. After years of being on the defensive, they came to suspect that the poll worker who made the six look like a one was a

Republican sympathizer who created the confusion on purpose to dent Gore's chances. Naturally, there is no way to know for sure.

As a postscript, it's worth pointing out that more fuzzy math popped up in a special election in September 2003, when New Mexico's Democratic governor, Bill Richardson, put his reputation on the line by taking two new state constitutional amendments to the people. The second amendment, regarding education funding, was particularly close, and the voting numbers changed almost daily from the night of the election until certification three weeks later. At one point the amendment was down by 2, then up by 122, then finally ahead by a margin of 195. In one county the *yes* and *no* numbers were switched after canvassing officials concluded they had been accidentally transposed. Republicans already alarmed in the wake of their narrow defeat in the 2000 presidential election found such movements in the vote totals distinctly fishy. They called for a recount but were told that under New Mexico law only candidates could request recounts. Since this was a ballot proposition, not a candidates' race, there was nothing they could do.

When they looked at the final official results for Amendment 2, the fishiness started to turn into a true stink. In two counties, Cibola and San Juan, the final tabulations had more votes than voters. More accidental transpositions, perhaps? Or bureaucratic sloppiness? Or proof that when it comes to electoral malfeasance, the two parties are separated not so much by morality or democratic scruples as they are by straightforward, naked access to power and the opportunity it affords one of them, in an appropriately degraded political culture and a tight enough circumstance, to do its very worst?

11
THE MIRACLE SOLUTION

★ ☆ ★ ☆ ★ ☆ ★ ☆ ★ ☆ ★ ☆ ★ ☆ ★

I always say, out of everything bad, something good happens.
—Theresa LePore, election supervisor, Palm Beach County, Florida,
looking back on the butterfly-ballot controversy and the
subsequent introduction of electronic voting

There are many ways to manipulate paper elections, but the scope of such an
attack is limited to one precinct or one county . . . The danger of a software
attack is that, while it takes a little more skill (but nothing extraordinary),
it can affect hundreds of counties simultaneously.
—David Jefferson, election security specialist, Lawrence Livermore
National Laboratory

WHILE THERESA LEPORE was still struggling through Palm Beach County's ill-fated punch-card recount, her reputation in almost as many tattered pieces as the chad littering the counting room floor, she was asked by a reporter how much it would cost to install a new voting system. "A lot of millions," she answered sharply. "And if you go to a new system, it has its own inherent set of problems."

Within a few months, though, she was singing a very different tune. In April 2001 LePore flew out to Riverside County, California, to observe the nation's first countywide touch-screen computer voting system, and she fell instantly in love. Voters, she enthused, would appreciate the fact that the Sequoia Pacific AVC Edge machines did almost all the work for them, automatically flitting from race to race as soon as each choice had been registered, and presenting a summary screen to double-check the full list before the votes were formally cast. Election administrators would love the machines, because they were fast, smooth, and relieved them of the tortuous work of vote tabulation. There was no chad to worry about, because there were no paper ballots. The nightmare of recounts, still vivid in LePore's memory, was all but eliminated since there were no physical votes to recount.

LePore, admittedly, was not the only one to be impressed. Riverside's registrar of voters, Mischelle Townsend, had attracted national attention with her seemingly prescient decision to go all-electronic for the November 2000 election. *Wired News*, the journal of record of the high-tech industry, described her as some kind of prophet for the new millennium. "If the U.S. State Department is looking for a way to restore America's good name after the recent election blunders in Florida," it wrote, "it ought to let the world know about Mischelle Townsend's bold experiment." Townsend, for her part, was more than happy to bask in the glory. "I've been counting my blessings for the last 24 hours that I'm not Theresa LePore," she crowed at one point during the Florida recount fiasco. "My heart goes out to her."

What neither LePore nor *Wired News* reporter Farhad Manjoo (soon to evolve into a thoughtful and trenchant e-voting critic) knew at the time was that election night in Riverside was a near disaster. A couple of hours after the polls closed, the tabulation software overloaded and started deleting votes from the tallying system instead of adding them. Sequoia had to send in an emergency resuscitation team, creating a delay of several hours. The system was eventually righted, at least according to Sequoia, but Riverside's results were not published until two hours after those of neighboring San Bernardino County, then still using punch cards. In the down-ticket race for the Moreno Valley Unified School Board, one candidate had been comfortably in winning position when the machines went down—and was reported as such in the next day's *Riverside Press Enterprise* newspaper—only to find herself trailing when the count resumed, for no reason she could easily ascertain. Her demands for a full explanation met only with official intransigence. Townsend reacted to the setbacks simply by pretending they had not happened. In letters to the school board candidate, Bernadette Burks, she flat-out denied there had been any computer crash, saying only that the server "reached capacity" and needed to be "manually expanded." She also refused to acknowledge that Burks had ever been ahead in the count, despite the evidence of her own numbers. "Flawless" was how Townsend described the November 2000 election, and "flawless" was how she would go on to describe every subsequent election under her tutelage.

"Flawless" was also the catchword Theresa LePore used to cajole the Palm Beach County commissioners into spending $14.4 million on their own Sequoia system. The new touch screens were deployed in time for the March 2002 local elections, and they, too, failed at the first hurdle. Emil Danciu, a well-respected former mayor of Boca Raton, was flabbergasted to discover he had finished third in a race for a seat on the Boca Raton city council, since an opinion poll taken shortly before the election had put him seventeen points in the lead. Supporters began flooding his campaign office with stories that every time they tried to vote for him, the machine lit up the name of one of his opponents instead. Danciu also discovered that fifteen cartridges containing the vote totals from machines in his home precinct had been removed by a poll worker on election night, causing an unexpected delay in the final results. Some of the cartridges were subsequently found to be empty, for reasons that have never been adequately explained. Armed with a fistful of affidavits, Danciu sued for access to the Sequoia source code to see if it contained some fatal flaw. He was told, however, that the source code was considered a trade secret under Florida law and that even LePore and her staff were not authorized to examine it on pain of criminal prosecution. His suit was thus thrown out, and he decided it would be futile even to appeal.

Two weeks after the Danciu election, something even stranger happened. In the inland town of Wellington, a runoff election for mayor was decided by just four votes. Another seventy-eight votes, however, did not register on the machines at all. Since the runoff was the only race on the ballot, that meant—assuming for a moment the machines were not lying—that seventy-eight people had jumped in their cars, driven to the polls, *not* voted, and gone home again. The scenario beggared belief, but it was touted, with an absolutely straight face, by LePore. "She's defended the system almost to the point where it's been ridiculous," Danciu's daughter Charlotte, who represented him in court, commented later. "She treated us as though we were sour-grapes sore losers and basically blew us off as though we were imbeciles. The tenor of what she told us was that if people were too dumb to vote on electronic machines, they shouldn't be voting."

The response to the 2000 presidential election fiasco was off to an unpromising start, to put it mildly. As it later became clear, there were two fundamental problems with the touch-screen DREs. First, as computer scientists had been warning for years without anyone paying much attention, they were inherently unsafe because of their vulnerability to software bugs, malicious code, or hack attacks. Even in the best designed system, removing votes from the physical world and storing them exclusively in electronic form was a risky proposition, because there was no way of being sure that the data put into the machines during an election would be the same as the data later spat back out. Hence the strong recommendation of academic experts such as Rebecca Mercuri (Bryn Mawr and Harvard), Peter Neumann (SRI International), David Dill (Stanford), and others to create a system of paper receipts enabling voters to confirm their individual choices and providing election administrators with the wherewithal to conduct meaningful recounts. No DRE on the market in the immediate aftermath of the 2000 election was equipped to produce this kind of independent paper audit trail.

The second problem with the new-generation DREs was that they were poorly programmed by their manufacturers and inadequately tested by government-contracted laboratories charged with their certification. This was a well-kept dirty secret at the outset, making it all the easier for vendors to blindside political decision makers with grandiose claims about the machines' miracle-working powers. Because of the proprietary nature of the software, state and county officials had to take assurances about security almost entirely on trust. And take those assurances they did—because they badly wanted to believe in the new machines and because they didn't want to admit that the problems in Florida were caused by anything more complicated than the malfunctioning of outdated machinery. Their blindness to the profoundly political nature of the struggle in Florida happened to dovetail with their own set of exquisitely political considerations. Who, after all, could continue to accuse them of neglect when they were opting for the most expensive, most technologically advanced system on the market? What local election administrator was going to object to the money being thrown around, all of it feathering the nests of a pleasant coterie of commercial and political interests? Who, above all, would ever fret again about Florida-style meltdowns and endless litigation over vote totals when the joy of DREs was that they made recounts impossible? Concern for the integrity of the system somehow seemed a lot less exciting than these considerations, even as control of the electoral process was privatized to an even greater degree than it had been in the 1970s and 1980s. Later, as information started leaking out about the shortcomings of the DREs and the incompetence of their manufacturers, politicians who had already committed themselves to tens of millions of dollars in new equipment preferred to bury their heads rather than admit any mistake. This wasn't just a matter of wounded pride. In many ways, the shortcomings of the DREs—at least until they became too glaringly public—suited them just fine.

All that helps explain, among other things, why Florida ignored the central recommendations of a blue-ribbon panel established in the immediate aftermath of Hurricane Chad to figure out how to fix the state's voting woes. Jeb Bush appointed the twenty-one-member Select Task Force on Election Procedures, Standards, and Technology—composed of ten Democrats, ten Republicans, and one Independent—just forty-eight hours after the Supreme Court decision handing the presidency to his brother, impressing on them the need to come up with rock-solid proposals as quickly as possible. They in turn reported back ten weeks later with thirty-five recommendations. By far the most important of these was Recommendation 12, urging the secretary of state's office to certify a uniform voting system across all sixty-seven counties. Not the least of the considerations was the fact that Florida's patchwork of different systems, and the resulting variance in the treatment of people's votes, had given the Supreme Court the opening it needed to invoke the Constitution's equal protection provisions and close down the count. Recommendation 12 further stated that only one state-certified system met acceptable standards on cost, accuracy, and ease of set-up. That was the optical-scan system—with the added proviso that votes should be tabulated precinct by precinct, not centrally at county headquarters.

Governor Bush publicly endorsed the task force's findings, but they were promptly pulled apart by the state legislature. Republican Party interest was the supreme motivating factor. After all, why should a Republican-dominated political establishment have cared about creating a nonpartisan state canvassing board when it knew that by postponing reform in that area, it could continue to control all three slots on the board? Why should the legislature "review issues related to the restoration of voting rights to ex-felons with completed sentences," as the task force suggested, when the suppression of the ex-felon vote played directly into the GOP's hands? In a state where voter registration tipped slightly in the Democrats' favor, the Republicans found themselves in charge of almost everything—both houses of the legislature, the governor's office, and the bulk of county governments. This imbalance did not come about by accident. It was the result of deliberate distortion brought about principally through the gerrymandering of electoral districts, with a little extra help from the gradual conversion of traditional white voters in the redneck northern part of the state from Democrat to Republican. What party wouldn't want to play that advantage for all its worth and find ways to preserve and extend it?

The task force was lukewarm about electronic voting, pointing out that DREs made recounts "difficult" and citing a Cal Tech/MIT study released during the panel's deliberations showing that their discard rate was worse than for any other machine type except punch cards. The report made no mention of broader security concerns but nevertheless suggested that DRE technology was not yet ready for prime time. That determination had not the remotest effect, however, on fifteen of Florida's largest counties—most of them urban, many of them Democrat-leaning—which decided to go full-speed ahead with DREs regardless. The Republicans can only have been thrilled. While most of the counties where they were strongest were already fixed up with optical-scan systems, the most reliable available, their big-city Democratic opponents were opting for a technology that promised to lose or foul up a crucial proportion of its ballots.

The fact that this happened was largely down to one woman, the former secretary of state, Sandra Mortham, whom we met in the last chapter laying the groundwork for the notorious statewide felon purge list. After Mortham left public office, she became a state lobbyist for Election Systems and Software (ES&S), the largest voting machine maker in the United States, whose product line included the now untouchable Votomatic punch-card machine. It so happened ES&S was developing an electronic touch screen called the iVotronic and was very keen to sell it while memories of the 2000 election were still fresh—and before its association with the Votomatic condemned it to commercial oblivion. Mortham had all the right contacts, not only because of her previous job and her close ties to Governor Bush, but because she was simultaneously a lobbyist for the Florida Association of Counties (FAC). In other words, she was in the happy position of working both sides of the fence, her assignment in effect to talk herself into bringing ES&S and the county-level check writers into alignment. As an added bonus, she used her connections in Tallahassee to lobby on both her clients' behalf before the Florida legislature. The upshot: the iVotronic was sold to twelve counties, including Miami-Dade and Broward, for a total of $70.6 million. Miami-Dade spent $24.5 million, Broward $18 million. ES&S paid a percentage of its profits to the FAC, as well as a commission fee to Mortham personally.

Under such cozy circumstances, county officials in Miami-Dade forgot to ask any tough questions about their purchase, and the consequences were little short of calamitous. ES&S had promised Miami-Dade it could add a third language, Creole, to its touchscreen software in addition to English and Spanish, which were standard features. But the company neglected to mention that the trilingual package would have to be loaded separately via a dedicated flashcard that would drastically slow down each machine. When the iVotronics made their debut in the Democratic gubernatorial primary in September 2002, they took so long to boot up that the entire electoral machinery of Miami-Dade County ground to a halt. Many polling stations did not open until lunchtime, creating consternation from one end of the county to the other. To make matters worse, freak storms knocked out power to certain precincts for so long that the battery backup on many iVotronics ran out. Then, the tabulation machines went bananas. One Miami precinct reported 900 percent turnout; another showed just one ballot cast out of 1,637 registered voters.

Governor Bush was forced to declare a state of emergency in both Miami-Dade and Broward, which had experienced similar problems, and extended the opening hours of polling stations by two hours. Nobody was happy with the results of the election, least of all Janet Reno, the former U.S. attorney general, who strongly suspected that the eight-thousand-vote deficit separating her from her challenger for the Democratic nomination, Bill McBride, was inaccurate. Since recounts were impossible, however, there was nothing she could do, and after a week of back-and-forth that was uncomfortably reminiscent of 2000, she quietly conceded. "It turned out the county had purchased a prototype," said Lida Rodriguez-Taseff, a gutsy lawyer who founded the Miami-Dade Electoral Reform Coalition and quickly became a major thorn in ES&S's side. "This was an invention that had never been tested. We were the guinea pigs."

For the general election in November, officials decided to switch on the county's seven thousand voting machines twelve hours ahead of time. Because of the obvious security risks that entailed, the city had police patrols roaming the streets and guarding precincts all night long. The election division, in fact, took the extraordinary step of asking the police to run the entire election. The cost of the enterprise remained in dispute, with county election officials admitting to only a few million extra dollars, while the Electoral Reform Coalition says it was somewhere between eight and twelve million. Either way, the expense may have been unavoidable. As the Center for Democracy, a nonpartisan group monitoring the election, discovered, it took as long as seventy minutes to fire up each machine. Because of the way the system was set up, the terminals had to be turned on one after the other in sequence. Most polling stations took four to five hours to get ready. The results were not in dispute this time—everyone agrees Governor Bush won reelection fair and square—but problems and breakdowns were still glaringly evident. In Broward County, which spent $3.5 million to fix the problems it encountered in the September primary, more than one hundred thousand votes mysteriously disappeared and were not recovered until the day after the election. The county's deputy election supervisor, Joe Cotter, blamed it on "a minor software thing."

While the South Florida counties were rushing headlong into a technology they would later have cause to regret, the state of Maryland was taking a more deliberate approach but still wound up falling for the allure of the DRE against the experts' better judgment. Secretary of State John Willis saw the disasters of the 2000 election as an opportunity for a career-making act of boldness and pushed hard for electronic voting right from the start. A special committee reviewed the options and, over the objections of some members, voted in favor of DREs. Still, the committee laid down strict testing criteria and said any system purchased by the state must be capable of creating a paper audit trail for recount purposes. Logically, that should have eliminated all the electronic systems then available. But logic was not what was driving this decision. In late 2001 an Election System Evaluation Committee made up of technical experts from around the state looked at a number of formal DRE purchase proposals and concluded, even more forcefully than the previous panel, that none of the proposed vendors met the state's standards, because they didn't understand enough about the conduct of elections and because their machines were too new to have been adequately tested. As one of the five committee members, Baltimore County's information technology chief, Tom Iler, said later: "You don't want to be on the bleeding edge with critical systems . . . Why would anyone want to buy first-generation technology which is a lot more expensive than established technology, just to see it become obsolete very quickly?"

Why indeed? The state never answered that question, and never explained—largely because the media was kept in the dark—why it blithely ignored the committee's unambiguous recommendation to reject every last proposal on the table. Instead, it went ahead with an initial $13.2 million purchase of four thousand DRE terminals, from a company soon to become synonymous with the vulnerabilities and suspicions surrounding electronic voting, Diebold Election Systems. It didn't take long for things to start going wrong. By the time of the September 2002 primary, even the administrator of Maryland's State Board of Elections, Linda Lamone, was having doubts. Although she would admit no fault with the machines, she told a state government oversight committee that working with Diebold had been a logistical nightmare and that company employees charged with training poll workers were "not responsible people." The primary threw up the kind of problems that were soon to be reported all around the country: machines that refused to fire up or otherwise malfunctioned, screen alignments that froze or assigned votes cast for one candidate to a completely different candidate, and so on. To Lamone, however, these were nothing but teething troubles, and in July 2003 her office announced it was spending another $55.6 million to expand electronic voting statewide.

Stranger things still were happening in Georgia, where Cathy Cox—a secretary of state more ambitious than Willis—had her eye on a future run for governor and decided she wanted her state to be the first in the nation to go all touch–screen. In May 2002 she signed a $54 million contract with Diebold and immediately set about getting poll workers trained in time for the November midterm elections. Curiously, the technical adviser who designed Georgia's certification procedure for electronic voting, and who also lobbied hard for the new technology before the state legislature and in the media, had previously testified in Maryland that he didn't think DREs were ready for use and might introduce "unnecessary risk" into the election process. The adviser, Brit Williams of Kennesaw State University, had been hired as an expert by Maryland's Election System Evaluation Committee and, according to the text of their official recommendation, issued in October 2001, told them "he would not choose a touch screen DRE to replace existing inadequate systems for the 2002 election." Within a few months Williams appeared to have undergone a change of heart, however, because he told a meeting of the Georgia Technology Authority in January 2002 he saw no problem in rushing Diebold's AccuVote touch-screen system through the state certification process.

He might have done better to go with his first instincts. On June 10, just a few weeks after the Diebold purchase went through, six tabulation machines and a touch-screen voting terminal were stolen from a Ramada Inn in Macon where they had been set up for a regional training session. The loss was a colossal piece of incompetence, since the Ramada Inn turned out not to be a standard conference hotel but rather a drug rehabilitation halfway house, where even the employees came under suspicion of being in on the job. But the theft was also an extremely serious security breach, because a technically adept hacker who gained access to the tabulation machines and the associated GEMS election management software could effortlessly—and undetectably—alter the outcome of an election not only in Georgia but anywhere in the United States where Diebold machines were used. For more than two years state officials refused to acknowledge the theft had happened and would not even release logistical details about the June training schedule. Finally, the head of the state election division, Kathy Rogers, acknowledged the incident in response to a question from an international election monitor in September 2004. She insisted, however, that security was not an issue, because the software had been changed—she did not say when—and the equipment was most probably "at the bottom of the Chattahoochee." Voting rights activists had their doubts any thief would throw a functioning computer into a river and worried that the machines were still out there somewhere. No trace was ever found.

The same month as the computer theft, the Diebold terminals began demonstrating symptoms of serious malfunction. Rob Behler, an engineer working as a Diebold contractor at the company's Georgia warehouse, later reported that 25 to 30 percent of the machines were either crashing as they were being booted up or otherwise failing. In his account, which the company has never denied, Diebold came up with three successive software patches—one in June, one in July, and one in August—to remedy the problem. The booting problem was solved by the time of the November election, but it remained far from certain whether the patches were ever submitted for certification—a basic requirement under state and federal law. Once the election was over, an Atlanta graphic designer and budding voting rights activist named Denis Wright put in a formal request for a copy of the certification documents, only to be told by the assistant director of legal affairs in the election division that "no records exist in the Secretary of State's office regarding a certification letter from the lab certifying the version of software used on Election Day." The state lawyer said it might be possible to trace the documents through Gary Powell, an official at the Georgia

Technology Authority, so some of Wright's fellow activists wrote to him as well. Powell responded he was "not sure what you mean by the words 'please provide written certification documents.'"

Wright commented later: "If the machines were not certified, and that's certainly the way it looks, then right there the election was illegal." The secretary of state's office has never demonstrated anything to the contrary, while Diebold has since established something of a track record of running elections on uncertified software, with confirmed instances in California and Maryland.

The November 2002 elections in Georgia were screwy in more ways than one. The state had its share of machine malfunctions— terminals freezing, screen alignments going out of whack, and so on. In Fulton County, covering downtown Atlanta, sixty-seven memory cards containing an unknown number of votes went missing, delaying certification of the results there for ten days. In neighboring DeKalb County, ten memory cards went missing and were later recovered from terminals that had supposedly broken down and been taken out of service. Most troublesome, however, were the results of the races for governor and U.S. Senate, which suggested wild double-digit swings in favor of the Republican candidates from the final preelection opinion polls. Sonny Perdue became the first Republican governor to be elected since Reconstruction, thanks to a sixteen-point swing away from the Democratic incumbent, Roy Barnes. And Saxby Chambliss, the colorless Republican Senate candidate, pulled off an upset victory against the popular Vietnam War veteran Max Cleland, representing a nine- to twelve-point swing. Part of this movement was no doubt due to a viciously personal Republican television ad campaign launched against Cleland in the final days before the election, as well as a late campaign appearance on Chambliss's behalf by President Bush. Part of it can also be explained as part of the shift in allegiance of old-style white Southerners from the Democrats to the Republicans. But it wasn't just the opinion polls that were at variance with the result. The voting pattern was also drastically different from Georgia's open primary, conducted on old voting machines just two months earlier.

In twenty-seven counties in Republican-dominated north Georgia, Cleland unaccountably scored fourteen percentage points higher in the general election than he had in the primaries, while in seventy-four counties in the Democrat-heavy south of the state, Chambliss improved on his own standing by a whopping twenty-two points. Were these statistical anomalies, or was something fishier going on? In the absence of a paper backup, or of any hint of transparency from state officials, the question was for the most part unanswerable. Cleland and Barnes both chose to remain silent. But a specific problem did eventually emerge in Dooly County, a poor, predominantly African American area in central Georgia, where the two major candidates for governor received exactly the same number of votes, according to the official returns. This seemed distinctly odd, given the county's history of strong support for the Democrats, and evidence later emerged that the figures derived from a test run, not the election itself. When asked to confirm or deny this, the probate judge in charge of elections in the county declined all comment.

In his prescient survey of voting systems written in 1988, Roy Saltman of the National Bureau of Standards identified four problem areas in verifying the outcome of computerized elections: the absence of a proper audit trail, poor program design, trade secrecy provisions that stop public officials from examining those programs, and inadequate administrative oversight. The new DRE systems introduced in the wake of the 2000 election suffered from every one of these pitfalls. Saltman cited a handful of other relevant dangers, too, including inadequate poll worker training and insufficient financial resources to maintain and operate the machines. The risk, he wrote, was that these oversights would be tantamount to an "abdication of control over elections to vendors."

That abdication was in full swing by the time of the 2002 midterm elections and became even more apparent as more and more counties purchased electronic systems. Several administrators in smaller jurisdictions—in places like Dooly County, Georgia, say, or the redwood forests of northern California—cheerily admitted to anyone who asked that the machines were too complicated for them to understand, and they were more than willing to let the nice local representative from Diebold help out in any way he saw fit. The problem with that attitude was not that the Diebold representatives were necessarily incompetent or crooked. Clearly, many local administrators regarded their intervention as a benign service, on a par with calling out a technician to fix a home PC. The problem was that the administrators were accountable to the public to deliver honest, clean elections, while the voting machine companies were accountable to nobody except their shareholders.

The market is not without its own checks and balances, of course. A manifestly fouled-up election is not going to be good for business. But the market also has its own built-in distortions. The insidious thing about DREs is that they are perfectly capable of giving an outward appearance of efficiency, speed, and mathematical exactitude—the service promised in the contract—while concealing all manner of flaws, miscalculations, or worse within their hermetic electronic universe. The vendors have little or no commercial interest in drawing attention to problems, especially when it is so easy to cover them up. And the temptation for many local election administrators is to go along with the pretense of perfection, since they, too, have an interest in declaring their elections to be "flawless." Whatever their commitment to the integrity of the process—stronger in some cases than in others—they are also bureaucrats who, in the end, want everything to fit neatly into its designated box with a pretty ribbon tied on top. If there is no way for anyone to open that box and second-guess the contents, so much the better. As Lida Rodriguez-Taseff put it: "We have thrown millions and millions of dollars at correcting the outward signs of problems, without correcting the problems themselves."

What is violated here is, above all, the public trust. In his paper Saltman laid out four steps needed to earn that trust, irrespective of which voting system is used. They were:

1.   Ensuring prospective voters are entitled to vote at the venue in question, and making sure they are given the right set of offices and issues on which to cast their vote.

2.   Ensuring they can vote in secret and without intimidation.

3.   Ensuring their choices are recorded precisely, anony-
     mously, and in an easily countable form.

4.   Ensuring the votes are counted accurately.

Without a voter-verifiable paper trail, DREs offer no guarantee of
steps 3 and 4. There is no systemic obstacle to steps 1 and 2, but both
have been violated on numerous occasions since 2000. In the March
2004 primaries, for example, a foul-up in Orange County, California,
gave some voters the wrong set of lower-order races to vote on, while
in Maryland some voters complained that the Senate race failed to
appear on their digital ballots. The problems of voter intimidation and
confusion over precinct location, especially with regard to provisional
balloting, are already rife and dealt with elsewhere in this book.

   Another computer expert whose views on basic standards need
considering is Michael Ian Shamos of Carnegie-Mellon University,
whose work as an electronic voting systems examiner in Pennsylvania
was considered in chapter 9. Shamos has been a believer in e-voting
from long before its inception, because he sees it as the most difficult
system, ultimately, for the voters themselves to defraud. But he, too,
offers some caveats—his "Six Commandments," as he called them in
a 1993 research paper:

I.   Thou shalt keep each voter's choices an inviolable secret.

II.   Thou shalt allow each eligible voter to vote only once,
      and only for those offices for which she is authorized to
      cast a vote.

III. Thou shalt not permit tampering with thy voting system,
      nor the exchange of gold for votes.

IV.   Thou shalt report all votes accurately.

V.   Thy voting system shall remain operable throughout each election.

VI.   Thou shalt keep an audit trail to detect sins against Commandments II–IV, but thy audit trail shall not violate Commandment I.

Again, the new-generation DREs as originally brought to market fell short—particularly Commandments III (for lack of sufficient safeguards), IV (for lack of adequate backup), V (in cases where the machines malfunctioned or failed to start up) and, of course, VI. In a more rational universe, political leaders and election officials would have responded to the Florida meltdown by turning to the widely respected work of Saltman, Shamos, and others and establishing some basic standards to help acknowledge their past neglect and make sure the same mistakes weren't simply repeated or reconfigured. The fact that they didn't came down in the end to inertia, lack of willingness to confront an age-old problem they had always previously ignored, and also a peculiarly twenty-first-century combination of money and politics.

At the federal level, the Bush administration got off to a distinctly shaky start on electoral reform, showing little or no interest in its first eighteen months and doing absolutely nothing to prod the House and Senate into papering over their partisan disagreements and coming up with their own comprehensive new law. Perhaps Brother Jeb told the president that things were moving along just fine on a state-by-state basis. Perhaps the White House, not wishing to remind itself or others of the circumstances of Bush's elevation to the presidency, hoped the issue would simply go away. Whatever the explanation, it plummeted down the priority list to the point where, in the summer of 2002, the White House yanked $400 million in federal funding for new voting systems off the table. According to Doug Chapin of the Election Reform Information Project, who followed the whole thing, the cause of reform had been "left for dead."

Then the second Florida meltdown happened, and the White House, facing another round of ridicule and embarrassment, suddenly snapped to attention. In the space of just a few weeks, Congress passed, and President Bush signed, a comprehensive package called the Help America Vote Act, or HAVA, which promised a delirious $3.9 billion to state and county authorities to throw out their old punch-card and lever machines and replace them with state-of-the-art technology. All the earlier stumbling blocks—partisan disagreements on everything from voter identification, the composition of a new federal agency, and the proper level of federal enforcement—melted away as if by magic. Election administrators, who had rarely been graced with enough money for lead pencils, much less six- or nine-figure windfalls, could not believe their luck. With dollar signs dancing in their eyes, they wasted no time in grabbing their coats and going shopping.

What ensued was a largely unregulated business free-for-all in which the major vendors—principally, Diebold, ES&S, and Sequoia, with some peripheral action involving Hart Intercivic, a small company based in Austin—ingratiated themselves with local and state election officials in every way they could think of. They offered political campaign contributions and lavish hospitality at national conferences. They hired well-connected former public officials as lobbyists and rewarded administrators who purchased their systems with lucrative job offers in their rapidly expanding industry. We've already seen how ES&S used Sandra Mortham's contacts in Florida. In California, Diebold hired Deborah Seiler, the former head of the secretary of state's election division, as its West Coast sales representative, while Sequoia snapped up two other senior employees in the secretary of state's office. Sequoia also hired Kathryn Ferguson, an election official who had helped them win contracts in Las Vegas and Silicon Valley, and Michael Frontera, who as executive director of the Denver Election Commission had spent $6.6 million of his taxpayers' money on Sequoia systems.

Sometimes the favors were a little more subtle. In 2001 Riverside County ran into unanticipated legal trouble because California's new elections code, passed in conjunction with a state spending bill on new voting machinery, specified that all systems would henceforth be required to produce a paper version of each ballot cast. Not only did Riverside's Sequoia terminals not produce a paper audit trail, but they were not even fitted with printers to print out the individual machine vote tallies at the end of each election day, as Mischelle Townsend herself explained at the time in a memo to the secretary of state's office. The vote tally printouts, as well as the so-called zero tapes produced at the beginning of the day to demonstrate that the terminals were empty, were one of the few cross-checking mechanisms available in the absence of a full paper trail, but Townsend told her masters in Sacramento it saved the poll workers much time and effort simply to skip that stage. Luckily for her, Secretary of State Bill Jones was more than sympathetic, declaring that as far as he was concerned printers were "an optional item" and that the pertinent section of the elections code should not be read too strictly. After he left office in 2002, Jones was hired by Sequoia as a paid consultant.

Not only was this revolving door between public officials and voting companies ethically dubious. In some instances it was also downright crooked. In 2002 Arkansas secretary of state Bill McCuen pleaded guilty to taking bribes and kickbacks involving a precursor company to ES&S; the company executive who testified against McCuen in exchange for immunity, Tom Eschberger, remained with ES&S as a vice president. (Intriguingly, it was Tom Eschberger, then with ES&S precursor Business Records Corporation, who defended the Votomatics in the wake of the 1985 Dallas mayoral election. At that time, he told a Texas House hearing it was unrealistic to expect perfect elections. "People are going to have the best elections that well-intentioned honest people can run, and that well-intentioned honest companies can run," he said. Quite.)

In Louisiana, Sequoia's southern regional sales manager, Phil Foster, was also indicted in a kickback scheme involving his brother-in-law, David Philpot, along with a voting equipment salesman from New Jersey by the name of Pasquale Ricci and Louisiana's state commissioner of elections, Jerry Fowler. Philpot admitted overcharging the state for Sequoia equipment and passing some of the profits back to Fowler and Ricci. According to court documents, he gave Foster envelopes stuffed with as much as forty thousand dollars in cash on five separate occasions on the understanding that the money would be passed on to Ricci. Philpot, Ricci, and Fowler all pleaded guilty, while charges against Foster were dropped in exchange for his testimony.

Such corruption was perhaps inevitable in a climate where a restricted number of companies were able to shift fabulous quantities of substandard product at scandalously high prices. The old Votomatics had cost between $125 and $300 per machine. Optical-scan technology was even cheaper, because counties needed to buy only one or two ballot readers per precinct. The price of a single touch-screen voting terminal, by contrast, was around three thousand dollars, even more with a printer attached. (Another reason, if one was needed, why administrators didn't like the idea of paper trails: having recklessly blown their wad on the core machines, they felt compelled to economize drastically on everything else.) To glean some idea of the level of sheer economic irresponsibility, one need just look at the figures from Los Angeles County, the single largest elections jurisdiction in the country, with more than four million registered voters. In 2001 LA chose to replace its punch cards with a rudimentary optical-scan system called InkaVote, at a cost of $3 million. The county registrar-recorder, Conny McCormack, saw this as only a stopgap measure, however, pending the introduction of Diebold DREs at the staggering cost of $100 million. In other words, until a number of Diebold-related scandals stymied her ambitions, McCormack had every intention of ditching one of the best performing election systems and replacing it with what Cal Tech/MIT and others have described as one of the worst *for thirty-three times the price.* McCormack insisted that her long-standing friendship with Deborah Seiler, the Diebold sales rep, had nothing to do with the decision.

The nationwide rush to purchase DRE systems almost certainly inflated prices far beyond market rates. Anti–touch screen activists in Riverside County, appalled by the wanton use of their taxpayer funds, calculated they could go to a retail computer chain and pick out the component parts necessary to run DRE software for around $600 to $800 per unit. Bob Varni, the Votomatic salesman from the 1960s and early 1970s, told me he had looked into the economics of electronic voting in the mid-1990s and calculated he could pull a system together for a manufacturing cost of about $100 per unit. He found a Japanese source for the computer terminals at $80 a pop, and reckoned the software cost, spread over several tens of thousands of machines, would amount to $10 or less. Even allowing for opportunity costs and a decent profit margin, he saw no reason why DREs should retail for any more than $500 to $600 per unit.

Instead of allowing the vendors to peddle their wares county by county or—in the cases of Maryland and Georgia—state by state, it would have made much more sense for a single centralized authority to negotiate a reasonable bulk price for the DRE machines. Ideally, this would have been done by the federal government, which could have taken the opportunity to impose some degree of uniformity and minimum performance expectations. But the feds turned out to be sluggish, uninterested, and largely absent. HAVA called for the establishment of a sizeable oversight committee, headed by two Democrats and two Republicans, as well as a technical panel to determine standards for new voting machinery. Both, however, were constituted almost a year after the deadline laid down by the new law and were so underfunded that they had no meaningful way to carry out their mandate. As late as the 2004 presidential election campaign, the technical panel, known as the Election Assistance Commission, was struggling with just seven full-time staffers and had to abandon its plans to develop a national voting machine testing system. A few months later, the National Association of Secretaries of State, which never fancied being regulated in the first place, took advantage of a growing mood of budgetary austerity in Washington to issue an open call for the commission's abolition.

By the time the EAC was constituted, the debate over voting machinery had—incredibly—degenerated into a partisan dogfight, with critics of electronic voting seen as Democratic Party whiners, and Republicans, at least in Washington, insisting there was nothing wrong with the DREs at all. When the U.S. Commission on Civil Rights convened an expert panel to discuss a report it had compiled on HAVA implementation in April 2004, the Republican delegation walked out before the proceedings even began.

The misguidedly partisan twist to the debate was exacerbated by the perception, expressed loudly in Internet chat rooms and by some of the more heated voting rights activists, that the introduction of e-voting had concrete benefits for the Republicans. The anomalies of the 2002 midterm elections in Georgia and elsewhere certainly bolstered that impression. So, too, did the fact that Chuck Hagel, the Republican senator from Nebraska, had previously been chief executive of a precursor to ES&S, American Information Systems, and came into office with votes counted by his own company—a clamorous conflict of interest made worse by the fact that the newspaper championing his candidacy, the *Omaha World-Herald*, was itself a part-owner of AIS.

As it turned out, all three major vendors had ties to the Republican Party. In June 2003 Diebold's chief executive, Walden O'Dell, threw a fund-raising party in honor of Vice President Dick Cheney that raised six hundred thousand dollars—a sum lavish enough to earn him an invitation to spend the weekend at the presidential ranch in Crawford, Texas. O'Dell sparked a furor shortly afterward by sending out a fund-raising letter to one hundred of his fellow Republicans in which he declared that he was "committed to helping Ohio deliver its electoral votes to the president next year." There was no evidence to indicate that O'Dell meant anything underhanded by this, but it was an unfortunate choice of words, to say the least, at a time when his company was vying for consideration as a preferred voting machine vendor in Ohio. When his letter was leaked to the *Cleveland Plain Dealer*, it lit a firestorm of negative coverage across the country and probably did more than any other single incident to besmirch Diebold's name in the eyes of the country's voting rights advocates. Indeed, it became fashionable to see

Diebold as the spearhead of some dark conspiracy in which corporate America and the Republican Party had joined forces to undermine democracy and achieve a total lock on the levers of power.

Like all conspiracy theories, this one had some elements of validity,
not least the very real concern that a partisan programmer working
for Diebold or one of its competitors could hack an election without
detection. But the scenario was almost certainly overblown, for a
couple of reasons. First, the root problem was not the political
allegiance of the voting machine companies; it was the reliability of
their products. As Rebecca Mercuri put it: "If the machines were
independently verifiable, who would give a crap who owns them?"
Second, the idea that the big three manufacturers were somehow
corporate titans on a par with the Big Three automakers in Detroit
was laughable. Certainly, some real money had been put into the
industry, particularly in the wake of the Florida meltdown. Diebold,
previously best known for manufacturing bank ATM machines
(which, not insignificantly, produce individual paper receipts as a
matter of course), entered the U.S. elections game in 2002 when it
acquired Texas-based Global Election Systems (GES), itself a hodge-
podge of small precursor companies with names like AccuVote and
I-Mark. Sequoia was snapped up at around the same time by the
London-based company De La Rue, which owned 20 percent of
Britain's national lottery. (De La Rue sold again, in early 2005, to
Florida-based Smartmatic.) But we're hardly talking megabucks.
Even by Diebold's middle-ranking standards (annual revenues:
around $1 billion), the $24.7 million it paid for GES was chump
change. ES&S, the biggest of the three, isn't even quoted on the
stock exchange. It evolved as a patchwork of business interests
encompassing Texas oil money; the McCarthy Group, which
owns the *Omaha World-Herald;* and a succession of start-up companies mostly founded by Todd Urosevich, an IBM veteran, and his
brother Bob. Todd stayed with ES&S, while Bob ended up running
Diebold Election Systems—one of many indications that this
industry attracts only a restricted circle of people, none of them
exactly corporate high-fliers. The unflattering truth, as we saw in

chapter 9, is that election systems are of negligible interest to the tech bigwigs at IBM, Microsoft, or Dell. Voting machine companies were arguably at their most dynamic when they were small and tightly run by sharp operators like Bob Varni or Ransom Shoup. Now, though, executives at vendor companies have turned as mediocre as the county election officials that many of them once were. The result (with a few notable exceptions) has been a parade of small-timers, glad-handers, chancers, and dimwits who couldn't organize an effective large-scale political conspiracy and keep quiet about it if the lives of their girlfriends, wives, mistresses, and children all depended on it. The story of e-voting in America post-2000 is not one of intricate connivance and grand-scale dastardly thinking, but rather one of shabbiness, complacency, laziness, mutual back-scratching, small-town networking, conflicts of interest, petty ambition, even pettier revenge, and an appalling lack of basic critical thinking. That, in the end, has had as insidious an effect on the health of American democracy as any sinister corporate plot, and perhaps more so.

For evidence of the pathetically low intellectual level on which the elections business is conducted, one need look no further than a videotape of a January 2004 meeting between a Diebold sales representative and members of the Texas Voting Systems Examination Board, which the local chapter of the American Civil Liberties Union (ACLU) obtained through an open records request. It's oddly compelling to watch, in a soufflé-deflating, car-wreck-ogling sort of way. The state board members seem vaguely bored and distracted and lob only the softest of softball questions about security concerns, as though the political earthquakes being triggered in California and elsewhere over DRE failures were some faraway event of little consequence. The only time the members come fully to life is in their idle chitchat about airport security and timetable changes at Southwest Airlines, topics that seem to get their juices flowing much more readily than the complexities of election management software.

That said, the board members are certainly aware that all is not well. As they conduct a test election, they notice, for example, that a confusion between two precincts has led to a discrepancy in the overall vote count. One of them asks: "Is that okay with everyone, the tally on that vote isn't going to match?" To which the Diebold representative, Don Vopalensky, replies, utterly unflustered: "That's what we did last time."

A fair amount of time is spent on a glitch making it possible for a single person to cast multiple provisional ballots using the same assigned voter number. Again, this doesn't seem to trouble anyone unduly. Instead, it is suggested that precinct workers affix paper stickers to their list of voter numbers so they can check who has already voted—hardly a failsafe method, especially if one or more precinct workers chooses to abuse the system. Hence the following exchange:

UNIDENTIFIED BOARD MEMBER: I have two provisional ballots with the same number. What's going to happen?

VOPALENSKY: That's a procedural thing . . . If they make these little stickers or whatever, slap it on there. They should do that.

The exchange more or less peters out at that point, as one board member interjects: "Forget provisional, I just want to make sure this machine can add. Remember we've had machines recently that didn't add?"

When Adina Levin of the Texas ACLU's Cyber Liberties Project first obtained the tapes, she could scarcely believe her eyes and ears. "What we saw shocked us because all the security and reliability issues that have surfaced about these machines just were not being taken into account," she said. "We were expecting the same excruciatingly boring meeting. Instead, the stunning lack of rigor made it quite entertaining in a twisted sort of way." Six months after the January get-together, board member James Sneeringer reexamined the Diebold software and noted that the provisional ballot problem still had not been fully fixed. It was no longer possible to register multiple provisional ballots on the same terminal, he wrote in a report to the attorney general's office, but it could still be done using a different terminal each time. Sneeringer did not see this as a reason to withhold certification. Instead, he endorsed his own variant on the sticky label remedy. He also noted that it was relatively easy for someone with access to the tabulation software to break into the operating system while an election was in progress—a total security no-no. Again, Sneeringer did not see this as grounds for noncertification. Instead, he recommended conditional certification for one year, a period encompassing the 2004 presidential election. Levin commented: "This is like the lock on your front door being broken and saying, 'We'll have a locksmith come by in a year and fix it.'"

There is no reason to suppose that procedures are any laxer in Texas than they are in the rest of the country. Indeed, as we will see in the next chapter, there is abundant evidence to suggest things are this unedified most of the time, especially when the participants think they can keep well away from the glare of public scrutiny. After the Texas ACLU saw the tapes, it sued the state for access to the next meeting of the Voting Systems Examination Board. In response, the state first tried to argue that the board was not a formal governmental body subject to public scrutiny but was just a random collection of individuals. Then, when that patently absurd argument went nowhere in a hurry, the state postponed the next certification meeting indefinitely. Clearly, open government and the conduct of popular elections are regarded in some quarters as contradictory concepts.

12
BACKLASH

★ ☆ ★ ☆ ★ ☆ ★ ☆ ★ ☆ ★ ☆ ★ ☆ ★

We were caught. We apologize for that. We did not realize that when we have an off button on this machine, that it does not turn the system off.
—Bob Urosevich, CEO, Diebold Election Systems, before the California Voting Systems and Procedures Panel, April 21, 2004

It doesn't matter if it's gross incompetence. It doesn't matter if it's intentional deceit. The result is the same. They've been stringing us along. They've been jerking us around. And they've been doing a bait-and-switch on software that has resulted in the disenfranchisement of voters . . . , and that's disturbing. That's very disturbing to me.
—Marc Carrel, vice chair of the California VSPP, commenting on Diebold, April 22, 2004

IN JANUARY 2003 the owner of a small Seattle-area public relations firm was sitting in her basement doing online research into electronic voting when she made a startling discovery. Through a simple Google search, she stumbled on an open file transfer protocol site containing the source code for Diebold's AccuVote-TS touch-screen machine, as well as program files for the company's election management software, a list of voters' names and addresses from Texas, and a sheaf of voting data culled from a 2002 primary election in California. There were forty thousand files in all. The woman, Bev Harris, knew immediately that this material was never intended for public scrutiny. The fact that it was lying around where anyone could find it had to be a security breach of colossal proportions. But she also realized she had hit an informational goldmine, a unique opportunity to break down the barriers of secrecy surrounding the e-voting universe.

Harris was soon to establish herself as a kind of activist-in-chief on voting issues, *the* go-to person for whistleblowers, leakers, and information peddlers of all stripes anxious to expose the vendor companies and the public officials who bought and promoted their wares. She founded a Web site, www.blackboxvoting.org, and wrote a book, also called *Black Box Voting*, both of which became touch-stones, for a while, for a growing army of anti–touch screen activists. At the beginning of 2003, though, she was still new at the game, her main exposure to electronic voting being through an alarmist Philadelphia-based writer named Lynn Landes, who had done some research into the ownership of the major vendors and believed, without too much evidence, that a cabal of right-wing extremists was planning to use the machines to overthrow American democracy. Landes in turn was heavily influenced by a self-published book from the early 1990s called *Votescam*, whose authors, James and Kenneth Collier, not only warned of rigged elections in the future but also asserted that many, if not all, elections since the assassination of President Kennedy had probably been rigged as well.

Harris did some digging around the Diebold source code with the help of a group of computer programmer friends, establishing, for example, that it was possible to enter the voter database using a standard Microsoft application, Microsoft Access, and change votes without leaving any trace. She also noticed, in data from a California primary, that one of the vote summaries from San Luis Obispo County was time-stamped 3:31 PM—more than four hours before the close of polling, when communication between the individual voting terminals and the central tabulation system was strictly taboo. Here, surely, was a scandal of epic proportions. But when Harris first tried to interest the media in the story—she had a daughter who worked at the *Los Angeles Times*—she found herself firmly rebuffed. Nobody wanted to run a story challenging the security of the country's brand-new computer voting systems on the say-so of an amateur sleuth fond of scare stories about evil corporations.

Harris and her friends did one smart thing, and that was to have the files copied to a server in New Zealand, where they were out of Diebold's reach and, from a legal standpoint, unequivocally in the public domain. David Dill, a computer science professor at Stanford University who had known about the security leak for a while but was worried about the trade secrecy implications, immediately contacted some of the country's smartest minds on computer security and encouraged them to examine the source code now it was freely available. First out of the gate was Avi Rubin of Johns Hopkins University, who, together with two of his brightest graduate students, Tadayoshi Kohno and Adam Stubblefield, and Dan Wallach, a colleague from Rice University in Houston, tore through the code in one frenzied week in mid-July. What they found left them so incredulous they rushed a research paper into print and gave an exclusive advance version to the *New York Times* (which, ever the cautious handler of explosive challenges to conventional wisdom, printed it on page A12).

Over the coming days, as he made the rounds of television news studios, Rubin was to describe the Diebold code as amateurish, stunningly inadequate, and downright scary. He and his graduate students had found the first gaping flaw within half an hour—the fact that the password unlocking the system's encrypted data was written directly into the source code. This was a violation of the most rudimentary principles of cryptography. Not only did it mean that anyone with access to the source code had the means to break into the system at will. It also meant that every single Diebold machine was crackable by exactly the same means. As David Jefferson, an election security expert at the Lawrence Livermore National

Laboratory and a frequent consultant to the California secretary of state's office, later described it: "What [Diebold] did is create a big complex building, put locks on every door, use the same key for every lock, and then publish a picture of the key on the wall."

The full Hopkins/Rice report elaborated: "Cryptography, when used at all, is used incorrectly. In many places where cryptography would seem obvious and necessary, none is used. More generally, we see no evidence of disciplined software engineering processes . . . We also saw no evidence of any change-control process that might restrict a developer's ability to insert arbitrary patches to the code. Absent such processes, a malevolent developer could easily make changes to the code that would create vulnerabilities to be later exploited on Election Day." Specifically, it was possible through a variety of techniques to alter the outcome of an election without leaving a trace. It was relatively straightforward, for example, to produce homemade replicas of the "smart cards" given to each voter to gain access to the system and use them to cast multiple ballots. Insecurities in the data transmission system were potentially even more dangerous, especially if election results were sent by modem from the precinct to county headquarters. "Even unsophisticated attackers," the report said, "can perform untraceable 'man-in-the-middle' attacks."

Diebold was left floundering by the report. At first it tried to cast doubt on the authenticity of the code, saying it was more than a year old and a test version at that. This was later contradicted—albeit briefly—by a company spokesman who was quoted in a *Wired News* article saying it was in fact the code used the previous November in the midterm elections in Georgia, Maryland, California, and Kansas. (Diebold later retracted the spokesman's comments and substituted them with a much more cautious statement.) Rubin himself also came under attack, for failing to take account of security procedures in polling stations and the safeguards they might provide against the vulnerabilities he had identified, and for his own personal ties to VoteHere, a software company in direct competition with Diebold that had appointed him to its technical advisory board. Both of these criticisms were just, prompting frustration and even anger from

Rubin's contacts in academia and the media who felt he should have been more careful. But they also did nothing to diminish the power of his core criticisms, which were entirely vindicated in a string of subsequent studies and which were ultimately recognized by Diebold itself, at least tacitly, as it sought to assure nervous clients that the problems had been addressed and corrected.

The reverberations from the report affected more than just Diebold. The findings were also a direct slap in the face of the testing labs that had passed the software for federal certification. The three labs involved in examining and approving election software—Wyle, Ciber, and SysTest Labs—were nominally independent, but in practice they had at least a financial interest in being solicitous toward the voting machine companies, since they were paid directly for their services and competed with one another for the work. All three operated under conditions of strict secrecy, which had the undeniable benefit of keeping sensitive software away from prying eyes but also made it impossible, barring leaks or court orders, to make even a minimal assessment of the labs' competence. (SysTest Labs was based in Denver, while Wyle and Ciber operated in the shadow of NASA's Marshall Space Flight Center in Huntsville, Alabama, where they were also engaged in high-level defense work.) When Congress first mandated the Federal Election Commission to draw up minimum technical standards for electronic voting machines in the late 1980s—before then, the industry had worked in a regulatory vacuum—it neglected to give any direction on how those standards should be tested and enforced. This gaping administrative hole was eventually filled by the Election Center, a Houston-based nonpartisan lobbying group representing state and local election officials, which took it upon itself to accredit and oversee the labs, known as independent test authorities, or ITAs. But the Election Center never wielded any formal congressional authority, giving rise to a deeply unsatisfactory situation in which the integrity of the country's election machinery depended on a system that was both impenetrable and publicly unaccountable.

Things grew only murkier as the Federal Election Commission's original 1990 standards were rendered obsolete by giant leaps forward in computer technology. Starting in late 1998 the FEC began developing a new set of standards to take account of the rise of the Internet, the growing sophistication of code-writing languages and encryption techniques, the proliferation of computer worms and viruses, and other security liabilities. But when the new standards were published in 2002, the terms of their adoption became shrouded in ambiguity, not least because state and county agencies across the country were in the throes of a DRE-buying frenzy. No vendor wanted to review its entire product line while sales were so buoyant, and no election official wanted to be left empty-handed for months on end after throwing tens of millions of dollars at a system that was supposed to be flawless anyway. So the Election Center and NASED, the National Association of State Election Directors, decided to fudge it. Any new product *components*, they said, would have to conform to the 2002 standards, but vendor companies would not be required to update entire *systems* from top to bottom. The question of what constituted a new product component was left distinctly vague. Did a patch on a software program qualify, for instance, or only a brand-new software package? According to an official who helped draw up the FEC standards, the understanding was that the testing labs would have "a bit of leeway" to decide such questions for themselves. The practical consequence of that leeway, though, was that as late as the 2004 presidential election most, if not all, key components of computer voting systems were still meeting only the 1990 benchmark—about as effective, in digital terms, as assessing a modern washer-dryer by the standards of a tub and washboard. The WinEDS program used in Sequoia's tabulation software, for example, was still widely used, even though the language it was written in, Visual Basic, was well known for its vulnerability to virus writers. Had the 2002 standards been fully implemented, Sequoia would have been obliged to rewrite the program or scrap it.

Perhaps the biggest problem with the whole setup was how cozy the key players were with each other. The Election Center represented state and county officials who were clients of the machine vendors, and it also accredited testing labs that were clients of the machine vendors. If that wasn't already too close enough for comfort, the center also developed its own direct relationship with the vendors. In early 2004 the *Philadelphia Inquirer* unearthed an IRS filing showing that the center had received annual donations of ten thousand dollars from Sequoia over a four-year period. The center's executive director, R. Doug Lewis, acknowledged the payments, saying he had received other donations from ES&S and "probably" from Diebold as well. He didn't show any sign of embarrassment about these ties; indeed, his organization appeared to be proud of them. At a national conference of county registrars organized in Washington in August 2004, the Election Center held a welcome reception sponsored by Diebold, a graduation luncheon and awards ceremony sponsored by ES&S, and a dinner cruise on the Potomac and "monuments by night" tour cosponsored by Sequoia.

Little wonder, given such clamorous conflicts of interest, if the system failed so spectacularly. When the Hopkins/Rice report first came out, the man in charge of examining voting machinery in Iowa, a University of Iowa computer science professor named Doug Jones, was stunned to read about some of the encryption problems, because he had found exactly the same flaws when he inspected the software as far back as 1996. In those days the company was still called I-Mark Systems, not Diebold, but the software architecture was one and the same. Jones had forwarded his discoveries to both I-Mark and the testing authority, Wyle Laboratories, believing that the software as it stood should not be allowed to come to market. But his concerns were ignored. In its certification report, Wyle went so far as to write: "This is the best voting system software we've ever seen." Despite all evidence to the contrary, that belief apparently persisted for another seven years.

The inadequacy of the source code was acknowledged by Diebold's own technicians in the programming notes they embedded into the software. Phrases like "gross hack," "this doesn't really work," and "this is a bit of a hack for now" abounded. The inadequacies became clearer still after someone with access to a Diebold employee ID broke into the company's internal computer system in March 2003 and pulled out a large batch of internal company e-mails, which, six months later, found their way on to the Internet. Diebold has never disputed the authenticity of the e-mails, which not only elaborated on the Hopkins/Rice report's findings but also highlighted the slippery relationship between Diebold and the ITAs. Here, for example, is Tab Iredale, Diebold's vice president of research and development, telling his staff not to let Wyle know that the Diebold operating system was compatible with WinCE 3.0, a program used for handheld and PDAs—that is, devices that can communicate remotely. "We do not want Wyle reviewing and certifying the operating systems," Iredale writes in the e-mail, dated April 15, 2002. "Therefore can we keep to a minimum the references to the WinCE 3.0 operating system." Quite why the Diebold system needed to be accessed from the outside—a blatant security breach—is not explained. Or here again is Ken Clark, Diebold's principal engineer, acknowledging in October 2001 that the audit system can be accessed without a password and changed using Microsoft Access. Clark writes to a colleague that he had considered putting in a password requirement to stop dealers and customers doing "stupid things," but that the easy access had "got people out of a bind" in the past. He cites one instance of a programmer who "did some fancy footwork" on a file being developed in North Carolina. Astonishingly, the e-mail correspondence makes clear that the testing lab—in this case a precursor company to Ciber called Metamor—was aware of the Microsoft Access issue, but chose to go ahead with certification anyway.

The hacked e-mails also cast an unflattering light on Diebold's business ethics. One employee, Brian Clubb, used his resignation letter in October 2001 (when the company was still called Global) to deplore "the practice of writing contracts to products and services which do not exist and then attempting to build these items on an unreasonable timetable with no written plan, little to no time for testing, and minimal resources." Clubb added: "It also seems to be an accepted practice to exaggerate our progress and functionality to our customers and ourselves, then make excuses at delivery time when these products and services do not meet expectations." If that sounds like sour grapes from an employee on his way out, it is worth bearing in mind that very similar complaints later surfaced about Diebold in its dealings with the state of California, as we shall see shortly. And here is another broadside, this time from Ken Clark reacting to the possibility that Maryland or another state might insist on adding a voter-verifiable paper trail on systems it had already purchased. "Let's just hope that as a company we are smart enough to charge out the yin if they try to change the rules now," Clark wrote on January 3, 2003. Asked exactly what he meant by "out the yin," he responded: "Short for 'out the yin-yang' . . . Any after-sale changes should be prohibitively expensive. Much more expensive than, for example, a university research grant."

Every one of these revelations was exquisitely embarrassing for Maryland's State Board of Elections, which, just two days ahead of the Hopkins/Rice report, had approved $55.6 million in expenditures to expand its Diebold operation statewide. Baltimore County, right next to Johns Hopkins, put in a request almost immediately to be exempted from the statewide e-voting installation plan. (The request was turned down.) Close to panic, the state government decided to commission not one, but two follow-up studies on the Diebold software to determine just how much of the taxpayers' $55.6 million it had flushed down the toilet and how much could still be salvaged. The first of these studies, by the computer risk-assessment company SAIC International, identified 328 security weaknesses, 26 of them critical, plus a whole slew of other high-risk issues that would arise if the system were ever hooked up to a network. SAIC came out with a list of suggestions for mitigating at least some of the problems, but the details of its analysis were missing, because the state redacted two-thirds of its report before releasing it publicly.

The second study was conducted a few months later by Raba Technologies, a security company employing many former members of the National Security Agency, and proved quite a bit more interesting because it included a "Red Team" exercise to try to break into the system during a simulated election. For a start, Raba found that it took approximately twenty seconds to pick the two locks securing each of Maryland's sixteen thousand AccuVote-TS terminals, and that every one of the locks—thirty-two thousand in all—was identical. Hardly a confidence-builder. As for the software, it proved little better than pitiful. "We could have done anything we wanted to," one of the Red Team members, computer scientist William Arbaugh of the University of Maryland, said. "We could change the ballots [before the election] or change the votes during the election." Another team member concurred: "Diebold basically had no interest in putting actual security in this system . . . It's not like they did it wrong. It's like they didn't bother."

Amazingly, both Diebold and Linda Lamone, the state's top election official, took the Raba report as a vindication. That was because, in response to the question of whether the state could deploy the system for the March 2004 primary election, the report concluded that it could, albeit unsatisfactorily, as long as a number of mitigating steps were taken to address the security holes. The report made clear this was not a long-term solution and urged further far-reaching corrective steps between March and the November general election. "Ultimately," it concluded, "we feel there will be a need for paper receipts, at least in a limited fashion." Such misgivings were entirely absent, however, from the public statements given by Lamone, who described the system as "flawless" (that Mischelle Townsend word again), or Diebold's chief executive, Bob Urosevich, who said Raba had confirmed "the accuracy and security of our voting systems as they exist today."

Far from being called on their remarks, Lamone and Urosevich set the tone for election officials across the country who faced similar criticism over their e-voting systems. The attitude was: sweat out the crisis and, if necessary, deny the problem exists. Deny that security is an issue. Deny that any machine has ever been hooked up to a network. Insist that the software has been extensively tested in government laboratories, that DREs are "100 percent accurate," that elections involving them have always been "flawless." Argue that those who want a voter-verified paper trail don't appreciate the fact that a paper trail already exists, in the form of internal audit logs and other redundant data stored in the machines. Point out that touch screens are popular with voters and are an essential tool for compliance with the Americans with Disabilities Act. In fact, insinuate that e-voting critics, aside from being conspiratorial scaremongers, are also fundamentally hostile to the interests of paraplegics, the deaf, the mute, or the blind. In short: take all the high emotion inherent in the accusation that American democracy is being undermined, and throw it right back in the faces of the accusers.

Such was the approach taken by R. Doug Lewis of the Election Center in testimony he gave to the Senate Judiciary Committee on September 9—later ripped to shreds point by point by David Jefferson of the Lawrence Livermore National Laboratory. He described the e-voting critics as "well-intentioned people . . . [who] scare voters and public officials." And he went on: "Do not be misled into believing that elections are reliant upon technology which can be manipulated. The real question is whether there are sufficient and proper safeguards to make it highly improbable. And the answer to that is yes. It may be possible to do many things, but like time travel (which is theoretically possible), it is highly unlikely at this time."

Strange things started to happen, like the frequent appearances of Jim Dickson, a disabled rights activist, at election conferences around the country. Dickson, who later turned out to be taking money from the voting machine manufacturers, would argue that DREs were the only devices capable of giving him, as a partially sighted person, the experience of full participation in the democratic process. This was, of course, an absurd argument—what good does it do disabled people, or anyone else, if their votes are not secure?— but the very presence of Dickson and his guide dog made it awkward for able-bodied critics to say so in public. It was not until later that Natalie Wormeli, a severely disabled lawyer from Davis, California, came forward to rebut him with great force and eloquence. "I understand the wonderful moment of doing things independently. I've had those," she said. "But I refuse to be an impatient passenger in the back seat saying, 'When are we going to get there?

When are we going to get there?' I know we're going to get there, but we need to get there safely and with everybody on board."

For a few months at least, the spin-doctoring effort was remarkably successful, as the flurry of media attention stirred up by the Hopkins /Rice report subsided, and the country's abiding faith in the system was allowed to smother unpleasant reality. In California, which was gearing up for an unexpected gubernatorial recall election that October, the ACLU went so far as to sue for a postponement so there would be time to complete the process of replacing the old punch cards with DREs. (The suit was thrown out by the California Supreme Court, not out of concern for the new technology so much as a belief that the old technology would do just fine. Both systems, in the end, had their problems on election day.) In Georgia state officials were downright cocky about their Diebold system, helped by the fact that the state's only major newspaper, the *Atlanta Journal-Constitution*, had not given serious consideration to the problems unearthed by the country's leading computer scientists. In an extraordinarily blinkered piece that appeared in the Atlanta newspaper on the day of the California recall, columnist Martha Ezzard wrote:

> So smooth has been the transition [to electronic voting] that other states have been knocking on the Secretary of State's door to get advice. The crazies and skeptics have knocked on [Cathy] Cox's door, too, of course, certain that hackers will foil the system, that votes can be changed by satellites or by aliens from outer space . . . But on the integrity of its voting system, Georgia, not California, is the bellwether. Today feels like the right time to brag about it.

Clearly Ezzard missed a remarkable demonstration session on e-voting that Cox's office had organized at Kennesaw State University a couple of months earlier, when a group of Georgia voting rights activists asked the tough questions the *Journal-Constitution* didn't want to touch and completely wrecked what was meant as a charm offensive on Diebold's behalf. Computer programmer Roxanne Jekot, who had examined the Diebold source code and deemed it unworthy of her first-year students at Lanier Technical College outside Atlanta, consistently embarrassed the assembled officials, because she knew as much about the protocols for computer voting as they did, and sometimes more. A sample of the exchange:

> JEKOT: So if the poll worker turns the machine off and then turns it back on, what happens to the votes cast earlier?

> MULTIPLE RESPONDERS: They are stored in the machine, nothing happens to them. The count displayed on the screen is also still there.

> JEKOT: So, if in the user manual it says that when you turn the machine back on, the election just resets, the manual is wrong?

Or again, on the subject of terminals being connected by modem to the central tabulation system, which the officials vehemently denied:

> JEKOT: So James Rellinger, who installed all 159 of these county GEMS [election management software] computers in Georgia is incorrect when he says he put a modem in every one of these computers?

> BRIT WILLIAMS [designer of Georgia's e-voting procedures]: Yes.

> JEKOT: And are you telling me that the county employee who tells me that he can call up the GEMS computer from his home computer is—what? Lying?

> COX: That is absolutely not true, and if that's the case he'll be brought before the elections commission!

Jekot ended up challenging the secretary of state's office to let her try to hack a Diebold machine. On the spot, they said yes. But subsequently they told her that the software was off-limits because it belonged to Diebold and was not available for public inspection. Instead, they offered her an empty terminal with no software loaded on it. Jekot politely told them she didn't think that would do the trick. The Kennesaw demonstration was to be the last time Cathy Cox would appear in a public situation where she risked exposure to hostile questioning. A conservative watchdog group concerned about the integrity of the electoral process, the Free Congress Foundation, later did an audit of new voting systems around the country and deemed Georgia's to be the worst, giving it an F-minus grade. (The national average was C-plus.)

In other parts of the country, activists and a small number of journalists were proving equally skeptical about taking election officials and voting machine manufacturers at their word. In Riverside County, California, computer programmer Jeremiah Akin attended a preelection "logic and accuracy" test of the county's Sequoia touchscreen system ahead of the gubernatorial recall and was deeply disturbed by what he saw. These tests, administered on a state-by-state basis, are far from exhaustive at the best of times and prove little more than the machines' ability to turn on and off and perform the simplest of mathematical calculations. The machines are run in an artificial test mode, not live election mode, and are rarely, if ever, subjected to complex real-life scenarios like multiple-candidate races or runoff qualifications. But Akin complained that even the basic requirements of the logic and accuracy test were circumvented. In a lengthy written account of his experience, he said that he and five other observers were shepherded away from the machinery at crucial junctures and asked to sign a form certifying the successful completion of the test before it was even over. He also challenged a claim by Sequoia that its software was not prone to the same vulnerabilities as Diebold's, because it worked on a proprietary operating system independent of Microsoft. Akin noticed, and Sequoia subsequently conceded, that the WinEDS vote tabulation software ran on Microsoft Windows. (A few months later, a leaked report from Wyle Labs made clear that the software used in Sequoia's voting terminals was not exactly tailor-made either, but was based on a commercially available package called pSOS.)

Meanwhile in Alameda County, also in California, *Wired News* reporter Kim Zetter signed up for poll worker training and discovered that without any vetting her fellow trainees were entrusted with keys and combination numbers enabling them to gain access to the county's Diebold machines. Anyone with malicious intent would still have to break two tamper-resistant ties attached to each terminal's carrying case, but these were readily available for purchase over the Internet and thus easy to replace. There would be plenty of time for any mischief, since the DRE terminals and the memory cards used to operate them were left sitting in polling stations days before the election.

Someone paying close attention to these developments was California's secretary of state, Kevin Shelley, who had been concerned enough to form an advisory committee on DREs, representing all sides of the debate, as early as February 2003. The Ad Hoc Touch Screen Task Force reported back in July, expressing concern about a flurry of issues, including certification standards, ballot verification, security, and the trustworthiness of the vendor companies and their employees. In November 2003, just when the rest of the country appeared to be sinking back into complacency, Shelley took the decision to mandate a voter-verified paper audit trail for all DRE systems in time for the 2006 midterm elections. It was a bold move, because the task force, made up of county election officials as well as e-voting critics, had been split down the middle on the question and because no paper trail system had been certified for use in the state at that point. But it was also a prescient one. California set a national precedent, and within a month its example was emulated by Nevada, which upped the ante by insisting that its DRE systems be fitted with a paper trail even sooner, in time for the 2004 presidential election.

Largely because of Shelley's close attention to the issue, California became, over the next few months, Diebold's biggest nightmare—a state where everything persisted in going wrong for the company, and public officials refused to cut it the slightest slack. The starting point for the disaster was a new Diebold system, the AccuVote-TSx, which the company was determined to introduce in time for the March 2004 primary and had already presold to four counties. In October, Diebold promised Shelley's Voting Systems and Procedures Panel that federal certification of the TSx was imminent and that there was therefore no reason to hold up approval for its use in California. Not only was this not true—the TSx remained uncertified for several more months—but it also became apparent that Diebold had installed unapproved software in all seventeen Californian counties where it operated voting terminals, or tabulation machines, or both.

Diebold's letters to the secretary of state's office on the subject read like the frantic excuses of a high school student trying to explain to his teacher why he hasn't done his homework. "Today is a new day at Diebold Election Systems," a groveling Bob Urosevich wrote to Shelley on December 19. "Strong action is being taken immediately to reassure the voters of California and the rest of the nation that the sanctity of the election process is secure." But the strong action did not materialize. In fact, by February it transpired that Diebold had withdrawn its outstanding applications for federal certification and had instead submitted new applications for updated versions of the same software. In other words, it had restarted the clock on the whole process with less than a month to go before primary elections in California, Maryland, and other key client states. It had no back-up system to offer the affected counties, other than a lame suggestion that they use paper ballots instead. Shelley's office, understandably, hit the roof. "It is apparent . . . that you continue to 'fly by the seat of your pants,'" Undersecretary of State Mark Kyle wrote on February 8. "In view of the fact that Diebold was solely responsible for obtaining federal qualification, and that you have repeatedly represented to all concerned that you would obtain that qualification in a timely fashion, we find your attempt to palm off responsibility at this late date astonishing."

The primary itself was a mess. In San Diego and Alameda Counties, the devices used to generate individualized computer cards for each voter malfunctioned, creating a mini-meltdown. In San Diego County, more than half the polling stations failed to open on time, because the card devices' batteries mysteriously drained. Since none of the polling stations were stocked with more than a handful of paper ballots as a backup, thousands of voters—it was never established exactly how many—were simply turned away. In Alameda County the situation was better because a paper backup was available, but the batteries performed just as dismally. It turned out that the card device, known as a "precinct control module" (PCM), was still in development and had been approved only after county registrars begged the secretary of state to let them use it for the primary on a one-off basis. As an official report later remarked, the choice was "between using equipment that had not been fully tested and approved, or using no equipment at all." Diebold either had not realized, or had not informed its clients, that a design flaw caused the PCM battery to drain even when the unit was switched off. Diebold itself later conceded it was the equipment, not poll worker error, that caused the problem.

The primary disaster led to a series of extraordinary hearings in Sacramento at the end of April that amounted to an official inquisition into Diebold's shortcomings. Bob Urosevich was there, along with a heavy-duty lawyer and an army of back-up technical experts, and he plainly hated every minute. He was vague on the details, nervous under cross-examination, defiant at certain junctures, and strangely self-deprecating at others. "I'm not a rocket scientist," he began at one point. "We're not idiots, although we may act from time to time as not the smartest," he suggested at another, to guffaws from the gallery. His broad line of argument was that Diebold had followed the same certification procedures it always did, but that California had lumbered the company with an excessive number of last-minute objections and requests that proved impossible to fulfill in the limited time available. The members of the Voting Systems and Procedures Panel weren't buying. "Let me just say the spin was making me dizzy," vice chair Marc Carrel said after the Diebold delegation had left. "We keep hearing apologies. We keep hearing misleading statements . . . I'm disgusted by the actions of this company, and I think that we should . . . forward everything we've found to the Attorney General." The attorney general duly opened an investigation, and one week later Kevin Shelley issued a series of rulings banning the TSx system from California altogether and issuing a twenty-three-point security checklist for counties to follow if they wanted to use any other DRE equipment in the November election.

Shelley could conceivably have gone further, by decertifying *all* electronic voting machines pending the introduction of a voter-verified paper trail, as some activists had urged. That, though, would have left ten counties, representing millions of voters, scrambling for a viable system just six months out from a presidential election, something the Voting Systems and Procedures Panel counseled strongly against. As it was, his rulings were quite controversial enough, sending shockwaves through the election administration business from coast to coast and bringing the issue irresistibly to public attention with a forcefulness that the release of the Hopkins/Rice report alone had not managed. Across the country, many jurisdictions that had been considering the switch to electronic voting suddenly found themselves thinking twice, or dropping the idea altogether. In Florida and Maryland Shelley's actions helped embolden voting activists and public officials to sue their respective states for the introduction of an independent paper trail. In Washington his example coaxed several dozen previously reluctant congressmen into throwing their support behind a mandatory paper trail bill proposed by Rush Holt, a New Jersey Democrat who had come to Capitol Hill in a nerve-rackingly close election of his own, and spurred Hillary Clinton and Bob Graham to introduce similar legislation in the Senate. Even Ohio, home to Diebold's corporate headquarters, had an eleventh-hour change of heart about its plan to introduce DREs statewide in time for the presidential election. The state's top election officials had previously been undeterred by a technical study they commissioned, in which the products of all the major vendors, not just Diebold, were analyzed and found to be wanting. But the California decision proved to be one headache too many. Kenneth Blackwell, Ohio's secretary of state, decided he wasn't going to risk his reputation on machines that could not even be relied upon to turn on and off.

Shelley also sparked fury among election registrars in his own state. In Los Angeles County, Conny McCormack argued that Shelley's pronouncements had completely derailed her timetable for compliance with the Help America Vote Act (which was another way of saying it had derailed her plans to spend $100 million on a Diebold DRE system). And, she said, his response to the discovery of uncertified software merely demonstrated his lack of understanding of how elections operate. There was nothing wrong with using uncertified software, she contended, if it meant smoothing over some last-minute bumps—a point she made without reference to the melt-downs in San Diego and Alameda. In fact, she acknowledged, LA had been patching its machines as needed for more than thirty years. "We have not been dotting every i and crossing every t to certify all the software," she said. "It would be the biggest irony to me knowing that a change would help voters, only to have someone say that because we hadn't done it by such-and-such a date we couldn't do it."

This curiously lackadaisical attitude from one of the country's most experienced election administrators did not go down well with some computer scientists. Rebecca Mercuri responded: "Her admission that there have been infractions by officials and vendors in L.A. County for 30 years should be investigated by the state Attorney General. What is the point of certification at all, if election officials like Conny can just disregard it whenever they feel like [it]?" Nor did it go down well with voting rights activists like Kim Alexander of the California Voter Foundation, who noted that just before the gubernatorial recall election of October 2003, McCormack had asked Diebold to make last-minute software modifications to DREs used in early voting in her county without getting them certified. McCormack lashed back at Alexander, who had served on Shelley's Ad Hoc Touch Screen Task Force, saying she was so unqualified to comment it was "laughable." But McCormack did not refute the charge.

In Riverside County, Mischelle Townsend took her own

considerable rage one step further. She spearheaded a federal lawsuit arguing that Shelley's new security stipulations and his demand for the introduction of a paper trail by 2006 were unreasonable and very possibly unconstitutional. In her fury, she did not merely sue the secretary of state's office. She also sued four urban counties, including Los Angeles, in an eccentric effort to push the debate in the other direction and force them to switch to all-DRE voting systems before the November election. Her suit went nowhere fast—it was tossed out within two months—and in losing she inadvertently laid the ground for several legal precedents inimical to the DRE apologists' cause. Townsend and her fellow plaintiffs argued that installing DREs was the only way to comply with the Help America Vote Act. Not so, said the court, which noted that in any case the HAVA deadline was January 2006, not November 2004. Townsend said touch screens were the only system in compliance with the Americans with Disabilities Act, to which the ruling by U.S. District Judge Florence-Marie Cooper countered that accuracy and reliability trumped all considerations of voter access. Finally, Townsend argued that a voter-verified paper trail was a security and logistics liability, and in any case no reliable paper-trail system existed. By that stage, however, one paper-trail system had in fact been certified in California and was already deployed in Sacramento County. If Riverside was looking for a paper trail it could count on, it needed only to ask its trusted vendor, Sequoia, which had by then modified its system to comply with Nevada's requirements for the November election and cleared the required certification hurdles.

Of all the arguments deployed by the touch-screen apologists, the resistance to a paper trail was by some distance the most perplexing, and also the one most in need of unpicking. County registrars like Townsend and McCormack liked to highlight the merits of the backups already in the machines: redundant memory, printouts from the individual terminals, cartridges, smart cards, and so on. In practice, however, it was unclear whether the internal audit logs could be trusted any more than the official tallies, or even if election officials could be relied upon to produce them when asked. In the wake of the 2002 midterm elections in Georgia, activists spent more than a year firing off letters to request the "zero tapes," the printouts that poll workers are supposed to generate before the election begins to demonstrate that the terminals have no votes stored on them, but never received a thing in return. In Florida's Miami-Dade County, the head of the county technology department tested the redundant data generated by ES&S's iVotronic touch screens in May 2003 and found so many flaws he concluded the material was useless. The technician, Orlando Suarez, wrote a letter to county and state officials detailing his findings and urging them to get the software bugs ironed out, but they ignored him until the letter came to public attention more than a year later.

Perhaps nobody has challenged the principle of trusting the redundant data over an independent paper trail more succinctly than Jeremiah Akin, the Riverside County computer programmer. In his report on the logic and accuracy test he attended in September 2003, he likened the system to a supermarket that tells you how much you owe without showing you a receipt for your individual purchases. He wrote:

> If you asked to see your receipt, the cashier would say, don't worry, we print them all out at the end of the day to make sure no-one was incorrectly charged. If you asked to see your receipt at the end of the day you would be told that it is not possible. If you insisted that what was really happening was that you were getting no receipt at all, the store would reply by saying that you do get a receipt, you just aren't allowed to see it . . . How long would you continue to shop at that store?

As it happened, the redundant data question was to play a crucial role in a highly contentious election dispute that unfolded in Riverside County just a few months after Akin wrote those words, culminating in the biggest personal victory scored by anti–touch screen campaigners to date: the downfall of Mischelle Townsend. At issue was a county supervisor's race in the March 2004 election in which the incumbent, Bob Buster, struggled to reach the 50 percent threshold required to avoid a runoff against his nearest challenger, a late-surging newcomer to politics by the name of Linda Soubirous. A number of strange and inadequately explained events had unfolded on election night itself. First, the count ground to a halt for about an hour, much as it had on election night in November 2000. Then, when it resumed, Buster's percentage of the vote started climbing until he squeezed just over the 50 percent mark. During the halt in the counting, Soubirous's campaign manager and a volunteer saw two men sitting hunched over a computer in the vote tabulation room at county headquarters. Although one of them had a county employee's badge, both were in fact employees of Sequoia. What they were doing there has never been entirely clear. Sequoia said they were merely sending lists of data to the secretary of state's office, but the very fact that they were in the room was already a troubling violation of standard election management practices. Two days later one of them was again seen typing away at a terminal in the vote tabulation room, apparently after being logged on to the system by the county's chief technology engineer. Again, no clear explanation was forthcoming.

Soubirous requested a recount and hired a lawyer to help lodge formal requests for forty-four items of back-up data—audit logs, error reports, chain-of-custody reports on data passed around on cartridges or over Intranet systems, and so on. Only five of the forty-four items were ever produced. After Soubirous's lawyer, Greg Luke, wrote to express his dismay at Townsend's refusal "to provide information which has already been generated, and should have been retained by you in the ordinary course of your official business," Townsend's attorneys responded that the materials were "not relevant to the counting of ballots" and in many cases did not exist, for reasons they did not specify. The recount went ahead on Townsend's terms, without examination of the back-up data, and to the surprise of no one confirmed Buster's narrow victory. Greg Luke called this "a process that only Katherine Harris could love . . . an empty formality suitable only for banana republics or dictatorships."

He continued to press for the forty-four items as a matter of principle, but Townsend determined that handing them over would be tantamount to a second recount, which she wasn't about to grant.

Townsend might have thought she had won this particular fight, but the victory came at considerable cost to her credibility. Her claim to have run nothing but flawless elections with DRE technology was fraying badly, even as she persisted in making the claim to anyone who cared to listen. At the same time, a flurry of public records obtained by anti–touch screen activists was casting her in an ever more unflattering light. The activists established that she had accepted money from Sequoia for a promotional trip to Florida that far exceeded Riverside's annual gift limit for public officials. They showed that she had failed to file a declaration of personal economic interests in four of the six previous years, in violation of county rules. And they proved, by obtaining the relevant correspondence, that the high-priced Sacramento lawyers hired to defend her in the Soubirous recount had been retained without the permission of the board of supervisors, who only approved the considerable expenditure six days after the contract was signed. By mid-June, the pressure of all this—not to mention the federal lawsuit she had filed, plus the prospect of a lawsuit against her from Linda Soubirous—must have seemed almost intolerable. A resignation letter was penned and released to the public a week after it was submitted. Townsend, naturally, denied that her departure had anything to do with the growing disquiet at her job performance. After twenty-seven years in public administration, she said she was taking early retirement to nurse her father-in-law through knee surgery.

13

ROUND ON THE ENDS AND HIGH IN THE MIDDLE: ELECTION 2004

★ ☆ ★ ☆ ★ ☆ ★ ☆ ★ ☆ ★ ☆ ★ ☆ ★

Welcome to Ukraine
—*Republican protest banner in Olympia, Washington, during the Gregoire-Rossi gubernatorial recount, December 2004*

The word now is, if someone gives you a provisional ballot, turn around and run.
—*Bess McElroy, African American voter organizer, Miami*

IN JUNE 2004 armed plainclothes officers from the Florida Department of Law Enforcement (FDLE) knocked on the doors of more than fifty elderly residents of a black neighborhood in Orlando and asked them aggressive questions about the absentee ballots they had submitted in the city's mayoral election three months earlier. The line of questioning made clear that the ballots were suspected of being fraudulent, and that the voters might therefore have been pawns, consciously or not, in a criminal conspiracy. The visits terrified the life out of the interviewees, not least because the state police officers took off their jackets and exposed their firearms as they pounded their subjects with questions. One senior officer crossed his legs and tapped a nine-millimeter pistol in an ankle holster as he asked why exactly one woman had voted absentee in the first place. "I felt threatened, embarrassed and like I was being accused of being a criminal," one interviewee, Willie Thomas, later wrote in a statement. Many others told their lawyers they no longer wanted to vote absentee—an option open to anyone without restriction under Florida law—because they felt it was somehow illegal.

At the center of the FDLE investigation was a seventy-three-year-old neighborhood vote organizer, community activist, and noted ladies' man named Ezzie Thomas, who had distributed and witnessed 270 absentee ballot forms as part of his paid work for the successful mayoral candidate, Buddy Dyer. Dyer, a Democrat, had won the race on the first round, with 234 votes more than the 50 percent threshold needed to avoid a runoff. Dyer's closest opponent, Republican Ken Mulvaney, had been crying foul since election day, arguing that the absentee ballots witnessed by Thomas must have been fraudulent and that he therefore deserved a second shot against Dyer. The strange thing, though, was that by the time of the house visits, Mulvaney's allegations had already been investigated and dismissed, both by Orlando's city attorney's office, which cross-checked the ballot signatures against the application forms, and by the FDLE itself. "It was determined that there was no basis to support the allegations of election fraud concerning these absentee ballots . . . [T]he Florida Department of Law Enforcement considers this matter closed," read a May 13 letter from the agency to the state attorney in Orlando.

So what were the house visits about? Ezzie Thomas's lawyer, the local Democratic Party and, soon after, Bob Herbert of the *New York Times* became convinced they had nothing to do with vetting the integrity of the March mayoral election and everything to do with suppressing black votes ahead of the November presidential race. If that was their purpose, they were certainly successful, because Ezzie Thomas vanished for the duration of the campaign, and his neighborhood group, the Orlando Voters' League, lapsed into inactivity.

It is worth bearing in mind that Orlando was regarded as *the* swing city in *the* swing area—the so-called I-4 corridor—in one of *the* swing states. Al Gore had taken Orange County, including Orlando, in 2000, much to the surprise of local Republicans, who vowed not to let the Democrats pull off the same feat a second time. Orlando was also very much in the sights of the state party. President Bush's handpicked Republican candidate for Senate, Mel Martinez, had previously been chair of the Orange County Commission, and the Florida secretary of state responsible for conducting the election, Glenda Hood, had been mayor of Orlando immediately before Dyer. None of them liked the fact that the city was now being run by a Democrat, and indeed once the presidential election was out of the way the FDLE turned its guns on Mayor Dyer himself, successfully removing him from office in the wake of a highly questionable indictment related to the absentee ballot question in March 2005.

The electoral battle for Orange County was waged on many fronts, some of them entirely above board. The Republican county chair, Lew Oliver, was doing a bang-up job of organizing Orlando's sizeable Puerto Rican community and made sure a Latino name appeared in the Republican column of the local ballot for every race below president. The city generally was known for its moderate politics and relaxed attitude toward partisanship. Before working for Dyer, Ezzie Thomas had worked for both Hood and Martinez, performing very similar services in organizing absentee votes. But the high stakes of the presidency made the November campaign strikingly different from business as usual. Hood, who had developed a reputation as a consensus builder during her twelve years at city hall in Orlando, started issuing a stream of unmistakably pro-Republican election rulings from her office in Tallahassee, where she now served directly at the pleasure of the president's brother, Governor Jeb Bush. There were grounds, too, to be deeply suspicious of the role of the FDLE and its controversial chief, Guy Tunnell, also a Bush appointee. Tunnell was previously sheriff of Bay County, on the Gulf Coast, where he had engineered the demise of the Panama City's only African American nightclub in a concerted onslaught of raids, arrests, police searches, and temporary closures over the course of several months. The neighborhood complaints on which he claimed he acted were later deemed by a federal judge to be bogus, and the true motivation for his campaign against the Sun Dancer club tinged with "racial animus." Governor Bush chose to ignore this cloud over Tunnell's reputation at his confirmation hearing in August 2003, saying in response to the lone public complaint about it: "I can tell you that Guy Tunnell is as good a cop as this state has, and we've got a ton of good ones."

The FDLE's investigation of the Orlando Voters' League appeared to be based on a paragraph in the Florida statutes declaring it illegal to receive or offer "something of value" for absentee ballots. The only "something of value" to come to light, though, were the stamps Thomas and his volunteers stuck on some ballot envelopes on the voters' behalf, the kind of service any get-out-the-vote group might offer. As Thomas's lawyer, Joe Egan, commented: "A 37-cent postage stamp is a very interesting definition of racketeering." And that wasn't the only interesting legal interpretation the FDLE was making. Around the time of the house visits, Orlando's firefighters' union found itself under investigation over the legality of its leave bank, the fund set up to give members days off for political activities. The bank had been established under Mayor Hood, not Mayor Dyer, but no matter: the union was accused of colluding with the Democrats in city hall to set up an illegal slush fund for the presidential campaign. It may have been no coincidence that right before the investigation was launched, the state firefighters' union switched its presidential endorsement from Bush, whom it had supported in 2000 out of deference to his brother, to John Kerry. Within days, the FDLE launched a raid on city hall, television news crews in tow, and confiscated several computers. Intimidating interviews of union officials followed, including another instance in which an FDLE officer crossed his legs and tapped his finger against his ankle pistol.

The case went precisely nowhere. A grand jury looked at the allegations and concluded no laws had been broken. But the FDLE persisted with its investigation, which so terrified the local union head, Steve Clelland, that he did not dare attend a Kerry rally in Orlando, even in off-duty hours, for fear of perpetuating the accusation that he was abusing his office. Normally, the firefighters might have been instrumental in marshaling thousands of votes, but in the run-up to November they, like the voters' league, fell deathly silent. Mayor Dyer, for his part, wrote to Florida's attorney general asking him to get the FDLE off his back. Dyer's bad luck, though, was that he had himself run for the attorney general's job, making an adversary, if not an outright enemy, of his successful Republican opponent, Charlie Crist. Crist refused to issue an opinion either way.

Such was the vicious tone set for the grand presidential battle of 2004. And Florida's dirty, racially tinged tactics were not restricted to Orlando. A month before the FDLE swung into action in Orange County, Glenda Hood tried to revive the felon purge list that had been the object of such scandal four years earlier. Hood's office swore that the new list, forty-eight thousand names in all, was free of the glaring errors that had plagued its predecessor. County officials and voting rights activists, though, were not so sure. First, the new list was prepared by the consultancy firm Accenture, which had donated twenty-five thousand dollars to Republican candidates in Florida, and was based largely on figures provided by the Bush-beholden FDLE. Second, it was being thrust on the counties without warning five months before election day. That might sound like a long time, but given the tight schedule that under-resourced county officials had to follow, it meant in practice they would have little or no time to check the names for accuracy. CNN and the ACLU sued for access to the list, won their case, and discovered in short order that it was, once again, top-heavy with African Africans, including roughly two thousand ex-felons who had had their voting rights restored and should not have been purged at all. Most startlingly, the list included only sixty-one Hispanic names, a suspiciously tiny number set against the size of either the general Latino population or the Latino prison population. The fact that Florida's Hispanic voters lean Republican—largely because of the influence of the

Cuban exiles in Miami—was not lost on the state's major newspapers, which kicked up such a stink that the purge list was abandoned within days of being made public.

Hood tried her luck in numerous other ways. She insisted the counties put Ralph Nader's name on the ballot, despite a court order declaring his candidacy papers invalid. Nader ended up being a negligible factor in the election, but memories of his spoiler effect on the Democrats in 2000 were still vivid. (The issue was eventually resolved by the Florida Supreme Court, which ruled in Hood's favor.) She also directed county election supervisors to throw out registration forms where applicants had signed a statement declaring themselves U.S. citizens but forgot to check a citizenry box elsewhere on the form. Again, it was widely assumed that new registrants, especially recent immigrants and lower-income voters, would lean heavily Democrat.

Hood also campaigned hard to get rid of what limited manual recounts Florida's DRE machines could provide. When the courts told her she couldn't simply ban recounts, she came up with a devious rewrite of her original ruling. She decreed that the state would permit analysis of the computerized machines' internal audit logs in the event of a close race, but in case of any discrepancy, the counties would go with the original count. In other words: we will do recounts, but if the recounts change the outcome we will disregard them. Since the fifteen counties using DREs were predominantly urban and Democrat-leaning, and since recounts tend to help the majority party, this too was seen as a blatantly one-sided maneuver. "She is the political mouthpiece of Jeb Bush, a true partisan using her office to the best possible advantage of the Republican Party," the Democratic congressman Robert Wexler, an election reformer embroiled in a high-profile lawsuit with the state, said shortly before the election. "She is the mechanism Jeb and George Bush have employed to do everything in their power to make Florida a Bush state. And she doesn't care what people think, because she's not accountable to them." Unlike her predecessor Katherine Harris, Hood was appointed, not elected.

Similar suspicions of blatant partisanship also swirled around

Ohio's secretary of state, Kenneth Blackwell, whose own questionable decision making generated umpteen predictions in the media
that he would become the Katherine Harris of 2004. He, too, was a
Republican in a Republican-run state. Like Harris four years earlier,
he, too, was cochair of the state Bush campaign. To compound the
conflict of interest, he actually spent quite a bit of election season,
when his role called for him to be *super partes*, mustering support for
his own prospective run for the Ohio governorship in 2006. For all
that, the newspapers were a little off the mark to compare him with
the cartoon-cutout practitioners of Florida's electoral politics.
Blackwell was smarter and a lot more ambitious than Harris, and far
more autonomous and unpredictable than Hood. After all, he had
resisted the lobbying charms of Ohio-based Diebold and its enthu-
siastic, Republican fund-raising chief executive, Wally O'Dell, when
he canceled plans to go through with a major statewide buy of
DREs. He also ruled that Ralph Nader had not collected enough signatures to qualify for the Ohio ballot, to the frustration of some of
his fellow Republicans who wanted to split the anti-Bush vote.

Some of Blackwell's decisions, though, were real peaches. In early
September he sent a directive to county election officials telling
them to reject voter registration forms unless they were "printed on
white, uncoated paper of not less than 80 lb. text weight." Since
many lower-income, urban new voters (read *Democrats*) were pulling
forms out of the newspapers, whose pages were neither white,
uncoated, nor as heavy as he specified, the directive was viewed as
a blatant mechanism to trip up supporters of the opposing party.
Blackwell eventually rescinded the order, but not for three crucial
weeks, in which time an unknown number of otherwise valid registration forms were discarded. He also decreed, a few weeks before
the election, that provisional ballots would be counted only if they
were cast in the correct precinct. That, on its own, might not have
seemed excessively partisan—although provisional votes are more
commonly required by transient, more typically Democratic voters.
What made Blackwell's ruling worse was that it was accompanied by
a flurry of incidents in which door hangers and flyers printed on

official-looking paper gave voters in Democrat-leaning urban areas the wrong information on where to vote. Some people received phone calls telling them their polling place had been changed, when it hadn't. After a federal district court struck down Blackwell's ruling in late October, saying the secretary of state "apparently seeks to accomplish the same result in Ohio in 2004 that occurred in Florida in 2000," Blackwell flatly refused to comply, calling the judge a "liberal . . . who wants to be co-secretary of state." Blackwell eventually won the fight on appeal.

There were other run-ins between political operatives and the law, some of them involving criminal allegations. In Las Vegas a former employee of a pro-Republican voter-outreach firm triggered an FBI investigation after he testified that he had seen his boss systematically tear up and discard completed registration forms from declared Democrats, processing only those from Republicans. The former employee had retrieved a handful of the destroyed forms from his boss's garbage can to substantiate his account. The owner of the outreach company was a certain Nathan Sproul, the former head of the Republican Party in Arizona and a prominent member of the Christian Coalition, who shrugged off the incident as a minor aberration in an otherwise incident-free multistate operation. Las Vegas, however, was not the only place where his consultancy firm, Sproul and Associates, ran into trouble. In Oregon one of his employees admitted to a television interviewer in Portland that he, too, "might have" torn up Democratic registration forms, while in Medford, in the south of the state, Sproul employees were accused of trying to pass themselves off as members of a nonpartisan organization as a way of obtaining permission for a registration booth at a public library. In West Virginia there were complaints that Sproul workers were passing themselves off as opinion pollsters, asking people about their preference for president, then offering to register only those who said they favored President Bush.

It wasn't just Republicans who dabbled in nakedly partisan tactics. In Colorado a disenchanted volunteer for a pro-Democratic group, Moving America Forward, described how she and her fellow volunteers were instructed to ask voters whether they supported Ken Salazar, a Democrat, for Senate, or his Republican opponent, Pete Coors. If the answer was Coors, they were to say thank-you and walk away. If the answer was Salazar, they were to offer an absentee ballot form. This was less serious than the allegations against the Sproul workers, since it did not involve the destruction of completed forms, but it hardly fell into the realm of fair play. Some prominent Kerry-supporting groups sought to distance themselves from such tactics, saying they were the doing of an irresponsible minority, emphatically not endorsed by the organization, and detrimental to the cause. Most likely, neither side could legitimately claim much moral high ground. If there were fewer abuses—or, at any rate, fewer complaints—on the Democratic side, it was partly because of a near-universal, if flawed, preelection perception that greater turnout would automatically favor the Kerry campaign. In other words, if they cheated less, it wasn't because they didn't want to, but because they felt they didn't need to.

The 2004 election, as we now know, did not result in the meltdown many people predicted, largely because Bush's margin of victory was just comfortable enough to prevent litigation or more than background rumbles about the reliability and veracity of the result. It is nonetheless a compelling election to study, because the irregularities, glitches, and attempts at cheating cannot be waved away, as they were in 2000, as the anomalous consequence of a vote-by-vote fight to the finish. Aside from the exceptional emotional investment in the outcome—something generally regarded as a good thing in elections—what we saw unfold was something approaching *American democracy as usual*. The fact that everyone was on maximum alert for another Florida only meant that the material gathered was richer and the picture more complete. Each outrage might not, on its own, have made more than a marginal difference. Taking everything together, though, the electoral landscape was hardly a pretty sight.

In Denver, Republican election lawyer Scott Gessler admitted that his party routinely called up supporters who had requested absentee ballots and suggested they go to the polls and cast a provisional ballot as well, the hope being that at least a handful of them would have their votes counted twice. This he referred to as "gaming the system"—one tiny but significant legal step away from out-and-out fraud. All across the country, voters reported that operatives of both parties had called them and urged them to throw away their absentee ballots, citing bogus administrative reasons. Fox News, the cable news network cheerleading for Bush, put out an erroneous report warning students that if they registered to vote on campus rather than at home they might be committing a felony. The administrators, meanwhile, were playing their own games. In Milwaukee, the mayor, a Democrat actively campaigning for John Kerry, put in a request for 260,000 extra ballots for city residents in anticipation of high turnout, especially in the heavily Democratic black-majority wards, only to be rebuffed by the county executive, a Republican who was equally active in campaigning for George Bush, saying it was a needless waste of resources.

Such were the routine weapons of electoral combat. Two things, though, made the 2004 election a little out of the ordinary. The first was the mishmash of new rules and standards rushed into service because of the breakdowns four years earlier. In some states, especially ones like Arizona with relatively progressive election laws already in place, this worked out just fine: registration cards were sent promptly to new voters, absentee ballots were mailed out on time, and provisional ballots were handled professionally and quickly. Other states, however, experienced bureaucratic backlogs, carelessness, and at least the suspicion of deliberate obstruction of certain voter groups. Florida was, once again, the nation's poster child for electoral dysfunction. The predominantly Democratic voters of Little Haiti in Miami complained that in many cases they were either sent no registration card at all, or that duplicate cards arrived without warning with the wrong party affiliation. Registration drive organizers in black neighborhoods reported that there was little or no trust of the provisional balloting system. Their assumption was that if they had been left off the voter rolls, it was no accident, and the prospect of their provisional ballots being recognized was next to zero. Some of this sentiment was based on paranoia rather than provable fact, of which there was a noticeable shortage. It was certainly true, though, that acceptance of provisional ballots varied wildly around the country—as low as 8 percent in Oklahoma and as high as 77 percent in Colorado and Ohio.

The other thing that made 2004 different was the threat of terrorism, which was both a genuine cause for concern and also a pretext for further political jockeying. John Ashcroft, the U.S. attorney general, started talking about the threat of disruptions to the election as early as May, and his warnings were echoed during the summer by Condoleezza Rice, the national security adviser, and Tom Ridge, director of Homeland Security, who took the additional step of floating the notion of postponing the November vote in case of an attack. To at least some security experts, like the veteran CIA analyst and trenchant Bush critic Ray McGovern, this public grandstanding did not smack of wise precaution so much as reckless hubris hinting at the dismantling of the electoral system itself. Even if the threat was genuine, McGovern and others asked, what purpose did it serve to alarm the electorate without more specific information? Why talk of postponing the election when a presidential contest is not one election so much as fifty-one (one for each state, plus the District of Columbia)? Even if there was an incident in New York, or San Francisco, or St. Louis, or all three, why couldn't the vote be deferred in the affected precincts and allowed to continue everywhere else, if nothing else as a mark of defiance against the perpetrators of the violence? The House of Representatives clearly agreed with this line of argument, because, in a rare refusal to follow the Bush White House's lead, it voted 419-2 to deny any agency or individual the authority to postpone a national election.

Terrorism popped up periodically as a theme on a local level, too. In Palm Beach County, Florida, the hapless Theresa LePore was fighting for reelection as Palm Beach County's election supervisor in late August when, on the day of the contest, sheriff's deputies suddenly showed up at her office, surrounded the building with squad cars, and erected barricades marked "do not cross." Normally speaking, this would be deemed illegal, because the office was doubling as a polling station, and polling stations are supposed to be fully accessible and free of any police presence. In this case the deputies' arrival seemed particularly inappropriate, because county residents were voting for a new sheriff as well as a new election supervisor, suggesting a direct conflict of interest. It also looked bad because of the emotions riding on LePore's race. With mistrust of the machines and her office's handling of them a key election issue, many of her opponents were voting absentee and delivering their ballots in person; the closure of election headquarters was thus a direct impediment to getting their votes cast. (For reasons best known to LePore, her absentee ballot design had the voter's party affiliation printed on the return envelope, an invitation to targeted foul play by rogue postal workers or partisan county election staff.)

According to the sheriff's department, the episode arose in response to a possible terrorist threat. A local television station said the concern was something akin to the Madrid train bombings that had taken place on the eve of Spain's national election five months earlier. But the source of this supposed threat was never identified, and the very idea that West Palm Beach, Florida, would be the focus of a major international terrorist conspiracy defied belief. LePore ended up losing her race, against a declared election reformer with heavyweight backing from nationally prominent Democrats, but by a much narrower margin than expected. Susan Van Houten of the Palm Beach Coalition for Election Reform asked incredulously: "We're talking about one of the most hated politicians in the country, and she almost wins?"

In some states, such as Georgia, fear of terrorist sabotage was invoked as one more reason, alongside trade secrecy, why the public should not have access to the audit logs and other data generated by electronic voting machines. In Ohio on election night, a purported terrorist alert was the reason cited in Warren County, outside Cincinnati, for locking down the county administration building and barring reporters and independent observers from watching the vote count. County officials said they had received word from an FBI agent of a threat ranking 10 on a scale of 1 to 10. The agent in question was not named, however, and the FBI subsequently said they knew nothing about a terror threat on Warren County that night or any other night.

Throughout the 2004 campaign season, electronic voting machine malfunction remained an abiding theme. Certainly, the failures were not as spectacular as some over the previous two years, but that in and of itself was not necessarily grounds for reassurance. It just meant Diebold and the other companies had eliminated some of their most elementary mistakes—some, but not all. In August, Sequoia proudly showed off its new paper-trail system to California lawmakers, only to realize once the demonstration was under way that the computer was making elementary arithmetical mistakes on its Spanish-language setting. This was the system Sequoia was planning to deploy less than three months later in the election in Nevada, where it had already been certified for use. During preelection logic and accuracy testing, observers in Riverside County, California, and Palm Beach County, Florida, said they saw the Sequoia tabulation system crash multiple times—something the counties themselves sought to deny. The same observers reported at least a dozen more crashes in Riverside on election day itself. In North Carolina a tabulation system in Cartaret County made by Unilect turned out to have a far lower vote-holding capacity than advertised, leading to the irretrievable loss of about 4,500 ballots on election night and, once the dust had settled, a push in the state legislature to introduce a Nevada-style paper trail. In one precinct in Franklin County, Ohio, just outside Columbus, a computer error awarded 3,893 nonexistent votes to George Bush, a mistake that was quickly rectified but nevertheless raised suspicions, among those inclined to be suspicious, of a broader vote-stacking conspiracy.

These were just the highlights. Verifiedvoting.org, the voting rights group founded by David Dill of Stanford University, tracked more than twenty-three thousand complaints about e-voting on election day, and another eleven thousand complaints thereafter. As in previous elections, many voters said they pressed the button for one candidate, only to have the name of another pop up on the screen. Others complained of screen freezes, machines abruptly taken out of service, and other glitches, prompting worries that votes were either improperly recorded or lost when the terminal where they were stored went down. Given the nature of DREs and the secrecy surrounding their workings, it was impossible to know what impact these incidents had on the accuracy of the vote count, just as it was impossible to tell whether any given irregularity was a simple glitch or a deliberate spanner thrown into the works.

State and county officials were quick to hail the performance of their pricey systems. Georgia's secretary of state, Cathy Cox, claimed her state had witnessed its most accurate election ever, with only a 0.39 percent undervote. Others, though, were not so sure. Roxanne Jekot examined the printouts from four precincts in different Georgia counties and found that the undervote rate had been listed as 0 in every case. In a different category dubbed "# Times Blank Voted," however, the failure rate was as high as 8 percent, casting serious doubt on Cox's claims. Did this make any difference to the outcome? Where the presidency was concerned, almost certainly not. But as Kim Alexander of the California Voter Foundation commented: "People shouldn't confuse the absence of a meltdown with a success." And what was true of electronic voting was true of the election as a whole. A report by Electionline.org, the online arm of the Election Reform Information Project, concluded a few weeks after the election: "[W]hile the margin of victory exceeded the margin of litigation, it did not exceed the margin of concern."

Perhaps the single most disorienting factor in the 2004 election, and the one giving rise to the greatest number of theories that the vote was stolen, was the failure of the exit polls. These were conducted not by the Voter News Service, which had gone out of business in the wake of its own failures in 2000 and again in 2002, but by Mitofsky International, a hitherto respected private firm. Starting in the early afternoon of November 2, Mitofsky's numbers suggested that John Kerry was cruising to victory, with winning margins in

Ohio, Florida, Pennsylvania, and other swing states. Shortly before the polls closed on the East Coast, Kerry's prospects looked sweeter still, leading to great excitement at the scene of the Democrats' planned victory party in Boston. (Terry McAuliffe, the party chairman, punched the air outside his hotel and shouted, to nobody in particular: "He [Kerry] is a rock star. We're going to win, baby!")

In the weeks that followed, numerous pseudoscientific analyses and a couple of bona fide statistical studies asserted either that exit polls never lie (not true) or that the divergence between the polls and the official result were so stark as to be beyond the realm of statistical possibility. We don't know exactly what went wrong, partly because Mitofsky has not made all of its data public, but we have a pretty good idea. We know, for example, that there were too many women in Mitofsky's samples. We also know that Mitofsky's pollsters worked on a state-by-state basis, not county by county, so they had to make certain statistical assumptions about voting patterns in places where they were not present. Since almost every political analyst in the country assumed higher turnout would translate into a Democratic victory, it is quite likely that Mitofsky made the same mistake. The groundswell of Republican support in the rural counties of southern Ohio, say, was not anticipated, nor was it invented.

The problem with a lot of the "Kerry won" arguments was that their proponents were allowing wishful thinking to cloud their analysis and thus cherry-picking apparent anomalies and inconsistencies only in the states where a smallish shift could have altered the outcome. They did not, as a rule, look at the question of consistency from one voting system to another, or from one state to another. Had they done so, they might have seen a more compelling argument for the genuineness of Bush's victory. Not only did the president end up with three million votes more than his challenger nationwide, something even the wildest theorists couldn't find an argument to counter, but state by state, he also tended to outpoll Republican Senate and gubernatorial candidates, while Kerry ran quite a bit *behind* his fellow Democrats in much of the country. That's a pattern that screams weak candidate, not wronged winner.

Ohio became the focus of much of the anxiety, and much of the suspicion, largely because it was the last state to report preliminary results on election night, and because its twenty electoral votes were enough on their own to swing the final result one way or the other. Here, too, though, some of the statistical data inconveniently challenged the conspiracy theorists. First, Bush's margin of well over one hundred thousand votes proved well-nigh unassailable, even after a recount that was requested, and paid for, by the Libertarian and Green parties. That kind of number can't easily be created out of thin air by electronic tabulation machines, especially in a state relying almost exclusively on recountable paper ballots. Second, Kerry did too well in certain key areas to support any argument that his votes were suppressed according to some prearranged grand plan. In Cuyahoga County, in and around Cleveland, Kerry's margin of victory turned out to be forty-two thousand votes greater than Al Gore's in 2000. He also won in Stark County, around Canton, a bellwether part of the state that Gore had lost four years earlier.

None of this, of course, excuses the multiple failings of the electoral system or the overt attempts, big and small, to deny voters the chance to exercise their democratic rights. Perhaps the best way to regard the election in Ohio is not as another Florida, an exceptionally dysfunctional state subject to exceptional pressures, but rather as a thoroughly *unexceptional* place, where the problems distinguished themselves only by being subjected to extraordinary scrutiny. Ohio was far from the only state where the bureaucracy of elections, despite plenty of advance warning, could not cope with high turnout. (The *Charlotte Observer* said some places in the nonbattleground Carolinas looked "like Soviet bread stores, with lines spilling onto sidewalks and wrapping around buildings.") It was far from the only state where precincts suffered chronic voting machine shortages, or where those shortages were suspected of having been engineered deliberately for partisan advantage. In many parts of the country, voters reported that it took them as long as nine minutes to complete their extensive multirace ballots. Many precincts, however, needed to rush them through two or three times that fast to cope with the crowds. In some places, voters were given a time limit—three or perhaps five minutes—or they were constantly pestered by election workers to hurry up. That, on its own, almost certainly led to voters making mistakes, or leaving certain parts of the ballot blank even though they had a preference to express.

The greatest cause of concern in the Buckeye State was the lack of voting machines in urban precincts. In Franklin County a study by the Democrats of the House Judiciary Committee concluded that 125 machines listed as available on election day were never deployed. These were withheld almost exclusively within the city of Columbus, leading to average waiting times of anything from two to seven hours. Some precincts had noticeably fewer machines on hand than they had had for the primaries, when turnout was far lower. In the more conservative suburbs, by contrast, machines were more plentiful and there were hardly any lines at all. The single worst location was the campus of Kenyon College, in Knox County outside Columbus, where just two machines were set up to service thirteen hundred voters. (At that rate, assuming each voter took just three minutes to complete his or her ballot, it would still take more than thirty hours to get through everyone.) Some Kenyon students said they had to stand in line for ten hours. About sixty of them were still waiting to cast their ballots at 2:30 on Wednesday morning, by which time some of the networks had already called Ohio, and the election, for George Bush.

It was also in the inner cities where a preponderance of other problems were reported. In Toledo's Old West End, a predominantly African American, overwhelmingly Democratic part of town, one precinct opened ninety minutes late without explanation. A student observer said he saw more than one hundred people walk away in frustration, many of them commuters in a rush to get to work. The same precinct later ran out of regulation number 2 pencils needed to fill out the optical-scan ballots. In the vote count, Sandusky and Perry Counties showed significantly more votes recorded than eligible voters. In ten precincts in Cleveland, obscure third-party candidates did unaccountably well—215 votes for Michael Peroutka of the Constitution Party in one precinct in Cleveland's Fourth Ward, for example, compared with 290 for Kerry and 21 for Bush. The same precinct registered just eight third-party votes in 2000.

Every one of these reported irregularities appeared to be at the Democrats' expense, which explains why the streets of Columbus saw demonstration after demonstration by voting rights activists and disappointed Kerry supporters between election day and the final certification of the results on January 6. Kenneth Blackwell came under repeated fire from reporters and activists, who felt he was personally responsible. But Blackwell simply washed his hands of most of the problems. "County boards are responsible for buying their own voting machines," he told a news conference. If certain urban precincts had too few machines, it was the counties' fault, not his.

A San Francisco–based group called Votewatch took Blackwell at his word and proceeded to request copies of key election records from as many of Ohio's eighty-eight counties as possible. In the end, just twenty-six cooperated. None met Votewatch's requests in full. Six provided what Votewatch described as "primarily accurate copies of originals with a few missing non-critical items." In ten cases, less than half the critical items—signature rosters, ballot accounting reports, accumulated totals reports, and so on—were missing. In another ten cases, more than half the critical items were missing. It wasn't that the counties were necessarily withholding material. The impression gleaned by Votewatch was that the records were kept either shoddily or not at all, leaving the public "to blindly trust a process that has never undergone a thorough and independent audit." Like many of the more thoughtful analysts of the 2004 election, Votewatch's founder Steven Hertzberg said the most worrying aspects of the process were not the problems that came to light, but rather those that remained unknowable. "There are no criteria for distinguishing fraud from error, and no criteria for quantifying either," Hertzberg said. We can guess, in other words, that some part of George Bush's margin of victory in Ohio was improperly obtained. But we will never know for sure.

• • •

Two episodes in the 2004 election's aftermath illustrated just how much the atmosphere had soured, not improved, since the debacle of 2000. The first was yet another impossibly close statewide contest in Washington State, where Slade Gorton and Maria Cantwell had sat out their Senate recount so patiently four years earlier. This time it was the governorship at stake instead of the Senate. The Republican candidate, Dino Rossi, found himself 261 votes ahead after the initial count and was still a tantalizingly slim 42 votes in the lead after a machine recount. But then the Democrats requested, and obtained, a manual recount, at the end of which their gubernatorial aspirant, Christine Gregoire, inched ahead by 129 votes out of more than 2.9 million cast.

The fair play and civilized tone that had seemed so charmingly quaint in 2000 (prompting Gail Collins of the *New York Times* to joke that in Washington State they like to age their ballots in oak casks) was noticeable this time only by its absence. Both sides hired lawyers and launched public relations campaigns to spin the six weeks of recount uncertainty to their respective advantage. While Rossi was ahead, his staff argued that he had already won and it was time to put the electoral process where it belonged, in the past. Once he found himself trailing, however, he became inordinately interested in the niceties of balloting procedure, counting rules, and the competence of the state's election administrators. The Gregoire campaign, naturally, took a diametrically opposite tack, finding all kinds of irregularities to complain about until they realized the race was breaking in their favor.

The key to the election was King County, home to quintessentially liberal Seattle, where Rossi seemed determined to sniff out a Democratic plot hatched in the city's coffee bars and quirky postmodernist landmarks. Soon there was talk of dead people voting (true, but only in a small handful of unconnected cases), of activist judges making shockingly partisan rulings (such as a decision to allow a batch of overlooked, but valid, votes in King County to be included in the official tally—hardly a shocker), and of election officials allowing their personal political biases to sully the process. The Republican faithful amassed outside the statehouse in Olympia and made unflattering comparisons between their gubernatorial race and the blatant vote fraud under international scrutiny in the first round of Ukraine's ultimately rerun presidential election. It wasn't hard to understand Rossi's frustration after what amounted to little more than an administrative coin toss. In broader political terms, though, a lot of his accusations were plain silly. As a Democrat in a solidly Democratic state, Gregoire should never have had to fight so hard for every last vote and wasn't guilty of fiddling with votes so much as running a spectacularly lousy campaign. Sure, the electoral system turned out on close inspection to be deeply dysfunctional, but could anyone seriously say they were surprised?

The most promising anomaly unearthed by the Rossi campaign was King County's provisional finding that it had thirty-five hundred more votes than voters. Believing they had found their very own Holy Grail, the Republicans rushed to court on the eve of Gregoire's inauguration to claim that the election wasn't over after all. The judge, however, made clear he was in no mood to disrupt the orderly transition of power and laid out a timetable suggesting a legal battle lasting months if not years. King County, meanwhile, set to work "reconciling" its records and quickly reduced the vote gap from thirty-five hundred to eighteen hundred. The Democrats didn't seem too concerned. They murmured threateningly about examining the records of Republican-leaning counties and suggested that the whole matter should be settled in the (Democrat-controlled) state legislature instead of the courts. A Democratic lawyer, meanwhile, got together with his statistician brother-in-law and found disparities between absentee ballot and touch-screen machine totals in Snohomish County, just east of Seattle, that he said amounted to a "mathematical impossibility" favoring Rossi. Such was the progress of four years. In 2000 neither side could be totally sure who really won but accepted the flawed outcome anyway. In 2004 they fought like dogs and the result remained every bit as uncertain.

The second symptom of the souring national mood was California senator Barbara Boxer's decision to lodge a formal protest against the Ohio election results and force a two-hour debate on the Senate floor before the results could be certified. As Boxer herself conceded, the move was largely symbolic, since she was not disputing the outcome of the election, only the manner of its conduct. Four years earlier no senator had dared raise any objection to the much more dubious assignment of Florida's crucial twenty-five electoral votes, and Boxer felt it was important not to whitewash the system a second time. The problem with her action, though, was that it played right into the hands of the victorious Republicans, who refused to take her objections seriously and chose instead to paint Boxer as some off-the-planet conspiracist lunatic from what Tom DeLay, in the House of Representatives, described as the *X-Files* wing of the Democratic Party.

One of the few Republicans who bothered to speak in the Senate debate, Mike DeWine of Ohio, called Boxer's complaints "wild, incoherent [and] completely unsubstantiated." Vice President Dick Cheney, who presided over the session, spent much of the two hours sitting in a corner talking and laughing with his colleagues. Quite a few Democratic senators looked uncomfortable, too, and none joined Boxer's side in the end-of-debate vote. John Kerry, the most directly interested of the Democratic senators, wasn't even present. Like Dino Rossi, Boxer might have had good reasons for her protest, but in a polarized American political context could do little more than preach to her own choir. Ric Keller, a Republican congressman from Florida, told her to "get over it"—the twenty-first century equivalent of Boss Tweed gloating to his enemies about his less than transparent electoral victories in 1860s New York: "What you are going to do about it?"

Altogether, the Boxer episode highlighted a serious problem for the electoral reform movement in the wake of the 2004 election. Without a clear case of high-level vote theft, how could they capture the imagination of the broader public and make people realize the system was still very far from acceptable? How could they warn of the dangers of another Florida, or worse, without having to wait for another Florida actually to transpire? Regrettably, the reform movement did not help itself by peddling overheated theories about Republican vote theft based on either unreliable or non-existent sources offering no shred of credible evidence. Campaigners might have wanted to believe that the speaker of the Florida House had consulted a software expert on how to rig DRE machines, just as they might have wanted to believe tens of thousands of Kerry punch-card votes were systematically spoiled in Ohio. Because of the Internet, such theories were shared and propagated at lightning speed and took on the illusory appearance of hardened fact. But belief, on its own, was worse than useless, because it exaggerated a situation that was quite bad enough without exaggeration and opened the door to Tom DeLay and everyone else with a direct interest in dismissing election reformers as a bunch of politically embittered crackpots.

What the movement needed was a high-profile public advocate, one who could be authoritative, measured, and above party interest. Kevin Shelley, the California secretary of state who had pointed the way to more rigorous oversight of the electoral system nationally, might have been one such figure, but he became embroiled in a series of personal, and highly partisan, corruption scandals starting in the summer of 2004. Some of the allegations against him were very serious, including the suggestion, later confirmed by a state audit, that he misused federal election funds for his own political campaign purposes. In a few short months, to the delight of his many enemies in the voting machine industry and in county election offices, Shelley was reduced to the political equivalent of cold spit. When he resigned in February 2005, friendless and broke, he was given almost no credit in the California media for the earth-shaking reforms he had overseen.

That in turn portended badly for the broader movement for electoral reform. In a country already disinclined to believe that the system needed much reforming in the first place, Shelley's downfall was interpreted as an indication of how badly he had overreached, in his response to the voting machine vendors just as much as in his approach to political and personal ethics. That in turn made it difficult to imagine someone else taking up the same cause without being tarnished by association. Paradoxically, at a time when the electoral system's true colors were on uncharacteristically gaudy display—which is to say when winning was deemed much more important than fair play and whining considered the province of losers—the opportunities for effective protest and reform could not have been greater. And yet the chances of finding the providential figure the movement so badly needed seemed next to hopeless.

14
DEMOCRACY HERE AND THERE

★ ☆ ★ ☆ ★ ☆ ★ ☆ ★ ☆ ★ ☆ ★ ☆ ★

Absolutely everything is a violation! All these different systems in different counties with no accountability . . . It's like the poorest village in Africa.
—Dr. Brigalia Bam, chair of South Africa's Independent Electoral Commission, in Florida, September 2004

IN THE FALL of 2002, to the great amusement of the wider world, the United States played host to its first-ever international election-monitoring mission. It was not just any mission. The ten-man team from the Organization for Security and Cooperation in Europe (OSCE) included representatives from Russia and Albania—the sort of countries that until just a couple of years earlier, might have reasonably expected to receive lessons in democracy from the United States, not the other way around. "Whatever else it will be, it will be an experience," said Ilirjan Celibashi, the chair of Albania's Central Election Commission, as he left Tirana for Miami in late October.

It was not a large-scale operation. The team stayed just a few days, looking at the conduct of the congressional midterm elections in a handful of Florida counties, writing up a report full of encouragement for the electoral reform efforts then under way, and seeking to nudge them only very slightly further in the right direction. In the technical parlance of the OSCE's Office for Democratic Institutions and Human Rights, this was an assessment mission rather than a full-blown observation. Still, it was received with a bashful silence, bordering on excruciation, on the part of Florida officials who felt obliged to open up their precincts and election tabulation processes to the foreign visitors. The U.S. media hardly mentioned it at all.

Until the Bush-Gore meltdown in 2000, such a mission would have been almost unthinkable. In the late 1990s some OSCE member states had begun to wonder whether it wasn't worth looking at electoral standards in the established democracies as well as overseeing the transition from autocracy to pluralism in the more rugged outposts of the Balkans and Central Asia. At that stage, though, the organization had more pressing things to worry about, like the war in Kosovo, or the grudging approximations to democratic development in Belarus, Uzbekistan, and elsewhere. Looking at questions of voter registration, media access, provisional balloting, and counting procedures in Britain, France, or the United States seemed more like an abstraction than a necessity.

Then the electoral hurricane in Florida blew in, and perspectives began to change radically. Some of the more aggrieved OSCE member-states, especially those in the area of the former Soviet Union with less than sterling records of their own on free and fair elections, began murmuring about double standards and the "politicization" of the vote-monitoring process. In a wide-ranging discussion at a 2002 OSCE meeting on the so-called human dimension—which is to say, democracy, human rights, and free elections—delegates from both Britain and France freely acknowledged that their domestic systems were creaky and outmoded and depended to an unreasonable degree on the good faith of the bureaucrats and volunteers who staffed polling stations and organized the count of poorly secured paper ballots. The United States, however, was considerably less well disposed toward admitting its weaknesses. According to officials who were present at the meeting, American diplomats took umbrage at the idea there was the slightest thing wrong with their elections and certainly did not feel it was the place of economically and militarily inferior nation-states to poke their noses into America's domestic business.

Still, the topic refused to go away. OSCE election officials started adding a number of established democracies, not just the United States, to their mission agenda. They went to France and Turkey. They looked at local elections in Britain in 2003 and were on hand for the Spanish general election, overshadowed by the Madrid train bombings, in March 2004. The organization also commissioned a panel of experts to go over the 1990 Copenhagen Document, which had established the principal of election monitoring in OSCE member-states, and update it in the light of over a decade of practical experience. The idea was to determine the exact expectations for both established and emerging democracies. The panel raised a number of points that should have been troubling to politicians and election administrators in the United States, especially in regard to such fundamental principles as transparency and accountability. The fact that its report was roundly ignored in the United States, at least beyond the diplomatic community, probably came as little surprise to anybody, but it also set the stage for an increasingly acrimonious international showdown over the future of democracy.

The report laid out at least eleven OSCE commitments on which the United States could be said, without excessive overinterpretation of the fine print, to be falling short. These included the failure to set national standards for voting procedures, the failure to appoint impartial election administrators (the Katherine Harris/Glenda Hood factor), the widespread failure to register voters efficiently, the failure to provide adequate numbers of voting machines in many lower-income areas, and the lack of a "proportionate" policy on removing and restoring the voting rights of convicted felons. Quite a few of the unmet commitments related to third parties: the habit in the United States of freezing them out of the media, including candidates' debates, and generally denying them, in the words of paragraph 7.10, an "adequate opportunity . . . to inform the public about their candidacies and political programmes."

The United States was not, of course, the sole offender against the OSCE commitments, nor was it by any stretch of the imagination the worst. Still, the unavoidable reality of its shortcomings turned out to be a very convenient means by which the least savory of its fellow member-states could deflect attention from their own electoral malpractices. Already in late 2003 Russia and Belarus were hammering away at the double standards argument to push for a full-blown observation of the 2004 U.S. presidential election. Their indignation only grew as a series of political earthquakes rattled several former Soviet states in the course of 2004. First, the OSCE's reporting on Georgia triggered street protests and the eventual demise of Eduard Shevardnadze's government. Then it produced a critical evaluation of the Russian presidential elections, to the fury of President Vladimir Putin. The OSCE was also among the first and most prominent international organizations to denounce widespread fraud in Ukraine's presidential poll, leading to the so-called Orange Revolution, a second election, and the eventual defeat of Moscow's favored candidate, Viktor Yanukovich. By the end of 2004 the Russians were calling for urgent reform of the entire OSCE apparatus and threatening to veto funding of some of its core programs if the criteria for election monitoring were not overhauled—which is to say, watered down and reduced to little more than a technical checklist ducking the most important questions of fairness and transparency. "The Organization is not only ceasing to be a forum uniting States and peoples but, on the contrary, is beginning to drive them apart," Russia's foreign minister, Sergei Lavrov, warned OSCE ministers in Sofia in December 2004. "We need to devise a system of objective criteria [for elections] to be applied throughout the OSCE area . . . Election monitoring is not only ceasing to make sense but is also becoming an instrument of political manipulation and a destabilizing factor."

The OSCE, which had consistently built on the sterling work it had done in post-Communist Eastern Europe during the 1990s, was caught in the middle of what was effectively a revival of the Cold War rivalries between Moscow and Washington, with both sides merrily sacrificing principle to protect their own interests and find new ways to denigrate each other. Early on, the organization had understood something only imperfectly appreciated by some of its member-states: that the conduct of elections was a matter of political will as much as technical niceties. Now it found itself in a world where the lack of political will was not only affecting individual member-states; it was also poisoning relations between one bloc of members and another. The fault line ran a little farther east than the old Iron Curtain now that Poland, Hungary, the Czech Republic, and a handful of others had come under the European Union's sphere of influence. But the pivot between East and West, as it had been in the Cold War, and before that in the Europe of the post-Napoleonic order, was Vienna—by coincidence, the city where the OSCE had its headquarters. The organization did not want to capitulate to the increasingly autocratic tendencies of Putin and his regional allies. But neither did it want to pretend that the problems in the United States did not exist.

Just as it was agonizing about what kind of mission to send to the November presidential election, the OSCE then ran smack into a Republican versus Democrat partisan catfight. In July 2004 a Democratic congressman from Florida by the name of Alcee Hastings was elected president of the OSCE's parliamentary assembly, and he used the position as a bully pulpit to call for a full-scale observation of the Bush-Kerry contest—with a presence in many if not all the states, intensive monitoring of polling procedures by hundreds of observers, oversight of campaign practices and media campaigns over a period of months, and so on. The OSCE realized there was no way to acquiesce to such a request without being seen to be out to get the Republicans, especially in Florida, so it settled instead on a compromise: a "targeted observation mission," which would be bigger than a simple assessment but would restrict its focus to a handful of key states on election day.

In the end, nobody was happy. The OSCE appealed to European Union (EU) countries to supply observers, but almost no EU government wanted to risk the wrath of the United States. The entire EU ultimately provided just two people, both from the Netherlands. In the United States, meanwhile, the OSCE had to struggle mightily to gain access to polling stations. The State Department said it could not help, because elections were managed at state, not federal, level. The National Association of Secretaries of State said it could do little, because the rules of polling station access were set at county, not state, level. And individual county election supervisors, with a few honorable exceptions, were understandably reluctant to expose their inadequacies to global scrutiny. As a result, the OSCE presence was patchy, at best, with a less than ideal presence in Florida, Ohio, and Pennsylvania, and no presence at all in Georgia, where its requests for access were turned down cold. (Similar problems were encountered by other, less official international delegations, such as the Fair Elections International initiative organized by Global Exchange, which sent teams to five states but enjoyed only sporadic official cooperation.)

The OSCE put out a preliminary report right after the election, one of whose chief complaints, unsurprisingly, was the inadequacy of polling station access to nonpartisan observers, a requirement under the 1990 Copenhagen agreement. It also expressed concern about the lack of consistency in handling provisional ballots, described HAVA unflatteringly as "a work in progress" that did not properly address the need for minimum national standards, and made an oblique but unmistakably critical reference to "allegations of electoral fraud and voter suppression." As the winter months went by and the final document failed to appear—largely because OSCE officials, conscious of the minefield they were walking through, felt it had to be word-perfect—the pseudo-Cold War rhetoric started up again in earnest. The Belarusians began to accuse the OSCE of shying away from criticizing the United States. U.S. officials, afraid of the exact opposite, demonstrated their growing nervousness by placing a number of what one OSCE official described as "inappropriate phone calls" concerning the final report.

It wasn't that the report was likely to say anything that had not already been said by domestic critics of the U.S. electoral system. (It was not yet out at the time this book went to press.) And it wasn't as if the OSCE's concerns were likely to wind up on the front page of the *New York Times*. The point was that because of the tug-of-war between the Americans and the former Soviet states, the very democratic principles that had given the OSCE meaning and authority as an institution risked being sacrificed on an altar of geopolitical rivalries, in which everyone's position could justifiably be accused of bad faith. Neither side had sufficient incentive to clean up its act so long as it could argue that the other was behaving just as badly, if not worse. "It would be good if the United States became an example of effective follow-up," one senior OSCE official said somewhat wistfully in the wake of the 2004 election. It was clear, however, that he viewed such a scenario as less than likely. All the players, in the end, were uninterested in openness and accountability. They wanted to be allowed to indulge their bad political habits unhindered by the outside world. Hence the warning of an admittedly lowly figure on the international stage, the secretary-general of the Albanian foreign ministry, that the Copenhagen Document, and all the optimism it expressed about the future of democracy following the fall of the Berlin Wall, risked being reduced to "Legoland, a virtual reality."

There were other ways in which the dysfunctions of the U.S. electoral system spilled out into the international arena. Just as much as the countries of the former Soviet Union enjoyed bashing the United States for their own domestic political ends, they also made sure they undertook a careful examination of U.S. practices to see if any of them had any applicability back home. The process was, perhaps, not unlike the copycat vote thievery of America's big-city political machines in the late nineteenth century, the difference being that the pseudodemocracies of the Commonwealth of Independent States could use the United States not only as a role model, but also as a pretext and a cover. After all, if a voting technology was good enough for the greatest democracy on the planet, why shouldn't it be good enough for a tin-pot autocracy in Central Asia?

By far the biggest enticement was electronic voting. Perhaps some portion of public opinion in the United States could be induced to believe DREs were the harbingers of a free, fair, accurate, and speedily delivered electoral future, but it seems highly doubtful that legislators and government leaders in Kazakhstan were seduced by that particular line of argument. Rather, the Kazakhs gave every appearance of trying to sneak e-voting in by stealth, as though they were handling something volatile, explosive, and borderline illegal. E-voting was introduced into the country's March 2004 electoral law only on the third reading in its parliament, without prior public debate. Even then the percentage of precincts mandated to adopt it was left vague. The final decision on deployment was left to a special state committee, but nobody seemed to want to participate in the deliberations, and the committee remained unconstituted until five days before the first round of parliamentary elections in September 2004. In the end, about 10 percent of the country voted on electronic machines, but because of concerns that some of the machinery might not work, paper ballots were also universally available. Most voters chose paper.

Computer voting has also proved popular with officials in Russia, who have been developing electronic tabulation technology for years. In December 2004 poll watchers who were mistrustful of machine tabulators in Severodvinsk on the Arctic Coast established a major discrepancy between their unofficial manual tallies and the machine counts—something that hinted at the possibility of more widespread problems around the country. Ironically, when election officials in Severodvinsk were barraged with demands for a manual recount, they initially resisted, saying: "This isn't America!" In Armenia a Russian observer on an OSCE mission was overheard advocating e-voting to the local officials whose activities he was supposed to be observing, not influencing. He was sharply rebuked by his superiors, not only because it wasn't his place to make any such recommendation, but also because OSCE officials tend to view electronic voting with deep suspicion.

Most e-voting systems, after all, circumvent the OSCE's standard observation practices, because they remove the evidence from plain sight. They also transfer an uncomfortably large degree of authority over the election process, as the U.S. example clearly demonstrates, from official bodies with at least some public accountability to secretive, for-profit private companies.

In many parts of the world e-voting found itself on the agenda not just because of some vague inspiration from the United States, but also because one U.S. company or another was actively pushing it. By far the most active of the major U.S. vendors in this regard was ES&S, which by early 2005 was boasting on its Web site of a presence in the UK, France, Portugal, Guam, Canada, Japan, Hungary, and those redoubts of global democracy, Palau and the Mariana Islands. Not all of ES&S's ventures ended happily, however. In May 2000 Venezuela took the drastic step of postponing its presidential elections with just three days to go, because the electronic tabulation system provided by ES&S to count the country's optical-scan ballots was manifestly unable to cope with the tasks required of it. A preelection test of the ES&S software revealed deep flaws in the system and was denounced as "a simulation of a simulation." The Venezuelan military dispatched a special plane to Omaha, Nebraska, to pick up ES&S executives in a last-ditch attempt to fix the problems. ES&S claimed Venezuela had made an overwhelming number of last-minute changes to the candidate lists for lower-order races; the Venezuelans claimed ES&S had simply promised more than it could deliver (the same charge would later be made against the company in Miami-Dade County, Florida), and failed to provide the flashcards needed to boot up the ballot-reading machines accurately. ES&S was not the only culprit. Another U.S. company, Pennsylvania-based Unisys, had made mistakes in its handling of the voter registration database, and a Chicago-based contractor was late printing the ballots. Regardless of where the fault lay, though, the election postponement was regarded as a major embarrassment all around—newspapers called it the "mega-flop"—and ES&S was booted out of the country shortly afterward.

ES&S's experience in the Philippines, where it has manufactured many of its voting machines, was hardly any happier. It supplied sixty-eight optical-scan card readers for regional use in elections in 1996 and again in 1998, but was roundly criticized when the machines managed to read only 50 ballots per minute, not 150 as advertised, and could not even manage those accurately. In 2000 the company was asked to supply a registration database system and put forward a proposal for a centralized vote tabulation system, only to be accused of trying to pull strings in a rigged bidding arrangement and giving equipment demonstrations that were considered so unsatisfactory they were tantamount, in the words of one official from the Philippine Commission on Elections, to "a mock-voting system, and not a workable prototype system." Three years later the entire move to electronic voting in the Philippines was shut down by the Supreme Court, because the commission was found to have shown "reckless disregard" of its own bidding procedures. By that stage, ES&S, acting as part of a consortium with Unisys and others, had fallen from favor in any case. Even before the Supreme Court intervened, it had lost out to a rival consortium including election.com, the e-voting arm of the Accenture consultancy group, which happily accepted payment of more than one billion Philippine pesos— roughly $20 million—and then, after the contract was canceled, refused point-blank to return the money.

Curiously, the president of ES&S's international department continues to list his exploits in both Venezuela and the Philippines as "accomplishments" on the company Web site. Then again, that's par for the course for the looking-glass world of international voting-machine sales, which is just as unruly and chaotic as the domestic variety, only with the added twist that public opinion in the purchasing countries frequently finds itself reeling in disbelief at the sheer unscrupulousness and mediocrity of manufacturers hailing from the most economically advanced, most techno-savvy nation on the planet. To complicate matters, the money to buy the pricey computerized systems is frequently furnished in the form of loans from U.S.-influenced institutions like the Inter-American

Development Bank, with the active encouragement of the State Department. Pro-democracy activists in Latin America and elsewhere can justifiably ask if the purpose of the exercise is really to streamline and update their voting systems, or just to line the pockets of U.S. corporations. Some also fret about the possibility—much discussed but never substantiated—that some form of long-distance political control is being attempted. In the absence of hard evidence, and given the machines' woeful general lack of reliability, that suspicion has to be chalked up to paranoia, which is as widespread a phenomenon globally as it is domestically. That said, it is not paranoid to believe that at least some of the e-voting systems have been built to be rigged by players within the client country itself. We know that, because evidence has emerged in what is by far the biggest of the overseas e-voting markets, Brazil.

Brazil began experimenting with DRE technology in 1996 and by 2000 had extended it across the entire country, a vast operation involving the purchase of four hundred thousand terminals to serve some 117 million eligible voters. This put Brazil far ahead of the rest of the e-voting world, including the United States, and effectively turned the country into what Pedro Rezende of the University of Brasilia has described as a "guinea techno-pig." The equipment, a basic PC-compatible screen with a keyboard attached, was sold first by Unisys, then by a Brazilian company called Procomp. In 1999 Procomp became a wholly owned subsidiary of none other than Diebold, then making its first foray anywhere into the e-voting market. (Diebold wouldn't get into the U.S. elections business for another two years.) The operating system, bearing the distinctly Orwellian name VirtuOS, was developed by a Brazilian company called Microbase, which later took advantage of its contacts with American corporations and foreign trade institutions to clinch a major inventory software contract with the U.S. Army.

From the start, critics like Professor Rezende issued warnings about the dangers of an inaudible system, especially in a country with a colorful history of *bico de pena*, or vote fraud, and two long, painful interruptions to democracy itself during the twentieth century. At first, the skeptics were dismissed with the usual rhetoric about the inherent trustworthiness of new technology. But then, in 2000–2001 a major scandal erupted over the Brazilian senate's internal electronic voting system, and the entire political establishment was forced to sit up and pay attention. The affair began with the impeachment of an incorrigibly corrupt senator named Luiz Estevão and an ensuing attempt by rival factions within the senate to taint each other by association with him. At one point the president of the senate, Antonio Carlos Magalhaes, casually boasted to anticorruption prosecutors that he knew exactly who had voted to remove Senator Estevão and who had not. Unfortunately for him, the prosecutors were surreptitiously recording the conversation and subsequently leaked it to the media. Months of investigation followed, including a technical assessment by experts from the State University of Campinas, which showed that the senate voting system—designed by another Brazilian firm called Elizeu Koop—was compromised by eighteen different backdoors and other vulnerabilities. Not only was it possible for someone to spy on the supposedly secret votes of individual senators, but it was also possible to cast votes for members who were not present, with or without their authorization. A series of dramatic public confessions, first by another influential senator and then by the senate's head of technology, confirmed that the fix had indeed been in on the day of the impeachment vote. Elizeu Koop, the software company, originally insisted its system was "100 percent secure"; Brazilian television later reported that the software had instead been "built exactly to specification." In other words, the security holes appeared to have been ordered by the senate leaders themselves. Magalhaes resigned before he could be impeached, as did two of his high-profile senate colleagues.

The scandal had an incendiary effect on preparations for Brazil's 2002 presidential election. The clamor for a voter-verified paper audit trail, treated up to that point as a fringe issue that could safely be ignored by the country's election officials, grew so loud that a new law mandating just such a feature on every DRE terminal was

enacted almost immediately. The argument did not end there, however, and much of 2002 was taken up with wrangling over just how
many of the back-up voting slips should be examined on election
night. The supreme court justice responsible for overseeing the election didn't want to examine any of them, but he also knew that
public opinion needed placating. In the end, he agreed with the
Brazilian congress to make a random selection of 3 percent of all
votes cast and double-check them on a strictly nonbinding basis.
The 2002 election turned out to be a watershed that brought the
left-wing populist Lula da Silva triumphantly into office, but
election night was not without its glitches. About four hours into the
tabulation process, Lula's vote total suddenly dropped from more
than a million to minus forty-one thousand. Technicians at election
headquarters in Brasilia rebooted the system, and within minutes
Lula's original total was restored. Some of his supporters remained
suspicious, however, especially when he failed to win on the first
round, as many opinion polls had predicted. (He went on to win easily in the runoff.) Was the sudden vote drop the result of a format-
ting error, as the official explanation had it, or was something more
sinister at work?

Throughout the 2002 campaign season, electoral officials had
bad-mouthed the idea of a paper trail, calling it "unnecessary" and
"stupid," and positively gloated when a bag of back-up voting slips
was shown on the television news one morning sitting stranded on
the roof of a city bus shelter. What more proof did anybody need—
assuming the abandoned slip bag had not been planted to make a
political point—that the paper trail was a security liability, not an
asset? The closest race of 2002 was for governor of the Federal
District in Brasilia, in which the two leading candidates were separated by less than 0.1 percent of the vote amid multiple accusations
of voting irregularities and fraud. When the trailing candidate
requested an audit of the paper voting slips, the national election
board turned him down, saying there was no reason not to trust the
machine tally. As would later prove to be the case in the United
States, Brazil's electoral officials were clearly determined to prove

that electronic voting was failsafe and resisted with all their might any measure that risked casting doubt on their assertions.

There is nothing about e-voting that makes it inherently disastrous. On the contrary, as with all other kinds of technology, there is a right way to go about it as well as a wrong way, and in some parts of the world, at least, it has been handled with a heartening degree of caution and appropriate oversight. In Australia, the electoral commission in the Australian Capital Territory, the area in and around Canberra, has developed an open source code for DRE machines in conjunction with a private company hired through Australian National University. At all stages the public authorities, not the private company, have called the shots, and the software, which runs on the Linux operating system instead of Microsoft Windows, has been posted on the Internet, where it is freely available for public analysis and comment. So far, the Electronic Voting and Counting System, or eVACS, has received rave reviews. Security is a significantly reduced concern, because everyone can see exactly what measures the system has taken to protect its own integrity. That said, there has been considerable carping that eVACS does not include a paper trail, with a number of computer scientists saying it is never a good idea to do without a paper backup, however good the system might be.

The story has not been dissimilar in India, where 380 million voters cast their ballots on more than a million electronic machines in May 2004. These were rudimentary devices, running on very simple code and allowing each individual voter to enter his or her choices by pushing one of a line of buttons running down the side. The software was hardwired onto a microprocessor that could not be reprogrammed, and the machines were trip-wired so they would shut down if anyone tried to force them open. Election officials had the power to override the machines at any time if they suspected thugs were attempting to take over a polling station or cast multiple ballots by force. The machines were not only relatively cheap and easy to use, but they were also immune to many of the chain-of-custody or networking problems that have arisen in the United States. Once the balloting was over, election officials hand-carried the machines one by one to a central counting center. That's not necessarily a model other countries would want to emulate, but in India it ensured that any hanky-panky was limited to single machines or precincts and could not be extended over a wide geographical area.

In Europe the prime motivation for e-voting has not been the elimination of fraud, but rather the hope that the growing problem of voter apathy can be stemmed by making the process quicker and more painless. The Netherlands has been a pioneer in developing DREs, although it has focused almost exclusively on ensuring the technical solidity of the machines and given little or no thought to security measures or a paper backup. A Dutch system was almost introduced in Ireland in time for the June 2004 local and European elections, but the Irish Commission on Electronic Voting decided at the last minute to reject the system, because its experts had not been allowed to access the source code and test it to their satisfaction. That caution was widely welcomed by voting rights activists on both sides of the Atlantic. Britain, meanwhile, has forged its own path through a series of pilot projects overseen by its newish Electoral Commission. Since 2002 the commission has tried a bit of everything in selected constituencies—all-postal voting, e-voting, even Internet and text-message voting. Most computer experts are extremely dubious about voting online because of the Internet's singular vulnerability to hackers and infections, as was demonstrated by a trial Internet election in Toronto in January 2003 that was sabotaged by a Slammer worm attack. At the time of this writing, the British appear to be shying away from it, too.

One unexpected success story, curiously, has been Venezuela. After its bruising experience with ES&S, the National Electoral Council commissioned two young Venezuelan computer engineers to devise their own DRE system from scratch, complete with a paper audit trail. The opposition to President Hugo Chavez was skeptical at first, worrying that some kind of scheme was being cooked up and noting that the government owned 28 percent of one of the engineers' two companies. But when the system faced its first big test, in the tightly contested August 2004 referendum on Chavez's future, it came out looking remarkably good. The National Electoral Council conducted a paper audit of 192 machines, chosen at random, and found a variation of just 0.02 percent from the machine count. The Carter Center, which was in Venezuela to monitor the election, conducted its own paper audit of 359 machines from 150 different precincts. Although its error rate was considerably higher, closer to 1 percent, it, too, failed to find any major discrepancy. The referendum was not entirely flawless: in several hundred precincts, each of the two or three machines in a given polling station recorded exactly the same number of votes in favor of Chavez's retention, something the opposition said was a clear sign of vote rigging. An almost equally large number of precincts, however, manifested the same phenomenon in reverse, with clustered machines showing an identical number of no votes. The Carter Center consulted two foreign statisticians who said the coincidences, while odd, were within the realms of probability. In the end, the center chose not to imbue them with much significance, particularly since they appeared to cut both ways. Overall, the center reported, "the automated machines worked well and the voting results do reflect the will of the people."

Such confidence in the outcome would have been impossible, of course, without a paper trail, especially in a country like Venezuela where mistrust of governmental authority runs deep and an authoritarian populist leader like Chavez can be assumed to try everything he can to stay in power. There is an inescapable lesson for the United States here, especially for highly charged presidential battleground states like Ohio and Florida. If you want the public to have confidence in the results, you need to be able to demonstrate that the vote has been conducted fairly and counted accurately. It doesn't seem unreasonable to expect U.S. states interested in deploying and promoting DRE systems to rise to Venezuela's electoral standards. Or does it?

15

THE DEMOCRATIC FUTURE

★ ☆ ★ ☆ ★ ☆ ★ ☆ ★ ☆ ★ ☆ ★ ☆ ★

Imagine a political system in which votes are bought and sold freely in the open market, a system in which it is taken for granted that people will buy all the votes they can afford and use their power to get more money in order to buy more votes, so that a single magnate might easily outvote a whole city. Imagine a situation in which elections have become a mere formality because one or a few individuals are owners of a controlling number of votes. Suppose that nine-tenths of the members of the community are unable to exert any appreciable influence. Suppose, moreover, that the minority is entitled to very little information about what is being done. That is what the political system would be like if it were run the way business is run.
—E. E. Schattschneider, The Semisovereign People *(1950)*

DOES REPRESENTATIVE DEMOCRACY have a future, or is it just a phase we've been going through? The question may sound overblown and melodramatic at first. But it starts to seem quite a bit more pertinent on careful examination of America's political landscape in the wake of the 2004 presidential election.

Take the question of electoral disengagement—or, to use a less delicate term, voter ignorance. This is far from a new problem, but in 2004 it reached such disturbing heights one had to wonder how many people had the remotest idea what they were voting for. As a survey by the University of Maryland's Program on International Policy Attitudes (PIPA) showed, a majority of those who reelected George Bush did so on the basis of completely erroneous assumptions. More than 70 percent of his supporters continued to believe that Iraq had either weapons of mass destruction or a major program for developing them, despite official reports coming out right and left flatly stating the contrary; 75 percent believed Saddam Hussein had provided substantial support to al-Qa'ida, and 63 percent believed concrete evidence had been found to prove the link. Anywhere from half to three-quarters of the Bush electorate also believed the president was behind the Kyoto Protocol on global warming, that he was in favor of an international war crimes tribunal—even after he explicitly stated his opposition in one of the televised campaign debates—that he supported an international land mine treaty, and that he advocated stricter environmental and labor protections in international trade agreements.

Canvassers in the field found an equally dispiriting lack of familiarity with the central themes of the election, or indeed with the basic nuts and bolts of politics itself. Christopher Hayes, who spent time in the Wisconsin suburbs for the Kerry campaign, was stunned to discover seniors who not only could not differentiate between the two candidates' positions on Medicare (which is what he was there to explain), but did not even understand that health care was a political issue in the first place. Despite repeated attempts, he found it impossible to get through to them that their prescription charges and deductibles had anything to do with the political leanings of the man in the Oval Office. As Hayes asked in a remarkable account of his experiences in *The New Republic:* "How can undecided voters evaluate a candidate on issues if they don't even grasp what issues are?"

Some misconceptions were the result of willful deception promulgated by the White House, which was then insufficiently checked by a cowed Democratic opposition, and amplified by an excessively pliant, if not downright sycophantic, mainstream news media. Just

about the only point of agreement between Bush and Kerry supporters in the PIPA survey was that the administration itself had promoted the idea of a link between Saddam, al-Qa'ida, and weapons of
mass destruction. Granted, only one side of the political fence was
taken in by the deception, but that in itself was scant grounds for
comfort. It just meant that objective reality had become a partisan
issue: insist on the facts, and you immediately risked being identified
as an elitist, morally lax, latte-drinking liberal snob abhorrent to
"mainstream America," whatever that might be. One senior White
House official told writer Ron Suskind that facts were the province
of a minority henceforth to be known as the "reality-based community." "We're an empire now," he added, "and when we act, we create
our own reality." In other words: ignorance is to be encouraged as
long as it is politically useful. That's a defensible position, in a
realpolitik sort of way, but it is certainly not a democratic one. To
quote that august member of the reality-based community, Thomas
Jefferson: "If a nation expects to be ignorant and free, it expects what
never was and never will be."

The concept of empire, and with it the resurgence of a radical,
belligerent form of nationalism in response to the September 11
attacks, has a lot to do with the emergence of this new cultivation of
ignorance. Political disengagement is no longer to be regretted now
that America is waging an open-ended war against shady enemies
who could pop up anywhere, any time; it is to be embraced and even
encouraged. Proper debate and questioning of the country's leaders
are to be deplored and derided as unhelpful to the cause.
Appropriate political participation, in this view, comes down to
little more than cheering on the home team. The constant drumbeat of war, or the threat of it, is perhaps the only way to explain
how Bush's reelection campaign could dare take the unprecedented step of admitting only Republican Party loyalists to rallies and
speeches and having private security guards muzzle and expel any
hecklers who slipped through the screening process. At one appearance by Vice President Dick Cheney in New Mexico, attendees
were even required to sign a loyalty oath. Such tactics go against all

recognizable definitions of democratic speech, but the really unnerving thing is that much of the country appears to be fine with them. When Glenn Hiller, a graphic designer from West Virginia, obtained a spare ticket to a local Bush rally and interrupted the president to ask a question about Iraq's nonexistent weapons of mass destruction, he was not only drowned out by boos and insults from the rest of the crowd and shown the door. He also lost his job, because his employer found his behavior embarrassing. Free speech has thus been reduced to partisan fodder, too.

One of the problems with any form of expansionist nationalism is that a government that is willing to disregard the views and interests of other countries seen to be standing in its way is going to be tempted, sooner or later, to disregard the views and interests of dissenting domestic constituencies, too. This is the British scholar Anatol Lieven's gloomy, but far from implausible, assessment of the likely fallout from the Iraqi conflict:

> If the result of U.S. entanglement in the Middle East is also unprecedented embroilment in a series of conflicts, then this is likely to severely damage not only U.S. global leadership, but the character of U.S. nationalism and perhaps of U.S. democracy. Prolonged war may bitterly divide American society and create severe problems for public order, as it did during the Vietnam War; and it also may help push the U.S. government in the direction of secretive, paranoid, authoritarian and illegal behavior.

I should make absolutely clear that such authoritarianism is still a considerable distance away, and far from inevitable. The United States remains a country where free speech and the free exchange of ideas remain highly valued and largely intact. The problem with politicizing free speech, though, is that it can become a first stage toward assailing and eventually dismantling it. If America is attacked again on any scale—and expert opinion tells us such an attack, or series of attacks, is almost inevitable—the likelihood is that restrictions contained in the 2001 Patriot Act, or in the extralegal treatment of detainees deemed "enemy combatants," are going to start looking like very small potatoes indeed.

Even before September 11, there were worrying structural cracks in the architecture of American democracy, which have become only more pronounced since. Chief among these, perhaps, has been the merger of government with the aims and ambitions of corporate business—put another way, the triumph of special interests over the public interest. The United States went through something similar during the era of the robber barons in the late nineteenth and early twentieth centuries, and the results were not pretty: vast gulfs in wealth between rich and poor, mass disenfranchisement of the working class, racial segregation in the South, and, eventually, the bursting of the economic bubble and ensuing miseries of the Great Depression. In 1959 Seymour Martin Lipset wrote a famous paper arguing that middle-class stability was an essential component of a successful democratic system and indeed was the finest achievement of industrial capitalism. Wealth inequality was poison, he argued, because it ate at the very core of that achievement, and the stability that went with it, leaving only predators and their prey to fight over diminishing political spoils.

That inequality has expanded dramatically since the late 1970s, as corporate executive compensation packages have skyrocketed, even as manufacturing jobs with benefits and union protections have vanished and been supplanted by low-wage, low-security service-sector work. The richest fifth of U.S. households now enjoys more than 50 percent of the income, while the poorest fifth get by on just 3.5 percent. The average after-tax income of the top 1 percent is sixty-three times larger than the average for the bottom 20 percent— both because the rich have grown significantly richer and also because the poor have grown poorer; about 19 percent poorer since the late 1970s. The middle class, too, has been squeezed ever tighter. Every income group except for the top 20 percent has in fact *lost* ground in the last thirty years, regardless of whether the economy has boomed or tanked. The Republicans were certainly the most forthright in embracing these trends, starting with Ronald Reagan's trickle-down economic policies. But both major parties, with their increasing reliance on corporate donations to finance ever more expensive and empty election campaigns, share responsibility for them.

The regressive Bush tax cuts, the proposed privatization of social security, and the dramatic plunge back into deficit spending are just the latest, if also some of the most extreme, measures indulging the new generation of robber barons at the expense of the middle class. The political effects of this are not to be underestimated: nothing works like economic insecurity, especially when it is overlaid with fear of a hidden terrorist enemy, to create an alienated, resentful, and paranoid electorate that is willing to sign up for a radical nationalist program promising new forms of self-empowerment. The fact that this empowerment is largely illusory, strengthening and enriching only those forces undermining the system in the first place, is something they may not realize until the worst damage is already done.

The dangers of overpowerful corporations and the purchase of the political class were well appreciated at the time of the United States' foundation. Indeed, one can argue that the greatest achievement of the political system in the early years of the republic was not the separation of church and state, but rather the separation of economic and political power. As E. E. Schattschneider argued in his classic work, *The Semisovereign People,* the American system broke the monopoly stranglehold that economic elites had held over the political sphere during much of the history of Western civilization and opened society up to vigorous competition over both power and the accumulation of wealth. Conservative political thinkers have always liked to argue that capitalism and democracy are alternate manifestations of the same phenomenon, but really they are best defined, and are most efficient, in apposition to each other. "The public interest resides in the no man's land between government and business," Schattschneider wrote. "The public likes competitive power systems. It wants both democracy and a high standard of living and thinks it can have both provided it can maintain a dynamic equilibrium between the democratic and capitalist elements in the regime."

It is that equilibrium that is now getting lost again. And, strangely, the American public barely seems to be noticing. In the populist Republican mind-set that has now become predominant, business and the economy have magically been placed in a category beyond politics, a bit like health care in the minds of those Wisconsin seniors. It doesn't get discussed on talk radio, and receives only a fraction of the campaign-trail attention devoted to gay marriage, say, or stem-cell research, or fantasies of bombing terrorists back to the Stone Age. It is as though unfettered corporate capitalism were already a given—as though Americans had already accepted they were, as Thomas Frank felicitously put it in the title of one of his books, "one market under God."

Naturally, these issues all weigh heavily on the electoral system, which may be the centerpiece, indeed the very symbol, of democracy in action but is, first and foremost, a mirror held up to the totality of the political apparatus. We've seen that over and over in this book; in many ways the story of vote fraud and electoral malfeasance is also the story of democracy in the United States. One of the great fallacies of U.S. public life, which has been applied to countless developing countries, especially those being courted as U.S. allies, is that plentiful elections in and of themselves are a sign of robust democratic health. The premise does not hold in the United States, just as it does not hold in Haiti, or El Salvador, or Serbia— countries where the quality of civic life has fluctuated wildly even though elections have taken place on a more or less regular basis. Elections lose at least some of their democratic meaning in an unstable economy, or a civil war, or a society lacking basic infrastructure, or one where much of the voting population is fed government propaganda or no information at all. There is a long history of autocrats using elections, and the blessings they bring in the form of U.S. and other outside support, as a front to perpetuate themselves in power. Political scientists refer to this as "façade democracy," or, in a slightly less rigid setting, "casino democracy"—the concept being that you give voters just enough winning opportunities here and there to keep them interested, but that the house always finishes on top. In his international mediation work, Jimmy Carter likes to observe that "peace is more than the absence of conflict"; likewise, democracy has to be more than the ritual of holding elections.

One has to wonder if the sheer profusion of elections in the United States, with their tepid-to-dismal turnout rates, do not themselves sometimes act as a front, an excuse to say everything is fine and never mind the system's glaring shortcomings. Certainly, elections are little more than a charade in congressional and state legislative races where the district boundaries have been gerrymandered to death and super-protected incumbents may face no opponent at all. They are almost as farcical when complex, barely comprehensible ballot initiatives are put before the voters, and their outcome is determined almost exclusively according to the size of each campaign's television advertising budget. In the old days, political parties and interest groups would ply voters with alcohol and hard cash to win their support; now they bombard them with carefully crafted images in their living rooms. The platform may have changed, and what they do may no longer be deemed illegal, but the upshot is the same. Too often, the electorate is bought off, pure and simple.

One big difference between the present and the era of the original robber barons is that we now live in an integrated world economy where decisions taken in the United States more than ever affect the fortunes of the entire planet. The history of universal suffrage has been, primarily, a struggle for the enfranchisement of the non-propertied working classes. But now the United States, along with much of the rest of the developed world, has divested itself almost entirely of manufacturing jobs and many of its industrial labor needs to the Third World, where of course the underlings of the new global capitalism have no say in U.S. elections whatsoever. This is one reason why the leaders of both parties, Democrat and Republican, have become so much more conservative over the past half-century. It is difficult to envision success for a progressive, socially inclusive agenda when the domestic constituency for such a program is shrinking (not least because of the failure of the new service-sector underclass to organize as a significant political force), while those most in need of it—overseas factory workers, and the vast armies of the unemployed and underemployed struggling beneath them— have no sway other than the power of long-distance appeals for dignity and justice.

Is this what democracy in a globalized world should look like, or is there some major inconsistency here? Where are the political means to address the fact that four-fifths of the planet have access to only one-fifth of its riches? Since American politicians need to appeal only to American voters and address American concerns, and since only the top half of the socioeconomic heap turns out, U.S. elections have become, in essence, a choice between differing visions of elite self-interest. Granted, the competition between these visions can become quite heated, and the elitism is always larded with hefty doses of populist rhetoric to make it seem more far-reaching than it really is. But the genuinely broad political questions of our age—the architecture of global capitalism, and the role of the United States within it—are almost never subject to serious challenge. The fact that the United States has been without a serious economic or geopolitical competitor since the end of the Cold War has not exactly helped to spur debate. Not that there is anything inevitable about this: Ross Perot's anomalous third-party candidacy in 1992 showed how the North American Free Trade Agreement could fire up a national debate, and the anti–World Trade Organization protests in Seattle seven years later demonstrated an unmistakable public passion for global as well as local perspectives on jobs, labor rights, and capital investment. Periodically, renegade politicians of all stripes, not just from third parties, attempt to bust out of the straitjacket of politics as usual. It is not inconceivable that one day one of them will succeed. But as long as the corporate and political elites remain closely intertwined, the prospects for bringing these issues to the forefront of electoral politics remain dim.

It is often said, especially by those whose countries have felt the force of indelicate U.S. foreign policy interventions, that everyone in the world, not just Americans, should have a say in choosing a U.S. president. Occasionally, impish voices in Central America and elsewhere will suggest *only* foreigners should get to choose. In fact, the rest of the world exerts a greater influence than is sometimes recognized. The problem with that influence, though, is that it tends to come from select groups of highly organized expatriates who represent very specific policy agendas, not the totality of political opinion in their home countries or regions. The anti-Castro Cuban exiles in Miami exert control out of all proportion to their numbers, largely because they are a swing constituency in a swing state, with money to burn and voters they can mobilize to great effect. The American Israel Public Affairs Committee and other pro-Israeli groups have lobbied the political establishment so successfully that Congress and the White House not only continue to side unambiguously with Israel in the Middle East crisis, they are in fact more narrowly supportive of the hard-line Israeli position than public opinion in Israel is. Obviously, these trends are not good news for Palestinian Americans, or Jewish opponents of the Israeli settler movement, or Cuban moderates who believe dialogue, not confrontation, is the best way to foster economic and political reform. But as long as the presidential Electoral College continues to give undue weight to specific groups of voters in key battlegrounds, and as long as success in political lobbying depends on how much money interest groups can contribute to candidates' campaign funds, fairness, wisdom, and due consideration of multiple viewpoints are never going to be the driving forces of U.S. foreign policy.

What this adds up to is a crisis of political representation in an economically lopsided world. Its effects can be felt in many countries, not just the United States. The era of mass-movement parties is waning almost everywhere. In its place is a new form of politics in which voters, wooed by television imagery more than substantive policy debate, cluster around specific issues or abstract concepts like "morality," not a comprehensive ideological program. They behave, in other words, more like consumers than party supporters, making for a much more fragmented and uncertain political climate. The defects of the U.S. system are of particular significance in this overall shift, because the United States is the Western democracy most beholden to corporate money in its campaigning and lobbying practices, and because its electoral apparatus is so manifestly not equal to the tasks expected of it. Too often, as we have seen, it fails to attract voters to the polls, to give them real issues and competitive races on which to offer their opinions, and to make sure that their votes, once cast, are counted fully and accurately.

The good news is that at least some of these problems are fixable, given an appropriate degree of political will. There is often an expectation, at this stage of a book, for an author to take stock of the problems laid out in the preceding pages and, with all the wisdom he or she can muster (a pipe often helps), start proposing brilliant and original solutions. But in the case of the U.S. electoral system, there is little mystery about what needs to be done. The question has been examined over and over by think tanks, politicians, academics, election lawyers, voting rights groups, and computer experts. Since the 2000 election we have had the National Commission on Federal Election Reform, cochaired by Gerald Ford and Jimmy Carter; the Constitution Project's Forum on Election Reform, based at Georgetown University; the Voting Technology Project, jointly run by CalTech and MIT; as well as testimony and analysis from the Center for Voting and Democracy, the Election Reform Information Project, and countless smaller and less prominent groups. All of them, interestingly, have come up with more or less the same set of prescriptions (which makes one wonder why more of their excellent advice has not been heeded).

All agree that the system needs greater uniformity of standards, including clear rules for registration, absentee balloting, and provisional voting, as well as more rigorous oversight of both polling-station procedures and the purchase of voting machinery. No one defends the appointment of partisan election officials, much less the notion that the secretary of state of Florida or Ohio should be helping to run one of the presidential campaigns. There is consensus that optical-scan machines are the most cost-effective and least error-prone voting system, at least for now. Everybody wants accountability, starting with the possibility of meaningful recounts. If DREs are the future, everybody wants to make sure the software is properly vetted and accessible to government experts. Outside the elections business itself, there are few, if any, objections to the idea of a voter-verifiable paper audit trail.

One can add some broader, but no less sensible suggestions. Among them:

- Abolish the Electoral College and institute direct election of the president. Since this would involve changing the Constitution, one could take the opportunity to state clearly in Article II that final authority in presidential elections rests with the voters, not state legislatures. It might also be worth loosening the rules on election timing slightly, so if a major problem arises there would be no constitutional bar to rerunning an important vote, either partially or completely.

- Give candidates above a certain threshold equal, unpaid access to the broadcast media so they can explain and debate their ideas. The bipolar disorder of the major parties slinging meaningless mud at each other has got to stop. Better still, introduce full public financing of election campaigns, and tell all those corporate lobbyists to get in line like everyone else.

- Allow same-day registration, and have every precinct plugged into the same nationwide voter database to make sure people don't try to vote in more than one state.

- Institute a "none of the above" option for voters in all races, so blank portions of the ballot do not become an invitation to fraud. This would also help distinguish undervoting caused by machine error from the intentional variety.

- Institute automatic restoration of voting rights to felons who have completed their prison sentences. Consider allowing certain classes of felons to vote even behind bars, or leave it to the judge's discretion (but show no mercy to convicted election fraudsters).

- Make election day a holiday, move voting to the weekend, or allow voting to take place over several days, as is already happening in many states with early voting.

- Set up a public agency to develop source code for future DRE machines. Get a government agency, either state or federal, to negotiate a bulk purchase price on the machines to prevent gouging or corruption by county officials.

- Make every county conduct a compulsory recount of a sample 1 percent of the ballots, selected at random, to ensure statistical consistency. This already happens in some jurisdictions, but it should happen everywhere. Better still would be targeted recounts focusing on areas where voting was closest.

- Encourage greater experimentation with instant runoff voting and even proportional representation at local or state level, just to let people know there are other ways of doing things. The United States welcomes innovation in other spheres, so why not in elections?

The problem with these recommendations, of course, is that they remain meaningless unless someone in authority is prepared to take them seriously. One can imagine the objections: Too much government! Too much federal control over the states! Too much state interference with the counties! It is perfectly justifiable, of course, to ask whether certain steps wouldn't be too far-reaching for local authorities to swallow in one gulp. One can, and should, quibble over the details. But the broader point is this: the administration of elections, and of democracy more generally, is a question of political culture, to which all technical and logistical considerations are subordinate. If that culture is complacent, or rotten, or both, then all the technical solutions in the world won't make the slightest bit of difference. Change is hard. It's not as simple as replacing an outdated computer system or patching a malfunctioning piece of software. It involves shifting ingrained attitudes and changing institutional habits and trampling on certain people's deeply held, if misplaced, sense of personal pride and achievement. Fostering awareness and understanding of the problem certainly helps. But political cultures don't tend to change quickly unless something drastic happens—an unavoidable crisis, like the 2000 election, or some form of official behavior so egregious that everyone agrees it must stop and never be allowed to recur. Even then, the change is not necessarily for the better, especially when the two major parties have an ingrained interest in defending their duopoly more vigorously than the integrity of the process. And it would be foolhardy to predict how and when such a turning point might come again. It is clear by now that the response to the meltdown in Florida has been insufficient and, in many respects, wrongheaded. Chances are, some of the more blundering post-Florida missteps will be corrected before the 2008 presidential election. But others, most probably, will not.

What is true about improving the mechanics of voting is true also more generally. It is impossible to predict how long the intense love affair between corporate and political elites will maintain its ardor, or what effect it will have on America's long-term democratic health. History suggests that these things go in cycles. The orgy of deregulation in the 1920s eventually gave way to the New Deal and the emergence of a progressive Democratic Party, albeit one that was encumbered with a reactionary, segregationist wing in the South. One can envision a similar transformation taking place among the modern Democrats, especially if the model of top-down leadership, disdainful of its own core constituencies and overly dependent on corporate fund-raising, keeps losing them elections. Equally, one can imagine that the Bush Republicans will run out of steam sooner or later, if only because they are well on the way to bankrupting the federal government and demolishing the economic prospects of their grassroots supporters.

Worldwide, there are moves to conceive of a new, more democratic global future. The Seattle protests of 1999 were one starting point, even if they failed to establish much of a political foothold, and the annual World Social Forum, conceived as a counterweight to the business elite's World Economic Forum in Davos, is an intriguing incubator of ideas and alliances—what Carlos Fuentes refers to as the creation of "a new legality for a new reality." The rapid expansion of the European Union, meanwhile, is helping to redefine the contours of the old nineteenth-century nation-state and laying out a vision of political organization that is at once more regionally based and also more interdependent. Both the EU and China show signs of turning into full-fledged competitors to the United States, in the economic if not also the diplomatic sphere, which might go some way toward redressing some of the imbalances in the current hegemonic system.

That said, the immediate prospects for a more representative, more democratic future do not look good. In the Arab and broader Muslim worlds, frustration over the West's failure to encourage political pluralism or heed the concerns of impoverished populations has been a major spur to anti-Americanism and, at the fringes, has helped fuel the growth of radical militant groups like al-Qa'ida. By responding to the atrocities of September 11 in an almost exclusively confrontational and militaristic manner, the United States has only hardened the battle lines, extended conflict to places and peoples where no conflict previously existed, and squeezed the moderate middle on all sides. Whatever else this is, it is not a recipe for a more representative, more interactive, more equitable world.

It is also difficult to imagine how a belligerent, our-way-or-the-highway attitude on the part of the United States overseas can possibly lead to a deeper-rooted attachment to democratic ideals at home. I hope I am wrong about that. It would be comforting to think that a new spirit of democratic accountability and transparency could grow from the ground up, starting with pressures exerted by local reform groups and slowly working its way through the county, state, and federal systems. Some of that has already started to happen, thanks to the formation of national and transnational grassroots movements tapping into the mass communication potential of the Internet. Neither history nor established patterns of political behavior, however, argue strongly in favor of the short-term success of such initiatives. Just as the United States uses its geopolitical weight to enforce its will in strategic regions of the world, so, too, political parties understand the power they wield within their own domestic fiefdoms and are generally unafraid to use it. If they want to stack, rig, or steal an election, and they have the means and the infrastructural control necessary to pull it off, they will almost certainly do so, whatever rules are in place. After all, they've been doing it for two hundred years.

NOTES ON SOURCES

★ ☆ ★ ☆ ★ ☆ ★

PREFACE

Among the reactions to my piece on the conservative-libertarian Free Republic Web site was this comment: "It's great to see that the 'Pubbies are finally in the game. It's been discouraging to have to watch the 'Rats continually steal votes in election after election while the 'Pubbies were looking the other way" (posted by "Neanderthal" on October 15, 2003).

For those interested in reading more about the 1996 election in Albania, see the (diplomatically incendiary) report compiled by the OSCE's Office for Democratic Institutions and Human Rights based on its observation mission, http://www.osce.org/documents/odihr/1996/07/1176_en.pdf.

CHAPTER 1

The Carter quotes are taken from his radio interview with Terri Gross on NPR's *Fresh Air* (October 21, 2004). Much of the material on the 2004 election is taken from my reporting for *The Independent* and from the sources elaborated in chapter 13.

The 1946 Kansas City congressional election scandal is described in Estes Kefauver's 1950 Senate committee report on organized crime, among other places. Thanks to Sherry Bebitch Jeffe for her memories of Ex-Lax and the mystery voting-machine malfunction in Baltimore. James H. Gundlach's paper, *A Statistical Analysis of Possible Electronic Ballot Box Stuffing: The Case of Baldwin County Alabama Governor's Race in 2002*, is available at http://web6.duc.auburn.edu/~gundljh/Baldwin.pdf.

The material on the 1975 mayoral election in San Francisco was gleaned from newspaper articles in the *New York Times* and *USA Today*, some of the more general books on Jim Jones and the Peoples Temple (Jeannie Mills's *Six Years with God* and Deborah Layton's *Seductive Poison*), and a conversation with John Barbagelata's son Paul. On the more recent woes of the San Francisco elections office, I used my own reporting for *The Independent*, documents from the secretary of state's office, and coverage in the *San Francisco Chronicle*, particularly Philip Matier and Andrew Ross's reliably well-informed political column. The California Voter Foundation Web site (www.calvoter.org) also contains a useful archive of information and references.

On Lyndon Johnson, nothing touches Robert Caro's masterful multi-volume biography, *The Years of Lyndon Johnson*. His college years and the 1941 Senate race are described in Volume 1, *The Path to Power* (1982; New York: Knopf, 2002). Volume 2, *Means of Ascent* (New York: Knopf, 1990), is devoted almost exclusively to the gravity-defying 1948 Senate race.

For the postscript on Karl Rove, I drew on Melinda Henneberger's profile in the *New York Times* Sunday magazine ("Driving W.," May 14, 2000) and on James Moore and Wayne Slater's *Bush's Brain: How Karl Rove Made George W. Bush Presidential* (New York: Wiley, 2003).

CHAPTER 2

Mona Charen's op-ed appeared in the *Washington Times* on October 25, 2004. George Will's *Newsweek* piece was cited in Frances Fox Piven and Richard A. Cloward's *Why Americans Still Don't Vote and Why Politicians Want It That Way* (Boston: Beacon Press, 2000), which was a valuable spur to many of the ideas in this chapter. The Trilateral Commission report is called *The Crisis of Democracy: Report on the Governability of Democracies to the Trilateral Commission* (New York: New York University Press, 1975). Robert D. Kaplan's "The Future of Democracy" was the cover story in the December 1997 issue of the *Atlantic Monthly*. Benjamin Ginsberg's books include *Politics by Other Means* (New York: Basic Books, 1990), cowritten with Martin Shefter, and *Downsizing Democracy: How America Sidelined Its Citizens and Privatized Its Public* (Baltimore: Johns Hopkins University Press, 2002), cowritten with Matthew A. Crenson. The Cato Institute report, *When Ignorance Isn't Bliss: How Political Ignorance Threatens Democracy*, was published as a Policy Analysis on September 22, 2004, available at http://www.cato.org/pubs/pas/pa525.pdf. On Leo Strauss and the Straussians, I drew largely on two papers in the Spring 2004 issue of the journal *Logos*, Nicholas Xenos's "Leo Strauss and the Rhetoric of the War on Terror," and John G. Mason's "Leo Strauss and the Noble Lie: The Neo-Cons at War." Both are freely available online. I also read Mark Lilla's pieces in the *New York Review of Books* ("Leo Strauss: The European," October 21, 2004, and "The Closing of the Straussian Mind," November 4, 2004.

On the structural failings of the electoral system, issues of turnout, gerrymandering, and the Electoral College, I am deeply indebted to the work of the Center for Voting and Democracy (CVD), whose excellent Web site is at www.fairvote.org. CVD senior researcher Steven Hill wrote an outstanding, highly readable book called *Fixing Elections: The Failure of America's Winner Take All Politics* (New York: Routledge, 2002). I also interviewed CVD's executive director, Robert Richie, and was given an early peek at the organization's number crunching on the 2004 election. The International Institute for Democracy and Electoral Assistance's figures can be found at www.idea.int/vt/survey/voter_turnout_pop2.cfm. A couple of other useful books: Thomas E. Patterson's *The Vanishing Voter: Public Involvement in an Age of Uncertainty* (New York: Knopf, 2002), and Ruy E. Teixeira's oldish but still interesting *The Disappearing American Voter* (Washington, DC: Brookings Institution, 1992). Teixeira, a Senior Fellow at the Century Foundation and the Center for American Progress, continues to write interestingly on electoral politics at the Emerging Democratic Majority Web site (www.emergingdemocraticmajorityweblog.com) and elsewhere.

On the felon disenfranchisement question, the work of Christopher Uggen and his colleagues is a must-read: Christopher Uggen and Jeff Manza, "Democratic Contraction? The Political Consequences of Felon Disenfranchisement in the United States," *American Sociological Review* 67 (2002): 777–803, and Angela Behrens, Christopher Uggen, and Jeff Manza, "Ballot Manipulation and the 'Menace of Negro Domination': Racial Threat and Felon Disenfranchisement in the United States, 1850–2002" *American Journal of Sociology* 109 (2003): 559–605. Courtenay Strickland of the Miami ACLU's Voting Rights Project was very helpful on the Florida angle.

On the Electoral College, other sources besides the CVD included Gary L. Gregg's piece for the *National Review Online*, "Counting the Real People's Vote," posted October 27, 2004; Jack N. Rakove's essay "The E-College in the E-age," which can be found in a collection edited by Rakove titled *The Unfinished Election of 2000* (New York: Basic Books, 2001); and the work of Lawrence D. Longley; see, for instance, *The Electoral College Primer* (New Haven, CT: Yale University Press, 1996, with Neal R. Peirce, updated 1999).

CHAPTER 3

Some of the more provocative interpretations of the Constitution and the origins of American democracy can be found in Alexander Keyssar's *The Right to Vote: The Contested History of Democracy in the United States* (New York: Basic Books, 2000), and in Robert A. Dahl's *How Democratic Is the American*

Constitution? (New Haven, CT: Yale University Press, 2001). Also useful, especially on the Electoral College, is Jack N. Rakove's essay "The E-College in the E-age" (see chapter 2 notes for reference). More traditional readings of the Constitution and the Philadelphia convention include Catherine Drinker Bowen's *Miracle at Philadelphia* (Boston: Little, Brown, 1966), and Max Farrand's *The Framing of the Constitution of the United States* (New Haven, CT: Yale University Press, 1913). The quote from Michael Lind is taken from a January/February 1998 article in *Mother Jones*. On Jefferson and the 1800 election, I relied on Garry Wills's *"Negro President": Jefferson and the Slave Power* (New York: Houghton Mifflin, 2003), and one of his sources, Leonard L. Richards's *The Slave Power: The Free North and Southern Domination, 1780–1860* (New Orleans: Louisiana State University Press, 2000).

On the broader questions of the American system of government, I consulted the following: Richard Hofstadter's *The American Political Tradition* (New York: Knopf, 1948), Daniel J. Boorstin's *The Genius of American Politics* (Chicago: University of Chicago Press, 1953), Louis Hartz's *The Liberal Tradition in America* (New York: Harcourt Brace, 1955), and, most intriguingly, Samuel J. Huntington's *Political Order in Changing Societies* (New Haven, CT: Yale University Press, 1968).

On Andrew Jackson and Jacksonian democracy, the man to read is Robert V. Remini, both *The Election of Andrew Jackson* (Philadelphia: Lippincott, 1963) and *The Jacksonian Era* (Arlington Heights, IL: H. Davidson, 1989). *Jacksonian Democracy: Myth or Reality?* edited by James L. Bugg (New York: Holt, Rinehart and Winston, 1962), is a useful reader on the differing historical interpretations of the era, including an extract from Hofstadter's book and also from Arthur J. Schlesinger Jr.'s *The Age of Jackson* (Boston: Little, Brown, 1953), which is worth reading in its own right.

CHAPTER 4

Much of the voluminous literature on Tammany Hall and the Tweed Ring repeats the same well-worn stories without a great deal of analysis. The best, most intelligent account is probably Alexander B. Callow's *The Tweed Ring* (New York: Oxford University Press, 1966). M. R. Werner's *Tammany Hall* (Garden City, NY: Doubleday, 1928) has the virtue of completeness and reproduces many of the original documents and transcripts. George Washington Plunkitt's oral history, *Plunkitt of Tammany Hall* (recorded by William L. Riordan, New York: McClure Press, 1905), is a gripping read. John I. Davenport's self-published report, "The Election and Naturalization

Frauds in New York City, 1860–1870" (first issued in 1894), contains valuable documentary evidence. On machine politics more generally, the seminal reformist text is Lincoln Steffens's *The Shame of the Cities* (1904; New York: Peter Smith, 1948). Among the more accessible general histories is Fred J. Cook's *American Political Bosses and Machines* (New York: Franklin Watts, 1973).

For the background on the history of voting in the United States, see the early chapters of Eldon C. Evans's *A History of the Australian Ballot System in the United States* (Chicago: University of Chicago Press, 1917) and Joseph P. Harris's *Election Administration in the United States* (Washington, DC: Brookings Institution, 1934). One exhaustive, if dry-as-dust, resource on the history of electoral malfeasance is Chester H. Rowell's 1901 report for the House of Representatives, *A historical and legal digest of all the contested election cases in the House of Representatives of the United States from the First to the Fifty-Sixth Congress, 1789–1901* (Westport, CT: Greenwood Press, 1976).

For general insights into the development of U.S. democracy, the spoils system, and the evolution of big-city machines, I relied on, among others, Hugh Brogan's *Penguin History of the United States of America* (1985; London: Penguin Books, 1990) and D. W. Brogan's *Politics in America* (New York: Harper, 1954).

CHAPTER 5

The story of the 1876 election has been told many times, from many different perspectives; for example, in Keith Ian Polakoff's *The Politics of Inertia: The Election of 1876 and the End of Reconstruction* (Baton Rouge: Louisiana State University Press, 1973), in Sidney I. Pomerantz's chapter-long account in *The History of American Presidential Elections* (Arthur M. Schlesinger Jr., ed. [New York: Chelsea House, 1971]), and in the penultimate chapter of Mark W. Summers's *The Era of Good Stealings* (New York: Oxford University Press, 1993). The most useful, most analytically rewarding sources on which I've drawn here are Roy Morris Jr.'s *Fraud of the Century: Rutherford B. Hayes, Samuel Tilden, and the Stolen Election of 1876* (New York: Simon and Schuster, 2003), Louis W. Koenig's brief but insightful summary "The Election That Got Away," *American Heritage* 11, no. 6 (1960): 4–7, Eric Foner's magisterial *Reconstruction: America's Unfinished Revolution 1863–1877* (New York: Harper Row, 1988), which gives by far the most authoritative account of the political currents of the time, and the opening chapter of C. Vann Woodward's *Origins of the New South 1877–1913* (Baton Rouge: Louisiana State University Press, 1951). Chief Justice Rehnquist's book is *Centennial Crisis: The Disputed Election of 1876* (New York: Knopf, 2004).

CHAPTER 6

Both Parkman's essay, "The Failure of Universal Suffrage," and Winchell's "The Experiment of Universal Suffrage" appeared in the *North American Review*, Parkman's in July–August 1878 and Winchell's in February 1883. The most useful books on the suffrage restrictions of the late nineteenth century and the failure of the Australian ballot include Eldon C. Evans's and Joseph P. Harris's books (see notes to chapter 4), Keyssar's *The Right to Vote* (see chapter 3), Frances Fox Piven and Richard A. Cloward's *Why Americans Still Don't Vote and Why Politicians Want It That Way* (See chapter 2 for reference), Louise Overacker's *Money in Politics* (New York: Macmillan, 1932), J. Morgan Kousser's *The Shaping of Southern Politics* (New Haven, CT: Yale University Press, 1974), and C. Vann Woodward's *The Burden of Southern History* (Baton Rouge: Louisiana State University Press, 1960). On the Fourteenth and Fifteenth Amendments, I drew on Keyssar's *The Right to Vote*, Walter Dean Burnham's *Presidential Ballots 1836–1892* (Baltimore: Johns Hopkins University Press, 1955), and William Gillette's *The Right to Vote: Politics and the Passage of the Fifteenth Amendment* (Baltimore: Johns Hopkins University Press, 1965). For the 1896 election, I turned to Lawrence Goodwyn's *Democratic Promise: The Populist Moment in America* (New York: Oxford University Press, 1976), Michael Kazin's *The Populist Persuasion* (New York: Basic Books, 1995), Walter Dean Burnham's *Critical Elections and the Mainsprings of American Politics* (New York: Norton, 1970), especially the chapter on the "system of 1896," E. E. Schattschneider's *The Semisovereign People* (New York: Holt, 1950), and Kevin Phillips's biography *William McKinley* (New York: New Press, 2003). Ralph G. Martin's *The Bosses* (New York: Putnam, 1964) has a useful biographical chapter on Mark Hanna. On the Progressive Era, see Richard Hofstadter's *The Age of Reform* (New York: Knopf, 1955) and Robert H. Wiebe, *The Search for Order, 1877–1920* (New York: Hill and Wang, 1967), as well as Brogan's *Penguin History* (see notes to chapter 4).

CHAPTER 7

The Wilmington massacre is exhaustively described in H. Leon Prather Sr.'s *We Have Taken a City: Wilmington Racial Massacre and Coup of 1898* (Cranbury, NJ: Fairleigh Dickinson University Press, 1984) and discussed from numerous perspectives in *Democracy Betrayed: The Wilmington Race Riot of 1898 and Its Legacy*, edited by David S. Cecelski and Timothy B. Tyson (Chapel Hill: University of North Carolina Press, 1998).

On the South's downward spiral from Reconstruction to segregation and beyond, the giants are V. O. Key (*Southern Politics in State and Nation* [New York: Vintage, 1949]), J. Morgan Kousser (especially *The Shaping of Southern Politics* [see chapter 6 for references], but also *Colorblind Injustice: Minority Voting Rights and the Undoing of the Second Reconstruction* [Chapel Hill: University of North Carolina Press, 1999]), and C. Vann Woodward (*The Burden of Southern History* [see chapter 6 for reference], *Origins of the New South 1877–1913* [see chapter 5], and *The Strange Career of Jim Crow*, 3rd ed. [New York: Oxford University Press, 1974]). W. A. Dunning's essay "The Undoing of Reconstruction," which appeared in the *Atlantic Monthly* in July 1901, is of enduring value. The legal history is usefully traced in Pamela Karlan's essay "Equal Protection: *Bush v. Gore* and the Making of a Precedent," in *The Unfinished Election of 2000* (see chapter 3 for reference), and also in the work of Laughlin McDonald of the Georgia ACLU (*Racial Equality* [Skokie, IL: National Textbook Co., 1977], and *A Voting Rights Odyssey: Black Enfranchisement in Georgia* [New York: Cambridge University Press, 2003]). On the later period, other works consulted include Numan V. Bartley and Hugh D. Graham's *Southern Politics and the Second Reconstruction* (Baltimore: Johns Hopkins University Press, 1975), Steven F. Lawson's *Black Ballots: Voting Rights in the South, 1944–1969* (New York: Columbia University Press, 1976), Lani Guinier's provocative book of essays, *The Tyranny of the Majority: Fundamental Fairness and Representative Democracy* (New York: Macmillan, 1994), and the 2004 report by the NAACP and People for the American Way, "The Long Shadow of Jim Crow: Voter Intimidation and Suppression in America Today."

CHAPTER 8

There aren't as many good books about Chicago in the 1920s as one might think. Those that take a serious stab at examining the connections between local politics and organized crime include John Landesco's *Organized Crime in Chicago* (Chicago: University of Chicago Press, 1968) and James L. Merriner's *Grafters and Goo Goos: Corruption and Reform in Chicago 1833–2003* (Carbondale: Southern Illinois University Press, 2004). Some insights, from a rigorously unsensationalized perspective, can be gleaned from Douglas Bukowski's *Big Bill Thompson: Chicago and the Politics of Image* (Chicago: University of Illinois Press, 1998). The best retelling of the Pineapple Primary and the other electoral irregularities of the period is in Joseph P. Harris's *Election Administration in the United States* (see chapter 4 for reference), not least because Harris worked in elections in the city at the time. For a contemporary account from the reformist viewpoint, Charles Edward Merriam's *Chicago: A More Intimate View of Urban Politics* (New York: Macmillan, 1929) is highly recommended. Estes Kefauver's *Crime in America* (Garden City, NY: Doubleday, 1951), a book-length version of his famous Senate committee report, has a fascinating chapter on Chicago. Kefauver also writes about Kansas City, on which there is much more in Lyle W. Dorsett's *The Pendergast Machine* (New York: Oxford University Press, 1968).

On the Daley machine and the 1960 presidential election, there is the excellent *American Pharaoh: Mayor Richard J. Daley, His Battle for Chicago and the Nation* (New York: Little, Brown, 2000), by Adam Cohen and Elizabeth Taylor, and Edmund F. Kallina Jr.'s somewhat parochial but nevertheless richly researched *Courthouse over White House: Chicago and the Presidential Election of 1960* (Orlando: University of Central Florida Press, 1988). David Greenberg wrote an excellent summary of the issues swirling around the Nixon-Kennedy election for the online magazine *Slate* ("Was Nixon Robbed? The legend of the stolen 1960 presidential election," *Slate*, October 16, 2000). On the Giancana-Kennedy link, I've quoted largely from Seymour Hersh's *The Dark Side of Camelot* (New York: Little, Brown, 1997). For Nixon's dirty tricks in the 1972 campaign, see, among many others, Anthony Summers's *The Arrogance of Power: The Secret World of Richard Nixon* (New York: Viking Penguin, 2000).

CHAPTER 9

This chapter grew out of a series of interviews with some of the players in the voting machine wars, among them Bob Varni, Bill Rouverol, Kimberlee Shoup, Florida state senator Jim Sebesta, and Louisiana representative Emile "Peppi" Bruneau. Ransom F. Shoup II was invited to comment on the sections of the chapter pertaining to him, which he was shown, but ultimately chose not to confirm, deny, or elaborate on anything. Special thanks to Rebecca Mercuri, whose Web site, www.notablesoftware.com, is a valuable resource for scientific analyses of voting systems, and to Eva Waskell of Votewatch, who provided me with many useful documents, including Michael Ian Shamos's 1980 evaluation of the Votomatic, David Burnham's 1987 letter to Lance J. Hoffman of George Washington University, Mae Churchill's 1990 letter to the FEC and the hard-to-find 1988 report by ECRI, "An Election Administrator's Guide to Computerized Voting Systems." Thanks also to Kim Alexander, who told me about the priceless *Behind the Freedom Curtain*, viewable online via the Prelinger Archive at www.archive.org/movies/details-db.php?collection=prelinger&collectionid +19033.

I also relied on a number of media reports and scientific documentation. The Tampa scandals were well covered at the time by the *Tampa Tribune and St. Petersburg Times*, although Senator Sebesta provided extra details. AVM's woes were covered in a long 1996 article in the *Pittsburgh Post-Gazette*. The Shoup family saga was previously chronicled in *Philadelphia* magazine in 2001 (Christopher McDougall, "The Clan Behind the Curtain," May 2001, see www.phillymag.com/Archives/2001May/clan_1.html), although the piece got a number of its facts wrong. Contemporary media accounts substantiate most if not all of its retelling of the 1978 scandal in Philadelphia, however. The strange bidding process in New York in 1990 was covered exhaustively by the *New York Times*.

On the early history of lever machines, Joseph P. Harris's *Election Administration in the United States* (see chapter 4) is, once again, invaluable. Harris's own career is illuminated in an oral history available in the special collections of the University of California at Berkeley ("Professor and Practitioner: Government, Election Reform, and the Votomatic," interview with Harriet Nathan, Berkeley, Regents of the University of California, 1983).

The Shamos report is called *The Votomatic Election System: An Evaluation* (prepared for the Pennsylvania Bureau of Elections, Pittsburgh, 1980). Much of the early history of computer voting is covered admirably by David Burnham's pieces for the *New York Times* and, at extraordinary length, by Ronnie Dugger in his famous piece for the *New Yorker*, "Annals of Democracy: Counting Votes" (November 7, 1988). Many of the technical issues, as well as accounts of various breakdowns, including the 1985 mayoral race in Dallas, are covered in Roy Saltman's reports for the National Bureau of Standards: "Effective Use of Computing Technology in Vote-Tallying" (NBS, Final Project Report, March 1975) and "Accuracy, Integrity, and Security in Computerized Vote-Tallying" (NBS, August 1988, see www.itl.nist.gov/lab/specpubs/500-158.htm). The Ken Thompson quote comes from *Communication of the ACM* 27, no. 8 (August 1984): 761–63, and is available via Rebecca Mercuri's Web site.

Finally, on the fallacies of technological progress, see David F. Noble's books *America by Design: Science, Technology, and the Rise of Corporate Capitalism* (New York: Knopf, 1977) and *The Religion of Technology: The Divinity of Man and the Spirit of Invention* (New York: Knopf, 1998). Also see Lewis Mumford, *Technics and Civilization* (New York: Harcourt Brace, 1934) and *The Myth of the Machine: The Pentagon of Power* (New York: Harcourt Brace, 1970).

CHAPTER 10

The 2000 election produced an avalanche of media coverage, including my own for *The Independent*, on which I've drawn throughout this chapter. The Florida meltdown also produced an avalanche of books, of which the best are probably Jake Tapper's *Down and Dirty: The Plot to Steal the Presidency* (New York: Little, Brown, 2001), a breezy, vivid, highly readable account that is perhaps just a touch too keen to wish a plague on both political houses, and Jeffrey Toobin's *Too Close to Call: The Thirty-Six-Day Battle to Decide the 2000 Election* (New York: Random House, 2001), an equally engaging read, which perhaps gives a little too much credit to the Democrats. Both benefit enormously from the fact that the authors witnessed many of the events themselves and talked to many invaluable firsthand sources.

Much has been written, too, about the Supreme Court's *Bush v. Gore* decision. A good starting point is Vincent Bugliosi's polemic *The Betrayal of America* (New York: Thunder's Mouth Press, 2001). More measured academic considerations can be found in *The Longest Night: Polemics and Perspectives on Election 2000*, edited by Arthur J. Jacobson and Michael Rosenfeld (Berkeley: University of California Press, 2002), and in *The Unfinished Election of 2000*, edited by Jack Rakove (see chapter 2 for reference), especially the essays by Alexander Keyssar and Larry D. Kramer.

The Conyers report for the Democratic Investigative Staff of the House Judiciary Committee, "How to Make Over One Million Votes Disappear: Electoral Sleight of Hand in the 2000 Presidential Election" (August 20, 2001) is available online at www.house.gov/judiciary_democrats/electionreport.pdf. The Cal Tech/MIT report on the lost votes of the 2000 election is called "Voting—What Is, What Could Be" (July 1, 2001) and is available at www.vote.caltech.edu/Reports/2001report.html.

The New Mexico material was based on interviews with Mike Laurance, Al Solis, and Bill Wheeler of the Doña Ana County Republican Party, and Chuck Davis and Bill Barnhouse of the county's Democratic Party, as well as media reports and official returns published on the New Mexico secretary of state's Web site, www.sos.state.nm.us/.

CHAPTER 11

Some of the reporting in this chapter and in chapter 12 is new, and some of it is based on reporting I did on electronic touch-screen voting for *The Independent* and for *Los Angeles CityBeat* starting in October 2003. The main pieces on which I've drawn are "All the President's Votes?" *The Independent*, October 14,

2003), "Mock the Vote" (Los Angeles CityBeat, October 29, 2003), "Something Rotten in the State of Florida" (Independent, September 29, 2004), and, specifically on Riverside County, "Down for the Count" (Los Angeles CityBeat, June 24, 2004). Other pieces and their sources are referenced below.

The case against touch-screen voting without a voter-verified paper trail has been authoritatively made in the writings of Rebecca Mercuri, David Dill, Peter Neumann, Doug Jones, and others. The easiest jumping-off points for their work are via the Internet, particularly www.notable software.com (Mercuri's Web site), www.verfiedvoting.org (started by Dill, now a broader campaigning site), and www.cs.uiowa.edu/~jones (Jones's site). Roy Saltman's report for the National Bureau of Standards, "Accuracy, Integrity, and Security in Computerized Vote-Tallying" (August 1988), is available online at www.itl.nist.gov/lab/specpubs/500-158.htm. Michael Ian Shamos's Six Commandments come from a 1993 conference paper prepared for the CPSR (Computer Professionals for Social Responsibility) titled "Electronic Voting—Evaluating the Threat." For the Cal Tech/MIT studies on the performance of difference voting systems, go to www.vote.caltech.edu, where all their findings are archived. The specific report referenced, "Residual Votes Attributable to Technology: An Assessment of the Reliability of Existing Voting Equipment," was updated in March 2001.

The Florida material is based on interviews with Mercuri, Charlotte Danciu, Lida Rodriguez-Taseff, and other members of the Miami-Dade Electoral Reform Coalition, Ion Sancho of the Leon County elections office, and Kendall Coffey; on legal documents, as well as numerous media reports and materials from the Reform Coalition's Web site, www.reformcoalition.org. The report of the Governor's Select Task Force on Election Procedures, Standards and Technology (March 1, 2001) is available online at www.collinscenter.org/usr_doc/Election%20Report.pdf.

The Maryland material is based in part on a lawsuit filed by Linda Schade and other voting rights activists in August 2004 and accessible via Schade's TrueVote Web site, www.truevotemd.org/. I don't agree with some of the suit's interpretations, and the presentation of fact is occasionally muddled, but it is a valuable resource not least because of the scrupulous documentation of its own sources. I also talked to Schade and to Tom Iler, director of Baltimore County's Office of Information Technology, and obtained a copy of the October 2001 procurement committee findings, in which the state was urged not to go ahead with its purchase of DRE systems.

The Georgia material is based on official letters and documents; interviews with voting rights activists Denis Wright and Roxanne Jekot; two independent secondhand accounts of the Macon theft by Kathy Rogers, as well as an interview with one of the participants in the interrupted training session; statistical analysis of the 2002 midterm election results by Charles Bullock of the University of Georgia, first reported in the *Baltimore City Paper*, and various media accounts.

For Riverside County in California, much of the official information comes from documents obtained through public records requests. Riverside County's tabulation problems on election night in November 2000 were reported at the time in the *Riverside Press Enterprise*, never to be mentioned by the paper again. I also interviewed Bernadette Burks and obtained copies of her correspondence with Mischelle Townsend. The cost estimates on DREs came from Jeremiah Akin in Riverside County and from an interview with Bob Varni at his home in San Francisco.

On the politics of HAVA's passage, I spoke to Doug Chapin of the nonpartisan Election Reform Information Project. The U.S. Commission on Civil Rights report on HAVA, *Is America Ready to Vote?* is available via its Web site, www.usccr.gov. The Texas material comes from the official videotape of the January 2004 meeting, which I have seen, as well as an interview with Adina Levin, and legal documents available through her Web site, www.safevoting.org.

CHAPTER 12

Some of the best, most consistently reliable reporting on e-voting has been done by Kim Zetter of *Wired News*. Her piece "How E-Voting Threatens Democracy" (*Wired News*, March 29, 2004) is a good place to start, but it is also worth consulting the *Wired* Web site's whole Machine Politics archive at www.wired.com/news/evote/. Also recommended is Farhad Manjoo's work for Salon.com. Both writers have a strong technical grasp of the subject, more so than I do. Good archives of material on e-voting, including press coverage, can be found at www.verifiedvoting.org (David Dill's original site), www.calvoter.org (site of the California Voter Foundation, including a Weblog by Kim Alexander), and www.electionline.org (a particularly valuable day-to-day survey of press coverage run by the Election Reform Information Project in Washington). Bev Harris's book, which has good information in places but spotty-to-dubious analysis, can be accessed through her Web site, www.blackboxvoting.org, as can the cache of Diebold e-mails hacked from the company's internal computer system in March 2003.

The major reports on Diebold software are: Aviel D. Rubin, Dan S. Wallach, Tadayoshi Kohno, and Adam Stubblefield, "Analysis of an Electronic

Voting System" (Johns Hopkins University Information Security Institute Technical Report TR-2003-19, July 23, 2003; updated in *IEEE Symposium on Security and Privacy* 2004, IEEE Computer Society Press, May 2004, available at http://avirubin.com/vote.pdf); SAIC's "Risk Assessment Report: Diebold - Accu-Vote-TS Voting System and Processes" (prepared for Maryland Department of Management and Budget, September 2, 2003; available at www.dbm.maryland.gov/dbm_publishing/public_content/dbm_search/tec hnology/toc_voting_system_report/votingsystemreportfinal.pdf); and Raba Technologies, "Trust Agent Report: Diebold AccuVote-TS Voting System" (prepared for Maryland General Assembly Department of Legislative Services, January 20, 2004, see www.raba.com/press/TA_Report_AccuVote.pdf). The report commissioned by the state of Ohio into the equipment used by all three top vendors plus Hart InterCivic is the "Direct Recording Electronic (DRE) Technical Security Assessment Report" (prepared by the Compuware Corporation, November 21, 2003, available at www.sos.state.oh.us/sos/hava/files/compuware.pdf).

The California secretary of state's Web site has an admirably complete archive of official reports, rulings, and transcripts of public hearings (start at www.ss.ca.gov/elections/elections_vs.htm). The major reports commissioned in California are the "Ad Hoc Touch Screen Task Force Report" (July 1, 2003, see www.ss.ca.gov/elections/taskforce_report_entire.pdf), the "Report on the March 2, 2004, Primary Election" (April 20, 2004, see www.ss.ca.gov/elections/ks_dre_papers/march_2_report_final.pdf), and the "Staff Report on the Investigation of Diebold Election Systems Inc." (April 20, 2004, available at www.ss.ca.gov/elections/ks_dre_papers/diebold_report_april20_final.pdf).

Interviews for this chapter include conversations and e-mail exchanges with David Dill, Rebecca Mercuri, Kim Alexander, a former FEC member who did not want to be named, Conny McCormack, Mischelle Townsend, Diebold spokesman Michael Jacobson, Roxanne Jekot, Jeremiah Akin, Art Cassel, Brian Floyd, Linda Soubirous, and Greg Luke. My interview with McCormack appeared in *Los Angeles CityBeat* on May 27, 2004, see http://lacitybeat.com/article.php?id=942&IssueNum=51. David Jefferson's deconstruction of R. Doug Lewis's Senate testimony is at http://verify. standord.edu/EVOTE/Ecresponse.html. Roxanne Jekot's Web site, including her transcripts of the confrontation with state election officials at Kennesaw State University, is at www.countthevote.org. Akin's Web site, including his detailed eyewitness reports on Riverside's slipshod election management practices, is at www.exit.com/RiversideVoteTest/index.php. The Riverside County documents on Mischelle Townsend were kindly provided by Cassel. The Wyle report on Sequoia's operating system came out in the discovery phase of a federal lawsuit against the county filed by a disgruntled voter and was provided by Akin.

CHAPTER 13

The Orlando material is based on interviews with Joe Egan, Steve Clelland, Lew Oliver, and an official at city hall who requested anonymity, as well as legal documents and official correspondence. Thanks to Kevin Wood for legal documents on Guy Tunnell and Panama City, as well as a transcript of Tunnell's confirmation hearing.

Much of the 2004 campaign was exhaustively covered in the media, which generated much of the secondary material in this chapter. The Palm Beach County material is based on interviews with Susan Van Houten and Echo Steiner of the Coalition for Election Reform and Theresa LePore's successful challenger, Arthur Anderson. The invocation of terrorism in Georgia's refusal to release key election-related materials was made in a letter from Kathy Rogers, the state elections director, and provided by Roxanne Jekot. The Kim Alexander quote comes from a telephone interview; Terry McAuliffe's line about Kerry being a rock star I overheard as I passed McAuliffe near Copley Square in Boston on election night.

On Ohio and more general assessments of the 2004 election, I found the following particularly useful: the letter written by John Conyers and other Democratic members of the House Judiciary Committee to Ohio Secretary of State Kenneth Blackwell on December 2, 2004, in which they laid out numerous allegations of electoral improprieties; Electionline.org's briefing on the 2004 election, available at their Web site, www.electionline.org; Curtis Gans's postelection analysis for the Committee for the Study of the American Electorate, available at www.gspm.org/csae/; and Votewatch's report on its Ohio audit, available at its Web site, www.votewatch.us. I also interviewed Steven Hertzberg by telephone. Thanks to Rebecca Mercuri, among others, for helping to analyze the exit polling.

The Gregoire-Rossi race was extensively covered in the Seattle dailies and also the *Seattle Weekly*. The study of Snohomish County's votes is at www. votersunite.org/info/SnohomishElectionFraudInvestigation.pdf. For my account of the so-called Boxer's Rebellion in the Senate, which I watched on television, I also relied on firsthand accounts in the *San Francisco Chronicle* and at Salon.com.

CHAPTER 14

A lot of the material on election monitoring and broader questions of democratization in OSCE member-states is available at the Web site of the organization's Office of Democratic Institutions and Human Rights, www.osce.org/odihr. These include detailed reports on monitoring missions as well as the October 2003 document I cite, "Existing Commitments for Democratic Elections in OSCE Participating States." The paragraphs I identified as being problems for the United States are: 2.4, 3.2, 3.3, 4.1, 4.2, 4.3, 5.2, 5.4, 7.3, 7.10, and 8.3. I also spoke directly to senior officials from OSCE member-states and read the transcripts of speeches from ministers and delegations heads, which they kindly provided. I interviewed Ilirjan Celibashi briefly in October 2002. I also accompanied the Fair Election International mission to Florida in September 2004, which is when I interviewed Dr. Brigalia Bam. The group's report on the 2004 election is available at www.fairelection.us/fairelectionreport.pdf.

Venezuela's woes with ES&S were widely reported at the time, for example by *Latin America Weekly Report*, "Mega-elections called off at last minute; malfunctioning computers persuade Supreme Court," May 30, 2000. The material on the Philippines also came from reports in the local business press and from Namfrel, the National Citizens' Movement for Free Elections. On Brazil, a lot more has been published in Portuguese than in English, but see especially Pedro Rezende's paper "Electronic Voting Systems: Is Brazil Ahead of Its Time?" (*Cryptobytes* 7, no. 2 [Fall 2004], see www.rsasecurity.com/rsalabs/cryptobytes/CryptoBytes_Fall2004.pdf) and also, cowritten with Amilcar Brunazo, "Security Measures for Brazil's e-Vote, Act One: Preemptive Sampling," www.cic.unb.br/docentes/pedro/trabs/Brazilvote1.htm.

On e-voting in Australia, see Zetter, "Aussies Do It Right: E-Voting" (*Wired News*, November 3, 2003, www.wired.com/news/ebiz/0,1272,61045,00.html). On India, see Eric Weiner, "What the U.S. Can Learn from India's Electronic Voting Machines" (*Slate*, September 29, 2004, http://slate.msn.com/id/2107388). On European initiatives, see the Council of Europe's site on democracy, e-voting, and e-governance, www.coe.int/T/E/Integrated_Projects/democracy/. Reports from Ireland's Commission on Electronic Voting can be found at www.cev.ie. The activities of Britain's Electoral Commission can be followed at www.electoralcommission.org.uk. On the 2004 referendum in Venezuela, see the Carter Center report of August 21 at www.cartercenter.org. On some of the reported problems, see Zetter, "E-Vote Rigging in Venezuela?" (*Wired News*, August 23, 2004, www.wired.com/news/evote/0,2645,64687,00.html).

CHAPTER 15

The PIPA report, issued on October 21, 2004, is called "The Separate Reality of Bush and Kerry Supporters" and is accessible via the organization's Web site, www.pipa.org. Ron Suskind's stunning piece, "Without a Doubt," was the cover story of the New York Times Sunday magazine on October 17, 2004. Christopher Hayes's piece, "Decision Makers," appeared on *The New Republic's* Web site on November 17, 2004.

Among the books that were helpful in outlining the discussion on American democracy in a globalized world were Anatol Lieven's *America Right or Wrong: An Anatomy of American Nationalism* (New York: Oxford University Press, 2004), Carlos Fuentes's essays on globalization and civic society in *This I Believe: An A to Z of a Life* (New York: Random House, 2005), and two by Thomas Frank: *One Market under God: Extreme Capitalism, Market Populism, and the End of Economic Democracy* (New York: Anchor Books 2000) and *What's the Matter with Kansas? How Conservatives Won the Heart of America* (New York: Metropolitan Books, 2004). Lipset's essay is called "Some Social Requisites of Democracy: Economic Development and Political Legitimacy" (*American Political Science Review* 53 [1959]). The more recent figures on wealth inequality, drawn from census and congressional sources, I took from Charles Noble's paper *What John Kerry Won't Say about the "Two Americas"* (*Logos* 3, no. 4 [Fall 2004], see www.logosjournal.com/noble_election.htm). On the likelihood of future al-Qa'ida attacks and their possible effects on American civic society, see, for example, Richard A. Clarke's essay "Ten Years Later," the cover story in the January/February 2005 issue of the *Atlantic Monthly.* Schattschneider's book is referenced in chapter 6 above. Special thanks also to Tim Pershing of Brandeis University for discussing his doctoral thesis on definitions of democracy. The term "casino democracy" originated with him.

Among the recommendations for fixing the U.S. electoral system are those of the National Commission on Federal Election Reform (at www.reformelections.org), the Constitution Project's Forum on Election Reform (see www.constitutionproject.org), and the various reports of the CalTech/MIT Voting Technology Project (see www.vote.caltech.edu, as well as the references in chapters 10 and 11). I also read the testimony of Rob Richie of the Center for Voting and Democracy, given to the House Judiciary Committee on December 8, 2004 (see www.fairvote.org/righttovote/ohiotestimony.pdf). Specifically on electronic voting, Kim Alexander wrote a paper called "Ten Things Elections Officials Can Do to Secure the Vote This November" (California Voter Foundation, August 19, 2004, see http://calvoter.org/issues/votingtech/pub/081904Kasecurevote.html).

BIBLIOGRAPHY

★ ☆ ★ ☆ ★ ☆ ★

BOOKS

Bartley, Numan V., and Hugh D. Graham. *Southern Politics and the Second Reconstruction* (Baltimore: Johns Hopkins University Press, 1975)

Boorstin, Daniel J. *The Genius of American Politics* (Chicago: University of Chicago Press, 1953)

Bowen, Catherine Drinker. *Miracle at Philadelphia* (Boston: Little Brown, 1966)

Brogan, D. W. *Politics in America* (New York: Harper, 1954)

Brogan, Hugh. *The Penguin History of the United States of America* (1985; London: Penguin Books, 1990)

Bugg, James L., Jr., ed. *Jacksonian Democracy: Myth or Reality?* (New York: Holt, Rinehart and Winston, 1962)

Bugliosi, Vincent. *The Betrayal of America* (New York: Thunder's Mouth, 2001)

Burnham, Walter Dean. *Presidential Ballots 1836–1892* (Baltimore: Johns Hopkins University Press, 1955)

—. *Critical Elections and the Mainsprings of American Politics* (New York: Norton, 1970)

Callow, Alexander B. *The Tweed Ring* (New York: Oxford University Press, 1966)

Caro, Robert A. *The Years of Lyndon Johnson: Means of Ascent* (New York: Knopf, 1990)

—. *The Years of Lyndon Johnson: The Path to Power* (1982; New York: Knopf, 2002)

Cecelski, David S., and Timothy B. Tyson, eds. *Democracy Betrayed: The Wilmington Race Riot of 1898 and Its Legacy* (Chapel Hill: University of North Carolina Press, 1998)

Cohen, Adam, and Elizabeth Taylor. *American Pharaoh: Mayor Richard J. Daley: His Battle for Chicago and the Nation* (New York: Little, Brown, 2000)

Cook, Fred J. *American Political Bosses and Machines* (New York: Franklin Watts, 1973)

Crenson, Matthew A., and Benjamin Ginsberg. *Downsizing Democracy: How*

America Sidelined Its Citizens and Privatized Its Public (Baltimore: Johns Hopkins University Press, 2002)

Crozier, Michel, Samuel P. Huntington, and Joji Watanuki. *The Crisis of Democracy: Report on the Governability of Democracies to the Trilateral Commission* (New York: New York University Press, 1975)

Dahl, Robert A. *How Democratic Is the American Constitution?* (New Haven, CT: Yale University Press, 2001)

Davenport, John I. *The Election and Naturalization Frauds in New York City, 1860–1870* (New York: self-published, 1894)

Dorsett, Lyle W. *The Pendergast Machine* (New York: Oxford University Press, 1968)

Evans, Eldon C. *A History of the Australian Ballot System in the United States* (Chicago: University of Chicago Press, 1917)

Farrand, Max. *The Framing of the Constitution of the United States* (New Haven, CT: Yale University Press, 1913)

Felknor, Bruce L. *Political Mischief: Smear, Sabotage, and Reform in U.S. Elections* (New York: Praeger, 1992)

Foner, Eric. *Reconstruction: America's Unfinished Revolution 1863–1877* (New York: Harper Row, 1988)

Frank, Thomas. *One Market Under God: Extreme Capitalism, Market Populism, and the End of Economic Democracy* (New York: Anchor Books, 2000)

——. *What's the Matter with Kansas? How Conservatives Won the Heart of America* (New York: Metropolitan Books, 2004)

Fuentes, Carlos. *This I Believe: An A to Z of a Life* (New York: Random House, 2005)

Gardiner, John A., and David J. Olson, eds. *Theft of the City: Readings on Corruption in Urban America* (Bloomington: Indiana University Press, 1974)

Gillette, William. *The Right to Vote: Politics and the Passage of the Fifteenth Amendment* (Baltimore: Johns Hopkins University Press, 1965)

Ginsberg, Benjamin, and Martin Shefter. *Politics by Other Means* (New York: Basic Books, 1990)

Goodwyn, Lawrence. *Democratic Promise: The Populist Moment in America* (New York: Oxford University Press, 1976)

Greenfield, Jeff. *Oh Waiter! One Order of Crow!* (New York: Putnam, 2001)

Guinier, Lani. *The Tyranny of the Majority: Fundamental Fairness and Representative Democracy* (New York: MacMillan, 1994)

Harris, Joseph P. *Election Administration in the United States* (Washington, DC: Brookings Institution, 1934)

——. *Professor and Practitioner: Government, Election Reform, and the Votomatic*, interview with Harriet Nathan (Berkeley: Regents of the University of California, 1983)

Hartz, Louis. *The Liberal Tradition in America* (New York: Harcourt Brace, 1955)

Hersh, Seymour M. *The Dark Side of Camelot* (New York: Little, Brown, 1997)

Hill, Steven. *Fixing Elections: The Failure of America's Winner Take All Politics* (New York: Routledge, 2002)

Hofstadter, Richard. *The American Political Tradition* (New York: Knopf, 1948)

——. *The Age of Reform* (New York: Knopf, 1955)

Huntington, Samuel P. *Political Order in Changing Societies* (New Haven, CT: Yale University Press, 1968)

Jacobson, Arthur J., and Michael Rosenfeld, eds. *The Longest Night: Polemics and Perspectives on Election 2000* (Berkeley: University of California Press, 2002)

Kallina, Edmund F., Jr., *Courthouse over White House: Chicago and the Presidential Election of 1960* (Orlando: University of Central Florida Press, 1988)

Kazin, Michael. *The Populist Persuasion* (New York: Basic Books, 1995)

Kefauver, Estes. *Crime in America* (Garden City, NY: Doubleday, 1951)

Key, V. O. *Southern Politics in State and Nation* (New York: Vintage, 1949)

Keyssar, Alexander. *The Right to Vote: The Contested History of Democracy in the United States* (New York: Basic Books, 2000)

Kousser, J. Morgan. *The Shaping of Southern Politics* (New Haven, CT: Yale University Press, 1974)

——. *Colorblind Injustice: Minority Voting Rights and the Undoing of the Second Reconstruction* (Chapel Hill: University of North Carolina Press, 1999)

Landesco, John. *Organized Crime in Chicago* (Chicago: University of Chicago Press, 1968)

Lawson, Steven F. *Black Ballots: Voting Rights in the South, 1944–1969* (New York: Columbia University Press, 1976)

Lieven, Anatol. *America Right or Wrong: An Anatomy of American Nationalism* (New York: Oxford University Press, 2004)

Longley, Lawrence D., and Neal R. Peirce. *The Electoral College Primer* (New Haven, CT: Yale University Press, 1996, updated 1999)

Martin, Ralph G. *The Bosses* (New York: Putnam, 1964)

McDonald, Laughlin. *Racial Equality* (Skokie, IL: National Textbook Co., 1977)

——. *A Voting Rights Odyssey: Black Enfranchisement in Georgia* (New York: Cambridge University Press, 2003)

Merriam, Charles Edward. *Chicago: A More Intimate View of Urban Politics* (New York: Macmillan, 1929)

Merriner, James L. *Grafters and Goo Goos: Corruption and Reform in Chicago 1833–2003* (Carbondale: Southern Illinois University Press, 2004)

Moore, James, and Wayne Slater. *Bush's Brain: How Karl Rove Made George W. Bush Presidential* (New York: Wiley, 2003)

Morris, Roy, Jr. *Fraud of the Century: Rutherford B. Hayes, Samuel Tilden, and the Stolen Election of 1876* (New York: Simon and Schuster, 2003)

Mumford, Lewis. *Technics and Civilization* (New York: Harcourt Brace, 1934)

——. *The Myth of the Machine: The Pentagon of Power* (New York: Harcourt Brace, 1970)

Noble, David F. *America by Design: Science, Technology, and the Rise of Corporate Capitalism* (New York: Knopf, 1977)

——. *The Religion of Technology: The Divinity of Man and the Spirit of Invention* (New York: Knopf, 1998)

Overacker, Louise. *Money in Politics* (New York: Macmillan, 1932)

Parent, Wayne. *Inside the Carnival: Unmasking Louisiana Politics* (Baton Rouge: Louisiana State University Press, 2004)

Patterson, Thomas E. *The Vanishing Voter: Public Involvement in an Age of Uncertainty* (New York: Knopf, 2002)

Phillips, Kevin. *William McKinley* (New York: Times Books, 2003)

Piven, Frances Fox, and Richard A. Cloward. *Why Americans Still Don't Vote and Why Politicians Want It That Way* (Boston: Beacon Press, 2000)

Polakoff, Keith Ian. *The Politics of Inertia: The Election of 1876 and the End of Reconstruction* (Baton Rouge: Louisiana State University Press, 1973)

Prather, H. Leon, Sr. *We Have Taken a City: Wilmington Racial Massacre and Coup of 1898* (Cranbury, NJ: Fairleigh Dickinson University Press, 1984)

Rakove, Jack N., ed. *The Unfinished Election of 2000* (New York: Basic Books, 2001)

Rehnquist, William H. *Centennial Crisis: The Disputed Election of 1876* (New York: Alfred A. Knopf, 2004)

Remini, Robert V. *The Election of Andrew Jackson* (Philadelphia: Lippincott, 1963)

——. *The Jacksonian Era* (Arlington Heights, VA: Harlan Davidson, 1989)

Richards, Leonard L. *The Slave Power: The Free North and Southern Domination, 1780–1860* (New Orleans: Louisiana State University Press, 2000)

Riordan, William L. *Plunkitt of Tammany Hall* (New York: McClure Press, 1905)

Rowell, Chester H. *A historical and legal digest of all the contested election cases in the House of Representatives of the United States from the First to the Fifty-Sixth Congress, 1789–1901* (Westport, CT: Greenwood Press, 1976; first published by the U.S. House, 1901)

Sabato, Larry J., and Glenn R. Simpson. *Dirty Little Secrets: The Persistence of Corruption in American Politics* (New York: Times Books, 1996)

Schattschneider, E. E. *The Semisovereign People: A Realist's View of Democracy in America* (New York: Holt, Rinehart and Winston, 1950)

Schlesinger, Arthur M., Jr. *The Age of Jackson* (Boston: Little Brown, 1953)

—, ed. *The History of American Presidential Elections* (New York: Chelsea House, 1971)

Steffens, Lincoln. *The Shame of the Cities* (1904; New York: Peter Smith, 1948)

Summers, Anthony. *The Arrogance of Power: The Secret World of Richard Nixon* (New York: Viking Penguin, 2000)

Summers, Mark W. *The Plundering Generation: Corruption and the Crisis of the Union 1849–1861* (New York: Oxford University Press, 1987)

—. *The Era of Good Stealings* (New York: Oxford University Press, 1993)

—. *Party Games: Getting, Keeping, and Using Power in Gilded Age Politics* (Chapel Hill: University of North Carolina Press, 2004)

Sumner, William Graham. *What Social Classes Owe to Each Other* (New York: Harper, 1883)

Tapper, Jake. *Down and Dirty: The Plot to Steal the Presidency* (New York: Little, Brown, 2001)

Teixeira, Ruy A. *The Disappearing American Voter* (Washington, DC: Brookings Institution, 1992)

Tocqueville, Alexis de. *Democracy in America* (New York: Penguin Books, 1984)

Toobin, Jeffrey. *Too Close to Call: The Thirty-Six Day Battle to Decide the 2000 Election* (New York: Random House, 2001)

Werner, M. R. *Tammany Hall* (Garden City, NY: Doubleday, 1928)

Wiebe, Robert H. *The Search for Order, 1977–1920* (New York: Hill and Wang, 1967)

Williams, T. Harry. *Huey Long* (New York: Knopf, 1969)

Williams, Walter. *Reaganism and the Death of Representative Democracy* (Washington, DC: Georgetown University Press, 2003)

Wills, Garry. *"Negro President": Jefferson and the Slave Power* (New York: Houghton Mifflin, 2003)

Woodward, C. Vann. *Origins of the New South 1877–1913* (Baton Rouge: Louisiana State University Press, 1951)

—. *The Burden of Southern History* (Baton Rouge: Louisiana State University Press, 1960)

—. *The Strange Career of Jim Crow*, 3rd ed. (New York: Oxford University Press, 1974)

ARTICLES/REPORTS/OFFICIAL DOCUMENTS

Behrens, Angela, Behrens, Christopher Uggen, and Jeff Manza. "Ballot Manipulation and the 'Menace of Negro Domination': Racial Threat and Felon Disenfranchisement in the United States, 1850–2002." *American Journal of Sociology* 109 (2003): 559–605

California Secretary of State's Office. *Ad Hoc Touch Screen Task Force Report* (July 1, 2003, available at http://www.ss.ca.gov/elections/taskforce _report_entire.pdf)

—. *Report on the March 2, 2004 Primary Election* (April 20, 2004, available at http://www.ss.ca.gov/elections/ks_dre_papers/march_2_report_final.pdf)

—. *Staff Report on the Investigation of Diebold Election Systems Inc.* (April 20, 2004, available at http://www.ss.ca.gov/elections/ks_dre_papers/diebold_ report_april20_final.pdf)

The Caltech/MIT Voting Technology Project, *Residual Votes Attributable to Technology: An Assessment of the Reliability of Existing Voting Equipment* (Version 2, March 30, 2001, http://www.hss.caltech.edu/%7Evoting/CalTech_ MIT_Report_Version2.pdf)

—. *Voting—What Is, What Could Be* (July 1, 2001, available at http://www. vote.caltech.edu/Reports/2001report.html)

Compuware Corporation. *Direct Recording Electronic (DRE) Technical Security Assessment Report* (prepared for Ohio Secretary of State, November 21, 2003, available at http://www.sos.state.oh.us/sos/hava/files/compuware.pdf)

The Constitution Project's Forum on Election Reform. *Building Consensus on Election Reform* (Georgetown University Public Policy Institute, August 2001, available at http://constitutionproject.org/eri/CPReport.pdf)

Dunning, W. A. "The Undoing of Reconstruction," *Atlantic Monthly* 88 (July 1901)

electionline.org, *Briefing: The 2004 Election* (December 16, 2004, see http://www.electionline.org/site/docs/pdf/ERIP%20Brief9%20Final.pdf)

Governor's Select Task Force on Election Procedures, Standards, and Technology. *Revitalizing Democracy in Florida* (March 1, 2001, available at http://www.collinscenter.org/usr_doc/Election%20Report.pdf)

Greenberg, David. "Was Nixon Robbed? The Legend of the Stolen 1960 Presidential Election," *Slate*, October 16, 2000.

Gundlach, James H. "A Statistical Analysis of Possible Electronic Ballot Box Stuffing: The Case of Baldwin County Alabama Governor's Race in 2002" (paper presented at the Annual Meetings of the Alabama Political Science Association, Troy, Alabama, April 11, 2003, available at http://web6.duc.auburn.edu/~gundljhBaldwin.pdf)

Henneberger, Melinda. "Driving W." *New York Times* Sunday Magazine (May 14, 2000)

Kaplan, Robert D. "The Future of Democracy" *Atlantic* (December 1997)

Koenig, Louis W. "The Election That Got Away" *American Heritage* 11, no. 6 (1960): 4–7

Lipset, Seymour Martin. "Some Social Requisites of Democracy: Economic Development and Political Legitimacy," *American Political Science Review* 53 (1959)

Mason, John G. "Leo Strauss and the Noble Lie: The Neo-Cons at War" *Logos* 3, no. 2 (Spring 2004)

NAACP/People for the American Way Foundation. "The Long Shadow of Jim Crow: Voter Intimidation and Suppression in America Today" (Summer 2004, available at http://www.naacp.org/inc/pdf/jimcrow.pdf)

National Commission on Federal Election Reform. "To Assure Pride and Confidence in the Electoral Process." (University of Virginia Miller Center for Public Affairs and the Century Foundation, August 2001, available at http://www.reformelections.org/data/news/full_report.pdf)

Noble, Charles. "What John Kerry Won't Say about the 'Two Americas.'" *Logos* 3, no. 4 (Fall 2004), see http://www.logosjournal.com/noble_election.htm)

Parkman, Francis. "The Failure of Universal Suffrage." *North American Review* (July–August 1878)

RABA Technologies. "Trust Agent Report: Diebold AccuVote-TS Voting System" (prepared for Maryland General Assembly Department of Legislative Services, January 20, 2004, available at http://www.raba.com/press/TA_Report_AccuVote.pdf)

Rubin, Aviel D., Dan S. Wallach, Tadayoshi Kohno, and Adam Stubblefield. "Analysis of an Electronic Voting System." Johns Hopkins University Information Security Institute Technical Report TR-2003-19, July 23, 2003; updated in *IEEE Symposium on Security and Privacy 2004*, IEEE Computer Society Press, May 2004; available at http://avirubin.com/vote.pdf

SAIC (Science Applications International Corporation). "Risk Assessment Report: Diebold AccuVote-TS Voting System and Processes." Prepared for Maryland Department of Management and Budget, September 2, 2003; available at http://www.dbm.maryland.gov/dbm_publishing/public_content/dbm_search/technology/toc_voting_system_report/votingsystemreportfinal.pdf

Saltman, Roy G. "Effective Use of Computing Technology: Vote-Tallying." National Bureau of Standards, Final Project Report, March 1975, available at www.vote.caltech.edu/Reports/NBS_SP_500-30.pdf

——. "Accuracy, Integrity, and Security in Computerized Vote-Tallying." National Bureau of Standards, August 1988, available at http://www.itl.nist.gov/lab/specpubs/500-158.htm

Somin, Ilya. "When Ignorance Isn't Bliss: How Political Ignorance Threatens Democracy." Cato Institute Policy Analysis, September 22, 2004, available at http://www.cato.org/pubs/pas/pa525.pdf

Uggen, Christopher, and Jeff Manza. "Democratic Contraction? The Political Consequences of Felon Disenfranchisement in the United States." *American Sociological Review* 67 (2002): 777–803

U.S. Commission on Civil Rights. "Is America Ready to Vote?" Election Readiness Briefing Paper, April 2004

U.S. House of Representatives, Democratic Investigative Staff, House Committee on the Judiciary. "How to Make Over One Million Votes Disappear: Electoral Sleight of Hand in the 2000 Presidential Election" (August 20, 2001, available at http://www.house.gov/judiciary_democrats/electionreport.pdf)

U.S. House of Representatives, Status Report of the House Judiciary Committee Democratic Staff. "Preserving Democracy: What Went Wrong in Ohio" (January 5, 2005, available at http://www.house.gov/judiciary_democrats/ohiostatusrept1505.pdf)

Winchell, Alexander. "The Experiment of Universal Suffrage." *North American Review* (February 1883)

Xenos, Nicholas. "Leo Strauss and the Rhetoric of the War on Terror." *Logos* 3, no. 2 (Spring 2004)

INDEX

★ ☆ ★ ☆ ★ ☆ ★

voter fraud, 7-14
  Chicago, 152, 153, 157
  cities, 79
  1876 election, 95-96
  1960 elections, 161-167
  2004 elections, 287-288
first known in presidential election, 69
  first reported, 78
  Florida, 212, 284-285
  New York City, 73-77
  Philadelphia, 89
  in rural areas, 88
  secret ballots, 113-118
  voting machines, 183-185
  see also chain voting; election fraud;
    repeat voters; vote purchasing
voter ignorance, 315-318
voter intimidation, 111, 127, 132, 148,
  155, 161, 240, 275-277
Voter News Service, 204
voter registration, 301, 326
  fraud, 2, 11, 14, 161-164, 212, 281-
    282, 284-285
  qualifying tests, 34, 114, 134, 136-
    137
voter turnout, 31, 34
  decline, 122-123, 137
  2000 elections, 205
  increase, 69, 71, 90, 146, 155
voting machines, 7-8
  certification, 236-237, 266
  2000 elections, 205-207
  electronic voting machines (DRE), 3,
    15, 196-197, 226-227, 231-233,
    238-241, 244-250, 251-273, 287,
    327 (see also individual machines
    and companies)
  insufficient numbers, 290-291, 301
  lever machines, 164, 175-176,
    180-185
  optical-scan machines, 230-231, 244,
    308, 325
  in other countries, 306-314
  punch-card machines, 175-180, 185-
    200, 206-207
  purchasing scandals, 173-180
  rigging, 178-180, 192
  software and security issues, 227-
    229, 250-255, 259-260, 312,
    325-326
  thefts, 235-236
  vendor control, 191, 238-242,
    246-247
  voter fraud, 183-185
voting rights, 239-241, 270
  Constitution on, 36-37, 118,
    219-220
  felons, 43, 46-47, 135, 147-148,
    211-213, 301, 326
  limits on, 33-34
  white males, 67

see also African Americans; universal
  suffrage
Voting Rights Act of 1965, 146
Votomatic punch-card machines, 175-
  180, 185-197, 206-207, 231

Waddell, Alfred Moore, 129, 132
Wallace, George, 169
Wallach, Dan, 253
Washington, George, 58
Washington (state), 201-202, 293
Watanuki, Joji, 29
Watergate, 168
Watson, Tom, 126
Wayne, Anthony, 78
Weldon, Curt, 167
Wells, Madison, 98-99
West Virginia, 192, 282
Wexler, Robert, 280
white supremacists, 129
Will, George, 30, 215
Williams, Brit, 235, 263
Willis, John, 233
will of the people. see popular sovereignty
Wilson, Henry, 118
Winchell, Alexander, 109
Wolfowitz, Paul, 38
women's suffrage, 123
Wood, Fernando, 14, 83-84
Wormeli, Natalie, 261
Wright, Daniel, 128
Wright, Denis, 236-237
Wright, Silas, 128
Wyle Labs, 255, 257-258, 265

Zangara, Guiseppe, 157
Zetter, Kim, 265